# THE SYLVAC STORY

The History and Products of

SHAW & COPESTAKE LTD.
SYLVAN WORKS,
LONGTON,
STOKE-on-TRENT

AND

THOMAS LAWRENCE (LONGTON) LTD.
FALCON WORKS,
LONGTON,
STOKE-on-TRENT

1894–1982

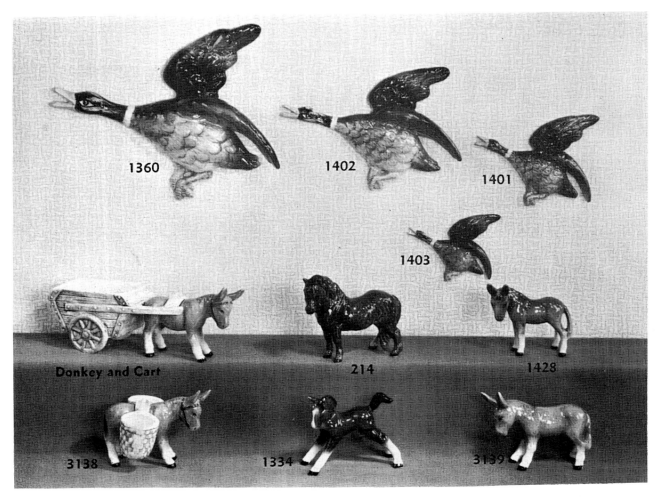

A typical selection of SylvaC available in the 1960s. Here you see the four flying ducks, the smallest of which, Number 1403, was a much later addition. They were sold in two sets. Large size set consisted of 1360, 1402, and 1401. Small size set contained 1402, 1401, and 1403.

Inside Front Cover: Ellen Whitehouse left, and Kath Amison right, in the factory shop about 1978. This is a poster which was produced about the time of the opening of the new shop, in 1978.

Inside Back Cover: One side of a leaflet issued about 1978, showing maps of various SylvaC showrooms.
Cover photographs: Front by George Caple, numbers 2425 and 2430.
Back by Brian Stalley, number 1209.

# CONTENTS

# ACKNOWLEDGEMENTS

Whilst compiling this information I have received considerable help from many people, and wish to thank the following:

Mrs. Jeanette Holdcroft, whose parents the late Mr. & Mrs. Reginald Thompson gave so much information, and for her kindness and hospitality during our visits.

Mr. Malcolm Chapman, who has contributed greatly to this information, Mrs. Rita McGeary, Mrs. Kath Day, who gave us our first leads in the research and her many friends. Mr. George Matthews, Mr Harold Clowes, Mr E.J. Dennis, Mrs. E. Hull, Mr. G.G. Barlow, Mr. E. Roy Taylor, Mrs. Helen Evans, Mr W.D. Holt who were all connected with the Shaw & Copestake or Falcon Ware factory, for additional information.

Miss Angela Lee, Curator of The Gladstone Pottery Museum for access to records. Miss Valerie Baynton, Curator of the Sir Henry Doulton Gallery. The staff of the City Museum and Art Gallery, the Hanley Library, and Longton Library, Stoke-on-Trent.

The late Olive Caple, Jayne L'Epine-Smith, David Richards for lending items from their SylvaC Collections. George Caple for spending many hours taking photographs for the first edition.

Local historians Malcolm Harris and Peter Landon, who have supplied old maps, documents, photographs and books of the area of Longton, and carried out research on my behalf.

From Australia: John and Marge Stiles who write unfailingly every month with news and photographs of new mould numbers, also Marie Hammond, Helen Jamieson, Lance Edwards, Paul Burt, Rosemary Woolger, Penny Sorrell, Sue Mann, who have made amazing finds 'down under'.

Jean Simms, Jackie Kaldenberg, Tony and Jackie Chew, Paul and Denise Tripp, James Brooks, Rachel Leeming who keep me regularly advised of any new information.

Brian Stalley for the hours spent perfecting his schedule of Story and Companion illustrations, and for his valued advice on SylvaC and Falcon Ware.

Mrs. B. Gorman, Mrs A. Morgan, Ms. M. Norton, Mr. J. Poley, Ms. P. Rowse, Mrs. M. Stonley, Ms. F. Daniel, Mrs. A.P. Hand, Mrs. J. Hallsworth, Mrs. G. Leatherbarrow, Mrs. S. McNeill, Mr. J. Miller, Mrs. J. Pearson, Ms. C.R. Roberts, Mrs. A. Sewell, Miss L.A. Smith, Mrs. S. Walton, Mrs. D. Jay, Mrs. J. Oxford, Mr. S. Rumsey and the many other collectors who have sent valuable information.

Mick and Derry Collins, who founded the SylvaC Collectors Circle, and have generously shared the results of their research.

Anthony Van De Weord for his excellent contribution to our knowledge of Shaw & Copestake in the form of his book Shaw & Copestake, A Collectors Guide to Early SylvaC 1894–1939.

Above all I am indebted to my husband Peter for all his support and encouragement, he has uncomplainingly accompanied me around Stoke-on-Trent, all the Antique Fairs, searched through volumes of books, taken video films and photographs, and has been largely responsible for the publication of this book.

Photographs by Peter Lepino, George Caple and Harold K. Bowen who kindly went to the Gladstone Pottery Museum to take photos from the Pottery Gazettes. Special thanks to the Gladstone Pottery Museum, and Tableware International, for allowing photographs to be taken from the Pottery Gazette.

Published by Pottery Publications, 7 Merton Park Parade, Kingston Road, London SW19 3NT.
Phototypeset by Intype, Woodman Works, Durnsford Road, London SW19 8DR.
Printed by The City Press, Biddles Limited, Walnut Tree House, Woodbridge Park, Guildford, Surrey.

First Edition 1989
Second Revised Edition 1995     ISBN 0 9514889 2 9

A display of SylvaC in the old Shaw & Copestake showrooms about 1940.

▲ Miss Dorothy Ridgeway, Company Secretary Shaw & Copestake Ltd., in the company showrooms c1950.

▼ Mrs. May Alcock, Company Secretary Thomas Lawrence (Longton) Ltd., in the company showrooms c1950.

# FOREWORD

Most of the world's greatest artists only achieved fame after their death. In a manner of speaking, the same situation applies to Shaw & Copestake Ltd. When in 1982, at the instigation of professional advisers, it was recommended that the company cease manufacturing and go into voluntary liquidation, none of the directors or the employees realised that the firms products would become collectors' items.

During the life-time of the company and its associate company Thomas Lawrence (Longton) Ltd, an immense number of ceramic products were developed and produced. The variety of these creations was fantastic. In many cases unique market leaders in their own field. From the very ornate highly decorated Victorian styles of vases and bowls of the early days, to ingenious table accessory items, to natural animal studies, to coloured glaze cachepots and floral containers, and of course the matt finish rabbits, dogs and other caricature animals which are so much sought after to-day, to name but a few of the vast SylvaC range.

As each new shape was modelled, it was given a shape number and in some cases a name. Unfortunately from the collector's point of view, these shape numbers did not follow in strict numerical or chronological order. This, to a large extent was due to the combination of the product numbers from two different factories. At this point I must mention the tremendous work undertaken by the author in compiling some sort of order out of the chaos of these numbers – a task made all the more difficult by the disappearance of the limited documentary evidence in existence at the time of the closure of the company.

Many of the company's products were the inspiration of the late Richard Hull Junior, who although no artist himself, had the unique talents of knowing what the market required and of being able to guide both artists and technicians into the production of the items which he had in mind. In its way this book may be regarded as a tribute to the man whose inspiration was responsible for the creation of so many of the pieces which collectors seek to-day. I am sure that he would have appreciated this narrative which records so much of the work to which he devoted his life.

I knew Richard Hull for most of my life, until his death in 1977. For nearly thirty years I was employed as accountant, company secretary and subsequently director of the company, which he did so much to build. It was very much a 'family' business in which the employees felt so much a part of the family. Richard Hull always endeavoured to foster that atmosphere to the extent that he earned the factory nick-name of 'father'. Throughout my time it was always a happy company. When in the recession of the early 1980's I had the unpalatable job of announcing the closure of the company, there was none of the bitterness amongst the employees at the prospect of redundancy usually associated with such events – just a deep sense of sadness at the end of an era of which they had all been a part. It is nice to know that Shaw & Copestake Ltd, will 'live on' through this book.

Finally may I congratulate Susan Verbeek, who together with her husband Peter, has undertaken months, even years, of research work in compiling the material necessary for this book. I am sure it will be of a particular help to collectors and to all who are interested in SylvaC Ware.

MALCOLM D. CHAPMAN
Ex Director of Shaw & Copestake Ltd.

# INTRODUCTION

I started to collect SylvaC in 1986, my first SylvaC treasure was a green matt dachshund, number 1332, (£2.50 at Shere Village Hall, Surrey). I had been looking for a green matt bunny, but couldn't find one and bought the dog instead, fortunately it had a SylvaC mark on the base, which inspired me to look for other SylvaC animals. It was the late Olive Caple who pointed me in the direction of Shaw & Copestake, she and her husband George had been collecting SylvaC for some time. I picked up snippets of information from dealers, but there were no books specifically written and very little about the subject elsewhere. I soon became very interested and tried to find out if there were any catalogues or brochures, the only information I could find was that SylvaC was originally produced by Shaw & Copestake Ltd, and the works had been taken over by another firm, I had no idea of the address or whereabouts of the premises.

1986, was the year of the Garden Festival in Stoke-on-Trent, my husband Peter and I had planned to visit the Festival, and were studying the leaflets sent. Glancing through the Factory Visits list I noticed 'Crown Winsor (formerly Shaw & Copestake, Longton)' our first clue, I telephoned immediately and arranged a visit. We met Mr. W.D. Holt, general manager, who gave me a catalogue and brochure, and took us round the show rooms, but he told us no early records of Shaw & Copestake Ltd., had been retained. A visit to the factory shop was our first introduction to Mrs. Kath Day, manageress, who was very helpful, and we were surprised to see quite a lot of SylvaC still for sale, some marked Crown Winsor, but much of it had the impressed mark of SylvaC. Kath Day suggested we met Mr. Malcolm Chapman, a former director, who had an importing business just down the road, we called on him the same day. Malcolm Chapman was very co-operative and friendly, and had a wonderful memory, working with him was Rita McGeary also an ex-employee of Shaw & Copestake. We were very pleased with the progress we made on our first trip to the Potteries, we arrived home with a list of contacts and some catalogues.

Our second visit to Stoke-on-Trent was very exciting, having followed up various leads, we met Mr. Reginald Thompson, who had been with Thomas Lawrence and Shaw & Copestake for over 60 years, employed as decorating manager, and chief designer. I could hardly contain my delight at the thought of meeting this great man, who had spent all his life working with Falcon Ware and SylvaC. He was tucked way in a little bungalow in Blurton, with his charming wife Gladys, both were being well looked after by their devoted daughter Jeanette Holdcroft. He was in very poor health, but perked up considerably during the times we visited, really relishing talking about all his years of toil in the Potteries. Sadly he passed away in April 1988, before publication of the first SylvaC Story in 1989. What we found on our visit was that Reginald Thompson had many old catalogues, which Jeanette had searched out for us, he very kindly gave these to me. I was so pleased I was able to record all Reginald Thompson's recollections on video tape, otherwise they would have been lost for ever.

We returned to Stoke-on-Trent many times, gathering more information and researching in the Museums and Libraries, and looking through pottery magazines. Kath Day also organised several Shaw & Copestake reunions at her home, and I was able to meet many of the former employees, who reminisced about their time at the Sylvan Works. All the interviews are on video tape, which caused great hilarity when we played it back to them, but it is an important record of what it was like to work at the Shaw & Copestake factory.

We also spent many a happy hour at the British Museum Newspaper Library in Colindale, wading through books, and of course we were still searching the Antique Fairs for pre-war items. I also made contact with many collectors of SylvaC, who were hearing about my researches, and seemed to assume I was writing a book on the subject. This had not been the original intention, the research had been for my own information, to make my collection more interesting. Every time we went to an Antique Fair, the SylvaC dealers told me about the book I was writing, and wondered how it was getting on. It was at this point that Olive Caple insisted I was quite capable of producing a book, I certainly had enough information, and I suddenly found myself launched on a rather formidable project. Please bear in mind I am not a professional writer, only a collector like yourselves, and I am learning, like you, about Shaw & Copestake and Thomas Lawrence all the time.

I was gradually gathering together a reasonable amount of literature and the register of mould numbers was considerably improved when Mr. Malcolm Chapman chanced upon the mould maker's registers, which immediately filled in a large number of gaps. I contacted the printers of the original catalogues, every agent still traceable, hoping for catalogues or photo negatives, also Tableware International, formerly The Pottery Gazette, and the local Staffordshire newspapers, without success. Not surprisingly printers do not keep examples of all their work, and no-one could have foreseen such interest in Shaw & Copestake. Photographers do not seem to keep negatives for any length of time either, so many of the photos have been reproduced from catalogues or the Pottery Gazette, which may reduce the quality of the print slightly.

However, I have managed to collect a large number of catalogues, dating from 1936, also brochures, leaflets, and the SylvaC & Falcon Bulletin, which was issued spasmodically throughout the life of the companies. Thanks are due to the former directors and staff who have dilligently searched out this treasure trove of information for me.

Having eventually achieved the publication of The SylvaC Story in 1989, I now find (in 1994), that although the original print run has long since sold out, there is still great demand for the book. It seemed sensible, if I decided to reprint, to up-date it, as much more information has been found during the last five years. For instance, in the first edition, there were very few of the original old Shaw & Copestake mould numbers about, but now thanks to the efforts of collectors, and the publication of Anthony Van der Weord's book, a considerable number have been traced. This, of course, has made the register even more complicated, as so many of the numbers are duplicated. The general consensus of opinion was that I separate the Falcon and SylvaC numbers, forming two lists of the two and three figure numbers, and this I have done.

So I found myself once again facing the daunting task of completely retyping the register of mould numbers, incorporating new information, and re-styling it so as to make room for new chapters. I have also rewritten some chapters, up-dating with information which has since come to hand. There is still much to find out about Shaw & Copestake, and also Thomas Lawrence, and I hope if you find any new information you will write to me at the Pottery Publications address, so it can be shared with other collectors.

In 1991 I published my second book, The SylvaC Companion, which complemented The SylvaC Story, and is filled with more photographs and information. The two books give a good selection of Falcon and SylvaC ranges produced over the years, and I hope you find all you need to know in the two books, but if you require any further information do not hesitate to contact me, at the Pottery Publications address, and I will do my utmost to help you. I hope you find this book interesting and helpful in your quest for SylvaC.

# PART ONE

# CHAPTERS 1–13

# CHAPTER 1

# COLLECTING SYLVAC

Collecting SylvaC can become compulsive. It creeps up on you gradually. It may have started quite innocently with a green bunny or flying duck, but the consequences can be total absorption in a fascinating hobby. There are many different types of SylvaC collectors. The matt green only brigade, fawn matt (green being considered unnatural) lobby, jam & honey pot specialists, wall vase enthusiasts, cat collectors and another only vases, but the majority once having started, collect any Shaw & Copestake item. It has to be admitted some SylvaC is really awful, and is wrapped up out of sight. The floral lines, with handpainted flowers usually have pride of place, and no one can be called a true SylvaC collector unless they have a good sprinkling of rabbits.

The quality of SylvaC varies enormously, some items are very poorly finished, but the flying ducks, character jugs, prestige pieces and the hand painting on some of the vases fill one with admiration. The pixies and gnomes must also be part of a good collection, and the large novelty jugs and vases are undoubtedly a very good investment. Any large animal is also bound to increase in value, and is becoming quite a rarity. There are so many vases to collect, that one wonders if it is worthwhile, but surely now is the time to add to your collection while prices are still reasonable. I always buy anything which is reasonably priced, provided it is perfect. It also pays to inspect dealers displays carefully as the most unlikely items very often turn out to be SylvaC, and one can be quite pleasantly surprised.

A surprising find was a maroon highly glazed clog, with a Dutch embossed scene 4½″ long Number 2863, very clearly marked SylvaC. But my pride and joy has to be the Shaw & Copestake clock set, very ornate, with the early daisy mark in gold. Having sought one for a long time it was a real triumph to find it. There is so much to look for, and this is why you will find the Number Register so useful. Not all ware is SylvaC marked, their system was very haphazard, and it will be useful to look the number up to see if it relates to what you have. The most important attribute a SylvaC collector needs is a sense of humour, if only to cope with the squirrels and fawns nestling in woodland, and the crying onion!

The ash-trays are also an interesting part of SylvaC, although the bases may be the same, there are many different adornments, mostly unrecorded.

Fortunately is it not an expensive hobby with reasonably priced items still available. It is still possible to buy small posy bars and vases for just a few pounds. The price of SylvaC varies such a lot, according to condition and size. Obviously the larger items cost more, and the bunnies are now much scarcer. I have to admit to seeing very highly priced SylvaC Ware, and it obviously depends how much you desire the item in question. It is not really possible to give you a price guide, I can only advise you to compare the prices the dealers are asking.

Should you collect the Falcon Ware? In my opinion it is equally as interesting, and as much of Falcon Ware is also SylvaC it must be the same value. Equally Falcon Ware stands on its own merits, and the quality of original Falcon Ware is excellent. They brought out some very original ideas, but it is not quite so easy to find as SylvaC, or so well marked. Other potteries also used the Falcon Ware mark, so be sure it is from the Thomas Lawrence Potteries in Longton.

I have to admit I have slipped up on a number of occasions, and bought ware I thought was SylvaC, which has turned out to be, in most cases, by Price Bros. (Burslem) Ltd, Top Bridge Pottery, Burslem. They produced a very similar range to SylvaC, but it is very easy to make a mistake. Other potteries such as Devonmoor Art Pottery, and Crown Devon, also made similar wares.

One worrying aspect of collecting has been the recent appearance of possibly newly produced or re-decorated SylvaC. This has been causing us all some concern, and various items have been seen including, dogs, cats, rabbits, character jugs, celery and spring onion jugs, the stilton cheese dish, Tudor Cottage Ware etc. Some of these are poorly finished, and very often the decoration is of an unusual texture. Some dealers have bought the items in good faith assuming them to be genuine.

One of the character jugs I bought was a fawn colour, but had been given a coat of varnish which gradually peeled off. Many people have bought a set of three sitting cats, 1086–8, which have been given a crazed finish to make them look old, they are white but have flower transfers on them, not a traditional SylvaC style. We have also seen these cats in the National Trust shops in a plain white glaze. Another collector reports having seen the Falcon Ware figure of Jeanette with a most unusual SylvaC back stamp, which immediately raised his suspicions.

I have seen the large crouching rabbit 2955 in yellow glaze, with Limited Edition (dated), on the base, so we know exactly what we are buying, and it is not being passed off as genuine old SylvaC. There has recently been a resurgence of penguins, thimbles and harvest mice in biscuit ware (unglazed), which apparently came from the Sylvan Works when it went into liquidation. This is quite feasible as they are very reasonably priced, and would, presumably have been glazed if they had been recently produced.

Portmeirion Potteries Ltd, who bought the Sylvan Works in 1990, still produce five pieces of Vine range, either in white or hand painted (the colours differ from the originals). These are available direct from the factory, the current price of the hand painted versions range from £17.00 to £28.00 + p. & p. they have the Crown Winsor back stamp. A few other vase ranges and mugs were produced, all marked Crown Winsor, but are now discontinued. A separate company called the Lanedelph Pottery Company was formed to market these products.

Most of the SylvaC moulds are still at the Sylvan Works, under the protection of the Portmeirion Potteries Ltd, but some were missing when Portmeirion purchased the business. A selection of the original moulds had been taken away, and some given to creditors in lieu of payments. One can assume it is from these moulds the questionable SylvaC is emerging.

▲ A selection of SylvaC and Falcon Ware catalogues collected during research, dating from 1940. Centre front are the mould makers registers.

◄ The author, left, with Mrs. Kath Day, manageress of the factory shop, at the start of researching "The SylvaC Story", in 1986.

# PRICE'S
# MATT FIGURES

*The above range for Export are offered in four colours: Matt Green, Blue, Fawn and Oatmeal, fifteen different figures, all at the same selling price.*

# PRICE BROS. (BURSLEM) LTD.
## TOP BRIDGE POTTERY
### BURSLEM

An example of some Price Bros. animals, showing similarity to SylvaC ware. From the Pottery Gazette c1950s.

3339     5211

3459     5209

▲ The Prestige Range.

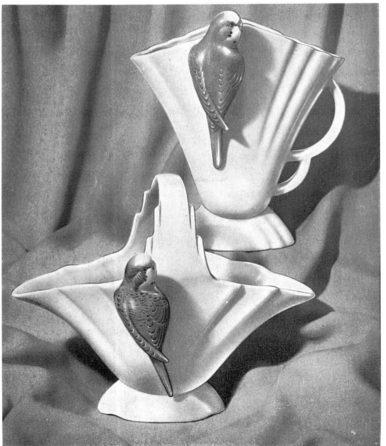

◄ The Budgerigar range. Jug 544, Basket 545.

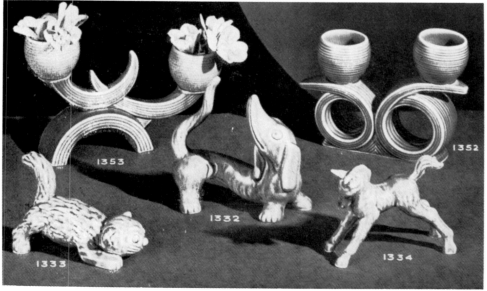

Pages reproduced from the 1940 catalogue.

Pages reproduced from the 1940 catalogue.

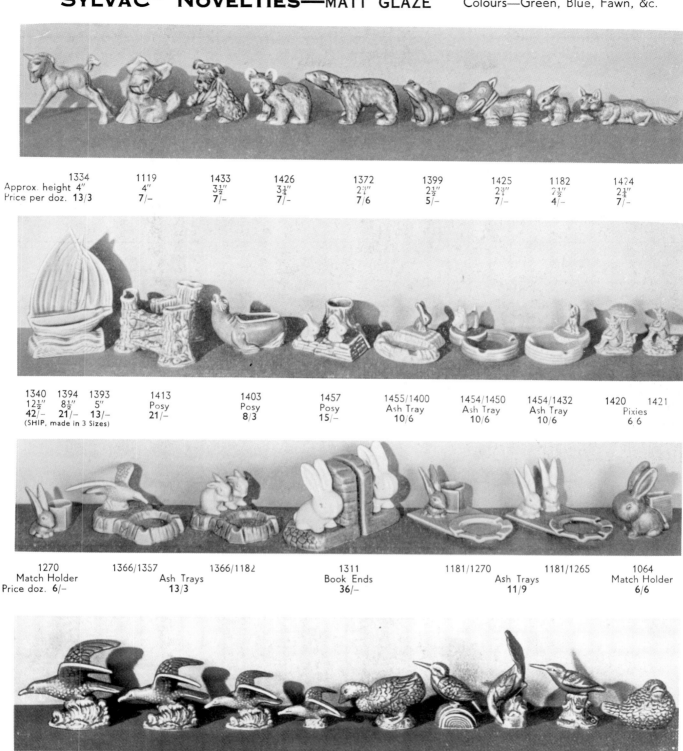

| 1334 | 1119 | 1433 | 1426 | 1372 | 1399 | 1425 | 1182 | 1424 |
|---|---|---|---|---|---|---|---|---|
| Approx. height 4" | 4" | 3½" | 3¾" | 2¾" | 2½" | 2¾" | 2½" | 2¼" |
| Price per doz. 13/3 | 7/- | 7/- | 7/- | 7/6 | 5/- | 7/- | 4/- | 7/- |

| 1340 1394 1393 | 1413 | 1403 | 1457 | 1455/1400 | 1454/1450 | 1454/1432 | 1420 1421 |
|---|---|---|---|---|---|---|---|
| 12½" 8½" 5" | Posy | Posy | Posy | Ash Tray | Ash Tray | Ash Tray | Pixies |
| 42/- 21/- 13/- | 21/- | 8/3 | 15/- | 10/6 | 10/6 | 10/6 | 6 6 |
| (SHIP, made in 3 Sizes) | | | | | | | |

| 1270 | 1366/1357 | 1366/1182 | 1311 | 1181/1270 | 1181/1265 | 1064 |
|---|---|---|---|---|---|---|
| Match Holder | Ash Trays | | Book Ends | Ash Trays | | Match Holder |
| Price doz. 6/- | 13/3 | | 36/- | 11/9 | | 6/6 |

| 1351 | 1350 | 1349 | 1357 | 1375 | 1328 | 1331 | 1330 | 1376 |
|---|---|---|---|---|---|---|---|---|
| Approx. height 5" | 4" | 3" | 2¼" | 3½" | 4" | 6½" | 4" | 3" |
| Price per doz. 24/- | 18/- | 12/- | 6/3 | 9/6 | 9/6 | 9/6 | 9/6 | 9/6 |

Pages from the 1940 Catalogue. Note number 1403 second row, the number which was re-used later for the smallest flying duck.

# "SYLVAC" NOVELTIES—MATT GLAZE

SEAGULL WALL PLACQUES—1543         1544         1545

1506        1500        1426      1521   1522   1520        LAMBS—1505 (6 in a Box)

1547      1485      1494      1573      1519      1561      1590      1504      1531

1528      1508      1518      1548      1512      1497      1534      1527

# "SYLVAC" NOVELTIES—CELLULOSE FINISH

788      769      1022   1086      992      1132      1320      1140      961      1211

Pages from the 1940 catalogue.

# CHAPTER 2

# HISTORY OF SHAW AND COPESTAKE

It is generally accepted that Shaw & Copestake was established in 1894. I have been unable to confirm the exact date of the founding of the Shaw & Copestake factory. Shaw & Copestake produced a 'History in Brief' for their customers, in which they gave the date as 1894, also adding that Mr. Richard Hull Senior joined the company in the same year. The obituary of Mr. Richard Hull Senior, in 1935, published in the Pottery Gazette, states he became a partner in the firm in 1900. Whereas the obituary of Mr. William Shaw, the founder of Shaw & Copestake, also to be found in the Pottery Gazette in 1951, gives the date of the partnership with Mr. Hull as 1898. Having studied all the relevant documents from the year 1894, the first mention of Shaw & Copestake is found in 1902. The address given is Drury Works, Normacot Road, but by 1904 the address has already changed to Sylvan Works, Normacot Road, as can be seen in the first advert. It has not been possible to establish if the name Drury Works was changed to Sylvan Works, or if it was a different location. From 1902 there are frequent mentions of Shaw & Copestake, in the Pottery Manufacturers Directories. So there are four different dates recorded, 1894, 1898, 1900 & 1902. Presumably the 1894 date, was recorded by the original directors of the company, in company records now no longer available, and we have to assume it to be correct.

The old works was situated opposite the site of the existing Sylvan Works in Normacot Road, Longton, Stoke-on-Trent, but has now been demolished. The site is used as a car park, only a short piece of wall remaining.

Mr. William Shaw and Mr. Copestake founded the business. Whether Mr. Copestake was connected with the well known Dewes & Copestake Pottery of Viaduct Works, Caroline St. Longton is not known. Mr. Copestake did not stay in the business long, only about six months. There are also other Shaws in the directories at around that time one being James Shaw, Albion Street, Longton. One can only speculate as to whether they were related. As William Shaw was very young when he founded the business, probably in his early 20s, one can reasonably assume he was financed by a relative, perhaps already in the business. He would also have had to be familiar with the business, and it seems more than likely his family were already associated with the Potteries.

Mr. Richard Hull senior bought Mr. Copestakes interest and became Mr. Shaws partner. This partnership continued until Mr. Hulls death in September 1935, when his son Mr. Richard Hull junior became Mr. Shaws partner.

In 1936, the business became a Limited Company. Mr. William Shaw continued to be a director until his retirement in May 1942, he died at the age of 76 on 31st December 1950. After Mr. Shaws retirement in 1942 Mr. E.J. Dennis became a director.

In 1938, Mr. Richard Hull and Mr. E.J. Dennis acquired Thomas Lawrence (Longton) Ltd, Falcon Pottery, Waterloo Street, Longton, Stoke-on-Trent. The Falcon Pottery was built in 1898 especially for Thomas Lawrence, and is still in existence. It is now used by the John Beswick Company, (part of the Royal Doulton Group). When Beswick took over the Thomas Lawrence Factory they found a room full of the Falcon backstamp, the room is still known as the Falcon Casting Room. The name Falcon appears quite frequently in the Beswick shape book, and it is more than probable these were pieces made in the Falcon Casting Shop. The name of the road was changed in the early 1950's to Barford Street.

Falcon Pottery was owned by Mr. Thomas Lawrence who founded it in 1888. In the 1920s or maybe shortly before, the business was taken over by his nephew Mr. John Grundy, whose daughter Miss Eileen Grundy married Mr. Richard Hull junior, thus amalgamating the two factories.

During the war years, the Shaw & Copestake Factory was requisitioned by the Government and used for storage. only the office and packing departments were available for use. Part of the Falcon Pottery was made available to Shaw & Copestake, and limited production continued under their own name. Shaw and Copestake were able to re-open their own factory in 1947.

A landmark in the history of the two firms was the opening of their own London Showrooms in 1953, at 30 Brooke Street, Holborn. Mr. H.W. Town was in charge of the Showrooms, he had previously been the Representative for London and the South East. Before they had their own premises they used London Agents, Mr. J.E. Holt, 60, Shoe Lane, Holborn, London for many years, and then Mr. J. Artis, Morley House, 26 Holborn Viaduct, London. The Scottish Agents were Mr. J. Crowe, 30, Gordon Street, Glasgow, and Messrs. Doleman &

The new combined offices and showrooms. The factory is at the rear. Photo taken about 1962 before the existing factory shop was opened.

▲ This Shaw & Copestake advertisement appeared in the Pottery Gazette on June 1st 1904.

◄ An article and photograph appeared in the Pottery Gazette on 1st April 1904. The following is an extract: "The group shown comprises the set of four pieces, consisting of centrepiece and stand, 21"h, with two side ewer-vases, 16"h. These have dark green ground with rich gold decoration. The same set is supplied in many decorative schemes; one with bronze green ground, richly gilt birds, foliage and handles, makes a handsome set well suited for a present. The vases are all artistic in outline and in ornamentation. The firm are very successful in their colour combination. Pale green and salmon ground, with hand painted flowers and gilt handles, celeste and gold ground, ivory and salmon ground, with colour and gilt foliage, make rich decorations."

Steward Ltd, 172, Buchanan Street, Glasgow. The Northern Ireland Agent was Mrs. H. Dean, 41, Donegall Place, Belfast, and the Eire Agents were Messrs T.G. Jones & Co., Ltd 1 Aston Place, Dublin.

Mr. Hull and Mr. Dennis's ambition for many years had been to build a new factory to combine the Shaw & Copestake and Thomas Lawrence Works, and this ambition started to be fulfilled in 1955. The new premises were positioned opposite the old bottle kilns in Normacot Road. In fact they had acquired some land on this site and offices and warehouses were already situated there. When more land became available, it seemed the ideal opportunity to build the finest and most modern factory in the Potteries. On January 22nd 1957 the first piece was made in the new building. The office block, showroom and warehousing units were completed in 1962. At this time they were employing 140 people. In 1962 Thomas Lawrence (Longton) Ltd, ceased trading under its own name and became fully merged with Shaw & Copestake Ltd by 1964. No more items with the Falcon Ware mark were produced after this date.

The post-war years saw not only a vast change in production techniques, but also changes in the marketing of the products: The export market continued to flourish and Shaw & Copestakes products were sent world-wide, about 30% of production being sent abroad.

Mr. E.J. Radford joined the Board in 1947, Mr. M.D. Chapman in 1962, and Mr. E.R. Taylor in 1974. Mr. Radford passed away in 1974, and Mr. Richard Hull in 1977. Mrs.

Richard Hull continued to be connected with the business until 1982.

During the late 1970s there was a steady decline in output due to the recession and Far Eastern competition, and 5 years later in May 1982 Shaw & Copestake went into voluntary liquidation. All production by the company ceased in that month. The land, buildings, plant and equipment were purchased by the North Midlands Co-Operative Society now known as the United Co-Operative Society, and leased to a workers Co-Operative known as Longton Ceramics. All the moulds, remaining stock and the name SylvaC were taken over by Longton Ceramics. This concern only lasted for 18 months, when the United Co-Operative Society took over the business, which was run in the name of Crown Winsor.

In June 1989, the business was sold once again and known as Crown Winsor (Pottery) Ltd. This company went into liquidation in November 1989, the factory and shop were finally closed in December 1989. The following spring the premises were bought by Portmeirion Potteries Ltd., and are now occupied by them. No production took place for the whole of 1990, during which time extensive renovation and installation of new equipment took place. Production commenced in January 1991 producing castware for the standard range of Portmeirion Pottery.

There was something special about working at Shaw & Copestake, it had such a happy atmosphere, and it was a very sad day for all when the company went into liquidation in May 1982.

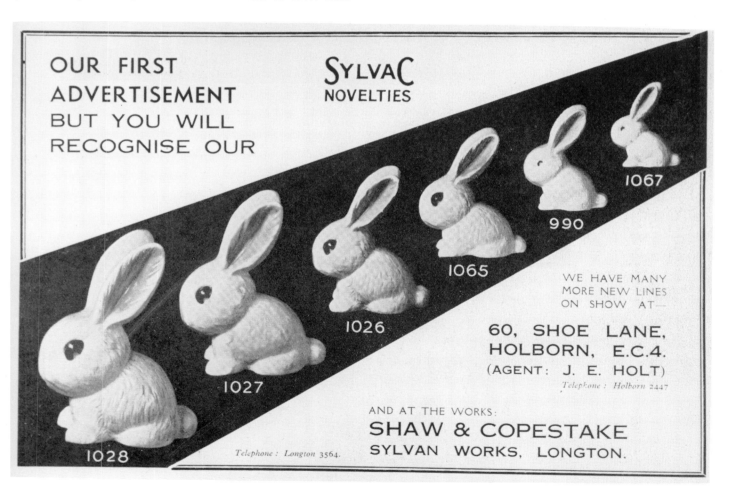

The first SylvaC advertisement appeared in the Pottery Gazette on January 1st 1936.

▲  Opening of the new London Showrooms in 1953. From left to right: Mrs. W.F. Wentworth-Shields, who officially opened the showrooms, Mr. W.F. Wentworth-Shields, Director of the British Pottery Manufacturers' Federation, Mr. Richard Hull, Managing Director, Mr. H.W. Town, in charge of the new showrooms and Mrs May Alcock Company Secretary of Thomas Lawrence (Longton) Ltd.

▼  A section of the new London showroom.

# CHAPTER 3

# HOW SYLVAC WAS MANUFACTURED

This is a description of the production methods used in the late 1940s in the old Shaw & Copestake factory which was probably built in the 1890's, and the Thomas Lawrence Factory built in 1898, until the opening of the new factory in 1957. Shaw & Copestake were always bringing in new methods of production, even in the old factory, and this was a continuous process. We find the old bottle kilns still being used, but alongside are new gas fired kilns. This chapter has been compiled from information found in the SylvaC and Falcon Bulletin, produced sometime between 1948 and 1951. These Bulletins were issued periodically, and were fully illustrated. I have been able to find the names of some of the workers, and have included these for your interest.

When a new article was suggested for production, the first stage was for the artist designer to sketch the subject to the exact size as required and showing all the detail. This drawing was then discussed by a committee of the heads of the production, decorating and sales department, along with the modeller, whose job it was to reproduce the drawing in either clay or plasticine. This committee discussed all the snags likely to occur when making or decorating the article, and also its feasibility as a saleable line. Once agreement had been reached and the design approved, the modeller reproduced the drawing exactly to scale.

From this original model, the mouldmaker prepared the first mould in plaster of Paris, called the block mould. This was done by marking out on the model the number of parts required for the mould, which would depend on the type of figure.

An intricate mould would be five to ten parts. Sometimes, the head or legs were made separately and stuck on the body in the making process. A mould was then taken of each of the parts of the block mould and this was known as 'the case'. From this case the parts of the working moulds were prepared, which when joined together make a complete working mould ready to be passed into the making departments.

The lines were manufactured in earthenware body, which had four principal ingredients, as follows:

STONE. This was obtained from Cornwall, when broken up and ground acted as a flux to hold the clays together in the body, and gave density to the finished article.

FLINT. The best quality came from France in the form of large pebbles. These, before use, were calcined or roasted and then finely ground. Flint gave the body its stability.

BALL CLAY. Came from Dorset or Devon, and was mined from the ground. It was a brownish tinted clay which gave the earthenware body its plasticity.

CHINA CLAY. Mined in Cornwall. After washing and weathering it was used to give the body its whiteness and helped with its plasticity.

The above ingredients were all mixed together in the correct proportions with water in a blunger to produce rough slip. The rough slip was run through very fine mesh lawns to remove any dirt, and then passed through magnets to remove any iron. This completed the process of preparing the earthenware clay. The surplus water was removed by passing the clay through a filter press, the solid clay was then passed through the 'pug' which made the clay more pliable and easy to handle.

To make a casting slip, a known weight of the made clay was mixed with water, silicate of soda and soda ash. The last two items acted as a medium to keep the clay particles in suspension, more fluid, and assist with the process of casting.

The casting slip was pumped up into the making shops from the slip house and when the moulds were assembled, they were filled with the slip and left to stand for approximately one hour. During this period the plaster mould, being porous, absorbed the water from the slip, where it was touching the mould. Consequently, when the surplus slip was poured out of the mould, it left a thin layer of clay adhering to the side of the mould. After being left to dry for an hour, the mould was opened and the cast clay piece removed. If any parts were made separately, they were stuck on in this wet state, which was a very skilled operation. The article was then left to dry, after which the seams etc., were carefully removed by an

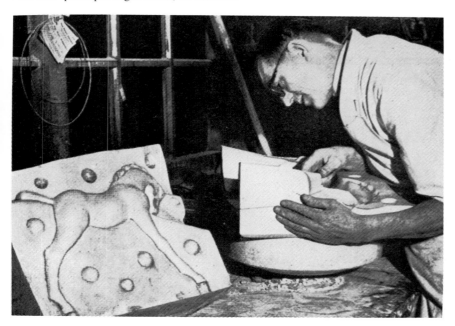

◄ Mouldmaking. Edward Walker, head mould maker at the Thomas Lawrence factory preparing mould in plaster of Paris.

◄ The sliphouse at the old Shaw & Copestake factory. Left, pugging the clay, centre, measuring the flint, right removing the magnet. On the far right is Mr. E.J. Radford works director.

◄ The casting shop at the old Shaw & Copestake factory. Left, filling moulds with casting slip, centre, emptying moulds, right, carrying finished clay to oven. Second from left is Mr. Frank Ridge who left in 1952.

◄ Fettling, in the old Shaw & Copestake factory. Removing surplus clay from seams with knife and sponge.

◄ Making flowers in the old Shaw & Copestake factory. The petals were made separately in the palm of the hand to be pieced together to form a flower. Individual flowers and leaves were then assembled together to form attractive flower groups.

► The continuous oven at the old Shaw & Copestake factory. Placing ware in saggers and carrying to placer. This picture shows the entrance to the continuous gas oven.

◄ The intermittent oven at the Thomas Lawrence factory. Carrying and filling saggers into the intermittent oven. When completely filled this entrance was built up with the fire bricks before commencing to fire. Williams Holmes is on the ladder, he left in the mid 1960s.

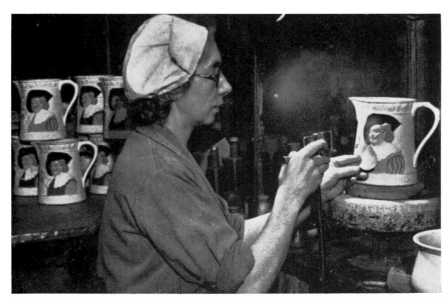

◄ Florence Key in the Thomas Lawrence factory aerographing or spraying the colour decoration on to the ware. Florence retired in the mid 1970s.

◄ Dipping house in the old Shaw & Copestake factory. Left to right, dipping biscuit ware in glaze, carrying ware to the kiln, aerographing colour, cleaning base of ware.

◄ Biscuit warehouse at the Thomas Lawrence factory. Brushing and cleaning the biscuit ware after biscuit oven fire.

◄ Glost oven at the Thomas Lawrence factory. Placing wares in trucks before firing.

◄ Glost oven at the Thomas Lawrence factory. Checking temperature on recorders and placing ware. James Brian clay manager is on the left, he retired in 1971.

◄ Glost oven at the Thomas Lawrence Factory. Drawing truck of fired ware from oven. On the right is E. Roy Taylor clay manager and later to become works director at Shaw & Copestake.

◄  George Wright in the decorating shop at the Thomas Lawrence factory, handpainting the wares. George retired in 1981.

◄  Decorating shop. Handpainting at the old Shaw & Copestake factory.

◄  The Thomas Lawrence warehouse. Back from left, Kate Worsdale, retired in 1973, Nellie Stewart, left in 1952. Front from left, Bill Tunicliffe, Janet Collis and Joan Ayres.

operation known as 'fettling'. The article had now finished its first stage of existence and was a very delicate piece of clay, neatly moulded and made to its own shape.

Completely round articles were machine made by a process called 'jolleying'. For this method, the clay after being 'pugged' was used in its plastic state. The machine rotated the mould, which formed either the inside or outside of the article, the other side being shaped by the application of a metal tool, brought down on to the clay in the mould by operating a lever.

Flower groups were completely hand made, each petal and leaf being made separately. They were formed in the palm of the hand from a roll of specially prepared plastic clay. The petals were pieced to-gether to form a flower and then assembled with the leaves into attractive flower groups.

The next stage was the first fire, known as biscuit firing. This was done in either intermittent bottle shaped ovens, fired with long flame coal, or a continuous gas kiln. The reason the Potteries was situated in Stoke-on-Trent was because of the deposit of long flame coal. Shaw & Copestake were using both methods, the most modern at that time being the continuous gas kiln, which was 82ft. long and rose to a temperature of 1160°C, and operated 168 hours per week. The ware was placed in fireclay containers known as saggers, these were placed in a small truck, each truck holding 12 to 16 saggers. A truck was placed in the oven at the entrance every two hours, and was slowly pushed through, taking 30 hours to reach the exit. Fifteen trucks were in the whole length of the continuous oven. The temperature rose gradually to 1160°C in the centre, and fell towards the exit end.

The intermittent bottle shaped oven was 16ft. in diameter and 18ft. high and held approximately 1,500 saggers. The filled saggers were placed in sixty columns of twenty-five saggers high in the oven, which was fired for 65 to 70 hours to a temperature of 1160°C. The firing took 12 to 15 tons of coal fed to nine fireboxes round the base. Before emptying the oven had to cool off for a period of 36 to 48 hours.

When the ware came out of the biscuit oven, it was hard and porous. After cleaning and brushing, if it was for underglaze decoration, it went straight to the decorating department. For example, animal models had the eyes painted in and the colour shading put on the body. They were then passed to the dipping or glazing department. White or coloured glaze ware went straight from the biscuit warehouse to the dipping department. In this department, the article was dipped into the liquid glaze of the colour required. This was a highly skilled operation as the dipper had to make sure the article only absorbed the correct amount of glaze, regardless of its porosity.

After cleaning the base, it was ready for the next stage of firing, which was done in a continuous electric glost oven, 97ft. long, rising to a temperature of 1060°C. This oven contained 17 trucks, one going into the oven every 96 minutes, taking 25 hours to go from end to end. The ware in this case was placed on siliminite shelves, each truck having five shelves. No two pieces had to touch one another when they were placed, or they would stick together and be a complete loss.

Some lines were ready for sale when they came from the glost oven, others had to go on to the decorating department for further painting, gilding or lithographing, etc., and were again fired to fasten the decoration on to the glaze, in a continuous enamel kiln rising to a temperature of 750°C.

The finished goods were selected and papered in the finishing warehouse, and then assortments were made up to the customers requirements. These assortments were packed in crates and casks and marked for their destination.

The SylvaC and Falcon fancy earthenware was shipped for 70 years to all parts of the world, and they had accredited representatives in all the principal countries.

When the new factory opened in 1957, the process was basically the same, except that all the kilns were either gas or electric. They also introduced a mechanised casting unit, and many small conveyors and mechanised aids. In 1964 they introduced a new packing system called 'Poly-tite', in which ware was packed skin tight.

The old Shaw & Copestake warehouse. First left Margery Addison, shipping clerk, second left Geoffry Abbott progress manager, retired in 1960, third right Roy Davies, despatch manager.

# CHAPTER 4

# PRODUCTS OF THE FACTORIES

### THE SYLVAC FACTORY

The early Shaw & Copestake products consisted of, and here I quote the Shaw & Copestake advert in 1904: 'Decorated Vases, Jugs, Flower Pots, Cheese Stands, Trinkets and Toilet Ware, and Fancy Earthenware', some of the vases were very large, being 21″ high. They were very ornate and heavily decorated with gold and a lot of hand painting, during this period the firm were employing about 25 men painters. Some of the designs from 1904 were reproduced in 1981 from an original Catalogue, (unfortunately lost), called, not surprisingly the 1904 Range.

During the First World War the firm used a lot of cellulose decoration, which consisted of painting with cellulose paint straight on to the biscuit ware, and no glaze being applied to the articles. This was a much cheaper finish, and although it did not wear very well, it was possible to use a more attractive range of colours than normal ceramic colours. Production of this type of decoration ceased in the early 1950s.

After the First World War and in the 1920s they produced clock sets in a very attractive style. These can be found in an assortment of colours and decorations. Also jug and toilet sets, in bold colours and decorations. Having dilligently searched for some of the older ware, I now have a fairly good idea of what was available. Some of the colour combinations were very strange, but presumably it was the fashion of the time.

In the late 1920s the first animals appeared, including a range of elephants in a black cellulose finish, also a swan and some gnomes for the garden.

In the 1930s a complete change came over the firms productions, a new matt glaze was introduced in blue, green, brown and ivory. This proved to be so popular that other colours were gradually introduced. Mr. Richard Hull junior developed this new finish,in conjunction with a local colour firm called Harrison & Sons (Hanley) Ltd. Some matt glazes continued until 1982. Every conceivable colour was eventually produced in a matt glaze, from black, through to white.

Although other potteries tried to copy this glaze, no one managed to produce it really successfully as it had to be fired at a lower temperature than the majority of kilns were able to achieve. The matt glaze was used on a large variety of Shaw & Copestakes wares, including animals, vases and jugs, tableware, book-ends and ashtrays. It was to contribute largely to their success. The hand-painted and cellulose ware continued to be produced as well. During the 1930s a large number of rabbits, dogs and animals and novelty vases were produced, called in the trade 'Fancies, for a popular class of trade'. They proved to be *very* popular and some lines were continued until 1982. They also produced some art deco vases, but it was the fancies that were becoming popular. Shaw & Copestake did not have their own designer at this time, and used freelance designers.

In 1935 Shaw & Copestake participated in the British Industries Fair for the first time, and from then on it became a regular event. The export side of the business continued to flourish. Other outlets emerged, for the fancies, and they were used as fairground prizes, seaside and holiday souvenirs, the bunnies were even filled with bath salts or cotton wool for the Christmas market. Flying ducks suddenly appeared, always recognisable because SylvaC (or Falcon) flying ducks always fly to the left, whereas most others fly to the right. Were SylvaC responsible for the first Flying Ducks? As the others all appeared around the same time it is impossible to say, and there is no record as to who modelled or designed them.

During the War years, when the Shaw & Copestake factory

was requisitioned by the Ministry of Defence, they moved into the Thomas Lawrence factory, which already belonged to them. Both firms continued with full production for export, and the home market was catered for as far as possible within the limits of the permitted quota. In an advert dated July 1942, they state 'SylvaC decorated ware has now been withdrawn for the duration of the War. Order your assorted crates of Jugs, Teapots, Beakers in White Finish'. Both firms were introducing new ranges throughout the war years, Shaw & Copestake produced a spitfire ashtray, Number 1667 and a fireplace ashtray complete with kitten Number 1622 in 1941. By 1947 Shaw & Copestake were back in their own factory and offering a wide range of earthenware fancies in semi-matt mottled glazes, bright-glazed colourings and coloured matt glazes. A particularly nice range brought out in 1949 was the blackberry tea and coffee set, made in primrose and pink.

During the next few years both factories were working at full pressure, using each others designs and marking items Falcon Ware or SylvaC. Thomas Lawrence already had their own designer and modeller, Mr. Reginald Thompson, and he was now designing for both factories, in conjunction with outside modellers.

During the 1950s and 60s, many new lines were introduced, wall plaques and floral brooches amongst them. A new logo was introduced in the 1960s, a Mr. SylvaC modelled by Mr. Thompson, but the brain child of Mr. M. Chapman, the commercial director, and was used for a number of years. It was used on the SylvaC labels, and catalogues and for general advertising. Mr. SylvaC was also made in the form of an ash tray, Number 3542, about 8″ high, which was given to dealers to display on their counters. One was on show in the SylvaC factory shop for many years.

A lot of advertising ware was made. A Leyland lorry ashtray Number 5404 made in 1977 is an interesting item, only about 1000 were made, for Leyland offices, it was designed by Mr. R. Thompson, and the paintress Vera painted only 10 a day as they were so intricate. A quantity of commemorative ware has been produced, and items especially for Fortnum & Masons, and Harrods.

In 1970 a Hollyberry range was introduced to decorate the Christmas table, and very attractive it looks too, with a dark green glaze and bright red berries. New designs were not quite so prevalent in the 1970s, the impression is of a gradual slowing down.

A few dog & horse head brooches and pendants were also made, a few thimbles and a new Tudor Cottage Ware was available in 1981, but only seven of the planned 30 pieces were ever produced.

By 1982 rumours were rife at the factory, it was obvious to the staff the firm were in trouble, the modellers were the first to realise, as they always work for a year ahead and work was scarce. The packers were on a two or three day week. Other potteries were also in difficulties, due to the economic climate. The Shaw & Copestake workers just hoped and prayed they would be able to survive, but it wasn't possible. When they were all called into the showroom, and told the bad news it still came as a terrible shock. Suddenly the majority of them were out of work, only a very small number of staff were kept on by the workers Co-Operative who took over the factory, using the name Longton Ceramics. This enterprise only lasted a short time, and it was taken over by Crown Winsor.

During their time (1984–1989) Crown Winsor sold many

Pages from the 1960 catalogue, showing novelty and floral ware.

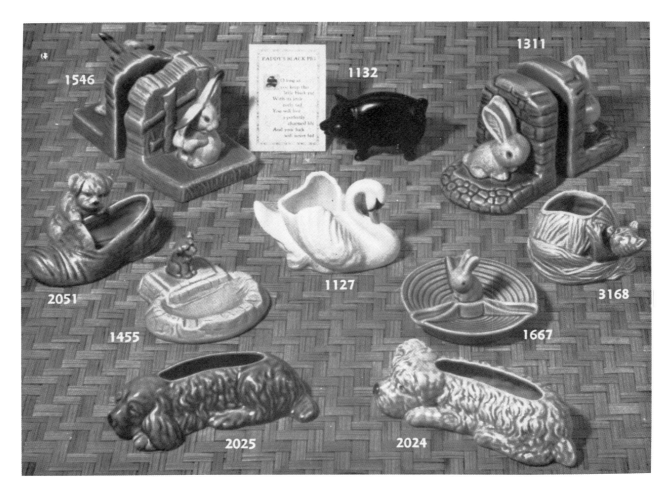

1546   1132   1311

2051   1127   3168

1455   1667

2025   2024

◄▲ Pages from the 1960 catalogue.

THE *SylvaC* DUCK FAMILY

HOLDER 2278         HOLDER 2277         HOLDER 707
DUCK FAMILY 2397    2398    2396         HOLDER 1127

▲ The 1904 range as shown in the 1980 catalogue.

▲ Novelty Money boxes.

▲ "Mine host". Falcon Ware.

▲ "Jeanette". Falcon Ware.

▲ Leyland lorry ashtray 5404. Owned by Vera Leese the paintress.

◄ Mr. SylvaC ashtray, with 'Toby' the dog, 3542. Modelled by Reginald Thompson, and used for advertising purposes. This one was seen in the factory shop. Note Mr. SylvaC has a teapot head, a wall vase body, uses the S and C for arms and legs and is holding a jardiniere. SylvaC is always spelt with a large S and C.

Bison 4732 8″ long                    Buffalo 4733 9½″ long.

SylvaC items in the factory shop, the dogs, character jugs, and cottage ware continued to be popular, and whilst there was demand, were still produced. The classical dogs were handpainted and mostly unmarked, but other items had the Crown Winsor back stamp. Some of the wares were white dipped only, with no added colours, the animals had no features, this finish was very often employed on biscuit ware that was already in the works when Crown Winsor took over the factory. Crown Winsor had no interest in promoting SylvaC, and although they used many of the original moulds they usually used their own back stamp.

From June 1989 the firm was taken over by Crown Winsor (Pottery) Ltd., but most of the management and staff remained the same. The range of products was very similar to previous years, but the new proprietor became a keen SylvaC fan wishing to promote and use the SylvaC moulds. Unfortunately this company went out of business in November 1989 and was finally closed in December 1989.

## THE FALCON FACTORY

The products of the Falcon Factory were very similar to the Shaw & Copestake Factory. They did not make table ware, but specialised more in toilet ware and trinket sets, along with the vases and jugs. They advertise Fancies and Novelties in 1928, but I have no idea what they were. Their ware is very nicely decorated with coaching scenes, glorious Devon scenes, cottages & hollyhocks and a flight of swallows. They also made childrens toilet ware.

They had a very strong export market, which continued thoughout the War years. During which time they also produced utility lines, jugs teapots etc. From this time, when Shaw & Copestake were using part of the Falcon Works, they were producing a considerable amount of SylvaC Ware.

After the Second World War, they brought out a range of table accessories, and the Cavalier Range, Numbers 300–309 was introduced in 1945, they apparently were producing a range of over 100 lamp bases and old English character studies for the U.S.A. In 1948 they introduced the English rose table accessory range which included a tea and coffee set. In 1950, they produced a lovely set of 'straw hat posies' which was featured in the Sunday Graphic in 1953 with a lady 'wearing' the hat. The range included wall vases, plant pots, and sweet dishes and are really nice collectors pieces Numbers 281/2/3, 299, 314/5. By 1957, they had moved out of Falcon Works, and joined Shaw & Copestake at the Sylvan Works. By which time they were both producing the same items. The Thomas Lawrence (Longton) Ltd., company ceased trading in 1962, and was finally wound up in 1964.

The Cavalier range and some character jugs as shown in the 1960 catalogue.

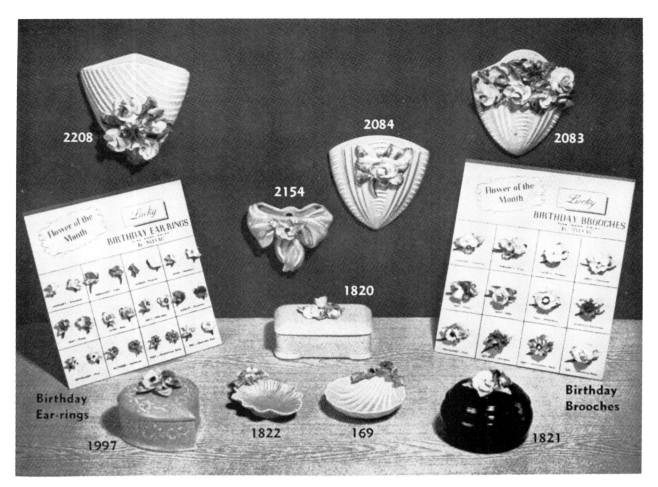

▲ Some earings, brooches and floral ware seen in the 1960 catalogue.

▼ Page from small leaflet issued in the 1950s.

### SEAGULL WARE M.102

| JUG 2086 | BOWL 2112 | WALL VASE 2079 |
|---|---|---|
| 6¼" High | 4¼" High    9½" Wide | 6¼" High |
| JARDINIÈRE 2113 | CANDY BOX 2111 | BASKET 2119 |
| 3¾" High    7½" Wide | 3" High    5" Wide | 6½" High    6½" Wide |

Two leaflets probably issued in the 1950s. These items were made in the Thomas Lawrence factory.

▲ Some rare items. From left back row: Duck 2396, Welsh lady character jug 1288, stag 3154, Vase 2314, Churchill cigar ashtray no number Falcon Ware, pig and piglet no number Falcon Ware, Paul 3112 Front row from left: gondola 384, shoveller 5122, tortoise 136, dish with lizard 431 Falcon Ware.

▲ From left: 1996 basket with dog 3657, 3560 wall with dog jumping, 31 slipper with dog, 2054 baskets (different sizes) with dogs 1400 and 3565, 3132 dog with panniers, 1484 top hat with kitten and dog, 596 barrel with dog (dogs can vary).

▲ Funnies. From left: Poodle 3428, sheepdog 3423, puppy 3114, tiny 1400, yawning 3433, puppy 3116, dachshund 3426, Yorkshire terrier 3432.

▲ Some of the ashtrays available in the 1940s. From left: 1366 with dog, 1455 with bunny, 1622 fireplace, 1667 with dog, 1454 with cat, 1455 with dog, 1366 with seagull two bunnies and dog, 1181 hare and match holder.

# CHAPTER 5

# SYLVAC ANIMALS AND PIXIES

## SYLVAC DOGS

Shaw & Copestake had already marketed at least 40 dogs before the start of the second world war, so the potential for dog ornaments had been realised. The first dogs were probably modelled around 1930, by a French modeller. Mr. Richard Hull travelled abroad extensively, in connection with the export trade, and had good contacts in France where many of his ideas came from.

The first known dogs are numbers 743 airedale and 752 pekinese, we then encounter the bulldogs very much in the style of Bonzo, numbers 1038, 1043 and 1044, 1117 was a dog with a large head, but the first well known dog was 1118, 'Monty the mongrel', he was produced for many years and appeared in a 1935 advert in the Pottery Gazette.

Undoubtedly the most popular of these pre-war dogs were the terriers, 1378, 1379 and 1380, they were still in production when the factory went into liquidation in 1982. They continued to be available in the Crown Winsor factory shop, in white glaze only, until they in turn went into liquidation. Other potteries jumped on this particular band wagon, and you have no doubt come across other almost identical terriers, which were blatant copies of the SylvaC models. This also applies to 1117 and 1118, the copies are very good and very difficult to detect except they have the all important mould number missing, and the dimensions are slightly different.

A set of 'Mac' dogs in five sizes comes high on the collector's list of priorities. The numbers are 1205–1209 and range in height from 5″–11″, as they have a registered design number it has been interesting to look this up at the Patent Office and discover they were designed by Otakar Steinburger, a Czechoslovakian modeller who was residing in Peckham. They were registered in 1932, but were not actually produced by Shaw & Copestake until 1936, which no doubt accounts for the many other similar unmarked pieces about. I used to think the story of 'Mac' 1209 with a golf ball was a SylvaC myth, but now I have seen one with my own eyes, and can confirm it is quite true.

From 1942 until c1947 most of the dogs were modelled at the Falcon Pottery, where Shaw & Copestake had joined Thomas Lawrence due to the Concentration of Industry scheme. Many were modelled by Mr. Reginald Thompson, the resident Falcon Ware designer and modeller, they were given the low two or three figure numbers.

About 1959 Mr. Thompson also modelled the popular 'Toothache dogs', known to the factory workers as Toby, numbers 2451, 2455, 3093 and 3183, usually in stone coloured matt glaze. They were produced until the 1970s, Toby also featured on the Mr. SylvaC figure, number 3542.

Many dogs continued to be modelled, including the caricature dogs of Stephan Czarnota, but mostly in the classical style and natural colours that Mr. Thompson favoured. Over 200 dogs were eventually produced, practically every breed was represented in the selection, from the St. Bernard to the Chihuahua. They also come with accessories such as pipe, slipper, ball and basket, and have varying expressions, comic, sad, happy, bashful and serious. SylvaC dogs are always collectable, but always be on the look out for recently produced wares that have not been made in the SylvaC factory, usually easy to spot because of the inferior quality of finish and glaze.

The very large dogs were produced in much smaller quantities, due to the space required to fire them, consequently making them quite scarce.

Shaw & Copestake, ever resourceful, used many of the dogs on vases, ashtrays, bookends, posies, bowls and novelty items.

Most dogs were designed by Mr. Reginald Thompson, but also by Stephan Czarnota, John Lawson, George Matthews, and of course Otakar Steinburger.

## SYLVAC RABBITS

Possibly the most popular of the SylvaC Ware are the round bunnies, Numbers 1028, 1027, 1026, 1065, 990, 1067, 1386 and 1400, ranging in size from 10″ to 2″. The price quoted in the 1940 catalogue for the 10″ Bunny Number 1028 is 26/- PER DOZEN! These bunnies are largely responsible for a lot of SylvaC collecting, as they seem to bring back the aura of the 1930s. Mr. Richard Hull returned from France one day in great excitement. He had seen our bunny, and knew he was on to something good. Mr. William Shaw, his partner, rather scathingly remarked 'No one is going to buy green rabbits'. However, Mr. Hull did go ahead, and produced one of the most successful lines. They were available in all colours and glazes, green matt being the most popular, and were produced from the 1930s until about 1975. In the 1972 catalogue they were reduced in number from the original eight to five, and were offered in the unusual colours of burnt orange, mustard and purple, glossy, of course. The matt colours discontinued about 1970. The larger bunnies were apparently also used as cottonwool containers, with the cottonwool protruding from the tail, also bathsalt containers, but how the bathsalts were retrieved I do not know.

Harry the Hare, Numbers 1300, 1299, 1298, 1265, were registered at the Patent Office by Shaw & Copestake in 1936. Registered Number 815840. Number 1298 was made until 1970, at which time it was produced in, fawn, green, turquoise and yellow matt. The others finished in the 1940s. They were all made originally in a wide variety of colours and finishes.

Lop Ear the Rabbit also appeared at this time, Registered Number 815839, (1936), Numbers 1302, 1303, 1304. They continued until 1975, also finishing in burnt orange, mustard and purple. The matt colours being discontinued about 1970. Another set of lop eared rabbits are 1525, 1526 and 1511, the difference being they were looking ahead, whereas the earlier lop ears were looking round.

There were also two sets of crouching rabbits available in the 1940s, three with ears up, Numbers 1389, 1388 and 1371, and three with ears down Numbers 1523 and 1530 and 1529. I also have a small crouching bunny with one ear up and one down, Number 1497 (1940s). The two bunnies kissing are Number 1534, after which there is a dearth of rabbits until the delightful set of ski-ing rabbits, made at the Falcon Pottery. Numbers are 25–29, and they are depicted, standing, injured and falling, nicely hand-painted in various colours, only between 2¼″ and 3½″ high. The first record of them is 1950 and they were only made for a short time.

Number 2955 a large crouching rabbit was seen in the 1960s for a short time, and Number 2980 an upright rabbit with bow tie, and protruding teeth, appeared in the 1960s, mostly seen in matt yellow.

The next series of rabbits was modelled in 1975, by George Matthews, Numbers 5289, 5290 and 5291, they were upright and

## TERRIER AND SCOTTIE DOGS

| | 1380 | 1379 | 1378 | 1209 | 1208 | 1207 | 1206 | 1205 |
|---|---|---|---|---|---|---|---|---|
| Approx. height | 11″ | 8″ | 5″ | 11″ | 9″ | 7½″ | 6¼″ | 5″ |
| Price per doz. | 34/6 | 18/6 | 7/3 | 33/- | 24/6 | 16/6 | 11/6 | 6/6 |

## DOGS

| | 1262 | 1261 | 1245 | 1259 | 1412 | 1118 | 1369 |
|---|---|---|---|---|---|---|---|
| Approx height | 8″ | 7¼″ | 5¾″ | 2¾″ | 9″ | 6¾″ | 5″ |
| Price per doz. | 36/- | 27/- | 20/- | 6/9 | 36/- | 13/6 | 7/3 |

| | 1227 | 1415 | 1121 | 1295 | 1122 | 1332 | 1123 |
|---|---|---|---|---|---|---|---|
| Approx. height | 5″ | 5″ | 4¾″ | 5″ | 3¾″ | 5½″ | 3½″ |
| Price per doz. | 11/- | 14/6 | 11/- | 14/6 | 11/- | 14/6 | 11/- |

Pages of dogs reproduced from a 1940 catalogue.

Two pages from a 1960 catalogue.

2451    2455    3183    1246    1247

2331    3179    3167    2473    3177

1414    2421    3182    3175    1415

3174    210    1548

176    203    209

18    115    188    177    116    114

◄▲ Pages
from a 1960
catalogue.

◄ Dachshund 177   Alsation 178.
Dachshund 188   Alsation 185.
From a 1950s leaflet.

◄ Corgis 3137 3133 3136
Corgis 3134        3135

▼ Vase 4528 Canine range.

## RABBITS

| | 1028 | 1027 | 1026 | 1065 | 990 | 1067 | 1386 | 1400 |
|---|---|---|---|---|---|---|---|---|
| Approx. height | 9¾" | 8¼" | 6¼" | 6" | 5" | 4" | 3" | 2" |
| Price per doz. | 26/- | 18/- | 12/- | 9/6 | 6/3 | 5/- | 4/6 | 3/- |

## HARES AND LOP-EARED RABBITS

| | 1300 | 1299 | 1298 | 1265 | 1389 | 1388 | 1371 | 1304 | 1303 | 1302 |
|---|---|---|---|---|---|---|---|---|---|---|
| Approx. height | 9¼" | 7½" | 6" | 3" | 7½" | 5½" | 3½" | 8½" | 7" | 5½" |
| Price per doz. | 21/- | 14/- | 7/- | 4/3 | 18/- | 12/- | 5/9 | 19/- | 11/6 | 7/- |

| | 1525 | 1526 | 1511 | 1492 | 1499 | 1498 | 1529 | 1523 | 1530 |
|---|---|---|---|---|---|---|---|---|---|
| App. hgt. | 8½" | 10½" | 13" | 5½" | 4¼" | 3¼" | 3¼" | 4½" | 5½" |
| Price doz. | 13/6 | 18/6 | 33/- | 13/6 | 7/- | 5/6 | 6/3 | 9/6 | 16/6 |

(Matt White with Coloured Beak)

Reproduced from a 1940 catalogue.

| 1146 | 1145 | 1144 | 1143 | 1142 | 1391 | 1390 | 1046 |
|---|---|---|---|---|---|---|---|
| Approx. height 9¾" | 8½" | 7¾" | 6¾" | 5¼" | 6" | 4½" | 6" |
| Price per doz. 24/- | 17/- | 11/3 | 9/- | 6/3 | 12/- | 6/3 | 6/6 |

| 1427 | 1374 | 1428 | 1414 | 1373 | 1431 | 1447 | 1422 |
|---|---|---|---|---|---|---|---|
| App. height 4¾" | 5" | 4¼" | 5¼" | 4½" | 3½" | 3½" | 4¾" |
| Price doz. 13/3 | 7/6 | 13/3 | 11/- | 7/6 | 13/3 | 14/- | 18/- |
| | | | | | | | (Made in 2 Sizes) |

▲  Pages from a 1940 catalogue.

Reproduced from the 1970s catalogue. Number 4707, 4708, 4709, 4710 and 4711

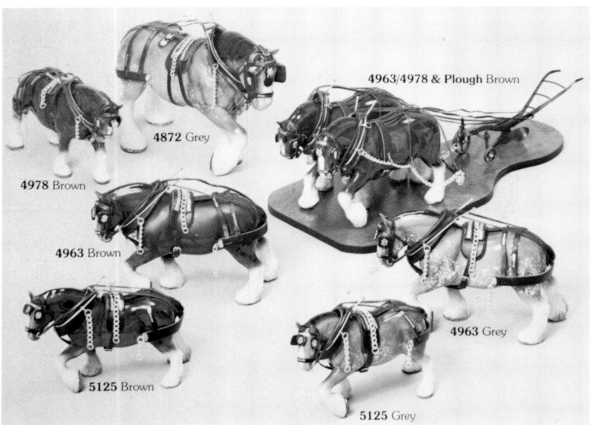

A selection from the 1980 catalogue.

A selection of SylvaC animals and birds.

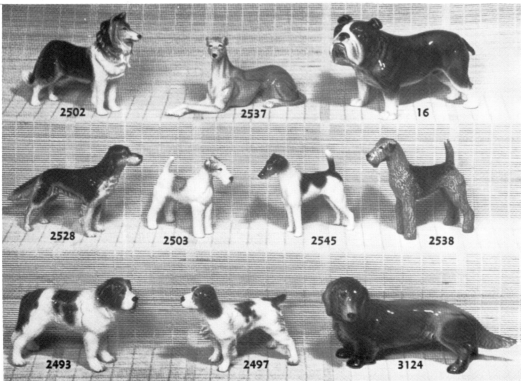

Horses and dogs from the 1960 catalogue.

lop eared, and fawn matt, and were available until 1982. In 1981, George Matthews modelled a childrens rabbit money-box, Number 5658, this rabbit has both ears down and is clutching a carrot, and that was the last SylvaC rabbit.

Rabbits of course feature quite a lot on ashtrays, bulb pots, bookends, vases and novelty ware, even wall vases.

The SylvaC bunnies were copied by many potteries, and it is sometimes difficult to tell them apart. As all SylvaC bunnies are numbered on the base (except the tinies), it is advisable to only buy clearly marked bunnies. Never be surprised at the unusual range of colours they can be found in. I hesitated for some time before buying a large cellulose orange hare, Number 1300, as the colour was so strange, but was delighted to discover later he was a genuine Shaw & Copestake hare. I have since discovered other cellulose decorated rabbits but would consider this finish quite rare. There is certainly plenty of scope for collectors of rabbits as the variations in sizes and colours abound, they are probably the most well-known and admired of the SylvaC ranges.

The largest round bunny, Number 1028, 10″, is very sought after and was made until 1975, it is possible there was also a larger one, but I have no definite confirmation of this. There are some gaps in the Register at this point, so it is quite possible. Perhaps a collector has this information.

## EARLY SYLVAC ANIMALS and BIRDS

Shaw & Copestake animals and birds are amongst the most highly prized of the majority of SylvaC collections. During our search for early examples I'm sure many were overlooked, until we learnt to recognise the colours that were used for the pre-war models, and also the outlandish comic attitudes of some.

When a collector rang and told me he had a pelican with a top hat, I was somewhat sceptical, but it was numbered 733 in the unmistakable style of Shaw & Copestake, and was quite genuine. A photograph of the pelican can be seen on page 73 of Shaw & Copestake, a Collectors Guide to Early SylvaC, along with pekinese 752, and airedale dog 743. They are all in a fairly distinctive mustard yellow cellulose, and were produced c1931. We still have no animals or birds registered before the kingfisher flower centre number 700 c1930, so far this is the earliest known model, until someone writes and tells me otherwise. The king-fisher was very enduring, and produced in many different decora-tions until early 1960s, it is partnered with various float bowls, numbers 436, 680, 711 and 726. One SylvaC enthusiast special-izes in collecting the kingfisher and float bowl, and has a wonder-ful selection in different colours and finishes. There is another bird flower centre very similar to 700, possibly a heron, with his head turned, it has no number, only a daisy mark, and is hand painted or plain white lustre, it may pre-date the kingfisher.

From a collector comes news of a monkey in a float bowl, number 747, the monkey is perched on a tree stump flower centre, and the bowl has embossed flowers around it, in a brilli-ant red and gold. I was a little startled to hear, from another collector in Lincolnshire, of a cockerel with glasses and a waist-coat, number 1179, and I was just wondering what-ever-next, when I received a phonecall about the three monkeys, hear, speak and see no evil, number 984, although I have yet to see a photograph, I understand they are quite small, about 1½″ high. The lesson we are learning is to pick up even the most unlikely looking object, because it might be Shaw & Copestake. Some-times it is possible to spot a colour or style which 'rings a bell', but we must obviously never disregard anything, however unlike Shaw & Copestake it may appear at first glance.

We are all very familiar with the elephants, free standing, on plinths and with howdahs. But there is also a range of camels, numbers 766, 767 and 772, and lions to complete this wildlife scene. The lions are much more complicated, and I have spent many hours trying to fathom them out, they start at 817 and continue until 825. They are either free standing, on plinths or with a tree stump vase, 823 and 824 are a matching pair with vases. The difficulty has been that the plinths are also numbered, so for instance 817 lion is sometimes on 820 plinth, but it is also free standing. The piece therefore has two numbers if it is with a plinth, a point which must be recorded with the utmost precision, together with the dimensions of lion on and off the plinth. The wildlife ranges were originally in cellulose, the camels either one colour or hand painted, the lions usually one colour cellulose in black or red, with shading or highlights. The elephants, some of which were produced for many years, were originally a black or red cellulose, sometimes a matt glaze, but generally in later years were a glossy black and occasionally 'flambe' red. The howdah on the elephants was beautifully handpainted with gold coloured edging, and there is even a small elephant posy from the same range 1153, all the trunks from this early range form an S for Shaw, making them easy to distinguish from other elephants.

The first cats appear to be of the laughing type 843 and 844, I haven't actually seen 844, but 843 is really delightful and I now have one of my very own. He is wearing a collar and bow tie, and carries on the comical theme of the pelican with the top hat. It is interesting to note the similarity between 843 and 5298 (page 27 TSC), which must of course be coincidental as designer George Matthews could not have seen the original. The contro-versial cat 981 is rather strange, he was described at first as a beaver, but we soon decided he was in fact a cat, sitting up in a begging position, which tends to give him an elongated neck, so far only seen in black cellulose. Puss in shoe 992, followed, and then the very popular frightened cat, or as some collectors call it, scaredy cat 1046, eventually joined by a big brother 1313 and tiny 1400. There is a wonderful range of crouching corkscrew tailed cats 1159/62/63/64 c1935 (page 35 TSC), fairly rare and usually in matt colours. Another early cat worth mentioning is 1286 (page 27 TSC), also fairly rare, I have this in my collection in blue, he is quite small only 4″h, has a long neck and startled expression, the mouth forming an 'OH'. A quick word about 1333 (page 15 TSS), a really Deco type crouching cat with flat edges, rarely seen, very collectable.

The wonderful family of ducks, Mr. Duck 1158, Mrs. Duck 1157, and Master Duck 1156 c1935 have really caught the imagination. Sometimes seen in colourful handpainted cellulose in varying condition, some pristine others flaking away, but they were also produced in matt glazes, which of course are more capable of surviving the years. I received a letter about Mr. Duck from my South African collector friend, who wrote that while staying with her sister in Richmond, Surrey she noticed a brown matt Mr. Duck in an antique shop. Although I didn't have precise directions I decided to rush over immediately. I searched numerous shops, eventually finding the right one only to be told it had been sold the previous day, despite having been on show for three weeks. I had missed Mr. Duck by a 'feather' (rather than a whisker), and was bitterly disappointed, especially as he was priced in the region of £15.00.

As you can see there were quite a few pre-war animals and birds, many of which I have not touched on here, but you will find them in the register of numbers at the back of the book. They were probably regarded as cheap novelty items, or fancies as they were known in the trade. During the war years and some years after, only 'seconds' (imperfect items) were allowed on to the home market, best quality were exported. This accounts for many having blemishes and marks which we have come to expect from SylvaC, and totally accept as part of the character of the wares.

◄ From left: Ducks 2396 and 1499, osprey 3339, golden crested grebe 3162, duck 1498, bird 1376. Front from left: mallard 5119, golden eyed duck 5120, shoveller duck 5122.

► Large foal at back Number 107, third row, from left: horse galloping no number, donkey 5131, second from left: donkey 1428, foal 1334, donkey 1374, mule 3384, front: foal 1447.

◄ Monkey 3141, Donkey 183, Cat 184. From a 1950s leaflet.

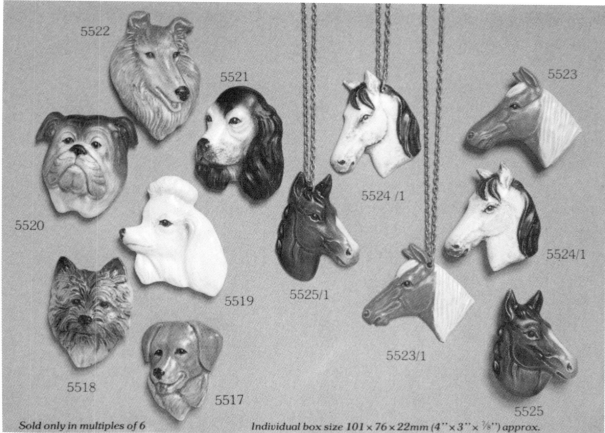

5522

5521

5523

5524 /1

5520

5519

5525/1

5524/1

5518

5517

5523/1

5525

**Sold only in multiples of 6**          *Individual box size 101 × 76 × 22mm (4" × 3" × ⅞") approx.*

Brooches and pendants as shown in the 1981 catalogue.

▲   Garden gnomes as shown in a 1950s catalogue.

## PIXIES AND GNOMES

It may surprise SylvaC collectors to learn that Shaw & Copestake produced a range of garden gnomes. The first appearing in the 1930s, Number 962, followed by seven others, Numbers 1024, 1092–5, 1097 and 1221. These were cellulose finished, the largest being 14" high and the smallest 4½" high. Numbers 1024 and 1221 were made until the late 1950s, but the others were discontinued in the 1940s. I am pleased to report several gnomes are now with collectors, and most have survived in excellent condition, presumably having been protected from outside elements. A new range was introduced in the 1950s and was available until the 1960s Numbers 74, 75, 81–83, 87, 108, 110, 113. The largest of this range was Number 110 which was 16" high and the smallest was 4¾" high, I was thrilled when a kind collector brought me gnome number 83 all the way from South Africa.

The first pixies were Numbers 1420 and 1421, the first is a pixie sitting under a toadstool, with a squirrel, and has the inscription 'Lucky Pixie' around the base, available from the 1930s until 1956. Number 1421 is a pixie in the same sitting position, but perched on a mound with a small toadstool behind him, this also is inscribed 'Lucky Pixie' 1930s until 1940s. They can be found in fawn/green/blue matt.

There are many pixies or gnomes attached to posies or bowls, 1480 and 1481 were the first examples. The round bulb bowl Number 1513 and 1514 is probably the one which evokes most memories, 'My grandmother had one of those', is a remark constantly heard. It is a woodland scene with recesses for gnomes and bunnies, originally in a matt glaze, but later in the M101 decoration, (See Chapter Six – Vases and Jugs).

Number 1513/4 was made from about 1940 until 1965. There followed a heart shaped posy Number 1963 in the 1950s and an oval bowl Number 2049, both with a gnome. Also in the 1950s was the wall vase Number 320 with a gnome on the front, one peeping over the top, and one round the corner, Number 353 is a log with a recess for a gnome and Number 355 a tree house jug with a gnome sitting at the door (sometimes a rabbit is found sitting at the same door).

If you want to start your day with a smile, you can do nothing better than collect the lazy pixies. These little fellows can be seen dozing off on a wheelbarrow 708, beside a toadstool 707, against a log and a basket 2275 and 2276, and a watering can and flowerpot 2277 and 2278. These posies can also be found with a gnome or mother rabbit, and the wheelbarrow sometimes contains hand painted flowers. They are not only matt glaze but come in glossy finish as well. A larger wheelbarrow number 747 also sports a pixie. These items sometimes have other gnomes or animals on them. They are mostly to be found in the matt glazes, but sometimes in a glossy finish.

A gnome on an upturned toadstool 2158 might be found but is quite rare, and a different gnome beside a yellow bamboo cane 2799 is another collectable item. Another pixie again is seen on bowls 2295 an acorn, 2289 a square container with a grass effect, 2339 and 2346 both with a grass and toadstool background.

Many people collect the pixies and gnomes, they are worth collecting for entertainment value alone. The pixie on the horseshoe vase, Number 4297, guarantees to bring you good luck from Ireland. But perhaps I do him an injustice, could it possibly be a Leprachaun?

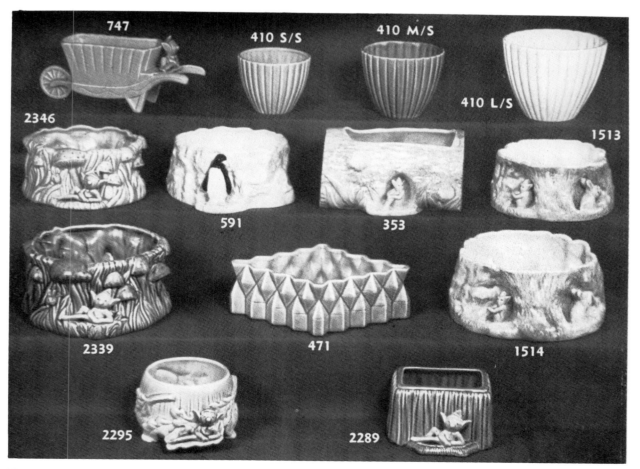

From a page in the 1960 catalogue.

Pages from a 1959 and 1960 catalogue.

# CHAPTER 6

# POPULAR SYLVAC WARE

### WALL PLAQUES AND WALL VASES

The best known of the wall plaques, is probably the set of four flying ducks, Numbers 1360, 1403, 1402 and 1401. The tiny 1403 came later, as the number was first used in the 1940s for a posy in the shape of a seal. The first Pottery Gazette advert for the ducks was in 1939, but they may have been available a few years before. SylvaC ducks always fly to the left, whereas other ducks more often go to the right. They were produced in green, blue and fawn matt glaze, as well as hand painted. They are also to be found with the Falcon Ware mark, and it is thought they were mostly made in the Thomas Lawrence factory.

There are three seagull wall plaques, also flying to the left, Numbers 1543–45, seen in a white matt glaze, and three swallows flying to the right Numbers 3156–58 in a dark blue glossy finish. All these birds are beautifully hand decorated in natural colours, and are really worth collecting.

Almost each range of wares had a wall vase, so there are plenty to collect. Some were decorated with hand painted flowers, others had budgies perched on them like Number 1956 which incidently has also been seen with a swallow attached. The budgies are green or blue. A blue tit on a coconut, Number 687, handpainted in natural colours, is one of the blue tit range.

There is a very unusual range of hats, a boater 733, a cap 721 a trilby 732, and girl's straw hats, numbers 278/9/80.

Quite a feature of a SylvaC Collection would be the bunny and mushroom wall vase, Number 323, and also the bunny and tree 354, and gnomes in the tree 320. Three dog head wall plaques, spaniel Number 88, scottie Number 89 and terrier Number 90 are also available in a handpainted finish. The dogs heads were given other numbers at one time (Numbers 25,26 & 27), these numbers conflict with the ski-ing bunny numbers, no definite explanation has emerged as to the reason for this.

Two very unusual wall plaques, designed by Mr. R. Thompson, were Numbers 327 and 329, 327 was a teenage boy's head and 329 a teenage girl's head. These were beautifully coloured, and are very rare.

In 1977 Mr. R. Thompson designed sets of martingales. They were ceramic discs which fitted into leather straps for hanging on the wall, available in a variety of decorations, such as horses, ships, French paintings, hunting scenes, dogs and Cries of London, Numbers, 5582/3.

The Cavalier Range also has a wall plaque plate, Number 5327.

### ASHTRAYS AND BOOKENDS

Shaw & Copestake made a large number of ashtrays. The most popular being the ashtrays Numbers 1181, 1366, 1454, 1455, and 1622. The adornments on these ashtrays varied a lot, but were usually rabbits, dogs, cats, birds, sometimes aeroplanes and cars. No doubt there are many I have not seen. They make a very interesting collection as you have two SylvaC items for the price of one. The later ranges, The Woodland Range and Riverside Range etc, all had ashtrays, with a small animal attached, and some of these continued until the 1980s, so there is enormous scope for a collection.

There were also many advertising ashtrays, such as the Mr. SylvaC with Toby the dog, 3542, the Leyland lorry 5404, Peter Rumsey Abergavenny 3467, Pipers Whisky ashtray Number 5436, and Guiness ashtray Number 5437. Then there are the novelty ashtrays such as the golf ball Number 4125.

The book-ends are more scarce. There were two different styles to start with, Numbers 1311, a brick wall effect, and Number 1546 a fence background. Sitting in front of which would be a bunny, dog, flowers or other item. Then came the horse at the stable door 2521, and the fish on a wave Number 2522, both very nicely finished items. I also note bookend Number 2826 in the Register, but have not yet seen this one.

### SYLVAC VASES & JUGS

Like a lot of the Stoke-on-Trent potteries, vases and jugs were the mainstay of the factory. They were produced continually from the start of the pottery at the turn of the century, to its end in 1982, changing styles to keep up or ahead of the latest trends. Experimenting with colours, designs and glazes, sometimes coming up with a real winner, others doomed to immediate failure. One winner that comes to mind is the acorn vase with the squirrel handle. It seemed to keep its appeal from the 1930s, through to the 1980s. It was first designed in 1935, (Numbers 1115 & 1195), then remodelled with a spout in the 1950s (Numbers 1958/9), and remodelled once again without the spout in the 1960s (Number 4068). The same applied to the vase with the stork handle, which was also modelled three times. Both these vases were also produced in miniature.

The hollyhock vase, the gnomes climbing into the mushroom vase, and the rabbits climbing into the furze vase, were not quite so popular, they were also remodelled, but didn't quite make it into the 80s.

Other vases in this style that dropped by the wayside earlier were the dragon handle vase 1116, and the stags head vase 1167, which didn't even make it into the 1940s. The monkey and coconut vase 1190, birds nest vase 1305 and budgie tail vase 1370, fared slightly better, making it into the 1940s. Real collectors items these early drop outs.

The animal vases were always an important feature of Shaw & Copestakes products, and they continued to bring out new combinations right up till 1977. The very first animal vase must have been the acorn vase, 1115, and the last was in the Harvest Time Range, Numbers 5243–5250 showing a little mouse nestling amongst the corn. In between those two ranges were the Woodland Range, with a squirrel or fawn, the Riverside Range with the swan, and the Giant Panda Range, with a panda that looks so surprised, and a bit put out at being there.

The smaller vases with an animal attached, such as the chimney pot, with either cat, owl or stork Number 2425 and the palm tree with hippo, giraffe or elephant Number 2430, were very amusing. Have you seen the dog dressed for tennis, and the city gent dog attached to vase Number 2660? Surely worth collecting for novelty value alone.

The Hyacinth leaf range Numbers 2452/3 etc, must be the most common SylvaC vase. This range was modelled by Mr. R. Thompson, in the 1950s and continued until 1982.

Every conceivable shape was tried out, some vases have shape names instead of numbers. When you consider the Falcon Pottery were also churning out masses of vases, it makes one wonder where they all went. But we have to remember the large export business that was built up over the years.

Jugs also seemed very popular, the large jugs that went with the toilet sets, and the sets of three jugs in different sizes. Some of which had the most lovely designs, others too gaudy for

|  | 1274 | 1138 | 1115 | 1195 | 1196 | 1318 | 1370 | 1305 | 1190 |
|---|---|---|---|---|---|---|---|---|---|
| App. hgt. | 8½″ | 10″ | 8½″ | 7½″ | 8½″ | 8¾″ | 7½″ | 8″ | 7″ |
| Price doz. | 33/– | 28/6 | 28/6 | 22/6 | 33/– | 33/– | 22/6 | 33/– | 33/– |
|  |  |  | (Made in 2 Sizes) |  |  |  |  |  |  |

|  | 1416 (Cellulose Finish) | 1451 | 1246 | 1312 | 1285 | 1284 | 1296 | 1423 | 1397 |
|---|---|---|---|---|---|---|---|---|---|
| App. height | 5″ | 5″ | 4½″ |  | 5¼″ | 3¼″ | 4″ | 2¾″ |  |
| Price doz. | 12/6 | 14/– | 9/6 | 30/– | 16/3 | 11/6 | 12/– | 7/– | 13/– |
|  |  |  |  |  | (Made in 2 Sizes) |  |  |  |  |

|  | 1487 | 1481 | 1513 | 1514 | 1480 | 1479 | 1484 |
|---|---|---|---|---|---|---|---|
| App. height | 4½″ | Diam. 8″ | Diam. 7″ | Diam. 8″ | Diam. 5½″ | Length 9″ | Height 3¼″ |
| Price per doz. | 13/6 | 23/– | M.85 36/– | 45/– | 16/6 | 15/– | 14/– |
|  |  |  | Matt 33/– | 42/– |  |  |  |
|  |  |  | (Made in 2 Sizes) |  |  |  |  |

From the 1940 catalogue.

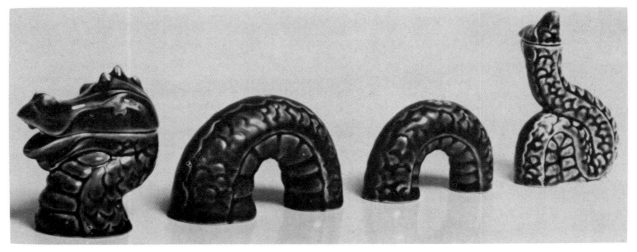

Sea monster cruet set 5468.

Jugs
and Bowls

JUG 1969

JUG 406

WALL VASE
SWALLOW

WALL VASE
BUDGERIGAR

JUG 1959 MADE IN TWO SIZES

JUG 455

JUG 1960

JUG 355

BOWL 468
MADE IN TWO SIZES

BOWL 1514
MADE IN TWO SIZES

▲ Page from a 1950s catalogue, showing unusual wall vase with swallow Number 1956.

3930

◄ Bull Number 3930, part of the Prestige range.

Bell 5535
120mm (4¾") *high*

L/S Tea Pot 4809 (4/5 cup)
146mm (5¾") *high*

Two piece Cruet 4832
90mm (3½") *high*

Coffee Pot 5537
228mm (9") *high*

Beaker 4817
115mm (4½") *high*

Breakfast/Salad Plate 4811
203mm (8") *across*

Cheese Dish 4815
178mm (7") *long*

Honey (or Preserve) Jar 4812
114mm (4½") *high*

Four piece Cruet 4832
228mm (9") *long*

The Croft range of table ware.

583  582  585  621  516

619  2172  2172  2172  2172

2184  3187  2184

4755/Pickled Cabbage  4565/Cucumber  4557/Bread  4753/Chutney

4553/Beetroot  5127/Beetroot  5048/Horseradish  4549/Apple  4750/Cole Slaw

4752/Piccalilli  4915/Tartare Sauce  4754/Parsley  5126/Onion  4756/Onion

A selection of SylvaC novelty tableware.

## WITH SOME POTS, THE ORIGINALITY IS ON THE OUTSIDE.

Frank Cooper's Original Oxford Marmalade
was created over 100 years ago for people who wanted something
highly distinctive and delicious.
It has a style all of its own, a pleasing individuality, just like
these conserve pots.
At a conservative estimate, in a hundred years no one's
come up with anything more original.

**FRANK COOPER'S** "OXFORD"
**ORIGINAL OXFORD MARMALADE**
COARSE CUT SEVILLE ORANGE
*Frank Cooper*

### THE TASTE OF INDIVIDUAL CHARACTER.
Frank Cooper Limited, 84 High Street, Oxford OX1 4BG

▲   The dogs head honey-pot was used recently in the FRANK COOPER'S Marmalade advertisement. Reproduced by kind permission of CPC (UK) Ltd. The FRANK COOPER'S OXFORD label is a registered trade mark of CPC (UK) Ltd., Esher, Surrey KT10 9PN.

◄   A display of the dogs head range, reproduced from a SylvaC catalogue. Numbers as follows: Cheese 1850, cruet 1715, toast rack 1990, butter 1818, honey 1849.

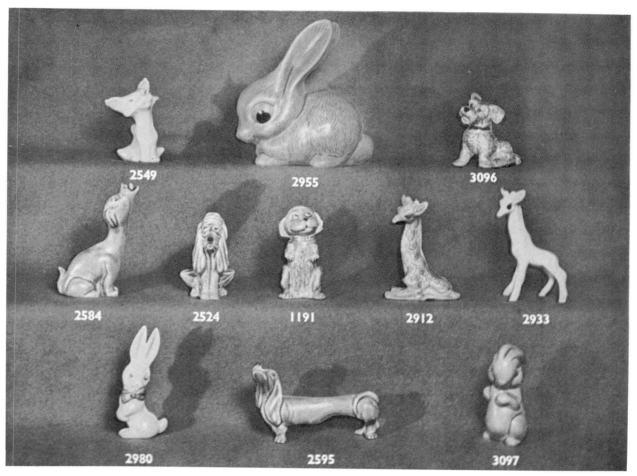

▲ Some unusual SylvaC animals.

Various novelty containers. Back row from left: 567 duck and barrel, 2425 chimneys with owl, stork and cat, 568 bowl with fawn. Front row from left: 2025 spaniel, 1457 tree stumps with bunnies, 2024 sealyham.

◄ The Tudor Cottage ware range.

▼ The sea provided much inspiration for SylvaC ware. These are just a few of the ranges. Back row from left: New shell 3524, coral 3907, Nautilus 2449. Front row: Dolphin 5188, Marina 4161, New shell 3532, boats 1394 and 1393.

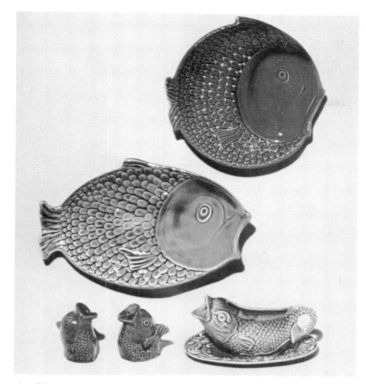

▲ Pisces range table ware.

▲ Cordon Brun range.

Teddy Nursery range.

▲ Zooline Nursery Range.

Novelty vases. Back row from left: 4297 pixie Ireland, 4227 scottie dog Scotland, 3711 harp Ireland, 4236 horseshoe Cheddar. Front row from left: 2656, 2658, 2655 all with lamb, 2600 with three different dogs.

words. It seems they loved any shade of mauve or purple, blended with any other colour that took their fancy.

All this changed in the early 1930s, when green, orange and fawn became fashionable. This progressed to the mottled look, a blend of greens and fawns decoration number M101, pale green and blue number M102, pink and green number M112, dark blue, green & fawn M106, shades of crimson M135, shades of blue M134, shades of fawn M105.

The cellulose ware was also given decoration numbers, and were very attractive and brightly coloured. This style of decorating finished in the mid 1950s. It was no longer available in the 1959 Catalogue.

## TOBY AND CHARACTER JUGS

There is a vast range of Toby and Character jugs. Mostly modelled in the 1960s by Longton New Art Pottery Co., Ltd., Parkhall Street, Longton, trading under the name of Kelsboro Ware. Shaw & Copestake purchased all the moulds from them. They were also produced with the Kelsboro Ware trademark, and the Crown Winsor mark. Although they are very fine pieces, it's a matter of opinion as to whether they are genuine SylvaC models. Shaw & Copestake and Thomas Lawrence did model their own character jugs, namely Punch (un-numbered) produced during the 1940s, 50s and 60s, Henry VIII also originally un-numbered until 1960s when it was numbered 4488 and, the Cavalier 306-re-numbered 4487 (1945–1965). Other original character jugs re-numbered are Number 4489 Yeoman of the Guard, Number 4491 William Shakespeare, Number 4492 George Bernard Shaw, Number 4486 Dick Turpin. These were re-numbered or given a new number to fit in with the sequence of numbers issued to the character jugs. Some of the really early ones can be found in the matt glazes, and the later models are carefully hand painted. The character and Toby jug numbers start at number 4400 in the Register of Numbers.

## SYLVAC TABLE WARE AND TEA SETS

Shaw & Copestake have always made a considerable amount of table ware, by which I mean jam pots, butter dishes, sugar bowls, teapots, jugs, cake plates, cruet sets, and everything to compliment the table setting. Also sometimes called table fancies. The most collectable of which must surely be the dogs head set. Would you believe, a little dogs head poking up from the butter dish, honey pot, cheese dish, cruet set, and toast rack. A really delightful set and available in either green/fawn or fawn/green. Numbers ranging from 1818 to 1990. (The honey pot was used recently in an advert for Frank Cooper's Marmalade.) 'There are many novelties of this type including the cow butter dish, 619, mouse cheese dish 621, and cat & mouse cheese dish 4525, also several cow cream jugs.

Of course the SylvaC honey pots are a legend, and are collected by many people. The range is quite extensive, the most popular being the strawberry, orange, pineapple, and blackberry, 582/5. But not many people know there is another range of fruit, with faces, Numbers 4895–4899 designed by George Matthews in the 1970s. There is a range of basket style containers with fruit decorating the lid, Number 4865, they all have the same number but with different lids. They used the same fruit lids for the leaf honey pots. Then there are the sports honies, made up of a golf ball, football, rugby ball, and bowls, Numbers 4712/8. Quite an amusing honey pot is the bee honey, looking very pleased with himself, he has obviously just eaten all the honey, 5383, designed by Mr. George Matthews in 1977. This is just a small example of what is available.

What can I say about the novelty pickle jars, and sauce bowls? There are at least fourteen of them, all with very bemused expressions, Numbers from 4549–5127 (not consecutive). I should hurry if you want to collect them, the prices are increasing all the time. George Matthews who designed most of these, has a lot to answer for.

There are not all that many SylvaC tea sets or coffee sets. By far the nicest was the blackberry tea set, made about 1949, and available in primrose or pink, numbers around 1862. Also very attractive was the butterfly range, the only piece I have seen is the honey pot, but there were other pieces as well. The numbers are a bit scattered, but start about 3554, they were designed by Mr. R. Thompson in the 1960s. There was also the Wyka Range, Totem Range, the Hollyberry Range for Christmas, and the Croft Cottage Range. The Avon tableware was one of the widest ranges, and was available with several different patterns, the most popular of which was Limegrove. The Cordon Brun Range was also quite extensive, including an 18 piece tea set and 15 piece coffee set. There was also the Medway Range, and a few items in the Brazil Range. There was a Pisces Range, of fish shaped tableware.

It was fitting that one of the last SylvaC designs was the range of Tudor Cottage table ware. Thirty items had been planned, but only seven were produced. Unfortunately there were no plates, cups or saucers to complete the set, but Mr. George Matthews really excelled himself with this design, it was made in 1981. How nice that the last SylvaC range was of such high quality.

## SMALL POSIES NOVELTY CONTAINERS AND MINIATURE VASES

Shaw & Copestake made many small posies, in a variety of shapes colours and designs. Many of these were attached to an animal or decorated with flowers. Some were pure novelty items, like the straw hat shapes, which in fact look very nice on the wall, there are two baskets, a hat pot, and posy bar in this range. One of the most popular posies was the curved posy Number 1479, which had either a small bunny or dog perched on one end, a similar design can be found with a lady draped over one end Number 1327. The round posy with three bunnies, Number 1312, is often to be seen, as is the round posy with the gnome in the centre Number 1480/1. There is also a heart shaped posy with gnome, the gnomes were sometimes replaced by animals. The squirrel eating from a bowl Number 1494 was also produced for quite a time.

All these small novelty posies are very fascinating, there are so many combinations. The dog on the slipper Number 31, and dog and shoe Number 2051, are really delightful, as are the dog posies Numbers 2024/5, the terrier and spaniel.

An interesting discrepancy has been found with posy Number 2054, which is an oblong basket, with a small dog. They come in two depths 1¾″ and 2¼″. There is also a round basket Number 1996, seen with a dog standing, or a little dog trying to climb in. Number 568 is a small bowl, with grass effect with either a fawn or rabbit. Number 3560 has a dog jumping over a wall, and Number 586 is a dog in a barrel. Number 586 is not numbered on the base, only stamped with a SylvaC mark.

Another set of novelty containers are Numbers 2798-owl on a tree trunk, 2799-gnome on a bamboo tree, 2800-fox with a pine-cone, 2807-two monkies and a coconut, all under three inches high. The kitten in a ball of wool, Number 3163 is either loved or hated. But should be part of the SylvaC collection, as should the kittens in a boot, Number 4977.

Small posies are also made as part of another range, as in the Woodland Range, Numbers 4231 and 4239, and the House in the Glen Range, Number 4890.

There are many miniature vases the most popular was Number 475-with the stork handle and 1993-with the squirrel handle. Another set being 4783–87, all 3″ or under. There is also a miniature tankard Number 4810.

The anenome posies came in three sizes, Numbers 123,126 and 127, and there is a very small container called sheaf, Number 1909 seen on its own or with hand decorated flowers.

This just gives you an example of a few of the items available, there are many more to be found.

## TANKARDS, MUGS AND BEAKERS

There is a large range of tankards, mugs and beakers to be found with the SylvaC mark. From the standard coffee mug, to the novelty sports tankards. Some tankards have been made to mark a special occasion, such as the Nottingham Forest Football Club Centenary Year-1965, Number 3488. Others were souvenirs, as 3546 for Jersey. There was an Age of Chivalry set of six tankards, all Number 4245 depicting different Earls and Princes. There are ten sports tankards, from soccer to sailing from Number 4719 to 4728 and six novelty tankards featuring a skull Number 4570, a drinking horn Number 4574, a riding boot Number 4584 and a fish in three sizes Numbers 4566,4567 and 4387. There is also D'Ye Ken John Peel Number 1614.

Most of the table ware ranges also included a beaker, Number 1600 in the Dahlia range, Number 4633-Hollyberry range, and Number 4801-Medway Range. There are also many individual coffee beakers in various designs.

Some SylvaC novelties as shown in the 1960 catalogue.

# CHAPTER 7

# TRADEMARKS AND LABELS

It is now thought by Shaw & Copestake experts, that the DAISY mark could have been used earlier than 1925, which is the date given in Goddens Encyclopaedia of British Pottery marks. It could possibly have been in use by 1912 and may even have been used sometime before that date. We have found an area in Longton called DAISY Bank, quite near the original William Shaw pottery, there was also a DAISY Bank Pottery, and this was probably the reason for using the DAISY symbol for marking the Shaw & Copestake wares. Made in England was incorporated into the early DAISY, and from c1935 SylvaC was also included.

The mould numbers were used early in the life of Shaw & Copestake and some of the original designs from the Sheaf Pottery Company and William Shaw pottery were absorbed into the Shaw & Copestake range. Decoration numbers were extensively used at this time, they were handwritten in gold or black, and referred to the type of decoration used on the ware. These were exclusive to Shaw and Copestake.

Most of the pre-second World War items do not have SylvaC impressed on the base. These moulds were obviously made before the SylvaC name was extensively used, but the mould numbers are very distinctive, and some of the wares have a SylvaC label attached. They started to impress the SylvaC name on the bases from about 1937, but it was very haphazard, and not all items were marked. They also used a rubber stamp on the base of unmarked ware. There doesn't appear to have been any definite system used, and many different labels and marks can be found, as can be seen from the examples shown. Although it may be possible to tell when a label or mark was FIRST introduced, Collectors must remember the haphazardness of the SylvaC system. Old labels seem to emerge on later models, and it is not a good idea to date by label. SylvaC labels even become mistakenly attached to non-SylvaC items. I have also been working on the theory that the SylvaC Ware in the slanting flowing style seen stamped on many of the wares, was used by the Falcon Pottery to mark the SylvaC items, but it hasn't been possible to complete this particular investigation.

In an attempt to date the SylvaC trade mark, I have spent some time at the Patent Office in London, where trade marks are registered. There was no trace of the SylvaC trade mark being registered before 1938.

You will notice the style of numbering differs on the ware made in the Falcon Factory, being embossed rather than impressed. Some of the later items also had a different style of numbering, using smaller figures.

### FALCON WARE

There are several different Falcon Ware marks. One with LG in the centre (Lawrence and Grundy), used in the 1930s. The falcon, the artists palette and the urn, with T. Lawrence above it, and Falcon Ware below it, were all probably 1940s.

In the 1950s Mr. Reginald Thompson designed the slanting flowing lines of SylvaC Ware and Falcon Ware, and back stamps were made. I have never seen any Falcon Ware labels, all the marks have been printed, stamped, or impressed on the base of the item. The very early Falcon Ware does not seem to be numbered. Most of it is named. Although the individual decorations were given numbers.

You have probably wondered at the significance of the additional letters or numbers sometimes found on the bases. It was probably the initial or mark of the mould maker.

J.H. Weatherby & Sons Ltd, Hanley, Stoke-on-Trent, also used the name Falcon Ware and Royal Falcon Ware on their products, this is incorporated in a Union Jack flag trademark. J.H. Weatherby & Sons Ltd., has NO connection with the Thomas Lawrence Ltd., Falcon Ware pottery.

1925–1937

1935–1940.

About 1920s.

1930s.

1930s.

1940s–1950s.

1940s–1950s.

1940s–1950s.

1950s.

1940s–1950s.

1960s–1980s.

1950s.

1940s–1950s.

1960s–1970s.

1940s.

1950s–1960s.

Label from 1960s.

Label from 1960s.

Label from 1970s.

From 1970s.

From 1980s.

Crown Winsor 1982+

Falcon 1920–1930s.

Falcon 1920s–1930s.

Falcon 1930s–1940s.

Falcon 1940s.

Falcon 1940s–1950s.

1940s–1960s.

1950s–1960s.

1950s–1960s.

1950s–1960s.

1950s–1960s.

Please note, in the absence of any records of the marking system used at the factories, these dates can be no more than a very general guide.

# CHAPTER 8

# POTTERY PERSONALITIES

## MR. WILLIAM SHAW. FOUNDER OF SHAW & COPESTAKE

MR. WILLIAM SHAW was born in 1874 and acquired his first pottery about 1894. Mr. Copestake, his first partner, only stayed a few months, and a new partnership was formed with Mr. Richard Hull, senior. Mr. William Shaw who was only in his early 20s when he started the business, retired from Shaw & Copestake in May 1942, having successfully run the business in partnership with the two Mr. Hulls for more than 40 years. He passed away on December 31st, 1950 at the age of 76. It is not yet known if Mr. William Shaw came from a family of pottery manufacturers. As there were several Shaws in the area also manufacturing earthenware, it is likely there was some connection. Mr. William Shaw also had a son connected with the business.

## MR. COPESTAKE

It is thought that Mr. Copestake only stayed in partnership with Mr. Shaw for a few months, possibly six. He then seems to vanish without trace. But there are other Copestakes in the same business in that area, the most well known being Dewes & Copestake. They were in business in 1896, and based in Caroline Street, Longton, Stoke-on-Trent, it is possible there was a connection. However although Mr. Copestake disappeared off the scene so quickly, his name carried on until 1982.

## MR. RICHARD HULL SENIOR-PARTNER IN SHAW & COPESTAKE

MR. RICHARD HULL SENIOR joined Shaw & Copestake shortly after it was founded. He was born in Frisby, Leicestershire on 11th August 1865, his parents were farmers. He came to the Potteries whilst very young, and began working in the pottery industry with a Mr. Joseph Ball, who was a manufacturer of china in Anchor Place, Longton, Stoke-on-Trent. Later he went to Canada, where for about six years he was in the employment of Gowans, Kent & Co, Crockery & Glass Importers, Toronto. On his return to the Potteries he joined Mr. Shaw at Shaw & Copestake, taking over Mr. Copestakes partnership, and was responsible for building up the large export business that continued successfully until the late 1970s.

During the First World War he was a volunteer guard and a special constable. He was a great sportsman, loved football, golf and shooting. He was a director of the Blythe Bridge Bowling and Tennis Club, a member of the Dunrobin Bowling Club, Meir Golf Club, Stockton Brook Golf Club, and also the Totteridge Club in South Herts. A wonderful character, who continued to participate in the business until his death on the 29th September 1935 at the age of 70. It is rather ironic that despite his love of sport and the open air he died of tuberculosis.

## MR. RICHARD HULL JUNIOR-CHAIRMAN & MANAGING DIRECTOR

MR. RICHARD HULL JUNIOR joined his father, Richard Hull senior at Shaw & Copestake in 1924, at the age of 18, and devoted his whole life to the running of the pottery. He was very proud of the fact that he started at the bottom of the business, and worked his way up. When his father died in 1935 Richard junior became Mr. Shaws partner and there began a successful, partnership until Mr. Shaws retirement in 1942. The business became a Limited Company in 1936. Although having no artistic talent himself, there is no doubt that Mr. Richard Hull knew exactly which wares were required by the market, and he was very clever at picking the designs that were successful. He was keen to promote the animal models and novelties and travelled all over the world looking for ideas. One of his greatest successes were the green matt rabbits, and they are still the most well known of SylvaC Ware. It was also his idea to use the SylvaC name, devised from the letters S for Shaw and C for Copestake, and incorporating the name of the factory, which was Sylvan. He continued to work at extending the export market, and was able to combine his love of travel with promoting the wares.

Mr. Hull was a founder member of The Ornamental Pottery Association, served on various Committees of the British Ceramic Manufacturers Federation, and was also a member of the organising panel for the pottery and glass section of the Blackpool Gift Fair. During which time he met many members of the Royal Family. Mr. Richard Hull junior died in 1977 at the age of 71, after several years of ill-health.

In the 1930s Mr. Richard Hull married Miss Eileen Grundy, daughter of Mr. John Grundy, Managing Director of Thomas Lawrence, Falcon Pottery. Which he eventually took over due to the untimely death of Mr. John Grundy.

Mrs. Eileen Hull, has been kind enough to assist in my research, and given me vital background information to enable me to build up a picture of her family. Although not connected with the day-to-day running of the pottery, Mrs. Hull was a sounding board for Mr. Hulls latest ideas for new wares. Mrs. Hull was the mainstay of the pottery canteen during the War, and ran it with great efficiency for the duration of the War, providing over 70 workers with a cooked meal every lunchtime.

## MR. E.J. DENNIS DIRECTOR FROM 1942

MR. E.J. DENNIS was a life long friend of the Hull family. After the untimely death of Mr. John Grundy of Thomas Lawrence (Longton) Ltd, Mr. Dennis took over Mr. Grundy's shares, to become a member of the board of directors with Mr. Hull, in 1938. He subsequently became a director of Shaw & Copestake in 1942, and despite being very involved with his own family business, took an enormous interest in the Falcon and Sylvan Works. He was always ready with a suggestion for the latest inovations in the pottery industry, and together with Mr. Hull, took great pride in the building of the new Sylvan Works, making sure the factory had all the most up-to-date equipment.

## MR. E.J. RADFORD DIRECTOR FROM 1947

MR. E.J. RADFORD became a director of Shaw & Copestake in 1947. He took a particular interest in the building of the new factory, which started in 1955. Mr. Radford passed away in 1974.

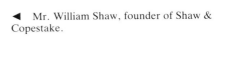
◄ Mr. William Shaw, founder of Shaw & Copestake.

▼ Staff Group c1960. Standing left to right: William Lake-Assistant Clay Manager, Malcolm Chapman-Commercial Director, Roy Davies-Dispatch Manager, Ivan Hallam-Representative Northern Area, Reginald Thompson-Senior Modeller/Designer, Gerrard Salt – Decorating Manager, Geoffrey Abbott – Progress Manager, Ronald Wright – Assistant Decorating Manager, James Brian – Clay Manager. Seated left to right: Eric J. Dennis – Director, Richard Hull – Chairman and Managing Director, E. John (Jack) Radford – Works Director.

## MR. M.D. CHAPMAN DIRECTOR FROM 1962

MR. M.D. CHAPMAN an accountant, joined Shaw & Copestake in 1955 assisting Mr. Richard Hull on the commercial side of the business, he was appointed a director in 1962. Mr. Chapman took an enormous interest in all aspects of the pottery, even suggesting designs. It was his idea to introduce a Mr. SylvaC, which was used for advertising purposes for a number of years. Mr. Chapman having a wonderful memory has been of considerable help in compiling information for this book. He has been able to put me in touch with many members of staff and directors, and is obviously very proud of his association with Shaw & Copestake. He was a personal friend of Mr. Hull junior, and fortunately has been able to remember all the vital information Mr. Hull passed on to him during their conversations. Thank goodness he was interested enough at the time to absorb all this information, and has passed it on for posterity.

After the liquidation of Shaw & Copestake, Mr. Chapman set up his own business, IMPORTING ceramics to Stoke-on-Trent, and appears to have found a surprisingly successful niche for what would seem to be an unlikely venture.

## MR. E.R. TAYLOR WORKS DIRECTOR FROM 1974

Mr. E.R. Taylor became a director of Shaw & Copestake in 1974 and remained with the company until 1982. He had previously been employed at the Thomas Lawrence Pottery as clay manager from 1948 until 1957. After spending a short time in Canada, he managed a small pottery in Wallasey, Cheshire. In 1961, he returned to Stoke-on-Trent, to start his own pottery. In 1971, faced with a compulsory purchase order on his premises, he accepted the position of works manager at Shaw & Copestake Ltd. Fortunately, Mr. Taylor has been able to identify lots of the photographs taken at the potteries.

## MR THOMAS LAWRENCE (Falcon Ware)

MR. THOMAS LAWRENCE founded his pottery, in Wharf Street, Stoke-on-Trent, about 1888. There is a wonderful paragraph in the Pottery Gazette May 2nd 1898 as follows: 'Thomas Lawrence, late of Wharf Street, Stoke-on-Trent, has removed to a commodius Pottery, which he has specially erected in Waterloo Street, Longton'. He was interested in photography, and before the turn of the century had attempted to decorate a vase with a photograph of his nephew John Grundy. Mr. Lawrence retired to Colwyn Bay, but still visited the pottery every week, staying the night with his nephew John Grundy, who eventually became managing director of the Falcon Works.

## MR. JOHN GRUNDY (Falcon Ware)

Mr. John Grundy, was managing director of Thomas Lawrence, Falcon Works, from about 1920. He was the nephew of Thomas Lawrence, who founded the business.

Thomas Lawrence became a limited company in September 1938. Sadly just three days after the limited company was formed Mr. John Grundy died. Mr. Grundy was to have been governing director and chairman of the new company. Mr. Richard Hull, his son-in-law, and Mr. E.J. Dennis stepped in, and Mr. Dennis took over Mr. Grundys shares in the business. Mr. Grundy was a very talented artist, and was mostly to be found in the decorating shop, working on the latest design. He was happiest when he had a paintbrush in his hand, and was much respected by his workforce. He knew every one of his employees by their first name. His remaining family take great pride in the paintings and drawings still in existence. He loved to hand paint the vases and several examples of his work still exist.

He was also very proud of the fact that he paid 2d. per week insurance to the local Cottage Hospital for each of his employees, so they could be well looked after if they were taken ill.

Although of an artistic nature, he was an equally astute business man, and it was a flourishing company that Mr. Richard Hull and Mr. E.J. Dennis took over in 1938.

Richard Hull Senior.

Thomas Lawrence.

Richard Hull Junior.

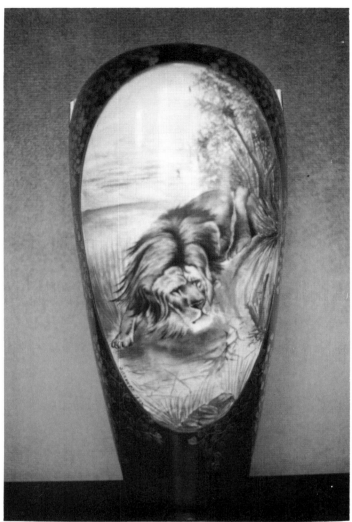

▲  An early attempt by Mr. Thomas Lawrence to decorate pottery by photography. The photograph is of Mr. John Grundy, his nephew.

▲  A vase handpainted by Mr. John Grundy in 1897 at the Thomas Lawrence factory.

◄  Leopard 1458 9½″ high, and Spaniel 1462 11″ high. As shown in the 1940 catalogue.

# CHAPTER 9

# DESIGNERS AND MODELLERS

## MR. REGINALD THOMPSON B.E.M

Mr. Thompson joined Thomas Lawrence (Longton) Ltd, in 1917, at the age of 14. He was employed as a painter, painting at the benches and extending lithos. As his outstanding artistic talent became apparent, he was awarded a scholarship to the Hanley School of Art, where he completed the course for pottery, decorators and designers, with distinction. After completion of the course he applied for the position of decorating manager at the Thomas Lawrence Works. Mr. John Grundy, the managing director, gave him a six months trial, and he subsequently became the youngest decorating manager in the Potteries at the age of 19, in 1922.

After the amalgamation of Shaw & Copestake Ltd and Thomas Lawrence (Longton) Ltd., in 1938, Mr. Thompsons designs were used at both factories, and he became chief designer. He finally retired in 1978 having completed the staggering total of 62 years loyal service, and was awarded the British Empire Medal in recognition of his services to the pottery industry.

You will be able to see in the Register of Numbers Mr. Thompsons numerous and varied designs and models. He made a very important contribution to the success of the factories. When the new factory was built and the two potteries merged together, Mr. Thompson found he was not only designing, but managing the decorating department, training the paintresses, as well as modelling. It was soon realised this was too much for one person and after discussion with Mr. Richard Hull some of the responsibility was delegated to other employees. Mr. Thompson then specialised in designing, modelling, training, and quality control. Some of his models were inspired by his love of gardening, particularly the Wishing Well, Dovecote, and Blue Tit ranges. His much loved cairn terrier, Wendy, 3447, was modelled in 1963, and even the stray cat he befriended, 5236, now has a place in SylvaC history. Some of his finest work can be seen in the Prestige range, and the Cavalier range. He also made several figures for the Falcon factory, unfortunately un-numbered, but marked Falcon Ware. One was called Jeanette, and was a young lady with flowers, one was a crinoline lady, another was called Bretton Girl.

It is difficult to mention all his work but the MR. SYLVAC ashtray was particularly well done. Mr. Thompson had a good rapport with Mr. Richard Hull junior, the managing director, and between them they would work out the various models, with perhaps Mr. Hull giving him the initial idea, and Mr. Thompson being able to produce exactly what was needed. Mr. Thompson had his own special brand of humour which can be seen in the pixie range, the tennis playing dog Number 2660 and the kitten in a ball of wool, Number 3168.

Mr. Thompson was a very quiet unasuming gentleman, who perhaps did not receive the recognition due to him. A man of many talents, artist as well as modeller he was sorely missed by everyone when he retired in 1978. He continued working for Shaw & Copestake Ltd until the age of 75, and then only due to illness did he finally retire. His whole life had been spent in the Potteries, he never took a holiday, and only once ventured abroad to Italy, accompanying Mr. Richard Hull on a business trip. Mr. Thompson died in April 1988 at the age of 85. Fortunately I was able to meet him several times, and have the conversations on video tape. It was particularly interesting to learn of the terrible working conditions prevalent at the time he started work in 1917, and the gradual improvement until the time of his retirement in 1978. When he first started work he would use the Potteries Electric Tramway, which played a large part in linking the six towns together. Mr. Thompson was a wonderfully talented man and it was a privilege to know him. It is fitting that so much of his work is now being collected and appreciated. It was a great joy to him, in the last months of his life to know of the interest being taken in his work. He loved to reminisce about his life at the Falcon and Sylvan Works.

## MR. STEPHAN CZARNOTA

Stephan Czarnota joined Shaw & Copestake Ltd., possibly in the late 1950s or early 1960s, and came originally from Hungary. He left Shaw & Copestake about 1966, to work freelance. During his time he modelled a large variety of wares. He was particularly good at the caricature models, and will be remembered for the range of long faced dogs Numbers 2938, 2950 and 2951 modelled in the early 1960s. (This information from Mr. M. Chapman, as the Mould Makers Register does not give modellers names until about 1963.) Also the Funnies range of dogs 3422–3433. He particularly enjoyed the humerous side of modelling, but also produced some classical dogs and animals, and many vases and flower pots.

## MR JOHN LAWSON

John Lawson joined Shaw & Copestake as a trainee modeller, working with Mr. Thompson and Stephan Czarnota in the 1960s but left before 1966 to emigrate to America. He seems to have modelled a considerable amount of ware in that time, including animals, vases, and also the Pebble Range of vases and bowls, of which a considerable amount is still to be seen. His initials are also by the Prestige piece of the otter with fish, Number 3459. But Mr. Reginald Thompsons daughter Jeanette, remembers her father bringing this model home to paint, and rather assumed her father had also modelled it. It may have been a combined effort, which I believe was the case with other models. His models can be identified in the Register of Numbers. He was replaced by Mr. George Matthews.

## MR. GEORGE MATTHEWS

George Matthews joined Shaw & Copestake in 1966, and stayed until liquidation of the company in 1982. He trained at the Newcastle School of Art, his first job in the pottery industry, was with the Boston Pottery, Sandiford, where he was taken on as a modeller. But as this was such a small pottery, and modelling was not required on a continual basis he found that he was asked to help in other departments, such as the mould making section, setting kilns, carrying ware etc. It was with this good grounding of all aspects of the pottery industry that he was taken on as Mr. Reginald Thompsons right hand man. George Matthews displays an amazing talent for all types of modelling, including animals, tableware and vases. He joined Shaw & Copestake at the height of their success, and his talents certainly meant this continued for many years. It is difficult to pick out any special models as they were all of such high quality, but perhaps the bust of Sir Winston Churchill, Number 5165, modelled in 1974, and the Tudor Cottage Ware Numbers 5670–5676 modelled in 1981 are worth a special mention.

◄ Reginald Thompson in the Thomas Lawrence factory c1949, supervising the painting of hat bands. In the background other workers are lithographing nursery ware. Left foreground is Gladys Hill.

► George Matthews working on the bust of Churchill, Number 5165, in 1974. The workshop as you can see was in an old part of the building, and was originally used by Cyples Colour Works before being incorporated into Shaw & Copestakes factory.

◄ Reginald Thompson sketching the Hyacinth Leaf range. This range was introduced about 1959 or 1960, but the photograph was taken after 1962 which suggests it was specially posed for a brochure.

George also had a very special relationship with Mr. Reginald Thompson, and visited him frequently during the last months of his life, a gesture that was so appreciated by the Thompson family.

After George Matthews was made redundant in 1982, he started his own business. He now makes the most beautiful resin based models of woodland and animals scenes under the trade name of Sandringham. Who knows, you may see a resemblance to some SylvaC animals in the Sandringham models.

## FREELANCE MODELLERS

OTAKAR STEINBURGER was a freelance modeller and designer in the early 1930s, he came originally from Czechoslovakia, but lived in Peckham, London. He modelled 'Mac' the scottie dog range, Numbers 1205–1209, and possibly dogs Numbers 1261/2 and 1245, which seem to be in a similar style. I was able to look up the registered number of the scottie dogs, at the Patent Office in Holborn, London, and I noticed that on the same date in 1932, Mr. Steinburger also registered many other designs, of dogs and other inventions. So I do feel that some of the early dogs were his designs.

MR. CHEADLE did quite a lot of work for Thomas Lawrence or Shaw & Copestake before the War, of which there is no record. The first recorded model is Number 3311, bowl with bird. Mr. Cheadle also designed some of the Feather Range in the 1960s, but there is very little of his work recorded. Mr. Thompson thought Mr. Cheadle may have modelled the tiny figures of Pete, Pam and Paul, Numbers 3111/2/3, and also the ski-ing rabbits, Numbers 25–29.

MR. WOOLLAM also designed or modelled from the 1930s, but once again there is no record of his work, only a few items in the Feather Range in the 1960s, and a cup and saucer in the Magnolia Range Number 3547.

MR. ARNOLD MACHIN M.A. designed and modelled a futuristic range of animals Numbers 3151–54. These included a cat, horse, tigress and stag, and were made at the Falcon Pottery. Mr. Machin also advised on the type of decoration most suitable for his designs.

MR. RICHARD DENNIS, son of the director Mr. E.J. Dennis also designed one or two items. One of which was a mug Number 4682, with owl embossed.

Some other initials are also given in the Register. These were sometimes the mould makers initial, and it is not known if they modelled the items. Some initials have been untraceable, and it is possible they were errors made by the person entering the information.

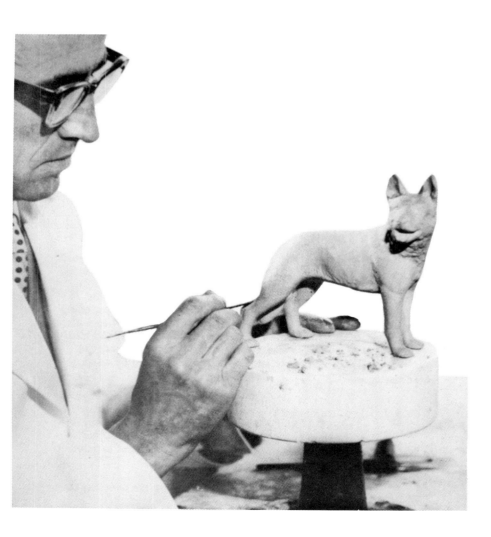

Stephan Czarnota modelling alsation Number 3170.

# *Thank you for your custom—*

## *PLEASE TELL YOUR FRIENDS*
## *WHERE WE ARE.*

# *Sylvac* **FACTORY SHOP**

# SHAW & COPESTAKE LIMITED

SYLVAN WORKS, NORMACOT ROAD, LONGTON, STOKE-ON-TRENT, STAFFS.

**OPEN MONDAY TO SATURDAY 10.00 a.m. TO 5.00 p.m.**

Advertising leaflet used until closure of Shaw & Copestake.

◄ Modus 80 animals.

5213

5212

5210

5238

▼ Assyria range. Vase 4573, plate 4690, fern pot 4678, small vase 4693, bowl 4699.

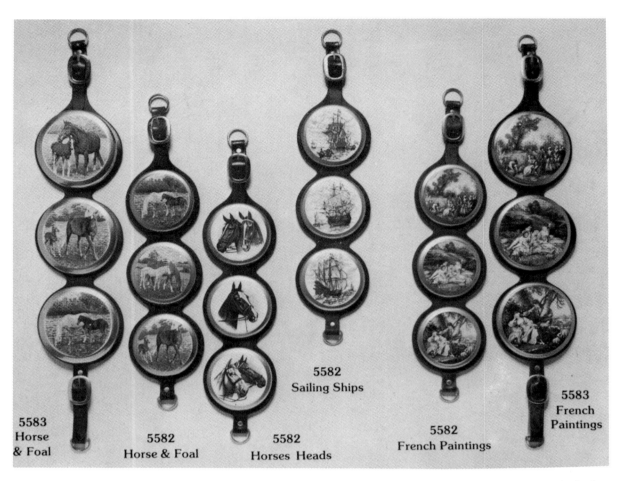

5583
Horse
& Foal

5582
Horse & Foal

5582
Horses Heads

5582
Sailing Ships

5582
French Paintings

5583
French
Paintings

▲ Martingales, from page in the 1981 catalogue.

3154

*SylvaC* WARE
MADE BY SHAW & COPESTAKE LTD, LONGTON, STAFFORDSHIRE

3151

3153

3152

◄ Black and white matt animals designed by Arnold Machin M.A., can also be found in other colours and finishes.

Old Shaw & Copestake vases from about 1910. From left Number 509, Number 371, Number 432, Centre Vase Number 578. All with very ornate decoration, and bearing the early daisy mark.

Shaw & Copestake jugs, probably 1920. Blue jug has daisy mark and is hand painted with a boat on a lake scene. Others are marked Silvo and are attractively decorated.

(*top left*) Clock set about 1920s. Clock Number 605 and vases Number 606. They all have the daisy mark.

(*bottom left*) Clock set about 1920s. Clock Number 605 and vases Number 606. With swan decoration, all have the daisy mark.

(*above*) The jugs are both Number 573. The jug on the left has the daisy mark with SylvaC in the centre. The clocks are number 605, decorated with roses and a Japanese lady. The dressing table items are hand painted with the boat on the lake scene and have the early daisy mark.

(*below*) Wild duck range in cellulose finish with embossed design. From left vases Numbers 650 and 785, clock Number 649, (the clock face is not original), vases Numbers 1858 and 650, in the front, trinket box 804.

Dragon handle jug Number 1116. Note the flames on the bottom left.

Very rare Art Deco jug Number 1147.

A collection of SylvaC cats. Numbers from left top row are: 2549, 5298, 5300, 5107 large siamese, 184, 1046. Bottom row 1485, 1296, two white kittens in the centre 104, 3168, 4977, small siamese in front: 102.

On the left Collon Number 2 vase, decorated with a boat. On the right Number 679 from the Evening Fantasy Range.

A 1939 setting for SylvaC ornaments. Note the rare matt coloured flying ducks, the dancing lady Number 920 and in the hearth lizard Number 1467.

A fine example of horse and rider Number 4707 (formerly Falcon Number 21), with hounds Number 4709.

(*far left top*) Novelty bowls. Top row from left: Numbers 569, 1513, and 587 (rabbit hutch). Middle row from left: Numbers 548, 355 and 689. Bottom row from left: Numbers 572, 353, 2049.

(*top left*) Top row: Wyka range tableware. Middle row: Dovecote range tableware. Bottom row: Blackberry range tableware.

(*far bottom left*) SylvaC honeypots. Note: Strawberry with face, second from left top shelf. Honey bee, fourth from left middle shelf and Butterfly range, third left bottom shelf.

(*bottom left*) Top row Numbers: 2295, 1514, 282 (Falcon Ware). Middle row: Numbers 591, 1510, 550. Bottom row Numbers: 469, 473, 2512.

(*top right*) Two ashtrays Number 1366, with seagull Number 1357 and dog number 1433.

(*middle right*) Lop Ear the rabbit in three sizes Numbers 1304, 1303 and 1302.

(*below*) Back row from left: Giant Panda range money box Number 5576, Riverside range vase Number 4377, Harvest range vase Number 5246, Woodland range vase Number 4233. Front row from left: Woodland range tray Number 4293, House in the Glen range 4890, Squirrel range posy Number 2468, Woodland range posy trough Number 4231, Riverside range vase Number 4393.

Character and Toby jugs. Numbers from left top row: 4431, 4401, 4460, 4439. Numbers from left bottom row: Punch no Number, Henry VIII originally un-numbered given 4488, 4440, 4411, Cavalier 306 re-numbered 4487.

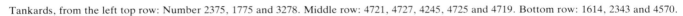

Tankards, from the left top row: Number 2375, 1775 and 3278. Middle row: 4721, 4727, 4245, 4725 and 4719. Bottom row: 1614, 2343 and 4570.

# CHAPTER 10

# THE SYLVAC SALES STORY

I had always harboured a secret wish, that once The SylvaC Story was published (1989), it would inspire ex-employees of Shaw & Copestake to write to me. I had to wait until July 1992 before this happened, when I received a letter from Mr. Harold A. Clowes, former senior sales representative and export manager. Mr. Clowes was slightly put out because I made no mention of him in the book, and scant reference to the sales story of Shaw & Copestake, which he rightly stated was an important part of the success of SylvaC. I HAD attempted to trace the sales story, but the few contacts I had were unable to help, and I did not know of the whereabouts of Harold A. Clowes. It gives me much pleasure to have the opportunity now to correct this sorry state of affairs, and Harold has proved to be the teller of a wonderful sales story, he recalls many fascinating anecdotes, which I know you will find interesting.

In the words of Mr. Harold A. Clowes:

## EARLY DAYS

I know little of the particular sales methods of Shaw & Copestake before the first world war, but the usual way in the pottery industry was for distribution to be mainly through wholesalers, with the added help of one or two agents. The valuable London market was usually handled by an agent who generally had an office/showroom in the Holborn district, thus enabling buyers to conduct much of their business in one area.

## BETWEEN WARS AND DURING SECOND WORLD WAR

Wholesalers featured largely in distribution, but Thomas Lawrence employed as agents a father and son named Emery who travelled around carrying stock which they sold to retailers from their van.

Shaw & Copestake had a bright young man named Bill Coates, who after returning from war service was offered the chance to travel for them as an agent. To help make the agency worthwhile they also obtained the agency for him from their very good friends the china manufacturers Hudson & Middleton Ltd, just a little way up Normacot Road, Mr. Coates was very successful. When the second world war came, the Shaw & Copestake works was taken over by the Ministry of Supply, and production concentrated at the Thomas Lawrence works. Mr. Coates was directed to war work, but had the forsight to register himself as a wholesaler, consequently he was able to obtain the occasional crate of export rejects, which he then passed on to his old customers.

## IMMEDIATE POST WAR

Almost everything had to be for export, the only items for the home trade being export rejects. No selling was required, every retailer was glad of any ration the factories cared to spare him. Richard Hull had the bright idea of opening his own retail shop, and premises were taken in a town in Cheshire, Mr. Emery junior was manager. In the days when two people standing outside a shop caused an immediate queue, this was at first a success. When the euphoria died down Richard Hull handed over the shop to Mr. Emery, the early success was not sustained and I gather the shop soon closed.

In the meantime Billy Coates had decided to find pastures new and purchased a half share in a very nice retail china and glass shop in Paignton, called Church's China Shop.

## SETTING UP THE SYLVAC TERRITORIES AND SALES TEAMS

In 1946 I was appointed area representative for the South West and South Wales for the firm I had joined in 1937, British Heat Resisting Glass Co, Ltd., manufacturers of Phoenix Oven Glass (now long since defunct). One of my customers was Church's China Shop in Paignton, and it was here I met Billy Coates. We got on very well and he regaled me with tales of his career with Shaw & Copestake. In about 1948 Phoenix showed at the British Industries Fair in London, and it was here I met Richard Hull for the first time.

In 1952, on one of my trips to Paignton, Billy Coates mentioned Mr. Hull had offered him his old position, which he declined. I decided to apply, and wrote to Mr. Hull. The result was that my wife and I were invited to his home for Sunday lunch, we were treated like old friends, and I was given the job. This was the first time they had appointed a full time sales representative with car provided. (Actually I had Mrs. Hull's Rover.)

The territory covered was South and West Wales up as far as Aberystwyth, Cornwall, Devon, Somerset, Gloucestershire, Wiltshire, Dorset, Hampshire and the Isle of Wight. The move proved successful for all concerned, and in 1953 Mr. Harry Town joined the firm on a similar full time basis, his area was London, Kent, Surrey, Sussex and Essex. The London showroom was opened the same year, and Mr. Town divided his time between the showroom and travelling. In 1956/7 his place was taken by Mr. Guy Westray, who continued with the firm for the next 20 years. In Scotland we had agents Doleman and Steward Ltd., Glasgow.

Next to join the team was Mr. Ivan Hallam, who had previously worked in the Shaw & Copestake warehouses. He was appointed to cover North Wales, the Midlands, the North West and the Isle of Man and eventually added the whole of Ireland to his territory. The final gap in the coverage of the country was filled by the appointment of Mr. Stewart Bowns, his territory was the North of England, North Eastern counties, Eastern England and East Anglia.

## TYPES OF BUSINESSES SUPPLIED

In the 1950s we supplied gift shops, glass and china shops, hardware stores, departmental stores and a few florists. Unfortunately, the higher class shops, whilst admiring some items, rather squirmed when they turned the pages and saw purple bunny rabbits and comical dogs. My own idea, which might have solved the problem, of having two catalogues, one under the Shaw & Copestake name and the other under Thomas Lawrence's name showing only high class items, was never acted upon.

Over the years outlets changed, departmental stores no longer bought individually, buying being centralised, this meant you were either 'in' or 'out' nationwide on the whim of one buyer. However, other opportunities presented themselves with the opening of garden centres, stocking bulb bowls and plant pots, kitchenware shops and trendy boutiques looking for 'way out' items. For many years very good business was done with Boots stores, but this declined in later years when a committee was formed to choose which products to stock.

▲ The SylvaC sales team Christmas 1977, at the launch of the New Cavalier range. Back left to right: Lionel Goldsmith, Guy Westray, Stewart Bowns, Eric Dennis (Director), Harold Clowes, Joe Henderson, Malcolm Chapman (Director).
Front left to right: Ivan Hallam, Stuart McNaught.

► The Paris Exhibition. Circa 1964.
The late Lord Derwent (Trade Minister), leaving the Shaw & Copestake stand, watched by Richard Dennis and Harold Clowes.
Both photographs kindly lent by Harold Clowes

## WHO'S WHO AT HARROGATE

Mr. G. Abbott, who has been on our Staff since 1946, was for the first seven years of his business career at the Shelley Potteries Ltd. He then joined the staff at Messrs. William Hudsons, Manufacturers of Sutherland China. In 1936 he became London agent for Messrs. H. M. Williamson & Son, and during the 1939–45 War was employed at the Royal Ordinance Factory at Swynnerton. He will be at the Harrogate Gifts & Fancy Goods Fair with Mr. Clowes and Mr. Town, in Room No. 201 at the George Hotel.

Mr. G. Abbott

Mr. H. A. Clowes joined our staff in August, 1952, as representative for South-West England and South Wales. On leaving school he was with a Birmingham Furniture Firm in the Production Office. In 1936 he joined the British Heat Resisting Glass Co. Ltd., Manufacturers of Phoenix Oven Glass in their Sales Office. Throughout the 1939-45 War he was in the Royal Air Force. On his return to civilian life he rejoined the Phoenix Glass and was appointed Sales representative for the South-West and South Wales.

His efforts since he commenced with us have been most satisfactory and we have every confidence that he will go from strength to strength.

Mr. H. A. Clowes

Mr. H. W. Town joined our Staff as a part-time representative in June, 1952, and from January 1st, 1953, will be full time representative for London, and South West England. Previously he was with Messrs. Lourie & Co., Ltd. and Messrs. Johnstone & Co., Ltd. and Messrs. Heppners Ltd. when he covered the Midlands and the North. He had experience of the retail trade as Branch Manager of some of the Lawley China & Glass Stores. In September, 1939, he joined the London A.R.P. Service and on being invalided out of same, he opened his own business in Folkestone. In August, Mr. Town, after leaving our works for home, had a very serious Motor accident and was in the Stafford Infirmary for some time. He is now fit again and we hope that he, too, will meet with success in his new appointment.

Mr. H. W. Town

A page reproduced from the SylvaC and Falcon Bulletin, Spring 1953, giving an interesting write-up of the Shaw & Copestake sales team at the Harrogate Gifts and Fancy goods Fair.

## ℬ.ℐ.ℱ. 1952

An illustration of a portion of our Stand at the British Industries Fair, Earls Court, held in May, 1952. It shows the large vase modelled and decorated specially for the Exhibition, by our Mr. J. Brian and Mr. R. Thompson. The vase is almost five feet in height and decorated in "Cotswold," the pattern illustrated on the opposite page.

A page reproduced from the SylvaC and Falcon Bulletin, Spring 1953, showing the five foot high vase which was made specially for the British Industries Fair, Earls Court, May 1952. It is displayed on the Shaw & Copestake stand, on which can be seen many other interesting items.

## BEST SELLING LINES

What was 'in' one year was often completely 'out' the following year. There was no explanation for the change in fashion and demand. Some lines went on selling steadily year after year, other fluctuated wildly, and many never got off the ground. For every four or five ranges of ten or twelve pieces only about one proved a success. When one considers the expense of designing, mould making and producing, as well as marketing, it can be seen that we were in a very high risk business.

Among the great successes were Woodland, Riverside, Croft, Hyacinth, Pebble, Marina and Maple ranges. Toothache dogs, mint sauce boats, onion bowls, the various sauce bowls, stork and acorn jugs etc were also very successful. Matt dogs, and in the early days rabbits, were a good seller. (Myxomatosis put paid to the dear old bunny trade!'). Hand painted dogs, toby and character jug sales rose and fell from year to year with no logical explanation, I can remember at a sales conference being told there were enough stocks of toby and character jugs to last for three years, within a year the demand had changed so much that each sales area was on a ration system. There was a great demand in the mid 1970s for leather harnessed shire horses, this lasted for a short time before dying a complete death. Ranges which produced poor sales were usually withdrawn, often after their first year.

When I joined the firm in 1952 the garden gnomes still featured on a full colour page of my catalogue, but they were soon withdrawn, and I cannot recollect ever taking an order for them. The lazy pixies were not really a popular line, except as Cornish or Devon pixies.

## THE EXPORT MARKET

In pre-war and immediate post second world war days export orders emanated from appointed agents based in various countries. As collectors will readily appreciate, SylvaC was a peculiarly British product with an appeal to the home market or to people of British origin or history. Consequently the countries to which it had the greatest empathy were Australia, New Zealand, South Africa, and to an extent, Canada. Mr. Hull made one or two visits to South Africa, usually combining business with pleasure.

In 1958 Mr. Hull was not satisfied with the amount of business our agents in Canada were providing, I was therefore asked to go on a two month tour of Canada to see what could be done to improve sales. I repeated similar trips until 1964. In 1962 I took out a very nice new kitchen ware range (later re-numbered and called NOUVEAU Kitchen Ware). It came in bright colours with handpainted kitchen utensils in an embossed band around the edge. Samples had been laboratory tested and passed, and I had an excellent trip with this range, particularly the red, gathering in many orders and I returned to England in buoyant mood. However, the first consignment of red sent to the T. Eaton Store in Montreal, when unpacked, showed bad peeling of the glaze. The ultimate result was that this had to be withdrawn and all orders cancelled.

In the early 1960s, Mr. Hull thought it was an opportune time to investigate the possibilities for SylvaC on the Continent. At that time Western Europe was a virtual closed book to us with scarcely a single account there. I was asked to plan a trip, and visited Paris, Brussels, Hanover, Frankfurt, Hamburg, Amsterdam and the Hague. In the following years further trips ensued, in 1964, assisted by Mr. Eric Dennis's son Richard, we had a stand at an exhibition in Paris, but together with other British pottery firms, this was not a success.

In the late 1970s I went on two further European trips, and in 1980 toured Spain, Andorra, and Italy, again this was very hard going, as not many of our products seemed to appeal to the European market. This turned out to be the last of my continental trips as the demise of Shaw & Copestake began to loom, not that we had much expectation of that at the time.

In the mid 1970s Lionel Goldsmith, based in Manchester, was appointed as a freelance agent to cover the U.S.A. He already held several agencies with Stoke pottery firms, making regular visits to the States. He boosted SylvaC sales in the U.S.A. but even having customers in such diverse places as the Falkland Islands, Canaries, Kuwait and Norfolk Island in the South Pacific, the SylvaC export sales did not amount to a very large percentage of the total turnover.

Strange as it may seem the Channel Islands counted in Government statistics as an export market. From the late 1950s to the middle 1960s an annual trip was made by Malcolm Chapman, but as his responsibilities at the works increased he relinquished this pleasant task to me, and the Islands remained a lucrative market to the very end.

◄ Storage jar number 2586, Reg. No. 897228
Honey pot number 2555, Reg. No. 897226
Both with embossed band of kitchen utensils. Later renumbered and called Nouveau Kitchen Ware. (See above)

# CHAPTER 11

# THE AUSTRALIAN CONNECTION

The Australian connection began as early as 1903, when agencies were set up in the Colonies. Many of the wares were specifically made and decorated for the special requirements of the Australian market. The cellulose ware vases were colourfully decorated with koala bears, and indigenous flowers and greenery. The Sydney Harbour Bridge, mould number 727 registered design number 758626 (1930), was specially modelled (as a twin vase), and embossed with Australian wildlife, it was usually hand painted in cellulose.

In 1928 Messrs E.G. Page & Co. Ltd., 52, Clarence Street, Sydney N.S.W. were appointed agents and they represented the company for many years, having a friendly business relationship with Shaw & Copestake. On the off chance they were still operating I asked a contact in Sydney to check them out, but they are not in the telephone directory, so presumably have now ceased trading. Messrs. H.C. Hawley & Co. of Liverpool were the English agents for E.G. Page & Co. Ltd., and they acted for Shaw & Copestake from 1903 for at least 50 years.

In the 1940s Messrs. T.W. Heath Ltd, of Melbourne, represented Thomas Lawrence Ltd., and their representative Mr H. Hills visited the works in 1948 to select samples. The OLD Falcon Ware, pre-SylvaC, also seems quite prolific in Australia, and many lovely and unusual pieces have been found.

Exports continued to Australia until Shaw & Copestake ceased trading in 1982. It was still a steady outlet, although by this time the orders were somewhat reduced compared with the early days. This would account for the difficulty there is in finding any great quantity of post-1970s SylvaC. As well as the exported wares, obviously a small amount of SylvaC was transported on British migrant ships, but this was probably very insignificant. Such was the quantity of SylvaC in the area that I know of one dealer who, having made a good contact, was actually importing bunnies back to this country, only a few years ago.

In March 1989 I received a letter from Maylands, West Australia, requesting two copies of The SylvaC Story. This came as some surprise, as, although I knew of the good export trade to Australia, it hadn't really occurred to me there would be any SylvaC enthusiasts there, thinking this was a peculiarly British eccentricity. Shortly after the first order, I received enquiries from bookshops, and in 1990 had my first contact with the All Arts Bookshop, Woollahara, New South Wales, who have since become the main distributors of SylvaC books. The All Arts Bookshop is one of the best antiques bookshops in Australia covering all spheres of antiques and collectibles.

I gradually began to receive a steady stream of correspondence from Australia, Tasmania and New Zealand, and discovered, much to my surprise our Australasian friends are as fanatical about SylvaC as we are, and appeared to have equally large collections. This is not entirely for nostalgic reasons only, as many have no connections with the U.K. at all, and have just found the Shaw & Copestake and Thomas Lawrence unique products an irresistible pleasure to collect.

My first contact, Helen, from Maylands specialises in Falcon Ware, but generally products from both factories are sought. In 1990 Penelope wrote from North Sydney, she was able to furnish me with details of several new numbers, and explained that most of her collection was found at local antique markets, outlying antique shops, and Carter's Giant Antiques Fair, an annual four day event in Sydney, which attracts traders from all over Australia, she was also able to recommend the All Arts Bookshop as a suitable distributor, and check on the old agents E.G. Page & Co. Ltd., to see if they were still operating. I had the pleasure of meeting Penelope and her husband, when they were visiting here. Marie, also from Western Australia, visited us, and I was amazed by the photographs of her collections, not only of SylvaC and Falcon Ware, but other British potteries. One particularly welcome visitor was Rosemary, who brought me, all the way from Western Australia, the rare Falcon Ware parrot flower centre, which, needless to say is very treasured.

In April 1991, I received yet another letter, from John and Margaret Stiles, who appeared to be very keen. John called himself a 'Sylvacaroon' who had collected over 200 pieces in three years. He told me about a SylvaC bunny he had owned in the 1940s, and that he had grown up with SylvaC. Having just

MR. E. G. PAGE

## Twenty-five Years

Mr. E. G. Page is the founder member of Messrs. E. G. Page & Co. (Pty.) Ltd., of Sydney, N.S.W., Australia, who have represented "SylvaC" for twenty-five years. It has been a quarter of a century of very happy and friendly business relationship and may it continue for years to come. Mr. Page married the sister of the late Mr. F. S. Tyler who was our New Zealand agent for many years.

◀ Photograph and write-up taken from the SylvaC and Falcon Bulletin, dated Spring 1953.

▲ Pierrette number 930 and footballer number 989 Reg. No. 787779.

▲ Jug number 1419 and bowl number 1565 both decorated with Australian 'Gum nut flowers'.

► Baskets numbers 1473 and 1496.

▼ Vases number 1165, one with the 'Gum nut' decoration.

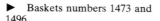

▼ Vases number 540.

◄ Top from left: Three Silvo jugs, jug 1147, Silvo jug. Bottom from left: Two daisy marked jugs, jug number 1139, jug number 1410 with koala bears, jug number 1406.

► Back: 700 kingfisher in 680 bowl, 1039 kingfisher vase in 436 bowl. Front: 700 in 726 bowl, 957 poppy in 722 bowl, 700 in 711 bowl.

◄ Top from left: Plant pots 718, 693, 715 and 714. Bottom from left: Vase 698, Sydney Harbour Bridge 727, 700 in bowl 722, Sydney Harbour Bridge 727, vase 728.

◄ A selection of Falcon Ware jugs.

► Rose Bowls all number 559 with different designs.

◄ Top from left: Jug 1794, Falcon 'Heron' jug, jug 1794. Bottom from left: Jug 1417, Falcon jugs 222 and 216, Falcon vase.

purchased a copy of my book, he decided to let me know of the N/I numbers in his collection, and listed his latest purchases.

This was the start of a correspondence which has continued regularly ever since. Every month John and his wife Margaret write to me, listing their purchases, and telling me of the adventures they experience on their various expeditions. They have found numerous new numbers, and a considerable amount of pre-war Shaw & Copestake, including the Sydney Harbour Bridge. Each letter is accompanied by a selection of photographs, so I can see for myself the decoration and shape of new purchases. It is thanks to John and Margaret that many of the old Shaw & Copestake numbers have been traced.

John and Margaret live in Queensland, which is situated between Brisbane and the Gold Coast (Surfers Paradise). It's difficult for us to realise the size of Australia, and John explained this beautifully in one of his letters: *'You can cut out a map of England, Scotland and Wales and fit it in between Sydney and Brisbane. The weather is so variable, after the Bush fires (1994), we were in the grip of monsoon rains and cyclonic floods and winds.'* John's previous letter had a different story to tell *'Even too hot to go in the pool as the sun is so fierce your head cooks in minutes'*.

However despite all these trials and tribulations John and Margaret are intrepid explorers of antique fairs, fleamarkets and junk shops. Like all good collectors they are often up at an unearthly hour to be first in the queue, and this has really paid off as they arrive home with a wonderful assortment of Shaw & Copestake and Falcon Ware trophies. They have now made contact with other Australian collectors, one of whom was lucky enough to find the pierrette 930 and the footballer 989, in New Zealand. I haven't met John and Marge yet, but this will be rectified later this year (1994), when they are returning to England for business reasons. However, I received a phone call from him last year, which was an experience in itself. We were on holiday at a remote country cottage in the depths of Suffolk, when our mobile phone rang, this isn't unusual, but it was 1 a.m. in the morning. My husband answered and handed it to me with the words, 'it's for you, it's a SylvaC collector', well I know you are all very keen but I thought this was taking it to extremes! It turned out to be John from Australia, the reception wasn't all

that good, so I hung out of the window, hoping to hear better. Can't you just picture me, in a remote cottage, hanging out of the window in the middle of the night trying to gather my wits about me, discussing SylvaC?

John has found several crinoline ladies, quite a few gnomes and the rare 1203 dog. He has a large collection of the early lions, some on plinths and with vases, black and dark red cellulose. He has a large number of colourful cellulose vases with most interesting decorations, and even a very early matching jug and vase numbered 19 and 30 with the daisy mark at the base of the handle. He doesn't have much luck with the later dogs or face-pots, they are about but not in abundance. He has cornered the market with pre-war pieces, as very few are marked SylvaC, or have the daisy mark, and he was able to spot them before others knew of their origins. This has changed lately, as more dealers and collectors begin to recognise pieces, which is inevitably reflected in the prices, but John and Margaret are still hunting and still manage to unearth the odd Shaw & Copestake relic that has lain on a dusty shop shelf for a long time. John must have one of the foremost SylvaC collections in Australia, and it all started because of a little blue bunny. This is John's story:

*'I used to live in Walthamstow, London, and one day saw a little blue bunny in the window of a shop called Garnhams. I managed to buy him by running errands to earn some money, but during the Blitz he disappeared, and I didn't think any more about it. I met Margaret, we married and had a family, in 1972 we moved to New Zealand, and in 1978 transferred to Australia. About four years ago we decided to go to an Auction, and sitting on a shelf was the blue bunny, of course I HAD to have him, and then there was no turning back. Now, four years and thousands of miles later I have over 700 pieces of SylvaC and Falcon Ware, many one offs and unique, but each one having a special spot and memory in my heart. I dedicate this to my darling wife Margaret who (after a great deal of training) is able to sniff out a piece at fifty paces, and without whom none of this would have been possible.'*

John is very keen to contact like minded SylvaC collectors, and if you write to him via the Pottery Publications address I will pass your letters on.

◄ Jug number 19 and vase number 30, there is a gold Daisy mark at the base of the jug handle.

This and the preceding photographs in this chapter are all from the collection of and photographed by John Stiles, from Queensland. As they were originally in colour, but have been reproduced in black and white, the quality may not be quite up to standard.

▲ Vases number 861, from the collection of and photograph by Lance Edwards, from New South Wales. Lance kindly sent me a whole album of photographs of his collection.

◄ Vase number 1174, from the collection of and photograph by Penny Sorrell, also from New South Wales. Penny keeps me informed of any interesting purchases she has made, and I was able to meet her when she visited the U.K.

# CHAPTER 12

# THE SYLVAN SCENE IN LONGTON

## LONGTON, STOKE-ON-TRENT

It is interesting to note from local reference books that in 1660 Longton was a small village of less than 200 people. By 1865 Longton had grown into a borough of 20,000 accommodating 61 potteries and the 1991 Census shows a resident population of 12,860, with the number of working potteries and ancillary establishments in the region of 60.

## SHEAF POTTERY COMPANY c1894–1900

It was c1894, in the heyday of the Longton pottery industry that Mr. William Shaw acquired the Sheaf Pottery Co. Shaw & Copestake's own official History of the Company gives this year as the founding date. Many years ago Mr. Malcolm Chapman, former director of the company, informed me the company was originally called Sheaf Art Pottery, but I could find no wares with this name, and no immediate connections with Shaw & Copestake. It wasn't until I received a letter from local historian Peter Landon, in 1989, who spent his childhood in the area, that I saw a glimmer of light, Peter mentioned SHEAF Passage, and the Old WheatSHEAF Public House. It seems the NEW Sylvan Works was built over part of Sheaf Passage, a small section of which still exists and is found off Webberley Lane (previously School Lane). The Old Wheatsheaf Public House was in Normacot Road, opposite the OLD Sylvan Works, and was demolished in 1949. The final piece of the jigsaw was put into place when an original half-tone printing plate bearing the name Sheaf Art Pottery was found when Crown Winsor (Pottery) Ltd went into liquidation in 1989, and many of the old Shaw & Copestake papers were taken out of the Sylvan Works to see light of day for the first time for many years.

During my original researches I found advertisements in the Pottery Gazette and information in the Manufacturers' Directory for the Sheaf Pottery Company, the first in April 1895 and again in June 1895, the address in both cases was Normacot Road. Sheaf Passage was off Normacot Road, and led to St. James School and School Lane (now Webberley Lane), so the original pottery was probably in that vicinity. The next mention in the Pottery Gazette is in March 1896 'Sheaf Pottery moved from Normacot Road to T. Walters old pottery in Commerce Street'. Commerce Street, is just a little way down the road on the right towards Longton town centre. There is a mention again in 1899 and 1900 'Sheaf Pottery, Commerce Street – Late F.A. Spruce.'

## WILLIAM SHAW 1901

In January 1901 the name of the pottery changed to William Shaw and the address is given as King Street, which was the next turning along from Commerce Street (the road is now cut in two, and called Berry Lane and Kingscross Street).

## SHAW & COPESTAKE 1902

In 1902 the company acquired the name Shaw & Copestake and the address is given as Drury Works, Normacot Road, but in 1904 the works are called SYLVAN Works. Parts of Normacot Road were originally called Furnace Road, Wheatsheaf Road and Drury Street, Possibly Drury Works was renamed Sylvan Works, there were also adverts for a Drury Pottery Co in Normacot Road in 1896. Or perhaps they made yet one more move before finally settling in the Sylvan Works. The removal of the company to presumably larger premises in 1902 coincides with the appearance of the additional name Copestake, possibly Mr. Copestake already owned Drury Works, or Mr. Shaw felt he needed some more investment in the company, and invited Mr. Copestake to become a partner. The Copestake family had a history of investing in local businesses for short periods.

You may wonder how one can be sure the three companies' were connected, and apart from the fact they showed the same range of vases in all the advertisements, I received the following information in February 1988, from Mr. Malcolm Chapman former director of Shaw & Copestake. *'I did at one time see a 1904 catalogue, the products were produced under the name of Sheaf Art Ware and not SylvaC. Basically the products consisted of very ornate vases and bowls, many of them of quite considerable size, heavily decorated with gold and a lot of hand painting. I seem to remember Mr. Hull advising me that during this period the firm were employing as many as 25 men painters.'*

## THE SYLVAN WORKS

The Sylvan Works was situated between Chadwick Street, and Park Passage, facing Normacot Road, opposite the Old Wheatsheaf Public House. Directly behind them, facing Uttoxeter Road were Gladstone China, Roslyn China and Park China Works. On the corner of Chadwick Street (named after a local doctor) and Normacot Road was the Sea Lion Public House, behind which were a few houses, the John Shaw Pottery 'Burlington Ware', and Evans the Undertakers (now Gladstone Staff Car Park'). Incidentally Shaw & Copestake also had a yard in Chadwick Street. Park Passage was originally a narrow cobbled gas lit passage leading from the High Street (now Uttoxeter Road) to Normacot Road. It was a short cut between the pottery factories, very poorly lit, and especially dark in winter, the smoke adding to the darkness. It was not advisable to use the passage and considered unsafe for children going to St. James School, it was eventually closed and the land purchased by Taylor and Tunnicliffe, Electrical Porcelain Manufacturers, whose factory was the other side of the passage. Park Passage took its name from the adjacent Park China Works.

Shortly after Mr. Shaw and Mr. Hull purchased the Sylvan Works (Mr. Richard Hull became a partner in 1903), they began acquiring land the opposite side of the road, on this land they built a warehouse and workshop. Included in this transaction were terraced houses in Sheaf Passage and Normacot Road, which were eventually demolished, and the buildings of the Cyples Colour Works, which is still part of the existing Sylvan Works.

The Cyples building was used by the SylvaC modellers, and you can see George Matthews on page 76 actually working in a room in the old building. George Matthews was thrilled to join such a prestigious firm, and looked forward to designing and modelling in this most up-to-date factory. He was somewhat crestfallen when he was shown his quarters in the oldest most dilapidated part of the Sylvan Works. The Cyples family arrived in Longton in 1763, and played an important part in the pottery industry of the area.

## MAP OF LONGTON AREA SHOWING PLACES OF
## INTEREST PAST AND PRESENT

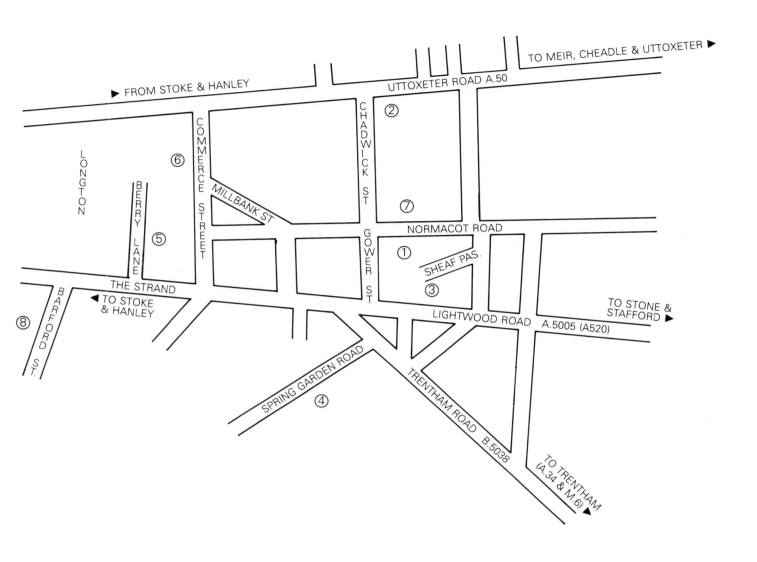

**LEGEND FOR MAP:**

1 Sylvan Works now Portmeirion Pottery Ltd

2 Gladstone Pottery Museum

3 St. James School, now the St. James Ceramic Design Centre

4 Daisy Bank Pottery, renamed Gainsborough Works

5 Berry Lane, formerly King Street, site of William Shaw Pottery, exact position unknown

6 Commerce Street, site of Sheaf Pottery, exact position unknown

7 Site of OLD Shaw & Copestake pottery

8 Barford Street, formerly Waterloo Street, site of the Thomas Lawrence, Falcon Pottery, now occupied by John Beswick Ltd.

## SHAW & COPESTAKE 1940s AND 1950s

I quote an extract from Peter Landon's letter received in 1989, in which he graphically describes the area during his schooldays, whilst the OLD Sylvan Works was still in operation and before the NEW Sylvan Works was built:

*'I attended St. James's Church School, which is behind the present Sylvan Works (now Portmeirion Potteries Ltd), the school stands, but only just! The NEW Sylvan Works was built over Sheaf Passage, which was the original lane to the school from Chadwick Street and Normacot Road. I remember raiding the OLD Shaw & Copestake tip for the bunnies that could be painted at home using water colours. The tip was next to Sheaf Passage, and terraced homes also stood on the site of the present buildings, as well as a corner shop. The Wheatsheaf pub also stood, and opposite was another pub called the Sea Lion, the wall of the pub is still standing'.* (Wall demolished 1944, photograph exists.)

The new Sylvan Works were ready for occupation in 1957, the old factory was used for warehousing only and finally sold to Taylor and Tunnicliffe c1962, who owned adjacent property. They demolished the buildings shortly after purchase. The Sea Lion public house, adjacent houses and the John Shaw Pottery have all been demolished, and now provide car parking facilities for the Gladstone Pottery Museum. The OLD Sylvan Works was a stark dismal three storey building, similar to others in the area, and seemed to be surrounded by other pot banks and bottle ovens.

## THE SYLVAN WORKS 1994

From 1894 to 1982 the Sheaf Pottery Co, the William Shaw pottery and Shaw & Copestake have centred around this small area of Longton, unfortunately many of the buildings have now been demolished, but if you look carefully, you can still catch some of the atmosphere of the area. It was fortunate that the Gladstone China Works was saved and is now the Gladstone Pottery Museum, a complete working example of a typical 19th century Staffordshire potbank. Potbank is the local term always used for a pottery works. The museum was founded in 1974, and is internationally recognised as a leader amongst industrial museums. It has recently been renovated and improved transforming the Museum into a major tourist attraction complete with modern amenities. A new circuit around the museum is being created and the demonstration and display facilities are being upgraded to restore the pottery to how it was around 1910.

The whole of this Shaw & Copestake area is now part of a European Urban Pilot Project which is refurbishing and uplifting the image of the area. I quote from their brochure: *'The project centres on the faded splendour of the Gladstone St. James Quarter, which nevertheless retains many attractive reminders of its past as one of England's major nineteenth century pottery centres.'* This includes various facelifts, landscaping, lighting and repairs to Normacot Road, including the area outside the Sylvan Works. St James School is being repaired and the interior converted to 21 design studios to become the St. James Ceramic Design Centre. The Roslyn China Works is also to be renovated and become craft studios, linked to the Gladstone Pottery Museum.

Many of the road names were changed in the early 1950s to alleviate confusion of the other five pottery towns having the same names. Well known local inhabitants have been immortalised in this way, amongst the new names were Barlow St, Webberley St and Barker St, all Longton Master Potters. Some changes also took place in 1832 and 1856, and all these are listed in a wonderful book called Longton Potters 1700–1865, by Rodney Hampson, published by The City Museum and Art Gallery, Hanley, which has been an enormous help. It became quite a problem for the post office when presented with a letter addressed, for example, to High Street, Stoke-on-Trent, when each of the six towns forming Stoke-on-Trent also had a High Street.

Situated a short distance from the Sylvan Works, to the west of Longton was an area called Daisy Bank, there was also a Daisy Bank Pottery, the road is now Spring Garden Road. It would be nice to think this gave Mr. Shaw the idea of using the daisy mark as a back stamp for his products. There are two rather tenuous connections with Shaw & Copestake, one is the land of both potteries was originally owned by the same Heathcote family, but as they owned much of the area this is probably not surprising, and the other that until 1830 the tenant of Daisy Bank was a John Drury which you remember was the name of the Shaw & Copestake works in 1902.

I do hope you will try to visit the Shaw & Copestake area, where so much activity took place all those years ago, perhaps you will look for some of the places mentioned. Portmeirion Potteries Ltd., will no doubt be pleased to see you in their factory shop, and they have kindly informed me that it may be possible for small (no more than 10) pre-arranged groups to be shown around the works, the factory shop is open most days, but please check the hours on 0782 326412 before travelling. The Gladstone Pottery Museum can provide you with refreshments, as well as an informative tour, 0782 319232/311378. You can even stay for bed and breakfast at Mr. Shaw's old home, Clovelly Guest House, Blythe Bridge, telephone 0782 398958.

**Clovelly Guest House**
92 Uttoxeter Road, Blythe Bridge, Stoke-on-Trent, Staffordshire ST11 9JG. Tel: (0782) 398958

◀ During our researches we thought it would be interesting to see the former home of Mr. William Shaw. It seems fortuitous that 'Clovelly' is now a Guest House, where collectors can stay when touring the area, or visiting the places of interest shown on the map. I believe there is now a small collection of SylvaC at Clovelly, which the manager and his wife have bought to recreate the Shaw & Copestake atmosphere. On the left is a reproduction of a business card given to me by manager Mr. William Marsden, on our visit. All SylvaC collectors are made most welcome.

# CHAPTER 13

# COLLECTOR'S PICTURE PARADE

**A selection of photographs sent in by SylvaC collectors**

▲  Dog number 72 (Falcon number), often seen but never photographed for any publication.

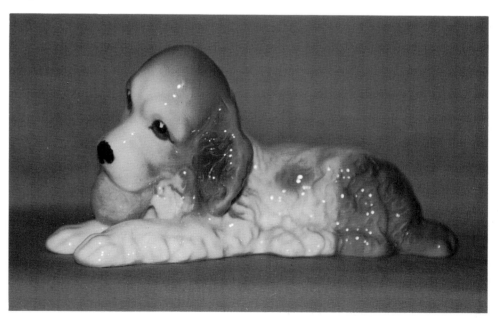

▲  Spaniel with ball, number 3276, to go with spaniel with slipper, and spaniel with pipe. Both dogs from the collection of and photographed by Jan Powell.

◄ Terrier dog resting, number 3318, from the collection of and photograph by David Richards.

► Manx cat, 'marmalade' colour, number 4077, from the author's collection.

◄ Bowl, mottled fawn, with green and white leaves draped over side, number 2513. From the collection of and photograph by Steve Rumsey.

◄ Cat, number 2795, one of a set of three. A very interesting design, this cat is quite flat, with see through eyes, and is coloured brown and white.

► Cat, number 981. This is an unusual pose for a cat, and quite difficult to photograph, but I can vouch for the fact he is a delightful character. Both cats from the collection of and photographed by Jackie and Tony Chew.

▲ This little blue dog is about 3½″ high, and because he is so cute I have included two views. The number is 129? (we would love to know the last figure). From the collection of and photograph by Jackie and Tony Chew.

▲ This cockerel has yellow feathers, orange comb, brown coat, blue waistcoat and is wearing spectacles. The number is 1179, lucky owner is Jean Simms, photograph by J. Murfet.

▲ Not a very rare dog, but a delightful addition to any collection. Number 73 (Falcon number), from the author's collection.

◀ Camel, number 772. The camel is sand coloured, the base and howdah dark green, and the saddlebags etc are gaily coloured.

▶ Both vases are numbered 709, although they have different Spanish designs, both photographs from the collection of Tracy Stevens.

▲  Outside vases numbered 1110, centre vase 1126, all from the Bachanti range, from the collection of and photograph by Bridget Gorman.

▲  Two pink and white cats with black stripes and green bows. Number 3406 on the left and number 3407 on the right. From the collection of and photograph by Jackie and Tony Chew.

▲ Lantern bookends number 4976. These are copper coloured, one has a green 'light' and the other a red light. From the collection of and photograph by Fabienne Daniel and Alan Morris.

▲ Very elaborately embossed 'Chinese' vases, in colourful cellulose. Number 703, from the collection of and photograph by Jackie and Tony Chew.

▲ Commemorative plaque, no number, on the back is inscribed: ROYAL VISIT SOUVENIR 1949, and in the centre Sylvac Ware (with a small 'c'). From the collection of and photograph by Jackie and Tony Chew.

▼ Smooth haired fox terrier number 3314, black and white. From the collection of and photograph by Jayne Richards.

▲ Bath Salts container from the Mosaic range, number 4966, decorated with a fish on the lid, and a sea horse. From the collection of and photograph by Jackie and Tony Chew.

▼ Master Duck has orange beak, wings and tail, yellow face, blue and black cap, brown coat with black collar. Number 1156, lucky owner is John Poley, who also took the photograph.

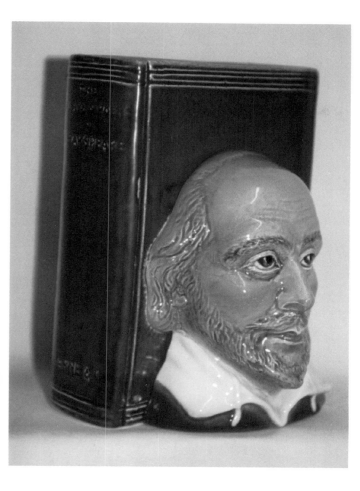

◄ Book vase, number 2841. Title of book is THE PLAYS & POEMS OF SHAKSPEARE, (note the unusual spelling). The book is brown, and the head in natural colours. From the late Mr. Reginald Thompson's collection.

► Ivy range jug number 2071, collected and photographed by Jackie and Tony Chew.

◄ Interesting wrought iron, and wood grain effect plant pot in natural colours, number 4763, from the collection of Mary Reynolds.

► Honey pot from the Tapestry range, beige ground with pink rose transfer, number 5631, photographed by Timothy Mark, and from his collection.

◄ Posy trough from the Begonia range, white ground with natural coloured begonia leaves, number 3867, from the collection of and photograph by Lucy Wood.

# PART TWO

# EXPLAINING THE REGISTER OF MOULD NUMBERS

## SHAW & COPESTAKE, SYLVAC AND FALCON WARE

PLEASE NOTE: The first part of this register lists the FALCON WARE MOULD NUMBERS ONLY, and does not contain any SHAW & COPESTAKE NUMBERS which follow at the end of the Falcon Ware list.

I have obtained more mould numbers since The SylvaC Story was first published in 1989, but I am still learning and constantly re-appraising original opinions. Many of the Shaw & Copestake numbers have now come to light and this has resulted in the need for separate schedules for Falcon Ware and Shaw & Copestake numbers.

Dating Falcon Ware has proved very difficult as only one item appears to have a registered design number. Research has shown most of the numbers probably date from 1942, when Shaw & Copestake shared the Falcon Works, due to the Concentration of Industry scheme, taking all the moulds and patterns with them. As the Falcon Ware factory was transferred to the new Sylvan Works in 1957, I have assumed the wares date between those times i.e. 1942–1957. However this doesn't take into account the early pre-war Falcon numbering system, which means some of the vases were incorporated into the new list, or else ignored and the number given to a new item, with the inevitable result of two pieces with the same number.

Where possible each entry has been checked many times in order to avoid errors, occasionally it has not been possible to verify information sent by collectors. Some collectors assume if a piece of pottery has a number on the base it must be SylvaC, this is not the case as other potteries also numbered ware, I have even been given the number of a Czechoslovakian jam pot! I hope I have managed to sift out all the red herrings. Dates and measurements can only be approximate, and must be regarded as a guide rather than absolute. I am sure many of you will have two vases of the same number which differ in height, and even in the official catalogues the measurements vary. The page numbers of illustrations is also given where applicable. There are no decoration details as so many colours and methods were used. If I have details of SylvaC being re-issued this is also noted.

Abbreviations: h=height • l=length • acr=across • dia=diameter • c.s.=clay size • s/s=small size • m/s=medium size • l/s=large size • p=page • TSS=The SylvaC Story • TSC=The SylvaC Companion • SCC/16=SylvaC Collectors Circle News Letter issue 16 • N/I=no information • Reg.No=Design number registered at the Patent Office, it is possible to date the original registration • OM=Outside modelled • RW=Ronald Wright • HH=Harry Hudson (mould maker) • EB=Eric Baker (mould maker) • TH=Tom Hudson (mould maker) • RT=Reginald Thompson • JL=John Lawson • SC=Stephan Czarnota • GM=George Matthews • C=Mr.Cheadle • W=Mr.Woolam • JB=J.Brian • JR=J.Radford • AM=Arnold Machin • 1982+=continued to be made after demise of Shaw & Copestake

# FALCON POTTERY MOULD NUMBERS
## c1940 – 1957

THESE ARE FALCON WARE MOULD NUMBERS USED AT THE THOMAS LAWRENCE LTD, FALCON WORKS AND DO NOT CONTAIN ANY SHAW & COPESTAKE NUMBERS, WHICH APPEAR FURTHER ON IN THE SCHEDULE.

| Number | Description | Approximate Size and end of production date | Number | Description | |
|---|---|---|---|---|---|
| 1 | Deer | | 27 | Rabbit on skis fallen p37 TSS | 2¼"h |
| 2 | N/I | | 28 | Rabbit on skis p37 TSS | 3¼"h |
| 03 | Girl sitting with doll SCC/16 (number referred to as 30 in error) | 6½"h | 29 | Rabbit on skis p37 TSS | 3"h |
| | | | 30 | N/I | |
| | | | 31 | Dog on slipper p38 TSS | 6"l |
| | Numbers 3–5 are also to be found on three terriers similar to 1378/79/80 these are NOT Falcon or S & C | | 32 | N/I | |
| | | | 33 | Lizard | |
| | | | 34 | Dog | |
| 4–8 | N/I | | 35 | Dog | |
| 09 | Choir boy | 6"h | | Numbers 34 and 35 are often seen on two dogs sitting, with one ear down, they are usually in a matt green glaze, ENGLAND is impressed on the base. I have had NO confirmation they are Falcon 36–38 N/I. Number 36 can be found on a "playing dog", with legs joined together, this is NOT Falcon Ware, and has been attributed to H. Wain, (Melba Ware), see SCC Newsletters 15 and 16. | |
| 10–14 | N/I | | | | |
| 15 | Horse standing p48 TSS p105/106 TSC | 6¾"h –1982 | | | |
| 16 | Bulldog standing p48 TSS p22 TSC | 5¼"h 8"l –1982+ | | | |
| 17 | Bison p34 TSS (number changed to 4732 in 1970) | 5"h 8–9"l | | | |
| 18 | Spaniel dog sitting p41/42 TSS p19 TSC | 5"h –1982 | | | |
| 19 | Borzoi dog lying | 4"h | 39 | Red riding hood | |
| 20 | Dog | | 40 | Rhino | |
| 21 | Horse and rider p45/85 TSS (number changed to 4707) | 8½"h 9½"l | 41 | Elephant | |
| | | | 42 | Cat | |
| 22–23 | N/I | | 43 | Duck jug p137 TSC | 4¾"h |
| 24 | Bird wall plaque | | 44 | Rabbit jug p137 TSC | 5"h |
| 25 | Rabbit holding skis p37 TSS | 3½"h | 45 | Dog jug p137 TSC | 5"h |
| 26 | Rabbit injured p37 TSS | 3"h | 46 | N/I | |

| No. | Description | Dimensions |
|---|---|---|
| 47 | Bulldog | |
| 48 | Rhino | |
| 49 | Lion/Leopard | |
| 50 | Camel | |
| 51 | N/I | |
| 52 | Bison standing | 8¼"h 12"l |
| 53 | Wolf/Bison | |
| 54 | Eagle | |
| 55 | Pony | |
| 56 | Buffalo (number changed to 4733 in 1970) p34 TSS | 5½"h 9½"l –1975 |
| 57 | Dog | |
| 58 | Lamp | |
| 59 | Pelican/Bird | |
| 60 | Horse | |
| 61 | N/I | |
| 62 | Lion | |
| 63 | Giraffe | |
| 64–65 | N/I | |
| 66 | Sealion | |
| 67 | Cairn Terrier standing | 4"h |
| 68 | Elephant standing p47 TSS p31 TSC | 9"h –1982 |
| 69 | Bear | |
| 70 | N/I | |
| 71 | Lamp/Eagle | |
| 72 | Scottie dog standing p103 TSS | 5¼"h 6½"l |
| 73 | Dog sitting p106 TSS | 4¼"h –1960s |
| 74 | Gnome p124 TSC | 6¾"h –1960s |
| 75 | Gnome p124 TSC | 6"h –1960s |
| 76–80 | N/I | |
| 81 | Gnome p124 TSC | 8"l –1960s |
| 82 | Gnome p52 TSS | 8"l –1960s |
| 83 | Gnome p52 TSS | 8"h –1960s |
| 84 | N/I | |
| 85 | Tiger | |
| 86 | N/I | |
| 87 | Gnome p52 TSS | 7¼"h –1960s |
| 88 | Spaniel head wall plaque "Grouse" | 3½"h |
| 89 | Scottie head wall plaque "Mac" (appears in 1944 advert) | 4"h |
| 90 | Terrier head wall plaque "Bob" | 3½"h |
| 91 | N/I | |
| 92 | Elephant standing p47 TSS p31 TSC | 4"h –1982 |
| 93 | Lion lying | 2¼"h 6¾"l |
| 94 | Bull | |
| 95 | Horse | |
| 96 | Chimpanzee l/s p47 TSS p31 TSC | 7"h –1982 |
| 97 | Chimpanzee s/s p47 TSS p31 TSC | 4½"h –1982 |
| 98 | Chimpanzee s/s p47 TSS p31 TSC | 4"h –1982 |
| 99 | Cat sitting p47 TSS | 5"h –1970 |
| 100 | Kitten sitting p47 TSS | 2¾"h –1970 |
| 101 | Kitten standing p47 TSS | 3"h 3¼"l –1970 |
| 102 | Kitten playing p47/84 TSS | 2¼"h 4"l –1970 |
| 103 | Kitten lying p47 TSS | 1¾"h 2¾"l –1970 |
| 104 | Cats in basket p84 TSS | 4¼"h |
| 105 | Mouse crouching l/s (see 4990) | 3½"l |
| 106 | Mouse sitting up s/s | 1½"l |
| 107 | Foal p50 TSS sim to 108/109 | 12"h –1960s |
| 108 | Foal standing | 8"h –1960s |
| 108 also | Gnome p52 TSS | 10"h 14½"l –1960s |
| 109 | Foal standing | 5½"h –1960s |
| 109 also | Giraffe | |
| 110 | Gnome p52 TSS | 16"h |
| 111 | Girl | |
| 112 | Boy | |
| 113 | Gnome p124 TSC | 11"h 16"l –1960s |
| 113 also | Boy | |
| 114 | Spaniel p41/42 TSS | 7"l –1975 |
| 115 | Spaniel p41/42 TSS | 3"h –1975 |
| 116 | Spaniel p41/42 TSS | 3¼"l –1975 |
| 117–118 | N/I | |
| 119 | Cottage | |
| 120 | N/I | |
| 121 | Candlestick | |
| 122 | Bowl | |
| 123 | Dish anenome posy | 8½"dia –1960s |
| 124 | Horse | |
| 125 | Horse | |
| 126 | Dish anenome posy | 7½"dia –1960s |
| 127 | Dish anenome posy | 10¼"dia –1960s |
| 128 | Wall vase | |
| 129 | Posy hat, also with flowers p31 TSS | 4½"dia –1960s |
| 130 | Penguin standing | 6⅛"h –1960s |
| 131 | Penguin stooping | 4¼"h –1960s |
| 132 | Penguin | 4"h –1960s |
| 133 | Penguin | |
| 133 also | Hippo | |
| 134 | Bear sitting upright p30 TSC | 5½"h |
| 135 | Horse | |
| 136 | Tortoise trinket/cigarette box p37 TSS | 6½"l |
| 137 | Bird | |
| 138 | Swallow | |
| 139 | Wall plaque | |
| 140 | Horse | |
| 141 | Foal | |
| 142 | Bear standing | 2½"h |
| 143 | Flower holder | |
| 144 | Flower holder | |
| 145 | Scottie dog standing, sometimes with tartan coat p41 TSS | 3⅝"h –1982+ |
| 146 | Scottie dog crouching p41 TSS | 2⅜"h –1965 |
| 147 | Scottie dog standing p41 TSS | 2¾"h –1965 |
| 148 | Scottie dog sitting p41 TSS | 2¾"h –1965 |
| 149 | Dog and chair | |
| 150 | Holder rabbit | |
| 151 | Posy holder with platform for small rabbit also with flowers | 1¼"h |
| 152 | Swan posy with flowers p31 TSS | |
| 153 | Wall vase | |
| 154 | Ashtray | |
| 155 | Bulldog standing p41 TSS | 3¼"h –1965 |
| 156 | Wall vase | |
| 157 | Dog | |
| 158 | Squashed top hat cat on rim dog on side | 3"h |
| 159 | Elephant | |
| 160 | Dog | |
| 161 | Dog and bowl | |
| 162 | Terrier dog lying | 1¾"h 7½"l |
| 163 | Spaniel dog sitting | 6"h |
| 164 | Cat | |
| 165 | Top hat with kitten playing on rim SCC/15 | 3¼"h |
| 166 | Two Sealyham dogs p23 TSC | 3⅛"h |
| 167 | Horse | |
| 168 | N/I | |
| 169 | Dish shell with flowers p36 TSS | s/s |
| 170 | Poodle dog sitting p41 TSS | 5¼"h –1970 |
| 171 | Container | |
| 172 | Bear | |
| 173 | Bear | |
| 174 | Bear | |
| 175 | Bear | |
| 176 | Boxer dog standing remodelled 1960s p42 TSS | 4¾" & 5¼"h –1975 |
| 177 | Dachshund dog standing p42/43 TSS | 3"h –1975 |
| 178 | Alsation dog lying with front paws crossed p43 TSS | 4½"h |
| 179 | Dog | |
| 180 | Container | |
| 181 | Top hat | |
| 182 | Boat | |
| 183 | Donkey sitting laughing p50 TSS | 5½"h |
| 184 | Vase | 14"h |
| 184 also | Cat boxing p50 TSS | 4¾"h |

| No. | | Description | Size |
|---|---|---|---|
| 185 | | Alsatian dog p43 TSS | 2¾"h |
| 186 | | N/I | |
| 187 | | Dog | |
| 188 | | Vase | 12"h |
| 188 also | | Dachshund dog sitting p42/43 TSS | 1¾"h –1975 |
| 189 | | Vase with two central circles (could be 681) | 8¼"h |
| 190–191 | | N/I | |
| 192 | | Vase slim shape p138 TSC | |
| 193 | | Vase | 10½"h |
| 194–195 | | N/I | |
| 196 | | Ginger jar with lid p67 TSC vase minus lid p102/144 TSC | 9½"h –1982 / 7½"h –1982 |
| 196 also | | Shoe | |
| 197 | | Ginger jar with lid p67 TSC | 10¾"h –1982 |
| 198 | | Plant pot p67 TSC | 5¾"h –1982+ |
| 199 | | Plant pot p67 TSC | 7"h –1982+ |
| 200 | | N/I | |
| 201 | | Tray | |
| 202 | | Candlestick, tulip shape, four leaf feet, scroll handle | 2½"h 4"w |
| 203 | | Setter dog running p42 TSS | 4¼"h –1965 |
| 204 | | Dog | |
| 205 | | Vase | 6¾"h |
| 205 also | | Foal | |
| 206 | | Vase narrow top | s/s |
| 206 also | | Foal | |
| 207 | | Vase | |
| 207 also | | Horse p48 TSS | 6"h –1960s |
| 208 | | Horse | |
| 209 | | Boxer dog sitting p42 TSS | 5½"h –1970 |
| 210 | | Dachshund dog on hind legs p42 TSS | 6½"h –1975 |
| 211 | | Dog | |
| 212 | | Dog | |
| 213 | | Foal | |
| 214 | | Shetland pony standing p2 TSS | 5"h –1982 |
| 215 | | Vase | l/s |
| 215 also | | Dog | |
| 216 | | Jug sim to 222 p138 TSC | 5½"h |
| 217 | | Jug | s/s |
| 217 also | | Dog | |
| 218 | | Jug p147 TSC | 5"h |
| 219 | | Jug | |
| 220 | | Vase narrow neck | l/s |
| 221 | | Vase p138/144 TSC | 15"h –1965 |
| 222 | | Jug sim to 216 p138 TSC | 7–7½"h –1970 |
| 223 | | Vase p67 TSC | 7½"h –1982 |
| 224 | | N/I | |
| 225 | | Vase p138 TSC | 6½"h –1960s |
| 226 | | Vase sim to 228 p138/147 TSC | 6½"h –1970 |
| 227 | | N/I | |
| 228 | | Vase sim to 226 p138 TSC | l/s |
| 229 | | Vase | |
| 230 | | Vase with handles p138 TSC | l/s |
| 231–232 | | N/I | |
| 233 | | Vase with handles p138 TSC | 8"h |
| 234–235 | | N/I | |
| 236 | | Vase p138/145 TSC | 8"h –1970 |
| 237 | | Vase oval p138 TSC | 7"h |
| 238 | | Vase round p138 TSC | s/s |
| 239 | | Vase with scalloped base p138 TSC | 8"h |
| 240 | | Vase diamond shape p138 TSC | 5⅛"h |
| 241–244 | | N/I | |
| 245 | | Jug sim to 222/216 | 3½"h –1960s |
| 246 | | Vase curvy top p147 TSC | m/s –1960s |
| 247–248 | | N/I | |
| 249 | | Jug p67 TSC | 6¾"h –1982 |
| 250–251 | | N/I | |
| 252 | | Bowl 'Mandarin' p105/144 TSC | 12"dia –1970 |
| 253 | | Bowl 'Thorpe' p145 TSC | 10"dia -1960 |
| 254 | | N/I | |
| 255 | | Lamp shape as 1807 vase p102/145 TSC | |
| 256 | | Cucumber dish Leaf Ware range | 10½"l |
| 257 | | Vase Collon | |
| 258 | | Vase two handles p103 TSC | 10"h –1960 |
| 259 | | Jug sim to 260/272 p67/101/144 TSC | 10"h –1982 |
| 260 | | Jug sim to 259/272 p101/144 TSC | 8"h –1960 |
| 261 | | Jug to match 264 Leaf Ware range | |
| 262 | | Tray with handles Springbok p47 TSC | |
| 263 | | N/I | |
| 264 | | Beakers to match 261 Leaf Ware range | |
| 265 | | Vase | |
| 265 also | | Tea pot Leaf Ware | l/s |
| 266 | | Honey Springbok range p47 TSC | |
| 267 | | Cream jug Springbok p47 TSC | |
| 268 | | Covered sugar Springbok p47 TSC | |
| 269–271 | | N/I | |
| 272 | | Jug sim to 259/260 p101/144 TSC | 12"h –1960 |
| 273 | | Jug sim to 292/293 p145 TSC | 12"h –1960 |
| 274 | | N/I | |
| 275 | | Vase Springbok p47 TSC | |
| 276 | | Vase Springbok p47 TSC | |
| 277 | | Bowl Springbok p47 TSC | |
| 278 | | Hat posy ring Reg. No. 857952 (1949) | 10½"dia –1960s |
| 279 | | Hat posy ring Reg. No. 857952 | 9"dia –1960s |
| 280 | | Hat posy ring p76 TSS (top photo) | 6"dia –1960s |
| 281 | | Hat flower pot | 8"acr –1960s |
| 282 | | Hat flower pot p86 TSS | 4"h 7½"acr –1960s |
| 283 | | Hat flower pot | 3¾"h 6"acr –1960s |
| 284 | | Tomato plate Leaf Ware range | |
| 285 | | Sweet dish Leaf Ware | |
| 286 | | N/I | |
| 287 | | Bowl on feet p105 TSC | 10"acr |
| 288–289 | | N/I | |
| 290 | | Sugar bowl Leaf Ware | |
| 291 | | Vase | |
| 292 | | Jug sim to 273/293 p145 TSC | 8"h –1960s |
| 293 | | Jug sim to 202/273 p145 TSC | 10"h –1960s |
| 294 | | Candy box Cavalier/Country scenes p151 TSC | 5½" l –1960 |
| 295 | | N/I | |
| 296 | | Mug | |
| 297 | | Twin tray Hydrangea p140 TSC | 9"l |
| 298 | | N/I | |
| 299 | | Hat nut basket | 7½"acr –1960 |
| 300 | | Jug Cavalier/Country p35 TSS p151 TSC | 5"h –1960 |
| 301 | | Jug Cavalier/Country | 6"h –1960 |
| 302–303 | | N/I | |
| 304 | | Jug Cavalier/Country p35 TSS p151 TSC | 3"h –1960 |
| 305 | | Jug Cavalier/Country p35 TSS p151 TSC | 2¼"h –1960 |
| 306 | | Cavalier Character jug (new no 4487) p88 TSS | 4¾"h –1965 –1982+ |
| 307 | | Jug Cavalier/Country p35 TSS p151 TSC | 4¼"h –1960 |
| 308 | | Beaker Cavalier | 4"h |
| 309 | | Jug Cavalier/Country p151 TSC | 6"h –1960 |
| 310 | | Sugar Cavalier/Country p151 TSC | 3"dia –1960 |
| | | The Cavalier range was first produced in 1945 | |
| 311 | | Straw hat | |
| 312 | | Beefeater Character jug (new no 4489 Yeoman of the Guard) p126 TSC | 4¼"h –1960 –1982+ |
| 313 | | Jar Cavalier | |

| | | | |
|---|---|---|---|
| 314 | Hat cake basket p76 TSS (top photo top left) | 7½″h 10½″acr –1960 | |
| 315 | Posy bar basket weave with ribbon | 6½″l –1960 | |
| 316 | Vase | | |
| 317 | N/I | | |
| 318 | Vase | | |
| 319 | Wall vase incised diamond pattern | 7¼″h | |
| 320 | Wall vase elves p54 TSS | 7½″h –1960s | |
| 321 | Wall vase scalloped rim p6 TSS | 8″h | |
| 322 | Jardiniere | | |
| 323 | Wall vase toadstool with rabbit p54 TSS | 7¼″h –1960 | |
| 324 | N/I | | |
| 325 | Teapot Country Scene p151 TSC | | |
| 326 | Sugar Country Scene | | |
| 327 | Wall plaque teenage boy's head | | |
| 328 | Honey Country Scene p151 TSC | | |
| 329 | Wall plaque teenage girl's head | | |
| 330 | Jug Acorn Squirrel sim to 1115/1195/1958/1959/1993/4068 p112 TSC | 6½″h | |
| 331 | Teapot Hydrangea p141 TSC | –1960s | |
| 332 | Honey Hydrangea p141 TSC | –1960s | |
| 333 | N/I | | |
| 334 | Jugs Hydrangea p140 TSC | sizes 1–4 –1960s | |
| 335 | Bowl shallow, Country scenes p151 TSC | 10″acr –1960s | |
| 336 | Jug | 10″h | |
| 337 | Triple tray Hydrangea p140 TSC | –1960s | |
| 338 | Cream jug Hydrangea p141 TSC | s/s –1960s | |
| 339 | Sugar Hydrangea p141 TSC | s/s –1960s | |
| 340 | Plate round p151 TSC Country scenes | l/s | |
| 341 | Plate round p151 TSC Country scenes | s/s | |
| 342 | Cheesedish Hydrangea p140 TSC | –1960s | |
| 343 | Bowl Hydrangea p140 TSC | l/s –1960s | |
| 344 | Jug Hydrangea sim to 350/351 p140 TSC | l/s –1960s | |
| 345 | Coffee pot Hydrangea p141 TSC | l/s –1960s | |
| 346 | N/I | | |
| 347 | Vase (unconfirmed) | | |
| 348 | Vase | | |
| 349 | Handbag vase | 5½″h | |
| 350 | Jug Hydrangea sim to 344/351 p140 TSC | s/s –1960s | |
| 351 | Jug Hydrangea sim to 344/350 p140 TSC | m/s –1960s | |
| 352 | Mug Hydrangea p140 TSC Hydrangea range first produced 1951 | –1960s | |
| 353 | Log container with recess for elf p53/86 TSS | 8½″l –1965 | |
| 354 | Wall vase tree with rabbit p54 TSS | 6″h –1960 | |
| 355 | Tree jug with elf or rabbit p57/86 TSS | 6¾″h –1960 | |
| 356–357 | N/I | | |
| 358 | Jug embossed lines and ferns | 6½″h | |
| 359 | Fruit dish two handles | | |
| 360 | Jug herring bone pattern with band of embossed flowers | 5¾″h | |
| 361–362 | N/I | | |
| 363 | Jug embossed band around centre | 9″h | |
| 364 | Jug embossed flowers rope handle, top and base | 6¼″h | |
| 365 | Sweet dish Hydrangea p140 TSC | –1960s | |
| 366 | Fruit dish Hydrangea p140 TSC | s/s –1960s | |

| | | | |
|---|---|---|---|
| 367 | N/I | | |
| 368 | Bulb bowl embossed leaves p142 TSC | 7½″dia | |
| 369 | Fern pot embossed leaves | 8″dia –1982 | |
| 370 | Vase | | |
| 371 | Jug embossed flowers and leaves | 7¼″–8½″h | |
| 372 | Tankard Pickwick | 5″h | |
| 373 | Tankard Tavern in the Town farmers boy | 5″h | |
| 374 | Tankard Old Bull and Bush farmers wife | | |
| | The above three tankards produced 1951 | | |
| 375 | N/I | | |
| 376 | Vase p147 TSC | 5½″h –1965 | |
| 377 | Bowl bird shape | 3½″h 8″l –1960s | |
| 378 | Bowl boat shape | –1960s | |
| 379 | Bowl pipe shape | –1960s | |
| 380 | Vase p102/144 TSC | 8″h –1960s | |
| 381 | Wall vase | | |
| 382 | Wall vase ribbon | 5″w –1960s | |
| 383 | Vase top handle p103 TSC | 10″h –1960s | |
| 384 | Galleon holder p37 TSS | 4⅜″h 6¼″l –1960s | |
| 385 | Vase sim to 387 without handles p102 TSC | 8¼″h –1960s | |
| 386 | Jug straight p101 TSC | 8″h –1960s | |
| 387 | Vase sim to 385 with handles p103 TSC | 8¼″h –1960s | |
| 388 | N/I | | |
| 389 | Bowl | | |
| 390 | Dish with cover | | |
| 391 | Cigarette box | | |
| 392 | Bowl | | |
| 393 | Cream jug p101 TSC | 3″h –1960s | |
| 394 | Cream jug p101 TSC | 3″h –1960s | |
| 395 | Jug | 3″h –1960s | |
| 396 | Bowl | | |
| 397 | Jug sim to crocus bud | 3″h | |
| 398 | Jug, rose, leaf handle | 3″h –1960s | |
| 399 | Dish with handles p147 TSC | –1960s | |
| 400 | Jug pineapple shape sim to 683/730 p66 TSS | 3″h –1982 | |
| 401 | Jug embossed leaves | 2¾″h –1960s | |
| 402 | Jug | | |
| 403 | Coffee Pot | | |
| 404 | Tea Pot | | |
| 405 | Tray | | |
| 406 | Dorothy bag jug sim to 453 p57 TSS | 7″h –1982 | |
| 407 | Jug | | |
| 408 | Basket | | |
| 409 | Jardiniere p92/104 TSC | 9½–10″l –1970s | |
| 410 | Flower pot p53 TSS | s/s 3¾″h m/s 4½″h l/s 5¼″h –1965 | |
| 411 | Flower pot | 4½″h –1960s | |
| 412 | N/I | | |
| 413 | Bowl Vine range re-introduced by Portmeirion Potteries | 12¼″l –1982 –1992+ | |
| 414 | Basket Vine range Re-introduced by Portmeirion Potteries | 10″l –1982 –1992+ | |
| 415 | Dish with handles | 11¼″l | |
| 416 | Posy, leaf shape also with butterfly | 1¼″h 7½″l | |
| 417 | N/I | | |
| 418 | Bowl p142 TSC | 7¼″dia –1960s | |
| 419 | Flower pot 'Tulip' | 4″h –1960s | |
| 420 | Jug with petal base | | |
| 421–422 | N/I | | |
| 423 | Jug vase | | |
| 424 | Toastrack | | |
| 425 | N/I | | |
| 426 | Flower jug sim to 427 p101/102 TSC | 6″h –1960s | |
| 427 | Flower jug sim to 426 p101/102 TSC | 9¼″h –1960s | |

| | | |
|---|---|---|
| 428 | Jardiniere | |
| 429 | Log | |
| 430 | N/I | |
| 431 | Tray with lizard p37 TSS | 7¼"l –1960s |
| 432 | Jug | |
| 433 | Vase, also with budgerigar | 8½–8¾"h |
| 434 | Vase | 8¾–9"h –1965 |
| 435 | Vase, also with budgerigar | 8¾–9"h –1965 |
| 436 | Bowl p54 TSS | 9½"dia |
| | This was an old 1930s S & C number but re-used in the Falcon factory until 1960s | |
| 437 | Bowl | |
| 438 | N/I | |
| 439 | Vase | |
| 440 | Vase | |
| 441 | Jug | |
| 442 | N/I | |
| 443 | Jardiniere with handles, vertical ridges | 5"h 11"l |
| 444 | N/I | |
| 445 | Jardiniere with handles, embossed waves | 5"h 13½"l |
| 446 | Tray | |
| 447 | Bowl | |
| 448 | N/I | |
| 449 | Fern Pot | |
| 450–451 | N/I | |
| 452 | Posy curved | 7"l |
| 453 | Dorothy bag jug sim to 406 | 3½"h |
| 454 | Posy | |
| 455 | Jug Dovecote range p57 TSS p148 TSC | 7–7¼"h –1960s |
| 456 | N/I | |
| 457 | Jug embossed Goulies and Ghosties, Goulie handle, VERY creepy, incised verse: "From Goulies & Ghosties and Long Leggity Beasties and things that go Bump in the night Good Lord Deliver Us" | l/s |
| 458 | Honey pot | |
| 459 | Table lamp embossed leaves | 6¾"h –1960s |
| 460 | Tray | |
| 461 | Flower Jug | 7"h 3"acr –1960s |
| 462 | N/I | |
| 463 | Jug p102 TSC | 5¾"h –1960s |
| 464 | Jug three 'spouts' | 5"h –1960s |
| 465 | Jug Vine range p148 TSC re-introduced by Portmeirion Potteries | 8"h –1982 –1992+ |
| 466 | Jardiniere | |
| 467 | Jardiniere | |
| 468 | Bowl round, stone wall, three platforms for frogs and lizards sim to 469 p57 TSS | l/s –1960s |
| 469 | Bowl sim to 468 p86 TSS | s/s 3⅜"h –1960s |
| 470 | N/I | |
| 471 | Bowl diamond shape goes with 480/481 p53 TSS | 3½"h 10¼"acr –1960s |
| 472 | Wall vase Vine range re-introduced by Portmeirion Potteries | 8"h –1965 –1992+ |
| 473 | Bowl, round, embossed acorns and leaves with recess for owl p86 TSS | 3⅛"h 7½"dia –1960s |
| 474 | Jardiniere with handles | |
| 475 | Miniature jug with stork handle sim to 1138/1960/4069 p66 TSS | 3"h –1982 |
| 476 | Miniature jug embossed hollyhocks sim to 1274 and 1962 p66 TSS | 3"h –1960s |
| 477 | Top hat with dog/cat | |
| 478 | Jug Vine range re-introduced by Portmeirion Potteries | 6"h –1982 –1992+ |
| 479 | Bowl with Australian flowers Sydney range p143 TSC | 12"acr –1960s |

| | | |
|---|---|---|
| 480 | Jug, diamond goes with 471/481 | 7"h –1960s |
| 481 | Posy bar, diamond goes with 471/480 | 8½"l –1960s |
| 482 | Tray (vase) | |
| 483 | Vase | |
| 484 | Bowl triangular | 10¼–10½"w –1960s |
| 485 | Bowl higher one side p105 TSC | 5½"h –1960s |
| 486 | Jug narrow p102 TSC | 9¼–10½"h –1960s |
| 487 | Jug wavy serpent handle | 6¼–7¾"h –1965 |
| 488 | Bowl wavy triangle p105 TSC (numbered 494 in error) | 4"h –1960s |
| 489 | Sauce boat p72 TSC | 12¾"l –1969 |
| 490 | Jug Sydney range p143 TSC | 8½"h –1960s |
| 491 | Sauce boat | 5½"h –1960s |
| 492 | N/I | |
| 493 | Shaving mug | |
| 493 also | Bowl two handles p105 TSC | 11½"l –1960s |
| 494 | Basket two horns p105 TSC (bottom line) | 3¼"h –1960s |
| 495 | Settee | |
| 496 | Vase | |
| 497 | Fruit dish Dovecote p86 TSS | 13"acr –1960s |
| 498 | Bowl | |
| 499 | Jug | |
| 500 | Fruit bowl Sydney range p143 TSC | 13½"acr –1960s |
| 501 | Jug Sydney range p143 TSC | 6"h –1960s |
| 502 | Bulb bowl | 4¾"h |
| 503 | Jardiniere | |
| 504 | Bowl | |
| 505 | Bowl | |
| 506 | Butter dish | |
| 507 | Lamp | |
| 508 | Bowl | |
| 509 | Basket Shell range p66 TSC | 6½"h –1970 |
| 510 | Jug Shell range p66 TSC | 9¼"h –1960 |
| 511 | Jug Shell range p66 TSC | 6¼"h –1960 |
| 512 | Jardiniere Shell p66 TSC | 14"l –1975 |
| 513 | Jardiniere Shell p66 TSC | 4¼"h 9¼"l –1975 |
| 514 | Jardiniere Shell p66 TSC | 6¼"h 6½"l –1975 |
| 515 | Vase | |
| 516 | Onion face bowl p59 TSS | 4"h –1989 |
| 517 | Vase | |
| 518 | Jug narrow | 4¾"h –1960s |
| 519–520 | N/I (Stop Press 520 Bowl with three holes.) | |
| 521 | Hat | |
| 522 | N/I | |
| 523 | Wall vase | |
| 524 | Wall vase Sydney range p143 TSC | 8"h –1960s |
| 525 | Tray oakleaf shape acorn posy container Reg. No. 873716 (1954) | 11½"l |
| 526 | Tray with leaf posy container | 8½"l –1960s |
| 527 | Tray with cone posy container | 8½"l –1960s |
| 528 | Tray with thistle posy container | 13"l |
| 529 | Butter dish, round Dovecote range | 5"dia –1960s |
| 530 | Cheese dish Dovecote p148 TSC | 4½"h –1960s |
| 531 | Fruit basket Dovecote | 11¼"acr –1960s |
| 532 | Teapot Dovecote sim to 577 | l/s –1960s |
| 533 | Sugar bowl Dovecote | 3"dia –1960s |
| 534 | Cream jug Dovecote | 3¾"h –1960s |
| 535 | Honey pot Dovecote p86 TSS | 4"h –1960s |
| 536 | Cucumber dish Dovecote p148 TSC | 12½"l –1960s |
| 537 | N/I | |
| 538 | Teddy Bear (unconfirmed) | |
| 539 | Squirrel (unconfirmed) (538 and 539 look genuine but a marked example has yet to be found) | 4¼"h |
| 540 | Lettuce dish Dovecote (should be with stand) p148 TSC | 8½"acr –1960s |
| 541 | Salad bowl Dovecote p148 TSC | 9½"acr –1960s |
| 542 | Cup with saucer/plate (T.V. set) Dovecote p148 TSC | 7¾"acr –1960s |

| | | |
|---|---|---|
| **543** | N/I | |
| **544** | Jug, also with budgerigar p14 TSS | 9"h –1965 |
| **545** | Basket, also with budgerigar p14 TSS | 8½"h –1965 |
| **546** | Jardiniere, also with budgerigar p72/73/92 TSC | 6½"h 10"l –1965 |
| **547** | Dish, shallow, also with budgerigar | 13"acr –1965 |
| **548** | Jardiniere Deco style also with budgerigar p86 TSS | 9½"l –1965 |
| **549** | Vase p72 TSC | –1960s |
| **550** | Bowl, as glacier with platform for penguin goes with 572/591 p86 TSS | 5" base 9¾"l –1960s |
| **551** | Jug | |
| **552** | Urn | |
| **553** | Urn | |
| **554–556** | N/I | |
| **557** | Jug Slymcraft range p76/102 TSC | 7–7¾"h –1982 |
| **558–559** | N/I | |
| **560** | Jug embossed leaves with recess for novelty goes with 568/2049 | 6½"h |
| **561** | Jug with tongue handle p101 TSC | 4½"h |
| **562** | Jug Slymcraft range p101 TSC | 6½"h –1960s |
| **563** | N/I | |
| **564** | Jug p102 TSC | 9"h |
| **565** | Vase | |
| **566** | Vase p102 TSC | 10"h |
| **567** | Novelty barrel with recess for duck sim to 569 p61 TSS | 2½"h –1960s |
| **568** | Bowl with recess for novelty goes with 560/2049 | 2¾"h 3¾"l (base) |
| **568 also** | remodelled with platform for novelty goes with 560/2049 p61 TSS | 2½"h –1960s 4½"l (base) |
| **569** | Novelty barrel with recess for duck sim to 567 p86 TSS | 4¼"h –1960s |
| **570** | Jug narrow | 11"h –1960s |
| **571** | Jug wider centre p102 TSC | 8¾–9"h –1960s |
| **572** | Jug as glacier with recess for penguin goes with 550/591 p86 TSS | 8"h –1960s |
| **573** | Vase | |
| **574** | N/I | |
| **575** | Vase | |
| **576** | Cup and Saucer Dovecote range, no number on items | –1960s |
| **577** | Teapot Dovecote range sim to 532 | s/s –1960s |
| **578** | N/I | |
| **579** | Vase | |
| **580** | Vase | |
| **581** | Basket | |
| **582** | Orange honey p59 TSS | 3½"h –1982 |
| **583** | Pineapple honey p59 TSS | 3½"h –1982 |
| **584** | Grape honey | 3½"h –1982 |
| **585** | Strawberry honey p59 TSS | 3½"h –1982 |
| **586** | Barrel container with little dog at one end (Dogs can vary) p38 TSS | 3"h –1960s |
| **587** | Rabbit hutch container with recess for rabbit p86 TSS | 4"h 8"l –1960s |
| **588** | Jug, squirrel on cone | |
| **589** | Bowl curved | 4"acr |
| **590** | Bowl | |
| **591** | Bowl, glacier, with recess/platform for penguin goes with 550 and 572 p53/86 TSS | 3¾"h –1960s |
| **592** | Bowl | |
| **593** | N/I | |
| **594** | Penguin, probably for 591 | |
| **595** | N/I | |
| **596** | Jug | |
| **597** | Bowl | |
| **598** | Bulb bowl | |
| **599** | Vase p72 TSC | –1960s |
| **600** | Vase | |
| **601** | Vase | |
| **602** | Vase | |
| **603** | Urn vase, lion handles p92 TSC | 10¼"h –1960s |
| **604** | Urn vase, lion handles | –1960s |
| **605** | Bowl | |
| **606** | Jug | |
| **607** | Vase | |
| **608** | Scorpion | |
| **609** | Punch bowl | |
| **610–613** | N/I | |
| **614** | Shell bowl | 2½"h 7"acr –1960s |
| **615** | Jardiniere Sea Shell range sim to 616/618 p92 TSC | 5¾"l –1970 |
| **616** | Jardiniere Sea Shell range sim to 615/618 p92 TSC | 9½"l –1970 |
| **617** | Flower pot Sea Shell | –1970 |
| **618** | Jardiniere Sea Shell range sim to 615/616 p92 TSC | 7¾"l –1970 |
| **619** | Butter dish with cow on lid. Produced later by various potteries in white glaze p59 TSS | 5"l –1982 –1983+ |
| **620** | Butter pot | |
| **621** | Stilton Cheese dish round with mouse on lid. Produced later by various potteries in white glaze p59 TSS | 6¾"dia (plate) –1982 –1983+ |
| **622** | Vase angular hour glass shape | 7"h –1960s |
| **623** | Vase p103 TSC | 7"h –1960s |
| **624** | Vase three tiered | 7"h –1960s |
| **625** | Vase fish shape | 7¼"h –1960s |
| **626** | Vase cone shape p102 TSC | 7¼"h –1960s |
| **627** | Vase | |
| **628** | Vase Classic range p91/94 TSC | 8"h –1982 |
| **629** | Vase Classic p91 TSC | 9"h –1970 |
| **630** | Vase Classic p91 TSC | 6"h –1975 |
| **631** | Bowl Classic p91 TSC | 6"acr –1975 |
| **632** | Vase Classic p91 TSC | 10"h –1970 |
| **633** | N/I | |
| **634** | Bowl | |
| **635** | Bowl | |
| **636** | Bowl p72/73 TSC | 10¾"l –1965 |
| **637** | N/I | |
| **638** | Bowl on feet | –1960s |
| **639** | Bowl p72 TSC | –1960s |
| **640** | Jardiniere handkerchief shape | 8½"h |
| **641** | Vase handkerchief shape | 8½"h |
| **642** | Bowl handkerchief shape | 11¾"l |
| **643** | Bowl handkerchief shape | 10¼"l |
| **644** | Vase handkerchief shape | 7"h |
| **645** | Wall vase Classic range p91 TSC | 9"h –1970s |
| **646** | Flower pot Classic p91 TSC | 5"h –1970s |
| **647** | Flower pot Classic | 4"h –1970s |
| **648** | Jardiniere Classic p91 TSC | 10"l –1970s |
| **649** | Bowl Classic p91 TSC | 8½"acr –1970s |
| **650** | Vase two entwined | 6"h –1960s |
| **651** | Vase | |
| **652** | Jardiniere handkerchief shape | 7"h |
| **653** | Wall vase handkerchief shape | 8"h |
| **654** | Tray | |
| **655** | Vase | 7"h –1960s |
| **656** | Vase vertical ridges p90 TSC | –1960s |
| **657** | Bowl | |
| **658** | Vase | |
| **659** | Wall vase | |
| **660–662** | N/I | |
| **663** | Bowl | |
| **664–665** | N/I | |
| **666** | Candle holder | |
| **667** | Candle holder | 4¼"h –1960s |
| **668** | Wall vase + handle | |
| **669** | Candle holder | |
| **670** | Candle holder | |
| **671** | N/I | |
| **672** | Candy box | |
| **673** | Dish shallow p72 TSC | –1960s |
| **674** | Vase p94 TSC | 5"h –1982 |

| | | |
|---|---|---|
| 675 | Vase incised swirls sim to 1571 p94/103 TSC | 5"h –1982 |
| 676 | Vase sim to 1562/3/4 p94 TSC | 5"h –1982 |
| 677 | Vase | |
| 678 | Vase opening to cone shape | 6"h –1970 |
| 679 | Vase plain cone shape also advertising Rowney paint brushes p85 TSS | 6"h –1975 |
| 680 | N/I | |
| 681 | Vase with two central circles (could be 189) | 8¼"h |
| 682 | Vase unsymmetrical decorative 'handles' | 6"h –1960s |
| 683 | Vase 'Pineapple' shape sim to 400/730 | 6"h –1970 |
| 684 | Vase sim to 1343 p94/103 TSC | 5"h –1982 |
| 685 | N/I | |
| 686 | Basket wicker pattern | 10½"h app |
| 687 | Coconut wall vase with blue-tit | 6½"h –1965 |
| 688 | Tree trunk vase with blue-tit | 7"h –1982 |
| 689 | Tree trunk triple vase with blue-tit p86 TSS | 6"h 11"l –1982 |
| 690–694 | N/I | |
| 695 | Bowl | |
| 696 | N/I | |
| 697 | Hand holding vase p31 TSS | 5"h –1960s |
| 698 | Pot | |
| 699 | Candle holder/pot | |
| 700 | (Using S & C number for Kingfisher) p54 TSS | 6½"h –1965 |
| 701 | Swallow-bowl | |
| 702 | Bowl usually with golden crested grebe (3162) p54 TSS | 11"acr –1960s |
| 703 | Barrel/barrow | |
| 704 | Jug | |
| 705 | Bowl | |
| 706 | Bowl | |
| 707 | Lazy Pixie novelty toadstool, used later with gnome, rabbit etc p32/54 TSS p112 TSC | 3"h –1970 –1975 |
| 708 | Lazy Pixie novelty wheelbarrow p31 TSS also 'Floral Lines' and with gnome | 5"l –1970 –1960 –1975 |
| 709 | N/I | |
| 710 | Vase, fish balancing on tail goes with 725 p90 TSC | 8"h –1960s |
| 711 | Vase p72 TSC | –1960s |
| 712 | Vase p72 TSC | –1960s |
| 713 | Wall vase p72 TSC | –1960s |

| | | |
|---|---|---|
| 714 | Jardiniere p72 TSC | –1960s |
| 715 | N/I | |
| 716 | Flower jug p72 TSC | –1960s |
| 717 | Tray | |
| 718 | Wall vase p73/90 TSC | 12½"acr –1965 |
| 719 | Tray | |
| 720 | Hat | |
| 721 | Cap wall vase p54 TSS | 4½"h –1960s |
| 722 | Hat | |
| 723 | Hat | |
| 724 | Shell bowl Nautilus range p70 TSC | 9"acr –1965 |
| 725 | Vase, fish balancing on head, goes with 710 p90 TSC | 9½"h –1960s |
| 726 | Wall vase Nautilus range p70 TSC | 8"h –1960s |
| 727 | Dish triangular p72 TSC | small –1960s |
| 728 | N/I | |
| 729 | Vase | |
| 730 | Vase pineapple shape sim to 400/683 | 10"h –1970 |
| 731 | Vase 'studs' down side | 9"h –1960s |
| 732 | Trilby hat wall vase p54 TSS | 4¾"h –1960s |
| 733 | Boater hat wall vase p54 TSS | 4¾"h –1960s |
| 734 | Vase sim to 751/752 | 8"h –1975 |
| 735 | Cactus in pot | 5"h –1960s |
| 736 | Cactus in pot p54 TSS | 5"h –1960s |
| 737 | Cactus in pot | 5"h –1960s |
| 738 | Cactus in pot | 5"h –1960s |
| 739 | Vase sim to 748/749 p73 TSC | 8–8¼"h –1965 |
| 740 | Vase | |
| 741 | Vase sim to 2337/2352 p73 TSC | 8¼–8½"h –1965 |
| 742 | Cactus in pot | 3"h –1960s |
| 743 | N/I | |
| 744 | Vase, uneven top | 5"h –1970s |
| 745 | Vase top opens out | 5"h –1970s |
| 746 | Vase studded decoration | 5"h –1970 |
| 747 | Wheelbarrow usually with pixie p53 TSS | 10½"l –1975 |
| 748 | Vase sim to 739/749 | 10¼"h –1960 |
| 749 | Vase sim to 739/748 p73 TSC | 6"h –1970 |
| 750 | Vase | |
| 751 | Vase sim to 734/752 | 6"h –1970 |
| 752 | Vase sim to 734/751 p73 TSC | 10½"h –1970 |
| 753 | Jardiniere Nautilus p70 TSC | 7½"h –1965 |
| 754 | Jug | |
| 755 | Vase | |
| 756 | Jardiniere Nautilus p70 TSC | 9½"h –1965 |
| 757–758 | N/I | |
| 759 | Shell pot | |

# SHAW & COPESTAKE AND SYLVAC MOULD NUMBERS

**From early 1900**

| | | |
|---|---|---|
| 19 | Jug ornate with narrow neck partner to 30 p98 TSS | 11"h |
| 20–29 | N/I | |
| 30 | Vase narrow neck two handles partner to 19 p98 TSS | 11"h |
| 31–35 | N/I | |
| 36 | Jug vase with narrow neck | 16"h |
| 37–74 | N/I | |
| 75 | Vase narrow neck curvy rim | 9"h |
| 76–126 | N/I | |
| 127 | Plant pot sim to 404 p36 TSC | 7"h 9"dia |
| 128–137 | N/I | |
| 138 | Vase narrow top wider at base | 10¾"h |
| 139–175 | N/I | |
| 176 | Clock with pillars | 16"h |
| 177 | N/I | |
| 178 | Spill vase | 4½"h |

| | | |
|---|---|---|
| 179–182 | N/I | |
| 183 | Plant pot | 5"h 5"dia |
| 184 | N/I | |
| 185 | Jardiniere | 5"h 4¾"dia |
| 186–229 | N/I | |
| | | |
| **Circa 1913** | | |
| | | |
| 230 | Clock very ornate | 11½"h 9"l |
| 231–254 | N/I | |
| 255 | Vase | 13¾"h |
| 256–261 | N/I | |
| 262 | Plant pot | 6½–6¾"dia |
| 263–272 | N/I | |
| 273 | Vase, with handles p35 TSC (top 2nd left) | 9½"h |
| 274–278 | N/I | |
| 279 | Vase Reg. No. 628381 (1913) | 11¾"h |
| 280 | N/I | |

**Circa 1914–1918**

| | | |
|---|---|---|
| **281** | Vase sim to 273 | 11½″h |
| **282–291** | N/I | |
| **292** | Vase Reg. No. 633217 (1914) | 9½″h |
| **293** | Vase with handles and curvy top Reg. No. 634174 (1914) | 11½″h |
| **294–301** | N/I | |
| **302** | Plant pot | 8″h 10″dia |
| **303–309** | N/I | |
| **310** | Vase | |
| **311–314** | N/I | |
| **315** | Plant pot on feet | 6″h 5¼″dia |
| **316–320** | N/I | |
| **321** | Vase | 9½″h |
| **322–334** | N/I | |
| **335** | Vase with handles | 10″h |
| **336** | Vase sim to 335 | 7½″h |
| **337** | Vase p35 TSC | 12″h |
| **338** | Vase sim to 337 | 13¼″h |
| **339–340** | N/I | |
| **341** | Plant pot | 6½″h 6″dia |
| **342** | Vase set sim to 335 | 7″h & 6″h |
| **343–346** | N/I | |
| **347** | Vase, two handles each side | 9½″h |
| **348–349** | N/I | |
| **350** | Plant pot on four feet | 5″h |
| **351–353** | N/I | |
| **354** | Vase sim to Holborn vase p20 TSS | 16″h |
| **355** | Vase on stand sim to 359 | 6½″h |
| **356** | N/I | |
| **357** | Jardiniere | 4½″h 4½″dia |
| **358** | N/I | |
| **359** | Vase on stand sim to 355 | 9¾″h |
| **360–361** | N/I | |
| **362** | Plant pot on feet | 4½″h 4½″dia |
| **363** | Vase sim to 364/365 | 7¼″h |
| **364** | Vase with handles fluted top and base sim to 363/365 SCC/11 | 9½″h |
| **365** | Vase very ornamental sim to 363/364 | 12″h |
| **366–370** | N/I | |

**Circa 1921**

| | | |
|---|---|---|
| **371** | Vase with handles p81 TSS | 10″h |
| **372–373** | N/I | |
| **374** | Vase with handles p35 TSC | 11¾″h |
| **375** | Vase fluted, handles | 12″h |
| **376** | Jardiniere with handles sim to 375 | 7″h 12¾″w |
| **377–378** | N/I | |
| **379** | Vase | |
| **380** | Vase sim to 376 | 5″h 8″w · |
| **381–386** | N/I | |
| **387** | Vase with handles | 11½″h |
| **388–398** | N/I | |
| **399** | Plant pot embossed shells and scrolls sim to 401 p168 TSC (top shelf right) | 4½″h 4½″dia |
| **400** | N/I | |
| **401** | Plant pot sim to 399 | 6¾″h 6¼″dia |
| **402–403** | N/I | |
| **404** | Plant pot sim to 127 | 7⅞″h 7″dia |
| **411** | Plant pot | 5¼″h 6¼″dia |
| **415** | Vase | |
| **416** | Vase sim to 418 | 10″h |
| **417** | Vase sim to 421 | |
| **418** | Vase sim to 416 | 7½″h |
| **419** | Vase with handles sim to 425/445 p35 TSC (top 2nd right) | 11½″h |
| **420** | Vase on square base | 11½″h |
| **421** | Vase oval sim to 446 p35 TSC (top 1st left) | 7½″h |

| | | |
|---|---|---|
| **422** | Vase square base narrow neck | 8½″h |
| **423** | N/I | |
| **424** | Vase sim to 540 | |
| **425** | Vase with handles sim to 419/445 p35 TSC (top 1st right) | 9½″h |
| **426** | Vase | 8½″h |
| **427–430** | N/I | |
| **431** | Vase sim to 432 | 8¼″h |
| **432** | Vase p81 TSS | 7½″h |
| **433** | Clock | 5¼″h |
| **433 also** | Vase to match 433 clock 433 originally plain later embossed figures Scello Ware (1928) and Wild Duck range (1932/3) | 4½″h |
| **434–435** | N/I | |
| **436** | Bowl also used with centre piece p54/96 TSS | 2½″h 9½″dia –1965 |
| **437–438** | N/I | |
| **439** | Vase narrow neck | 7½″h |
| **440** | Rose bowl on pedestal | 7″h 6½″dia |
| **441–444** | N/I | |
| **445** | Vase sim to 419/425 | 8½″h |
| **446** | Vase sim to 421 | 8½″h |
| **447–448** | N/I | |
| **449** | Vase with handles | 14″h |
| **450–464** | N/I | |
| **465** | Vase embossed fruits (unconfirmed) | 7½″h |
| **466–481** | N/I | |
| **482** | Clock plain | 12″h |
| **483** | Spill vase narrow waist | 4¾″h |
| **484** | Shaving/toothbrush mug | 4¼″h |
| **485–488** | N/I | |
| **489** | Bowl hexagonal | 3½″h 7¾″dia |
| **490–491** | N/I | |
| **492** | Rose bowl | 5¾″h 4½″w |
| **493** | Shaving mug | 3⅞″h |
| **494** | N/I | |
| **495** | Vase sim to 510 | 11½″h |
| **496** | Vase with handles sim to 509 | 11½″h |
| **497–508** | N/I | |
| **509** | Vase sim to 496 p81 TSS | 10″h |
| **510** | Vase sim to 495 | 9½″h |
| **511** | Vase sometimes with clock 520 | 11½″h |

**Circa 1925**

| | | |
|---|---|---|
| **512–519** | N/I | |
| **520** | Clock with pillars very ornate | 14″h 10½″l |
| **521** | Vase with handles | 12″h |
| **522** | Vase plain with upside down 'L' handles | 13¾″h |
| **523** | Dressing table tray | 13½″l |
| **524–537** | N/I | |
| **538** | Vase sim to 539/540/541/558/562 | 7¾″h |
| **539** | Vase sim to 538/540/541/558/562 | 8½″h |
| **540** | Vase sim to 538/539/541/558/562 p95 TSS | 8″h |
| **541** | Vase sim to 538/539/540/558/562 | 11½″h |
| **542–544** | N/I | |
| **545** | Vase | 6″h |
| **546** | Vase hexagonal sim to 548 | 8½″h |
| **547** | N/I | |
| **548** | Vase sim to 546 | 11¼″h |
| **549–555** | N/I | |
| **556** | Vase sim to 634 but wider at base | tall |
| **557** | N/I | |
| **558** | Vase sim to 538/539/540/541/562 | |
| **559** | Rose bowl with brass or silver plated grid, also found in 'Scello' ware c.1928 and embossed 'Wild Duck' range c.1932 p97 TSS | 4½–5½″h 7″dia |
| **560** | Jug p38 TSC | 8½″h |
| **561** | Vase | 7½″h |

| | | |
|---|---|---|
| 562 | Vase sim to 538/539/540/541/558 | 14″h |
| 563 | Jug | 6¾″ & 7¾″h |
| 564 | N/I | |
| 565 | Vase with handles | 11½″h |
| 566 | Rose bowl | 3″h 5″dia |
| 567 | Vase with handles | 11½″h |
| 568 | N/I | |
| 569 | Bowl Wild Duck | |
| 570 | Vase small handles embossed band around top | 8¼″h |
| 571–572 | N/I | |
| 573 | Jugs p83 TSS p38 TSC five sizes | 5″, 5¼″, 6″, 7″, 7¾″h |
| 575 | Rose bowl p35 TSC | 8½″h |
| 576 | Vase square base | 11″h |
| 577 | Vase | |
| 578 | Vase with handles p81 TSS p35 TSC | 6¾″h |
| 579 | N/I | |
| 580 | Plant pot on four feet | 4″h |
| 581 | N/I | |
| 582 | Vase ornate handles sim to 583 | 11¾″h |
| 583 | Vase sim to 582 | 13¾″h |
| 584 | N/I | |
| 585 | Vase | |
| 586 | Vase ornate with handles | 9½″h |
| 587 | Vase ornate with handles | 9½″h |
| 588–593 | N/I | |
| 594 | Tray Sylvo range | 13½″l 6″w |
| 595–599 | N/I | |
| 600 | Vase sim 610 & 611 p35 TSC | 9¾″h |
| 601 | N/I | |
| 602 | Plant pot sim to 603 | 5″h 6″dia |
| 603 | Plant pot sim to 602 | 5½″h 7″dia |
| 604 | Clock p37 TSC | 12″h |
| 605 | Clock heart shape p82/83 TSS | 9¼″h |
| 606 | Vase partner to 605 p82 TSS p42 TSC | 7¼″h |
| 607 | N/I | |
| 608 | Clock heart shape round or square centre | 11½″h |
| 609 | Vase partner to 608 | 9½″h |
| 610 | Vase sim to 600/611 | 7¾″h |
| 611 | Vase sim to 600/610 | 11⅝″h |
| 612 | N/I | |
| 613 | Vase | 8″h |
| 614 | Vase p42 TSC | 9¼″h |
| 615–620 | N/I (Stop Press 620 Tray) | |
| 621 | Vase | 13½″h |
| 622 | Vase | 14″h |
| 623–625 | N/I | |
| 626 | Vase sim to 627 | 7¾″h |
| 627 | Vase sim to 626 | 10″h |
| 628 | N/I | |
| 629 | Vase sim to 614 SCC/10 | 11½″h |
| 630 | N/I | |
| 631 | Bowl round on three feet | 7″dia |
| 632–633 | N/I | |
| 634 | Vase for spills | 6″h |
| 635 | Vase for spills, seen with silver rim | 4–5″h |
| 636 | Vase for spills sim to 634 | 8″h |
| 637 | Vase | 12″h |
| 638–639 | N/I | |
| 640 | Tray | |
| 641 | N/I | |
| 642 | Shaving mug | 3¼″h 6″l |
| 643 | Cheese dish oblong | 7½″l (base) |
| 644 | N/I | |
| 645 | Clock | 11½″h |
| 646–647 | N/I | |
| 648 | Vase Gothic style | 10½″h |
| 648 also | Clock Gothic style | 11½″h |
| 649 | Clock plain with oval or round face | 10″h |
| 649 | Clock embossed Wild Duck range c1932 p83 TSS | 10″h |
| 650 | Vase plain and embossed to partner 649 p83 TSS | 7½″h |
| 651 | Clock partners 652 SCC/13 | 8⅝″h 11¼″l |
| 652 | Vase partners 651 | 8½″h |
| 653 | N/I | |
| 654 | Sandwich tray, has matching plates unnumbered | 12½″l 6¾″w |
| 655–658 | N/I | |
| 659 | Vase plain and Scello ware | 9½″h |
| 660–662 | N/I | |
| 663 | Vase elaborate embossed Chinese scene sim to 703 | 12″h |
| 664–665 | N/I | |
| 666 | Jug octagonal | 6¾″, 7½″, 8¾″h |
| 667–674 | N/I | |
| 675 | Wall plaque | 11¾″l 8″w |
| 676–677 | N/I | |
| 678 | Vase sim to 679 | 10″h |
| 679 | Vase sim to 678 ornate handles scalloped top | 11″h |
| 680 | Bowl wavy edges shell like embossed pattern also partnered with 700 p96 TSS | 2½″h 8½″dia |
| 681–682 | N/I | |
| 683 | Butter/cheese dish | 3″h |
| 684–688 | N/I | |
| 689 | Plant pot embossed Lord and Lady | 4½″h |
| 690 | Plant pot embossed Lord and Lady scene (These scenes can vary slightly) SCC/11 | 5½″h |
| 691–692 | N/I | |
| 693 | Plant pot embossed Lord and Lady p96 TSS | l/s |
| 694 | Clock Lord and Lady | 6¼″h 5¼″w at base |
| 694 also | Vase Lord and Lady | 5½″h |
| 695 | N/I | |
| 696 | Clock Lord and Lady | 9¾″h |
| 696 also | Vase Lord and Lady with handles | 8½″h |
| 697 | Vase Lord and Lady with handles sim to 699 | 7¾″h |
| 698 | Vase Lord and Lady p96 TSS | 9¾″h |
| 699 | Vase Lord and Lady with handles sim to 697 | 11½″h |
| 700 | Kingfisher to go with float bowl 436/680/711 or 726 p54/96 TSS Swallow | 6½″h –1965 |
| 701 | | |
| 702 | N/I | |
| 703 | Vase elaborate embossed Chinese scene sim to 663 p109 TSS | 10″h |
| 704 | Plant pot Lord and Lady sim to 714/715 p37 TSC | 4¾″h |
| 705–708 | N/I | |
| 709 | Pair vases embossed Spanish scene each different p107 TSS | 10″h |
| 710 | N/I | |
| 711 | Bowl embossed flowers partnered with 700 p96 TSS | 3″h 11¼″dia |
| 712–713 | N/I | |
| 714 | Plant pot Lord and Lady sim to 704/715 p96 TSS | 6″h 6″dia |
| 715 | Plant pot embossed Lord and Lady sim to 704/714 p96 TSS | 7½″h 8½″dia |
| 716 | Jardiniere Lord and Lady | 11″dia |
| 717 | N/I | |
| 718 | Plant pot Lord and Lady straight sides p96 TSS | 6¼″h 6¼″w |
| 719–721 | N/I | |
| 722 | Bowl octagonal embossed with fairies p96 TSS | 11″dia |
| 723–725 | N/I | |
| 726 | Bowl embossed garden scene also partnered with 700 p96 TSS | 2½″h 9½″dia |
| 727 | Twin vase modelled on Sydney Harbour Bridge Reg. No. 758626 (1930) p96 TSS | 4½″h 8½″l |
| 728 | Bowl Lord and Lady p96 TSS | 6″h |
| 729–732 | N/I | |
| 733 | Pelican in top hat standing beside small 'rock' posy holder | 8″h |

| | | |
|---|---|---|
| 743 | Airedale terrier dog, also with vase 827 p37 TSC | 7"h 9"l |
| 744 | Clock with handles | 10½"h 10"w |
| 747 | Bowl embossed flowers with separate monkey flower centre | 7"d (bowl) 7"h (monkey) |
| 751 | Dog | |

**Circa 1931**

| | | |
|---|---|---|
| 752 | Pekinese dog standing | 6½"h 7½"l |
| 753–756 | N/I | |
| 757 | Plant holder Wild Duck sim to 812 Reg. No. 762858 (1931) | l/s |
| 758–765 | N/I | |
| 766 | Camel with saddlebags | 5½"h 6"l |
| 767 | Camel with saddlebags on plinth | 4¼"h 5½"l |
| 768 | Elephant standing | 4"h –1982 |
| 769 | Elephant standing p18 TSS | 6"h –1982 |
| 770 | Elephant standing | 7"–7¼"h –1982 |
| 771 | Elephant standing sometimes on plinth | 8¼"–8½"h –1982 |
| 772 | Camel standing with howdah and saddlebags sometimes on plinth p107 TSS | 7"–8"h 9"l |
| 773 | Elephant standing with howdah | 8½"h –1940 |
| 774 | Vase | 12"h |
| 775 | N/I | |
| 776 | Vase basket weave design, with embossed roses sim to 778 p37 TSC | 6"h 8"w |
| 777 | N/I | |
| 778 | Vase sim to 776 | 6¼"h 10¼"w |
| 779 | Cheetah | |
| 780 | Vase p42 TSC | 5"h |
| 781 | Spill vase slightly narrower waist | 4½"h |
| 782 | Vase Lord and Lady | |
| 783 | Clock (number is not clear) | 10"h 14½"w |
| 784 | Vase Wild Duck range p37 TSC | 7½"h |
| 785 | Vase Wild Duck range p83 TSS | 5¼"h |
| 786 | Bowl square Wild Duck partnered with 787 | 9"sq |
| 787 | Flying duck flower centre partnered with 786 | 7½"h |
| 788 | Elephant with howdah p18 TSS | 6"h –1940s |
| 789 | Elephant with howdah | 7⅜"h –1940s |
| 790 | Vase fan shape Wild Duck Reg. No. 768168 (1931) SCC/11 | 5¼"h 8¼"w |
| 791 | Vase Wild Duck range sim to 790 | 7"h |
| 792 | N/I | |
| 793 | Swan | 5¼"h 7½"l |
| 794 | Swan | |
| 795 | Swan p33 TSC | 7½"h 10"l |
| 796–797 | N/I | |
| 798 | Elephant with howdah | l/s –1940s |
| 799 | Vase Wild Duck Reg. No. 768695 (1931) SCC/11 | 9"h |
| 800 | N/I | |
| 801 | Vase Wild duck Reg. No. 768695 (1931) | 10"h |
| 802 | N/I | |
| 803 | Candleholder Wild Duck Reg. No. 769028 (1931) | 6"h |
| 804 | Box with lid Wild Duck Reg. No. 769029 (1931) p83 TSS | 3"h 7½"l 4¼"w |
| 805 | Box Wild Duck Reg. No. 769029 (1931) | 2½"h 6½"l 4"w |

**Circa 1932**

| | | |
|---|---|---|
| 806–808 | N/I | |
| 809 | Jardiniere Wild duck Reg. No. 769285 (1932) | 5½"h 9½"l |
| 810 | N/I | |
| 811 | Toilet set Jug Wild Duck Reg. No. 769699 (1932) | 10"h |

| | | |
|---|---|---|
| 811 also | Bowl Wild Duck range Reg. No. 769725 (1932) | 5"h 18"dia |
| 812 | Plant pot Wild Duck sim to 757 | 6"h 7"dia |
| 813 | Sam Weller character jug sim to 1231 | 9"h |
| 814 | Elephant with howdah | 4"h 5¼"l |
| 815 | Elephant standing | 4½"h –1982 |
| 816 | Elephant | |
| 817 | Lion free standing or on plinth 820 | 4¾"h |
| 818 | Lion free standing or on plinth 821 p25 TSC | 5¾"h |
| 819 | Lion free standing or on plinth 822 | 7"h |
| 820 | Plinth (for lion 817) | 8½"l |
| 821 | Plinth (for lion 818) | 10¼"l |
| 822 | Plinth (for lion 819) | 12"l |
| 823 | Lion on plinth with tree stump vase partner to 824 (handed) | 5½"h 9½"l |
| 824 | Lion on plinth with tree stump vase partner to 823 (handed) | 5½"h 9½"l |
| 825 | Lion and vase on plinth | 7¾"h 11"l |
| 826 | Elephant with howdah | 4½"h –1940s |
| 827 | Vase attached to dog number 743 p37 TSC | 4¾"h |
| 828 | Vase ribbed, Greek urn two handles | 8½"h |
| 828 also | Bowl Harvest Poppy probably partnered with poppy flower centre 957 | 9"dia (top) |
| | both above 828 numbers have been double checked by the collectors who have them | |
| 829 | Jug Egyptian range Reg. No. 774557 (1932) p42 TSC | 7¾"h |
| 830 | N/I | |
| 831 | Bowl Egyptian range Reg. No. 774557 | |
| 832 | Vase Egyptian range sim to 856 Reg. No. 774557 partner to clock 862 SCC/11 | 7½"h |
| 833 | Vase Egyptian range Reg. No. 774557 | 8¾"h |
| 834 | N/I | |
| 835 | Plant pot Egyptian Reg. No. 774557 | |
| 836 | N/I | |
| 837 | Rose bowl Egyptian range Reg. No. 774557 | 4¾"h 6"dia |
| 838 | Vase Egyptian range Reg. No. 774557 | 7"h |
| 839 | Vase Egyptian range Reg. No. 774557 p37 TSC | 7½"h |
| 840 | Portland vase with handles and narrow neck Egyptian range Reg. No. 774557 | 8¼"h |
| 841 | Vase Egyptian range sim to 838 with stand | 8"h |
| 842 | Goblin | 5½"h |
| 843 | Laughing cat with bow tie p27 TSC | 8½"h |
| 844 | Laughing cat sim to 843 with vase and detachable head | 8½"h |
| 845 | Goblin with vase | 7¼"h |
| 846 | N/I | |
| 847 | Figure, lady, Covent Garden fruit seller vase | 10"h |
| 848 | Bowl Harvest Poppy | 5¾"h 10½"l |
| 849 | Cheese dish 'From Southsea' | 5¼"l |
| 850 | Bird on tree SCC/18 | |
| 851–855 | N/I | |
| 856 | Vase Egyptian range round base sim to 832 | 7"h |
| 857 | Rose bowl tree trunk | 5"h |
| 858 | Posy tree trunk | 5"h |
| 859–860 | N/I | |

| | | |
|---|---|---|
| 861 | Vase wider top with embossed band around top originally with flower grid p99 TSS | 7¾"h |
| 862 | Clock Egyptian range partner to vase 832 Reg. No. 774557 | 9"h 7"w |
| 863–864 | N/I | |
| 865 | Figure, man, Covent Garden fruit seller vase | 10"h |
| 866–879 | N/I | |
| 880 | Figure, lady holding skirt | 8½"h |
| 881 | Figure, Spanish dancer p36 TSC | 9½"h |
| 882 | Vase | |
| 883 | Vase | |
| 884 | Vase | |
| 885 | N/I | |
| 886 | Vase with handle size 1 | 8"h |
| 887 | Figure, lady curtsying | 5"–5¼"h |
| 888 | Figure, lady in feathered hat and muff | 6½"h |
| 889 | Figure, lady in shawl and bonnet | 7¼"h |
| 890 | Figure, lady with flowers | |
| 891 | Dutch clog | |
| 892 | Plant pot | 6"h |
| 893 | Plant pot | 6¾"h 4¼"dia –1970s |
| 894–897 | N/I | |
| 898 | Jardiniere diamond shape with grid p71/104 TSC | 5¼"h 10"l |
| 899–900 | N/I | |

**Circa 1933**

| | | |
|---|---|---|
| 901 | Rabbit and match striker | |
| 902 | Ginger jar | 7¾"h |
| 903 | Ginger jar Harvest Poppy p37 TSC | 8¼"h (inc lid) |
| 904 | Vase Harvest Poppy | 7¼"h |
| 905 | Vase Harvest Poppy | 8¾"h |
| 906 | N/I | |
| 907 | Vase | |
| 908 | Vase Harvest Poppy | 7½"h |
| 909 | N/I | |
| 910 | Vase Harvest Poppy | 9"h |
| 911–916 | N/I | |
| 917 | Jug Carnations | 7"h |
| 918 | Rose bowl Harvest Poppy | 5½"h 6½"w |
| 919 | Figure, dancing lady p36 TSC | 8½"h |
| 920 | Figure, dancing lady p85 TSS p36 and back cover TSC | 8½"h |
| 921–925 | N/I | |
| 926 | Plant pot Egyptian range Reg. No. 774557 | 4¼"h 4¾"w |
| 927–929 | N/I | |
| 930 | Pierrette partner to 931 p95 TSS | 8¾"h |
| 931 | Figure Pierrot partner to 930 p36 TSC | 8¾"h |
| 932–934 | N/I | |
| 935 | Jug | |
| 936–939 | N/I | |
| 940 | Plant pot Palestine Ware | 7"h 7"dia |
| 941–942 | N/I | |
| 943 | Bowl Palestine Ware partner to 948 | 11"dia |
| 944 | Vase Palestine Ware p37 TSC | 6"h |
| 945 | Pot with lid Palestine Ware p37 TSC | 5¼"h 5½"dia |
| 946–947 | N/I | |
| 948 | Pastille burner Palestine Ware, partner to 943 | 9"h |
| 949–953 | N/I | |
| 954 | Cream jug | |
| 955 | Sugar bowl | |
| 956 | Cream jug | |
| 957 | Poppy flower centre possibly partnered with bowl 828 p96 TSS | 8"h |
| 958 | Rose bowl embossed Carnations/Cornflowers | 6"h |
| | I will refer to this range as | |

| | | |
|---|---|---|
| | Carnations | |
| 959–960 | N/I | |
| 961 | Shoe also with flowers p18 TSS | 5"l –1960s |
| 962 | Gnome standing p124 TSC | 5"h –1950s |
| 963 | N/I | |
| 964 | Jug Carnations p37 TSC | 7½"h |
| 965 | N/I | |
| 966 | Vase Carnations | 6"h |
| 967 | Vase Carnations | 8½"h |
| 968–969 | N/I | |
| 970 | Bowl/vase Carnations wider at centre | 6"h |
| 971–972 | N/I | |
| 973 | Posy vase with rabbits | |
| 974 | Jardiniere Carnations | |
| 975 | Vase | |
| 976 | Vase Carnations | |
| 977 | Vase Carnations | |
| 978 | N/I | |
| 979 | Vase Carnations | 8"h |
| 980 | N/I | |
| 981 | Cat sitting up on hind legs sim to 982 SCC/18 p105 TSS | 5½"–5¾"h |
| 982 | Cat sim to 981 | 8"h |
| 983 | N/I | |
| 984 | Three monkeys hear, speak, see no evil | s/s |
| 985 | Plant pot | |
| 986 | N/I | |
| 987 | Vase Carnations | 11"h |
| 988 | N/I | |
| 989 | Figure, footballer red and white striped shirt black shorts black socks with red tops Reg. No. 787779 (1933) p95 TSS | 8"h |
| 990 | Bunny round p21/44 TSS p28 TSC | 5"h –1975 |
| | Collectors report seeing dubious bunnies possibly recently re-issued or re-painted, take care when buying | |
| 991 | Lion | 3¾"h 7¼"l |
| 992 | Puss in shoe p18 TSS | 4"h 5"l –1940s |
| 993–999 | N/I | |
| 1000 | Mug ribbed | |
| 1001 | Flower jug | 7"h |
| 1002 | Vase | 11"h |
| 1003 | Posy holder round | |
| 1004 | Owl and tree trunk vase | 6⅞"h |
| 1005 | Spill vase | 6"h |
| 1006 | Urn vase with handles | 8½"h |
| 1007 | Vase sim to 1008 narrower at neck | 5"h |
| 1008 | Vase sim to 1007 | 8"h |
| 1009–1010 | N/I | |
| 1011 | Vase | 8¼"h |
| 1012 | Jug | 6"h |
| 1013 | Vase sim to 1014 | |
| 1014 | Vase sim to 1013 | 8½"h |
| 1015–1017 | N/I | |
| 1018 | Cat | |
| 1019–1020 | N/I | |
| 1021 | Pixie and toadstool | 2½"h |
| 1022 | Boy with banjo p18 TSS | 5"h –1940s |
| 1024 | Gnome kneeling p124 TSC | 4¾"h –1950s |
| 1025 | Vase Deco style | 7"h |
| 1026 | Bunny p21/44 TSS p28 TSC | 6¾"h –1970s |
| 1027 | Bunny p21/44 TSS | 8¼"h –1940s |
| 1028 | Bunny p21/44 TSS p28 TSC | 9¾"–10"h –1975 |
| 1029–1032 | N/I | |
| 1033 | Red Indian Chief, on rock p36 TSC | 7¼"h |
| 1034 | N/I | |
| 1035 | Figure, lady sitting holding jug and glass sim to 1080 | |
| 1036 | Red Riding Hood sim to 1081 SCC/12 | 7"h |
| 1037 | Girl with Donkey, on plinth | 7"h 8"l |

| | | |
|---|---|---|
| | partner to 1042 | |
| **1038** | Bulldog with bow sim to 1043/ 1044 | 3¾″h |
| **1039** | Vase with Kingfisher p96 TSS | 6″h |
| | | |
| **Circa 1934** | | |
| | | |
| **1040–1041** | N/I | |
| **1042** | Boy with donkey, on plinth partner to 1037 | |
| **1043** | Bulldog with bow sim to 1038/ 1044 | 7⅝″h |
| **1044** | Bulldog with bow sim to 1038/ 1043 p37 TSC (misprinted as 1004) | 8½″h |
| **1045** | Log with frogs | 9¼″l |
| **1046** | Cat frightened sim to 1313 p45/ 84 TSS p28 TSC | 6″h –1960s |
| **1047–1060** | N/I | |
| **1061** | Vase | |
| **1062–1063** | N/I | |
| **1064** | Bunny with holder or striker p17 TSS p27 TSC | 4–4¼″h –1956 |
| **1065** | Bunny p21/44 TSS | 6″h –1975 |
| **1066** | Rabbit | |
| **1067** | Bunny p21/44 TSS p28 TSC | 3¼–4″h –1975 |
| **1068–1069** | N/I *(Stop Press Flower Centre & Bowl)* | |
| **1070** | Flower jug ribbed sim to 1071 p71 TSC | 10½–11″h |
| **1071** | Flower jug sim to 1070 | 7″h |
| **1072–1074** | N/I | |
| **1075** | Vase embossed flowers sim to 1077 | 6½″h |
| **1076** | N/I | |
| **1077** | Vase sim to 1075 | 8¾″h |
| **1078** | Jug embossed flowers square base | 7″h |
| **1079** | N/I | |
| **1080** | Figure, lady holding glass sim to 1035 | 5″h |
| **1081** | Red Riding Hood SCC/12 | 5¼″h 3″acr |
| **1082–1085** | N/I | |
| **1086** | Cat sitting p18 TSS | 5¼″h –1982+ |
| **1087** | Cat sitting | 7″h –1982+ |
| **1088** | Cat sitting | 9″h –1940s |
| | These cats, and a matching 1085 are appearing on the market, white glazed and with flowers treat with caution! See comments SCC/17/18 | |
| **1089** | N/I | |
| **1090** | Mug to partner 1091 p45 TSC | 3½″h |
| **1091** | Jug to partner 1090 p45 TSC | 8″h |
| **1092** | Gnome standing sim to 1093/ 1094 p123 TSC | 8¼″h –1940s |
| **1093** | Gnome standing sim to 1092/ 1094 | 9½″h –1940s |
| **1094** | Gnome standing sim to 1092/ 1093 | 14″h –1940s |
| **1095** | Gnome with pot | 8¼″h –1940s |
| **1096** | N/I | |
| **1097** | Gnome with pot | 9½″h –1940s |
| **1098** | N/I | |
| **1099** | Cat and basket | |
| **1100–1107** | N/I | |
| **1108** | Vase with handle Deco top ribbed | 8″h |
| **1109** | Vase Deco style sim to 1384 p36 TSC | 7″h |
| **1110** | Vase with flower grid Bacchanti range p108 TSS | 7″h 5½″acr (top) |
| **1111** | Plant pot Bacchanti on three feet | |
| **1112** | Flower jug Bacchanti | 8″h |
| **1113** | Bowl Bacchanti p142 TSC | 5¾″h 10½″acr –1950s |
| **1114** | Jug embossed hollyhocks p42 TSC SCC/13 | 7¾″h |

| | | |
|---|---|---|
| **1115** | Flower jug, acorn with squirrel handle sim to 330/1195/1958/ 1959/1993 and 4068 p56 TSS | 8½″h –1950s |
| **1116** | Flower jug with dragon handle p84 TSS | 8¼″–8¾″h |
| **1117** | Dog sitting p37 TSC | 7″h |
| **1118** | 'Monty' the mongrel p40 TSS | 6¾″h –1940s |
| **1119** | 'Daisy' dog p17 TSS | 4″h –1956 |
| **1120** | Mongrel dog p39 TSC | 3¾″h |
| **1121** | Terrier dog p40 TSS | 4¾–5″h 6″l –1956 |
| **1122** | Sealyham dog p40 TSS | 3½″h 5½″l –1956 |
| **1123** | Comic Scottie dog p40 TSS | 3½″h 7″l –1940s |
| **1124** | N/I | |
| **1125** | Flower jug Bacchanti | 7″h |
| **1126** | Vase Bacchanti range p108 TSS | 8¾″h 4¼″acr (top) |
| **1127** | Swan posy holder p32 TSS p110 TSC. This was re-modelled in the 1980s, all dimensions smaller and high gloss finish | 3⅜″h 5½″l –1982 2½″w (wing to wing) 1982+ |
| **1128–1131** | N/I | |
| **1132** | Lucky Pig with card see 1486 for message also used as Caricature range money box p18/32 TSS p119 TSC | 2½–3″h 4″l –1982 |
| **1133** | Horn of plenty vase (unconfirmed) | 6½″h 6″l |
| **1134** | Witch pot jug shamrock partner to 1140 sim to 4186 | 2¾″h |
| **1135** | Witch pot shamrock sim to 4187 | 3¾″h 1940s |
| **1136** | Bowl | |
| **1137** | N/I | |
| **1138** | Flower jug with stork handle sim to 475/1960 and 4069 p56 TSS | 9½–10″h –1950s |
| **1139** | Flower jug diamond shape p96 TSS | 8½″h |
| **1140** | Witch pot sugar bowl shamrock, partner to 1134 sim to 4185 p18 TSS | 2¾″h |
| **1142** | Squirrel p45 TSS | 5¼″h |
| **1143** | Squirrel p45 TSS | 6¾″h |
| **1144** | Squirrel p45 TSS | 7¾″h –1940s |
| **1145** | Squirrel p45 TSS | 8½″h –1940s |
| **1146** | Squirrel p45 TSS | 9¾″h |
| **1147** | Jug Deco style p84/96 TSS | 6″h |
| **1148** | Vase Deco style | 7½″h |
| **1149** | Vase | 7½″h –1960 |
| **1150** | Flower jug ribbed sim to 1385 p71 TSC | 5¼″h |
| **1151–1152** | N/I | |
| **1153** | Elephant vase sim to 3239 | 3″h |
| **1154** | Whistling boy | |
| **1155** | N/I | |
| | | |
| **Circa 1935 SylvaC first used** | | |
| | | |
| **1156** | Master Duck p110 TSS p26 TSC | 4¾″h |
| **1157** | Mrs. Duck p26 TSC | 8″h |
| **1158** | Mr. Duck p26 TSC | 9″h |
| **1159** | Cat with corkscrew tail Reg. No. 806569 (1935) | 6¼″h |
| **1160** | N/I | |
| **1161** | Shy girl | |
| **1162** | Cat with corkscrew tail Reg. No. 806569 | 3¾″h |
| **1163** | Cat with corkscrew tail Reg. No. 806569 p35 TSC | 7¼″h |
| **1164** | Cat with corkscrew tail Reg. No. 806569 | 11″h 8″l |
| **1165** | Vase Deco style extraordinary shape like one vase on top of the other p95 TSS | 16½″h |
| **1166** | Vase | 20″h |
| **1167** | Vase stag handle | 8½″h |
| **1168** | Dish Oval | 2″h×11½″×7½″ |
| **1169** | Lucky pixie | 5¾″h |

| | | |
|---|---|---|
| 1170 | Girl partner to 1022 | 5″h –1940s |
| 1171 | N/I | |
| 1172 | Mr. Pig in cap and clothes | 6″h |
| 1173 | Vase Deco style p71 TSC | 7″h |
| 1174 | Flower jug p99 TSS | 10″h |
| 1175 | Jug Pilgrim shape p67/101 TSC | 6¼″h –1960s |
| 1176 | Vase ribbed p71 TSC | 7¼″h |
| 1177 | Vase ribbed | 8¾″h |
| 1178 | Flower pot ribbed | 7¾″dia |
| 1179 | Comical cockerel with glasses and waistcoat p106 TSS | 5½″h |
| 1180 | N/I | |
| 1181 | Ashtray with hare and striker number 1270 p17/38 TSS | 2½″h 6¾″l |
| 1182 | Rabbit as used on 1312 p17 TSS | 2½″h |
| 1183 | Cruet set ribbed | 2½″h 5″dia |
| 1184 | Honey pot ribbed p45 TSC | 4½″h to knob |
| 1185 | Butter dish round, ribbed | 6″acr |
| 1186 | Posy Bowl ribbed | 8″dia |
| 1187 | Spill vase ribbed | 4¼″h |
| 1188 | Dish ribbed | 1¼″h 5½″l |
| 1189 | Flower jug p67 TSC | 11½″h |

**Circa 1936**

| | | |
|---|---|---|
| 1190 | Vase two monkeys climbing into coconut sim to 2807 Reg. No. 809067 (1936) p56 TSS | 7″h –1940s |
| 1191 | Joey dog p61 TSS p39 TSC | 5″h –1965 |
| 1192 | Joey dog p39 TSC | 6″h |
| 1193 | Joey dog p39 TSC | 8″h |
| 1194 | Joey dog p39 TSC | 9½″h |
| 1195 | Flower jug acorn with squirrel handle sim to 330/1115/1958/1959/1993 and 4068 p56 TSS | 7½″h –1950s |
| 1196 | Flower jug mushroom with two gnomes sim to 1969 Reg. No. 809115 (1936) p56 TSS | 8½″h –1950s |
| 1197 | N/I | |
| 1198 | Cress dish and stand, ribbed | 11¼″l 7″w |
| 1199 | Dish oval | |
| 1200 | Rabbit | |
| 1201 | Vase p67 TSC | 5″h |
| 1202 | Alsation dog | |
| 1203 | Alsation dog p23 TSC | 9″h |
| 1204 | N/I | |
| 1205 | Scottie dog 'Mac' Reg. No. 778504 (1932) p40/41 TSS registered by Otaker Steinburger but not used by S & C until c1936 | 5″h –1970 |
| 1206 | Scottie Dog 'Mac' Reg. No. 778504 p40 TSS | 6¼″h –1940s |
| 1207 | Scottie dog 'Mac' Reg. No. 778504 p40/41 TSS | 7¾″h –1970 |
| 1208 | Scottie dog 'Mac' Reg. No. 778504 p40 TSS | 9″h –1940s |
| 1209 | Scottie dog 'Mac' Reg. No. 778504 p40/41 TSS p39 TSC also made with a golf ball in mouth | 11″h –1970 |
| 1210 | Jar vase | 7½″h |
| 1211 | Small bowl p18 TSS | 1¾″h |
| 1212 | Candle holder ribbed | 4–4¼″h |
| 1213 | Covered butter dish ribbed p45 TSC | |
| 1214 | Flower pot ribbed p67 TSC | 7″dia |
| 1215 | Flower pot ribbed | 8¾″dia |
| 1216 | Biscuit barrel ribbed p45 TSC | 7″h |
| 1217–1220 | N/I | |
| 1221 | Garden gnome with wheelbarrow p124 TSC | 7½–8″h 6″l –1950s |
| 1222 | Goblin sim to 842 | 4½″h |
| 1223–1225 | N/I | |
| 1226 | Clown's head wall plaque | 9″h 6″w |
| 1227 | Labrador dog standing p40 TSS | 5–5¼″h –1940s |
| 1228–1229 | N/I | |
| 1230 | Sarah Gamp character jug | 9″h |

| | | |
|---|---|---|
| 1231 | Sam Weller character jug SCC/14 | 6½″h |
| 1232–1234 | N/I | |
| 1235 | Posy holder diamond shape | 2″h 10″l |
| 1236 | N/I | |
| 1237 | Bridal pair? for top of wedding cake | 4″h |
| 1238 | Elephant in football clothes p29 TSC | 8″h |
| 1238 also | Bird | |
| 1239 | N/I | |
| 1240 | Bunny with vase embossed trees on vase | 6½″h |
| 1241–1242 | N/I | |
| 1243 | Dog, with collar SCC/13 | 9″h |
| 1244 | Dog, tall with collar | 10½″h |
| 1245 | Scottie dog standing p40 TSS | 5¾″h –1940s |
| 1246 | 'Sammy' Spaniel Reg. No. 813261 (1936) sim to 1247/3092 p42/56 TSS | 4–4½″h –1970 |
| 1247 | 'Sammy' Spaniel Reg. No. 813261 sim to 1247/3092 p42 TSS | 5¾″h –1970 |
| 1248 | Posy ring | 8″dia –1940s |
| 1249 | Posy bowl | 1½″h 6″dia |
| 1250 | Posy ring ribbed p16 TSS p45 TSC | 6″dia –1960s |
| 1251 | Posy holder diamond shape | 7″l |
| 1252 | Flower jug | 6″h |
| 1253 | Flower jug ribbed p67/102 TSC | 6″h |
| 1254 | Flower jug ribbed | 6″h |
| 1255 | Rabbit mat holder half rabbit (990) on front of base, rabbit shape only no ears or tail on back p45 TSC | 5½″h 3½″l |
| 1256 | N/I | |
| 1257 | Vase round | 7¾″h |
| 1258 | Sailor with cask HMS Flora on hat George Munro Ltd on base, sim to 1319 SCC/12/13 | 9″h |
| 1259 | Scottie dog p40 TSS | 2¾″h –1940s |
| 1260 | N/I | |
| 1261 | Scottie dog p40 TSS | 7¼″h –1940s |
| 1262 | Scottie dog p40 TSS | 8″h –1940s |
| 1263–1264 | N/I | |
| 1265 | 'Harry' the hare p17/44 TSS | 3″h –1940s |
| 1266 | Ashtray | |
| 1267 | Flower pot ribbed curvy top edge | 6¾″h 8″dia |
| 1268 | Flower pot ribbed | 9″dia |
| 1269 | Flower pot ribbed | 10″dia |
| 1270 | Hare match holder p17 TSS p27 TSC | 2¼″h –1956 |
| 1271 | Spill vase p104 TSC | 5″h –1960s |
| 1272 | Vase fan shape Shell range p66 TSC | 7¼″h |
| 1273 | Flower jug Rope range | |
| 1274 | Hollyhock jug sim to 476/1962 p56 TSS | 8½″h –1950s |
| 1275 | Vase fan shape Shell range | 6″h |
| 1276 | Flower jug Shell | 6″h |
| 1277 | Flower jug Shell p66 TSC | 7″h |
| 1278 | Fruit bowl Shell p66 TSC | 11″l –1970 |
| 1279 | Posy through Shell p66 TSC | 1½″h 12½″l |
| 1280 | Vase Shell p66 TSC | 8½″h |
| 1281 | Flower jug Shell | 9¾″h |
| 1281 also | Lamb | |
| 1282 | Flower pot Shell p66 TSC | 8″dia –1970s |
| 1283 | Flower pot Shell | 9″dia –1960s |
| 1284 | Lamb with tail up p56 TSS p27 TSC | 3¾–4″h –1940s |
| 1284 also | Lamb with tail down p47 TSS | 1940s–1968 |
| 1285 | Lamb sim to original 1284 p56 TSS | 5¼″h |
| 1286 | Cat startled p27 TSC | 4″h |
| 1287 | Cat | |
| 1288 | Character jug Welsh lady p37 TSS p27 TSC | 3½″h |

| 1289 | Character jug man p27 TSC | 2¾"h |
| 1290 | Eagle p27 TSC | 4"h |
| 1291 | N/I | |
| 1292 | Chicken ashtray p27 TSC | 4¼"h |
| 1293 | Duck ashtray p27 TSC | 3½"h |
| 1294 | Rabbit ashtray p27 TSC | 5½"l |
| 1295 | Scottie dog p40 TSS (described as Griffin in SylvaC catalogues) | 5"h –1956 |
| 1296 | Two kittens in basket p56 TSS | 4"h 4½"l |
| 1297 | N/I | |
| 1298 | 'Harry' the hare Reg. No. 815840 (1936) p44 TSS p28 TSC | 5¾–6"h –1970 |
| 1299 | 'Harry' the hare Reg. No. 815840 p44 TSS | 7½"h –1940s |
| 1300 | 'Harry' the hare Reg. No. 815840 p44 TSS | 9¼"h –1940s |
| 1301 | Jug | |
| 1302 | Lop-eared rabbit Reg. No. 815839 (1936) p44/87 TSS p28 TSC | 5¼–5½"h –1975 |
| 1303 | Lop-eared rabbit Reg. No. 815839 p44/87 TSS | 7"h –1975 |
| 1304 | Lop-eared rabbit Reg. No. 815839 p44/87 TSS | 8¼–8½"h –1975 |
| 1305 | Birds nest p56 TSS | 8"h –1940s |
| 1306 | Vase Rope range | 5½"h |
| 1307 | Vase Rope p90 TSC | 8½"h –1970 |
| 1308 | Vase Rope range | s/s |
| 1309 | Vase Rope range | 7¾"h |
| 1310 | Flower jug Rope | 6"h |
| 1311 | Book end with various novelties p17/32 TSS | 4¼–4½"h –1970 |
| 1312 | Round posy with rabbits p54/56 TSS | 8–8¼"dia –1960 |
| 1313 | Frightened cat sim to 1046 | l/s –1940s |
| 1314 | Posy bar ribbed | 1½"h 4½"l –1960s |
| 1315 | Posy bar ribbed p16 TSS | 6"l –1960s |
| 1316 | Posy bar ribbed | 8"l –1960s |
| 1317 | Posy bar ribbed | 12"l –1960s |
| 1318 | Flower jug 'rabbits climbing into furze' sim to 1978/4070 p56 TSS | 8¾"h –1950 |
| 1319 | Jolly sailor HMS Flora on cap sim to 1258 | 8½"h |
| 1320 | Shoe ashtray p18 TSS | 2"h –1960s |
| 1321 | Commemorative loving cup George VI | |
| 1322 | Toast rack | 2½"h 6½"l |
| 1323 | Bulb pot? | |
| 1324 | Posy ribbed 'Boomerang' shape | 2"h 10"l |
| 1325 | Posy ribbed diamond shape | 2"h 10"l |
| 1326 | Posy with figure on front p16 TSS | 3½"h –1940s |
| 1327 | Posy with figure one end p16 TSS | 3¼"h 8¾"l –1940s |
| 1328 | Woodpecker on log p17 TSS | 4"h –1940s |
| 1329 | N/I | |
| 1330 | Kingfisher on tree trunk p17 TSS | 4"h –1940s |
| 1331 | Bird with tail up p17 TSS | 6½"h –1940s |
| 1332 | Comical Dachshund p15/40 TSS | 5½"h 5"l –1940s |
| 1333 | Crouching cat p15 TSS | 4"h –1940s |
| 1334 | Foal/Zebra standing p2/15/17/50 TSS | 4–4¼"h –1970 |
| 1335 | Hip flask | 4"h |
| 1336 | Posy with figure to one side p16 TSS | 7¼"h –1940s |
| 1337 | Posy with flower seller p16 TSS | 6½"h –1940s |
| 1338 | Yacht sim to 1339 solid (no posy) | 6"h |
| 1339 | Yacht solid sim to 1338 (no posy) | 8¾"h |
| 1340 | Yacht sim to 1393/1394 p17 TSS | 12½"h –1940s |
| 1341 | Vase Deco style | 5¼"h |
| 1342 | Jug triple handle p101 TSC | 6¾"h –1960s |
| 1343 | Vase Deco diagonal lines sim to 684 p103 TSC | 9"h |
| 1344 | Flower jug p101 TSC | 9"h –1970 |

| 1345 | Vase Deco style | 9"h –1965 |
| 1346 | Vase Deco style sim to 2505 p94 TSC | 10½"h –1982 |
| 1347 | Vase sim to 1407 | 12½"h |
| 1348 | Jug Deco style | 12½"h |

## Circa 1937

| 1349 | Seagull on wave Reg. No. 823083 (1937) p17 TSS | 3"h –1940s |
| 1350 | Seagull on wave Reg. No. 823083 p17 TSS | 4"h –1940s |
| 1351 | Seagull on wave Reg. No. 823083 p17 TSS | 5"h –1940s |
| 1352 | Twin posy Deco Reg. No. 823084 (1937) p15 TSS | 5½–6"h 8"l –1940s |
| 1353 | Twin posy Deco Reg. No. 823082 (1937) p15 TSS | 6"h –1940s |
| 1354 | N/I | |
| 1355 | Vase Autumn range round embossed tree and leaves | 7"h –1960s |
| 1356 | Flower jug Autumn | 6"h –1960s |
| 1357 | Seagull on wave p17/87 TSS | 2¼"h –1940s |
| 1358 | Pot | |
| 1359 | Flower jug Autumn | 12"h –1960s |
| 1360 | Flying duck wall plaque sim to 1401/1402/1403 p2/15 TSS | 12"l –1975 |
| 1361 | N/I | |
| 1362 | Sugar shaker Deco style matches 1365/1368 | 5"h |
| 1363 | Jug Deco style partner to 1364 | 7¾"h |
| 1364 | Mug partner to 1363 | 3¼"h |
| 1365 | Jam pot Deco style matches 1362/1368 | 4¼"h |
| 1366 | Ashtray with novelty at one end p17/38/87 TSS | 5¾"l –1950s |
| 1366 also | Bird | |
| 1367 | Flower jug angular p101 TSC | 6"h –1960s |
| 1368 | Covered bowl to match 1362/1365 | 3¼"h 4¼"dia |
| 1369 | Puppy dog p40 TSS | 5"h –1940s |
| 1370 | Budgerigar vase p56 TSS | 7½"h –1940s |
| 1371 | Crouching hare p44 TSS | 3½"h –1940s |
| 1372 | Polar bear p17 TSS | 2¾–3"h |
| 1373 | Goat (kid) p45 TSS | 4½"h 4"l –1940s |
| 1374 | Donkey p45/50 TSS | 5"h 4"l –1940s |
| 1375 | Eider duck p17 TSS | 3½"h –1940s |
| 1376 | Bird p17/50 TSS | 3"h –1940s |
| 1377 | Pigeon | 4"h |
| 1378 | Terrier p40/41 TSS | 5"h –1982 |
| 1379 | Terrier p40/41 TSS | 8"h –1982 |
| 1380 | Terrier p40/41 TSS | 11"h –1982 |
| 1381 | Wall vase | 7¼"h |
| 1382 | Spaniel dog sitting matches 1461/1462 | 8"h –1940s |
| 1383 | N/I | |
| 1384 | Wall vase sim to 1109 p36 TSC | 7¼"h 8¼"w |
| 1385 | Wall vase ribbed sim to 1150 halved | 5"h |
| 1386 | Bunny p44 TSS p28 TSC | 3¼–4"h –1975 |
| 1387 | N/I | |
| 1388 | Crouching hare p44 TSS | 5½"h –1940s |
| 1389 | Crouching hare p44 TSS | 7½"h –1940s |
| 1390 | Koala bear on log p45 TSS p30 TSC | 4½"h |
| 1391 | Koala bear on log p45 TSS | 6"h |
| 1392 | Toast rack Deco | 2½"h 6½"l |

## Circa 1938

| 1393 | Yacht sim to 1340/1394 Reg. No. 826482 (1938) p17/62 TSS | 5"h –1950s |
| 1394 | Yacht sim to 1340/1393 Reg. No. 826482 p17/62 TSS | 8½"h –1960s |
| 1395 | Wall vase Shell range sometimes with flowers p66/105 TSC | 6¼–6½" –1960s |
| 1396 | N/I | |
| 1397 | Posy holder ribbed p56 TSS | 6"acr –1960s |

| | | |
|---|---|---|
| **1398** | N/I | |
| **1399** | Frog p17 TSS | 2½″h –1956 |
| **1400** | Bunny p17/41/44 TSS | 2″h |
| | Mouse p41 TSS | 1⅝″h |
| | Dog p38/41 TSS | 1⅞″h |
| | Cat p41 TSS | 2⅝″h |
| | Duck p4 TSS | s/s |
| | Teddy Bear | s/s |
| **1401** | Flying duck wall plaque sim to 1360/1402/1403 p2/15 TSS | 6½″l –1975 |
| **1402** | Flying duck wall plaque sim to 1360/1401/1403 p2/15 TSS | 9″l –1975 |
| **1403** | Seal posy p17 TSS | 3½″h 4½″l –1940s |
| **1403 also** | Flying duck wall plaque sim to 1360/1401/1402 p2 TSS | 5″l 1950s–1975 |
| **1404** | Flower jug p101 TSC | 6½″h –1960s |
| **1405** | N/I | |
| **1406** | Flower jug Deco p96 TSS | 11″h |
| **1407** | Vase sim to 1347 p103 TSC | 8½″h –1960s |
| **1408** | Serpent vase | |
| **1409** | Jug sim to 1410 p101 TSC | 5¼″h –1960s |
| **1410** | Jug sim to 1409 p101 TSC | 8–8¾″h –1960s |
| **1411** | N/I | |
| **1412** | Airedale Terrier standing p40 TSS | 9″h –1940s |
| **1413** | Triple vase rustic fence p17 TSS | 4½″h –1940s |
| **1414** | Scottie dog sitting p42/45 TSS | 5–5¼″h –1970 |
| **1415** | Skye Terrier standing p40/42 TSS | 5″h 7½″l –1970 |
| **1416** | Tree trunk vase with Koala bear p56 TSS | 5″h –1940s |
| **1417** | Jug p97 TSS | |
| **1418** | Jug p101 TSC p95 TSS | 8¼″h –1960s |
| **1419** | Jug Deco style | 11¼″h |
| **1420** | 'Lucky Pixie' toadstool and squirrel p17 TSS p30 TSC | 3¼″h –1956 |
| **1421** | 'Lucky Pixie' sitting on mound p17 TSS | 3″h –1940s |
| **1422** | Foal sitting sim to 1447 p45 TSS | 4¾″h –1940s |
| **1423** | Bear/panda p56 TSS | 2¾–3″h –1960s |
| **1424** | Fox p17 TSS p30 TSC | 2¼″h 6⅛″l –1960s |
| **1425** | Hippo p17 TSS | 2¾″h –1940s |
| **1426** | Bear/panda standing p17/18 TSS | 3¼″h –1956 |
| **1427** | Lamb looking at tail p45 TSS | 4¾″h –1940s |
| **1428** | Donkey standing also used with 3138 cart p2/45/50 TSS | 4⅜″h –1982 |
| **1429** | Vase diamond shape | 9″h |
| **1430** | N/I | |
| **1431** | Calf p45 TSS | 3½″h –1940s |
| **1432** | Cat sitting, one paw raised, seen on ashtrays etc p17 TSS | 2″h |
| **1433** | Terrier dog paw in sling sim to 1524 p17/41/87 TSS | 3½″h –1970 |
| **1434** | Cat lying down seen on ashtrays etc | s/s |
| **1435** | Cider jug 'Barrel' | 8″h –1940s |
| **1436** | Mug 'Barrel' p15 TSS re-modelled with different handle | 3½″h –1940s 1940s–1960s |
| **1437** | Honey 'Barrel' p15 TSS | 4½″h –1940s |
| **1438** | Butter or cheese covered dish round p15 TSS | 5″dia –1940s |
| **1439** | Cruet set four piece 'Barrel' p15 TSS | 1¾″h 4½″acr –1940s |
| **1440** | Butter or sweet dish 'Barrel' p15 TSS | 4″dia –1940s |
| **1441** | Cigarette container 'Barrel' p15 TSS | 3″h –1940s |
| **1442** | Match holder 'Barrel' p15 TSS | 1¾″h –1940s |
| **1443** | Sauce bottle holder or vase 'Barrel' p15 TSS | 3¾″h –1940s |
| **1444** | N/I | |
| **1445** | Mint sauce boat 'Barrel' p15 TSS | 5¼″l –1940s |
| **1446** | Biscuit jar 'Barrel' p15 TSS | 7″h to knob –1940s |
| **1447** | Foal sitting sim to 1422 p45/50 TSS | 3½–4″h 6⅝″l –1960s |
| **1448** | Bowl | |
| **1449** | Flower insert | |
| **1450** | Scottie dog, seen on ashtrays etc p17 TSS | s/s |
| **1451** | Stag p56 TSS | 5″h –1960s |
| **1452** | Character jug Mr. Pickwick p35 TSS | 6″h –1960s |
| **1453** | Character jug Mr. Micawber p35 TSS | 6″h –1960s |
| **1454** | Ashtray with space for novelty ribbed p17/38 TSS | 5¼″l –1940s |
| **1455** | Ashtray 'pond' with space for novelty p17/32/38 TSS | 4¾–5¼″dia –1965 |
| **1456** | N/I | |
| **1457** | Tree stump posy two platforms for rabbits etc p17/61 TSS | 3″h –1940s |
| **1458** | Leopard sitting has foot to mouth p74 TSS | 9½″h –1940s |
| **1459** | Serviette ring with 1265 hare, to go with 'Barrel' range p15 TSS | 3″h 3¼″l –1940s |
| **1460** | N/I | |
| **1461** | Spaniel dog sitting sim to 1382/1462 | 6″h –1940s |
| **1462** | Spaniel dog sitting sim to 1382/1461 p74 TSS | 11″h –1970 |
| **1463** | Character jug Neville Chamberlain | 6¼″h |
| **1464** | Tortoise p25 TSC | 2½″h 3¼″l |
| **1465** | N/I | |
| **1466** | Lizard on branch | 7″l |
| **1467** | Lizard p85 TSS | 7¼″l |
| **1468–1469** | N/I | |
| **1470** | Pepper and salt | |
| **1471–1472** | N/I | |
| **1473** | Basket Deco style p95 TSS | 6″h 10″l |
| **1474** | Holder with cat | |

**Circa 1939**

| | | |
|---|---|---|
| **1475** | Dog sitting with paw raised p39 TSC | 7¾″h |
| **1476** | Dog sitting with paw raised | 11″h |
| **1477** | N/I | |
| **1478** | Twin vase ribbed with space for novelty | 3¼″h |
| **1479** | Posy bar curved novelty at one end p56 TSS | 8½–9″l –1940s |
| **1480** | Posy oval with space for novelty sim to 1481 p56 TSS p90 TSC | 5½″dia –1960 |
| **1481** | Posy oval with space for novelty sim to 1480 p56 TSS | 8″dia –1960 |
| **1482** | Candleholder/ashtray ribbed sim to 1454 p6 TSS (above dog with paw in sling) | 5¼″l |
| **1483** | N/I | |
| **1484** | Top hat with kitten and dog Reg. No. 833892 (1939) p38/56 TSS | 3¾–4″h –1960 |
| **1485** | Candleholder with novelty in centre p18/84 TSS | 4–4¼″h –1960 |
| **1486** | Lucky pig sitting originally with card with the message: "PADDY'S BLACK PIG So long as you keep this little black pig with its little curly tail, you will have a perfectly charmed life and your luck will never fail." | –1940s |
| **1487** | Posy log with Koala bear at one end p56 TSS | 4½″h 6½″l –1940s |
| **1488** | Posy log | 1⅛″h 3½″l |
| **1489** | Vase | |
| **1490** | Vase p104 TSC | 4¾–5¼″h –1960s |
| **1491** | Vase p104 TSC | 4¾″h –1960s |
| **1492** | Duck sim to 1498/1499 Reg. No. 833893 (1939) p44 TSS p30 TSC | 5½–6″h –1940s |

| | | |
|---|---|---|
| 1493 | Kangaroo (probably the one on the right p5 TSS) | |
| 1494 | Squirrel eating from bowl p18 TSS | 4"h –1960s |
| 1495 | Vase | |
| 1496 | Basket p95 TSS | 6"h 10"l |
| 1497 | Rabbit one ear up p18 TSS | 2¼"h 3"l –1940s |
| 1498 | Duck sim to 1492/1499 Reg. No. 833893 p44/50 TSS p30 TSC | 3¼–3½"h 5½"l –1940s |
| 1499 | Duck sim to 1492/1498 Reg. No. 833893 p44/50 TSS p30 TSC | 4¼–4½"h –1940s |

**Circa 1940**

| | | |
|---|---|---|
| 1500 | Bear/Panda p18 TSS | 4½"h 8"l |
| 1501 | N/I | |
| 1502 | Dog | |
| 1503 | N/I | |
| 1504 | Dog with paw in basket p18 TSS | 3¾"h |
| 1505 | Lambs six in a box assorted colours and shapes p18 TSS sim to lamb on vases 2655/6/8 | s/s |
| 1506 | Bear/Panda p18 TSS | 5½"h |
| 1507 | N/I | |
| 1508 | Horse p16/18 TSS | 5"h –1960s |
| 1509 | Lop eared rabbit p16 TSS | 4"h –1960s |
| 1510 | Mushroom vase with lop eared rabbit p16/54/86 TSS | 5½"h –1960 |
| 1511 | Rabbit sitting up one ear down sim to 1525/1526 p44 TSS | 13"h |
| 1512 | Dog front paws down (playing position) p18 TSS | 3"h |
| 1513 | Round bowl with recess for rabbits and gnomes sim to 1514 p53/56/86 TSS | 7–7½"dia –1965 |
| 1514 | Round bowl with recess for rabbits and gnomes sim to 1513 p53/56/57/86 TSS | 8–8¾"dia –1965 |
| 1515–1516 | N/I | |
| 1517 | Leaf shaped ashtray in three sections with squirrel in centre p16 TSS | 4¾"h |
| 1518 | Squirrel sitting eating nut p18 TSS | 3½"h |
| 1519 | Stag standing on rock p18 TSS | 4¾"h –1956 |
| 1520 | Bear/Panda p18 TSS | 2⅛"h –1956 |
| 1521 | Bear/Panda p18 TSS | 1½"h –1956 |
| 1522 | Bear/Panda p18 TSS | 1¾"h –1956 |
| 1523 | Crouching rabbit sim to 1529/1530 p44 TSS | 4½"h |
| 1524 | Terrier dog with paw in sling sim to 1433 | 6"h |
| 1525 | Rabbit sitting up one ear down sim to 1511/1526 p44 TSS | 8½"h |
| 1526 | Rabbit sitting up one ear down sim to 1511/1525 p44 TSS | 10½"h |
| 1527 | Elephant sitting p18 TSS | 3½"h |
| 1528 | Dog scratching ear p18 TSS | 3½"h |
| 1529 | Crouching rabbit sim to 1523/1530 p44 TSS | 3¼"h |
| 1530 | Crouching rabbit sim to 1523/1529 p44 TSS | 5½"h |
| 1531 | Ashtray banjo shape p18 TSS | 5¾"l |
| 1532 | Ashtray angular with kissing rabbits p16 TSS | 3¼"h |
| 1533 | Setter l/s | 13¾"h |
| 1534 | Kissing rabbits p18 TSS | 2½"h |
| 1535–1536 | N/I | |
| 1537 | Strawberry pot with lid (on its side) | 3½"l |
| 1538 | Posy vase p104 TSC | 3½"h –1960s |
| 1539 | N/I | |
| 1540 | Stag 1519 on rock dish p16 TSS | 5½"h |
| 1541 | Bowl Cactus ribbed | 2"h 3"dia –1960s |
| 1542 | Bowl Cactus ribbed | 3"h 4"dia –1960s |
| 1543 | Seagull wall plaque p18 TSS | 4½"l –1960s |
| 1544 | Seagull wall plaque p18 TSS | 7¼"l –1960s |
| 1545 | Seagull wall plaque p18 TSS | 8½"l –1960s |

| | | |
|---|---|---|
| 1546 | Book end rustic "with assorted novelties" p16/32 TSS | 4½–4¾"h –1965 |
| 1547 | Ashtray mandolin shape p18 TSS | 5¾"l |
| 1547 also | Vase | |
| 1548 | Rough Collie dog p18/41/42 TSS | 5⅜–5½"h 8"l –1975 |
| 1549 | Vase | |
| 1550 | Corner vase | |
| 1551 | Cream jug p16 TSS | 3"h |
| 1552 | Beaker/mug p16 TSS | 3"h |
| 1553 | Cream jug p16 TSS | 3"h |
| 1554–1560 | N/I | |
| 1561 | Ashtray/night light stand flower shape p18 TSS | 4½"dia |
| 1562 | Vase sim to 1563/1564/676 p94 TSC | 7¾–8"h –1982 |
| 1563 | Vase sim to 1562/1564/676 p94 TSC | 9¾–10"h –1982 |
| 1564 | Vase sim to 1562/1563/676 p94 TSC | 11¾"h –1982 |
| 1565 | Bowl oval | 5½"h 10"l |
| 1566 | Galleon riding the waves p16 TSS | 4¾"h |
| 1567 | N/I | |
| 1568 | Vase sim to 1570 | 5"h |
| 1569 | Vase | |
| 1570 | Vase p103 TSC | 7"h –1960s |
| 1571 | Vase sim to 675 p103 TSC | 8½ & 10"h –1970 |
| 1572 | Cruet set Dahlia range p45 TSC | 3½"h |
| 1573 | Armchair ashtray p18 TSS | 2¾"h |
| 1574 | N/I | |
| 1575 | Vase p103 TSC | 6"h |
| 1576–1577 | N/I | |
| 1578 | Vase ridged p102 TSC | 8"h –1960s |
| 1579 | Mug Dahlia range p45 TSC | 3½"h |
| 1580 | Jug set size 2 Dahlia range size 3 (three sizes) size 4 p45 TSC | 6¼"h 5¼"h 4½"h |
| 1581 | Honey Dahlia p45 TSC | 4½"h |
| 1582 | Butter dish Dahlia p45 TSC | 4½"dia |
| 1583 | Sugar bowl Dahlia range p45 TSC | 3¼"dia |
| 1584 | Cream jug Dahlia p45 TSC | 3¼"h |
| 1585 | Teapot Dahlia p45 TSC | 6¼"h |
| 1586 | Cheese dish Dahlia range p45 TSC | 7¼"l |
| 1587 | Biscuit jar with cane handle Dahlia p45 TSC | 6½"h |
| 1588 | N/I | |
| 1589 | Single covered butter or single open butter or stacked in three Dahlia range p45 TSC | 4"dia |
| 1590 | Match holder floral or with rabbits p18 TSS | 2¼–2½"h –1960s |
| 1591 | Butter ration dish with or without lid p45 TSC | 7"l |
| 1592–1593 | N/I | |
| 1594 | Ashtray with novelty | |
| 1595 | Jug Dahlia range | 8"h |
| 1596 | N/I | |
| 1597 | Vase Dahlia round with narrower top | 4"h |
| 1598–1599 | N/I | |
| 1600 | Beaker Dahlia range | 4½"h |
| 1601–1604 | N/I | |
| 1605 | Jug Dahlia range | 6½"h |
| 1606 | N/I | |
| 1607 | Vase Dahlia range triangular opening on round top with handles extraordinary shape | 9½"h |
| 1608–1609 | N/I | |
| 1610 | Flower basket pattern sim to 1965–1967 | s/s |
| 1611 | Wall vase | |
| 1612 | Flower jug | 7"h |
| 1613 | Wall vase Dahlia band at top fluted to base very small | 4"h 1½"w (top), widest point 3", ½"w (base) |
| 1614 | Mug D'ye ken John Peel p88 TSS | 4"h |

| | | |
|---|---|---|
| **1615** | Vase | |
| **1616–1617** | N/I | |
| **1618** | Flower jug | |
| **1619** | N/I | |
| **1620** | Vase p72 TSC | 11″h –1960s |
| **1621** | N/I | |

**Circa 1941**

| | | |
|---|---|---|
| **1622** | Fireplace ashtray also with cat p38 TSS | 3½″h |
| **1623** | Jug p101 TSC | 6″h –1960s |
| **1624** | Jug sim to 1625 but with straight handle | 6″h –1960s |
| **1625** | Flower jug p101 TSC | 6″h –1960s |
| **1626** | N/I | |
| **1627** | Vase | |
| **1628** | Vase | |
| **1629–1634** | N/I | |
| **1635** | Jardiniere | |
| **1636** | N/I | |
| **1637** | Vase | |
| **1638–1639** | N/I | |
| **1640** | Jug | 7″h |
| **1641** | Flower jug | 6″h |
| **1642** | N/I | |
| **1643** | Vase | |
| **1644** | Vase Dahlia range | 8½″h |
| **1645** | Vase | Tall |
| **1646** | Puppy dog playing, partner to 1647 p39 TSC | 3″h |
| **1647** | Puppy dog sleeping, partner to 1646 p39 TSC | 3½″h |
| **1648–1650** | N/I | |
| **1651** | Vase embossed flowers and leaves small 'handles' on base | 7¼″h |
| **1652** | Vase round embossed flowers and leaves small 'handles' at top | 5¾″h |
| **1653** | Bowl embossed flowers p104 TSC | 5½″h 9½″l –1960s |
| **1654** | Sweet dish with two handles p105 TSC | 2″h 5″l –1960s |
| **1655** | Flower jug embossed flowers sim to 1782 p101 TSC | 8″h |
| **1656** | N/I | |
| **1657** | Basket | |
| **1658** | N/I | |
| **1659** | Lamb standing, head turned | 3¾″h –1960s |
| **1660** | Lamb standing, head turned Reg. No. 838603 (1941) | 5¾–6″h |
| **1660 also** | Toast rack | |
| **1661** | Lamb standing, head turned Reg. No. 838603 (1941) | 8″h |
| **1662–1666** | N/I | |
| **1667** | Ashtray round with novelty also Spitfire aeroplane p32/38 TSS | 5″dia –1965 |
| **1668–1677** | N/I | |
| **1678** | Duck skiing p30 TSC | 2″h |
| **1679** | Duck skiing p30 TSC | 2¾″h –1950s |
| **1680** | Duck skiing p30 TSC | 5¼″h |
| **1681** | Duck (probably to go on above skis) | |
| **1682** | Duck (probably to go on above skis) | |
| **1683** | Duck (probably to go on above skis) | |

**Circa 1942** Shaw & Copestake vacated their Works for the duration of the Board of Trade Concentration of Industry scheme, during the war. A portion of the Thomas Lawrence, Falcon Works was placed at their disposal, and they continued to trade under their own name. Shaw & Copestake were able to use their own offices and packing department at the Sylvan Works.

| | | |
|---|---|---|
| **1684** | N/I | |
| **1685** | Jug embossed p101 TSC | 7″h –1965 |
| **1686** | Vase | |
| **1687–1690** | N/I | |

| | | |
|---|---|---|
| **1691** | Lemonade jug/beaker | |
| **1692** | N/I | |
| **1693** | Teapot | |
| **1694** | N/I | |
| **1695** | Covered honey embossed leaves, handles sim to 1699 | 3″h |
| **1696** | Butter dish | |
| **1697** | Jug | |
| **1698** | Jug embossed leaves | 3″h |
| **1699** | Covered honey embossed leaves, handles sim to 1695 | 3½″h 4″dia |
| **1700** | Sugar bowl | 3½″dia |
| **1701** | Flower jug | |
| **1702** | N/I | |
| **1703** | Teapot | |
| **1704** | N/I | |
| **1705** | Jug | |
| **1706–1709** | N/I | |
| **1710** | Lemonade Jug | 10″h |
| **1711** | Mug embossed leaves | 3½″h |
| **1712** | N/I | |
| **1713** | Tomato tray | |
| **1714** | Bowl | |

**Circa 1943**

| | | |
|---|---|---|
| **1715** | Dogs Head cruet set | 7½″l –1960s |
| **1716** | Lemonade jug | |
| **1717** | Lemonade mug | |
| **1718** | N/I | |
| **1719** | Vase embossed leaves | 5½″h |
| **1720** | Cruet with handle | |
| **1721–1722** | N/I | |
| **1723** | Lamp | |
| **1724** | Lamp, Tree, 3 bunnies | 8″h |
| **1725** | Cruet | |
| **1726** | N/I | |
| **1727** | Teapot | |
| **1727 also** | Lamp embossed flowers ornamental handles | 5¾″h 3½″w (base) |
| **1728** | Cream jug to go with Dogs Head range | 3¼″h –1960s |
| **1729** | Jug | |
| **1730** | N/I | |
| **1731** | Vase | |
| **1732** | Vase p104 TSC | 9″h –1960 |
| **1733** | Tray | |
| **1734–1736** | N/I | |
| **1737** | Jug | |
| **1738** | Bowl on three feet | 8″dia |
| **1739–1743** | N/I | |
| **1744** | Jug | |
| **1745** | Jug p101 TSC | 6″h –1960s |
| **1746** | Jug embossed flower | 6″h –1960s |

**Circa 1944**

| | | |
|---|---|---|
| **1747** | Cheese dish Neptune range p46 TSC | |
| **1748** | Tray Neptune range p46 TSC | 11¾″l |
| **1749** | Teapot | |
| **1750** | N/I | |
| **1751** | Flower jug | |
| **1752** | Basket | |
| **1753** | N/I | |
| **1754** | Sugar bowl | |
| **1755** | Basket | |
| **1756** | Jug | |
| **1757** | Vase embossed wavy lines | 6″h –1960s |
| **1758** | Vase with ridges p102 TSC | 6″h –1960s |
| **1759** | N/I | |
| **1760** | Covered bowl | |
| **1761–1762** | N/I | |
| **1763** | Vase | |
| **1764** | N/I | |
| **1765** | Sugar bowl to go with Dogs Head range | –1960s |

## Circa 1945

| | | |
|---|---|---|
| 1766 | N/I | |
| 1767 | Dragon plate to match jug 1779 | 2½"h 13"l |
| 1768 | Sweet dish | |
| 1769 | Butter dish | |
| 1770 | Sugar bowl | |
| 1771 | Beaker | |
| 1772 | N/I | |
| 1773 | Basket | |
| 1774 | Bowl Cavalier range p34 TSS | 5"h 10"dia –1960s |
| 1775 | Tankard Cavalier range p88 TSS | 5"h –1960s |
| 1776 | Cheese dish Primrose range | |
| 1777 | 'Basket' posy p31 TSS p105 TSC | 3½"h –1960s |
| 1778 | Jug | |
| 1779 | Dragon jug to match plate 1767 | 9"h |
| 1780 | Basket embossed flowers to match 1782/1783 p105 TSC | 5½"h –1960s |
| 1781 | Vase embossed flowers to match 1791 | 6½"h |
| 1782 | Jug to match 1780/1783 sim to 1655 p101 TSC | 6½"h –1960s |
| 1783 | Bowl to match 1780/1782 p104 TSC | 4"h 6½"l –1960s |
| 1784 | Jug Deco style p102 TSC | 6¼"h –1960s |
| 1785 | N/I | |
| 1786 | Vase p104 TSC | 4½"h –1960s |
| 1787 | Vase Deco style p104 TSC | 4¼"h –1960s |

## Circa 1946

| | | |
|---|---|---|
| 1788–1789 | N/I | |
| 1790 | Jug | |
| 1791 | Sweet dish embossed flowers to match 1781 p105 TSC | 2¼"h 6¼"l –1960s |
| 1792–1793 | N/I | |
| 1794 | Jug, squashed p102 TSC (height error in TSC) p97 TSS | 4½"h –1960s |
| 1795 | Flower jug p102 TSC | 6"h –1960s |
| 1796 | Basket circle p105 TSC | 4½"h 6¼"l –1960s |
| 1797 | Tray Neptune range p46 TSC | 6½"l 5¼"w |
| 1798 | Twin tray Neptune range p46 TSC | 10½"acr |
| 1799–1800 | N/I | |
| 1801 | Jug Cavalier range p35 TSS | 7¾"h –1960s |
| 1802 | N/I | |
| 1803 | Vase | |
| 1804–1806 | N/I | |
| 1807 | Vase p102/145 TSC | 9¾–10"h –1965 |
| 1808 | Vase p145 TSC | 7½"h –1965 |
| 1809–1811 | N/I | |
| 1812 | Teapot Neptune range embossed seahorse | 5½"h |
| 1813 | Sugar bowl Neptune range embossed seahorse two handles | 2¼"h |
| 1814 | Cream jug Neptune range embossed seahorse | 2½"h |
| 1815 | Jugs Neptune range embossed seahorse | 3 sizes |
| 1816 | N/I | |
| 1817 | Vase | |
| 1818 | Butter dish Dog Head range p60 TSS | –1960s |
| 1819 | Posy basket also with hand painted china flowers | 4½"h –1960s |
| 1820 | Candy box p36 TSS | 3¼"h 5½"l –1960s |
| 1821 | Candy box p36 TSS | 3¾"h –1960s |
| 1822 | Sweet dish with flowers p36 TSS | 1½"h 5"l –1960s |

**Circa 1947 I have come to the conclusion that production continued until c1947 at the Thomas Lawrence Works, which accounts for some of the items from this period having a Falcon Ware mark. A 1948 Bulletin seems to suggest this. No doubt this was due to shortage of materials and continuing Board of Trade restrictions, and the Ministry of Supply, who had taken over the works, being unable to vacate the premises. Also new equipment had to be installed to make the Sylvan Works fully operational.**

| | | |
|---|---|---|
| 1823 | Bowl, also containing 8, 9 or 12 china flowers | 4"dia –1960s |
| 1824 | Flower jug p101 TSC | 8¾"h –1960s |
| 1825 | Ashtray, also with flowers in one corner oblong | |
| 1826 | Bowl diamond shape with flower grid p104 TSC | 5"h 7"l –1960s |
| 1827 | Bulb bowl embossed flowers p104 TSC | 3½"h 5½"l –1960s |
| 1828 | N/I | |
| 1829 | Bon Bon basket p105 TSC | 9"l –1960s |
| 1830 | Bulb bowl p105 TSC | 8½"l –1960s |
| 1831 | Vase, 'leaf' handles p103 TSC | 6½"h –1960s |
| 1832 | Vase p103 TSC | 8¼"h –1960s |
| 1833 | Vase p103 TSC | 8½"h –1960s |
| 1834 | Vase p103 TSC | 8½"h –1960s |
| 1835 | Vase p103 TSC | 8½"h –1960s |
| 1836 | Vase p103 TSC | 8½"h –1960s |
| 1837 | Vase p103 TSC | 8½"h –1960s |
| 1838–1847 | N/I | |
| 1848 | Bowl also with 5 or 7 hand painted flowers | 3"dia –1960s |
| 1849 | Honey Dogs Head range | 4¼"h –1960s |
| 1850 | Cheese dish Dogs Head range p60 TSS | 6½"h –1960s |

**Circa 1948 Production probably back at the Sylvan Works**

| | | |
|---|---|---|
| 1851 | Basket Wild Duck range | 8½"l –1950s |
| 1852 | Bowl Wild Duck range | 8"l –1960s |
| 1853 | Vase Wild Duck range | 6½"l –1960s |
| 1854 | Flower Jug Wild Duck range | 8½"h –1960s |
| 1855 | Vase Wild Duck range | 5"h –1960s |
| 1856 | Spill vase Wild Duck range | 5"h 3"w |
| 1857 | Vase Wild Duck Range | 8½–9"h 1960s |
| 1857 also | Lamp base as above | 8½–9"h |
| 1858 | Vase Wild Duck p83 TSS | 8½"h –1960s |
| 1859 | Plant pot Wild Duck square | 5"h 5¼"dia (top) –1960s |
| 1860 | Bowl Wild Duck range | 9½"l –1960s |

**Few new lines were designed at this stage, but the low Falcon Ware numbers were also from this period. Decorated wares were still available for export only, (apart from 'seconds', which could be offered to the home market).**

**Circa 1949**

| | | |
|---|---|---|
| 1861 | Dish diamond shape sim to 1862 Blackberry range (Some of this range can be seen p86 TSS) | 12½"l |
| 1862 | Dish diamond shape sim to 1861 Blackberry range | 10¾"l |
| 1863 | N/I | |
| 1864 | Fruit dish square Blackberry range | 8½"dia |
| 1865 | N/I | |
| 1866 | Jug Blackberry range | |
| 1867 | Honey Blackberry range | 4½"h |
| 1868 | Bowl with lid Blackberry range | 3"h |
| 1869 | Cream jug Blackberry | 2¾"h |
| 1870 | Honey Blackberry range | 3½"h |
| 1871 | Sugar bowl Blackberry | 2"h |
| 1872 | Cheese dish Blackberry | 2½"h 5–6½"l |
| 1873 | Toast rack Blackberry | 5¼"l |
| 1874 | Twin tray Blackberry | 10½"l |
| 1875 | Jug set Leaf Ware | 4½"h (3 sizes) |
| 1876 | Jug set      size 4 | 4"h |
| | Blackberry range   size 5 | 5⅜"h |
| 1877 | Shaving mug | 3¼"h 6"l |
| 1878 | Mug Blackberry range | |
| 1879–1881 | N/I | |
| 1882 | Candleholder | 1"h 4¼"acr |
| 1883 | Vase | |
| 1884 | Teapot | |
| 1885–1886 | N/I | |
| 1887 | Toastrack/butter leaf shape | 7¾–8"l 4"w |
| 1888 | Honey Leaf Ware | 3½"h |

| 1889 | Teapot Leaf Ware | 4½"h |
|------|------------------|------|

Circa 1950–1959 During the 1950's export markets became more restricted, and the Board of Trade removed restrictions on the sale of pottery to the home market. Purchase Tax was removed from bowls and some posies. The SylvaC animals although still taxed at the higher rate, were in great demand.

| 1890–1891 | N/I | |
|------|------|------|
| 1892 | Posy ring ribbed also with handpainted china flowers | s/s |
| 1893 | Posy ring | |
| 1894 | Sweet dish assorted flowers | 6"l |
| 1895 | N/I | |
| 1896 | Hawthorn tree with bird and spray of flowers | |
| 1897 | Ashtray 'crazy garden' assorted flowers | 5"dia |
| 1898 | Sweet tray assorted flowers | 5½"dia |
| 1899 | Posy sheaf with 5 or 7 flowers | s/s |
| 1900 | Dog standing (unconfirmed) | |
| 1901 | Pot | |
| 1902 | N/I | |
| 1903 | Candy box with flowers on lid diamond shape | 2¼"h 5"l |
| 1904 | Jug | |
| 1905 | Lamp base | |
| 1906 | N/I | |
| 1907 | Tray | |
| 1908 | N/I | |
| 1909 | Posy sheaf also with flowers p31 TSS | 2½"h –1960s |
| 1910 | Handled sweet dish | 4½"dia –1960s |
| 1911–1914 | N/I | |
| 1915 | Biscuit barrel | |
| 1916 | Biscuit barrel | |
| 1917 | N/I | |
| 1918 | Biscuit barrel | 8"h |
| 1919 | Sweet dish fluted with flowers | 6¼"dia –1960s |
| 1920 | Sweet dish fluted with flowers | 5"dia –1960s |
| 1921 | Sweet dish fluted with flowers | 7½"dia –1960s |
| 1922 | Posy vase | 2"h 2½"dia |
| 1923 | Posy vase | 3"h 3"dia |
| 1924 | Bowl ribbed | 3"h 3"dia |
| 1925 | N/I | |
| 1926 | Jug | |
| 1927–1928 | N/I | |
| 1929 | Teapot | |
| 1930 | Bowl also with flowers | –1960s |
| 1931 | Box | |
| 1932 | N/I | |
| 1933 | Handled sweet dish | 5½–6"dia –1960s |
| 1934 | Handled sweet dish | 6½–7½"dia –1960s |
| 1935 | Log tray | |
| 1936 | Mug | |
| 1937 | Honey Hobnail design | 4½"h |
| 1938 | Jug Hobnail design | |
| 1939 | Sugar Hobnail design | |
| 1940–1941 | N/I | |
| 1942 | Teapot | |
| 1943 | Jug set (three) | |
| 1944 | N/I | |
| 1945 | Cider jug | |
| 1946 | Cheese dish Hobnail | |
| 1947 | Twin tray | |
| 1948 | Honey with rabbit at side and bee on lid | 3¼"h 3½"w |
| 1949–1952 | N/I | |
| 1953 | Teapot | |
| 1954 | Bowl also with flowers | –1960s |
| 1955 | Sweet dish round flower | 4½"dia –1960s |
| 1956 | Wall vase half opened fan | 5¾"h |
| 1956 also | Wall vase usually with budgerigar, sometimes with swallow p57 TSS earlier version has Deco style flashes on sides | 8½"h –1960s |
| 1957 | Bowl also with flowers | 1¾"h 2½"dia –1960s |
| 1958 | Acorn jug with squirrel handle sim to 330/1115/1959/1993/4068 | 7½"h –1960s |

| 1959 | Acorn jug with squirrel handle sim to 330/1115/1958/1993/4068 p57 TSS | 8½"h –1960s |
|------|------|------|
| 1960 | Flower jug water lilies stork handle sim to 475/1138/4069 p57 TSS | 10"h –1960s |
| 1961 | Holder | |
| 1962 | Hollyock jug sim to 476/1274 | 8½"h –1982 |
| 1963 | Posy trough heart shape with elf | 8½"l –1960s |
| 1964 | Posy trough half circle p90 TSC | 6"dia –1960s |
| 1965 | Posy bar p90 TSC | 6"l –1960s |
| 1966 | Posy bar p90 TSC | 4"l –1960s |
| 1967 | Posy bar p90 TSC | 8"l –1960s |
| 1968 | Handled sweet dish | 5"dia –1960s |
| 1969 | Mushroom jug with gnomes sim to 1196 p57 TSS | 8½"h –1975 |
| 1970 | Jug squat p101 TSC | 5¼"h –1960s |
| 1971 | Jug squat p101 TSC | 5¼"h –1960s |
| 1972 | Wall vase | |
| 1973 | N/I | |
| 1974 | Honey pot | |
| 1975 | Box | |
| 1976 | Commemorative ashtray Coronation Elizabeth II | 6¼"l |
| 1977 | N/I | |
| 1978 | Flower jug, 'rabbits climbing into furze' sim to 1318/4070 | 8½"h –1960s |
| 1979–1981 | N/I | |
| 1982 | Fern Pot | |
| 1983 | Fern pot | |
| 1984 | Fern pot | |
| 1985 | Flower jug | |
| 1986 | Flower jug | |
| 1987 | Flower jug | |
| 1988 | Flower jug | |
| 1989 | Flower jug | |
| 1990 | Toast rack Dogs Head range p60 TSS | 2¼"h 6¾"l –1960s |
| 1991 | Basket | |
| 1992 | Posy trough p90 TSC | 6"dia –1960s |
| 1993 | Acorn jug with squirrel handle sim to 330/1115/1958/1959/4068 p66 TSS | 3"h –1982 |
| 1994 | Ashtray | |
| 1995 | Jug | |
| 1996 | Basket with dog 3567 looking in p38 TSS | 2"h (basket) –1960s |
| 1996 also | Girl | |
| 1997 | Candy box heart shape hand painted flowers on lid sim to 2022 p36 TSS | 4½"dia –1960s |
| 1998 | Barrel holder | |
| 1999 | Posy bowl | |
| 2000 | N/I | |
| 2001 | Shell dish with flowers sim to 2021 | –1960s |
| 2002 | Bowl | |
| 2003 | Ashtray | |
| 2004 | Bulb bowl | |
| 2005 | Ashtray | |
| 2006 | Jardiniere, also with three hand painted flowers | 1½"h 2"l –1960s |
| 2007 | Flower jug | |
| 2008–2018 | N/I | |
| 2019 | Tray Chrys Ware | |
| 2021 | Shell dish with flowers sim to 2001 | |
| 2022 | Candy box heart shape hand painted flowers on lid sim to 1997 | 3½"dia –1960s |
| 2023 | Posy bar | |
| 2024 | Sealyham dog posy p32/61 TSS | 2"h 7"l –1960s |
| 2025 | Spaniel dog posy p32/61 TSS | 2"h 7"l –1960s |
| 2026 | N/I | |
| 2027 | Bowl Ivyleaf range Reg. No. 874069 (1954) p68 TSC | 6"l –1960s |
| 2028 | Bowl | |
| 2029 | Chicken with vase tail | |

SylvaC 2030

| | | |
|---|---|---|
| 2030 | Basket | |
| 2031 | Jardiniere Chrys Ware | 4½″h 6″l |
| 2032 | Tray with holder Ivyleaf Reg. No. 874070 | 8″l –1960s |
| 2033 | Posy trough Ivyleaf p68 TSC | 7½″l –1960s |
| 2034 | N/I | |
| 2035 | Bulb bowl Ivyleaf Reg. No. 874069 | 9½″l |
| 2036 | Jug Ivyleaf range Reg. No. 874069 | 8¼″h –1960s |
| 2037 | Jug Ivyleaf range Reg. No. 874072 | 6″h –1960s |
| 2038 | Tray | |
| 2039 | Basket Ivyleaf range p67 TSC | 3½″h –1960s |
| 2040 | Tray | |
| 2041 | Bowl | |
| 2042 | Basket | |
| 2043 | Fern pot Ivyleaf range | 4″h –1960s |
| 2044 | Jardiniere (no handles) Ivyleaf p67 TSC | 7″l –1960s |
| 2045 | Jug Ivyleaf range | 2⅞″h –1960s |
| 2046 | Honey pot Ivyleaf range p68 TSC | 4½″h –1960s |
| 2047 | Fern pot Ivyleaf range p68 TSC | 5″h –1960s |
| 2048 | Mushroom bowl | |
| 2049 | Bowl with recess for gnome or other p86 TSS | 4¼″h 9″w –1960s |
| 2050 | Wall vase Ivyleaf range p68 TSC | 7½″h –1960s |
| 2051 | Slipper with dog p32 TSS | 3½″h 5½″l –1982 |
| 2052 | Wall vase Ivyleaf range sim to 2050 | 5″h –1960s |
| 2053 | N/I | |
| 2054 | Basket with platform for novelty (two sizes) p38 TSS | 1¾″h 5″l –1960s and 2¼″h 4¾″l |
| 2055–2059 | N/I | |
| 2060 | Boot bulb bowl | 4¼″h 8¼″l –1960s |
| 2061 | Acorn bulb bowl with squirrel handles sim to 2075 | 4½″h 11½″l –1960s |
| 2062 | Tree stump bulb bowl with dogs | 3½″h 7¼″l |
| 2063 | N/I | |
| 2064 | Cucumber tray Ivyleaf range p68 TSC | 13″l |
| 2065 | N/I | |
| 2066 | Cat | |
| 2067 | N/I | |
| 2068 | Salad dish with tray Ivyleaf range p68 TSC | 9½″l |
| 2069 | N/I | |
| 2070 | Table lamp Ivyleaf range | 6½″h |
| 2070 also | Vase as above | 6½″h |
| 2071 | Jug Ivyleaf range p111 TSS | 6″h |
| 2072 | Jug Ivyleaf range | 6″h |
| 2073 | Jug Ivyleaf range | 6″h |
| 2074 | Tomato tray Ivyleaf range | 9½″l |
| 2075 | Acorn bowl with squirrel handles sim to 2061 | 2½″h 6″l –1960s |
| 2076 | N/I | |
| 2077 | Jug Ivyleaf range | 8½″h |
| 2078 | Jug Ivyleaf range | 7″h |
| 2079 | Wall vase, with seagull or floral p36 TSS | 6¼″h –1960s |
| 2080 | Tray | |
| 2081 | Vase | |
| 2082 | Vase | |
| 2083 | Wall vase floral p36 TSS | 6″h –1960s |
| 2084 | Wall vase floral p36 TSS | 6″h –1960s |
| 2085 | Basket | |
| 2086 | Jug Seagull Ware p36 TSS | 6¼″h –1960s |
| 2087 | Flower jug | 6″h |
| 2088 | Cheese dish Ivyleaf p68 TSC | 3½″h –1960s |
| 2089 | Butter dish round Ivyleaf p68 TSC | 2½″h |
| 2090 | Bowl Ivyleaf range p68 TSC | 4″h 8½″w |
| 2091 | Wall vase Chrys Ware | 5¼″h 4¾″w |
| 2092 | Wall vase Chrys Ware | 9″h 7″dia |
| 2093 | Cream jug Chrys Ware p66 TSS | 3″h |
| 2094 | Jug Chrys Ware | 6″h |
| 2095 | Flower jug Chrys Ware | 7¼″h |
| 2096 | Flower jug Chrys Ware | 8½–9″h |
| 2097 | Bowl Chrys Ware | 4″h 6″l |
| 2098 | Bowl Chrys Ware | 9½″l |
| 2099 | Plant pot Chrys Ware | 4¼″h |
| 2100 | Plant pot Chrys Ware | 5¼″h |
| 2101 | Posy ring Chrys Ware | 5¾″w |
| 2102 | Posy bar Chrys Ware | 8″l |
| 2103 | Jug Chrys Ware | 5¾″h |
| 2104 | Jug Chrys Ware | 4¾″h |
| 2105 | Honey Chrys Ware | 4″h |
| 2106 | Honey | |
| 2107 | Tray | |
| 2108 | Basket Chrys Ware | 3¼″h |
| 2109 | Basket Chrys Ware | 4″h 6″dia |
| 2110 | Wall Vase | |
| 2111 | Candy box Seagull Ware p36 TSS | 3″h 5″w –1960s |
| 2112 | Bowl Seagull ware p36 TSS | 4¼″h 9½″w –1960s |
| 2113 | Jardiniere Seagull Ware p36 TSS | 3¾″h 7½″w |
| 2114 | Bulb bowl Autumn range | – 1960s |
| 2115 | Flower pot Autumn range | –1960s |
| 2116 | Jardiniere Autumn range | 3¼″h 7½″l – 1960s |
| 2117 | Jardiniere | |
| 2118 | Vase with handles Chrys Ware | 5½″h |
| 2119 | Basket Seagull Ware p36 TSS | 6½″h 6½″w –1960s |
| 2120 | Cat sitting | 5″h |
| 2121 | N/I | |
| 2122 | Mini jardiniere also with hand painted flowers p31 TSS p73 TSC | 2″h 5¼″l –1960s |
| 2123 | N/I | |
| 2124 | Vase Ivyleaf p68 TSC | 8½″h |
| 2125 | Vase | |
| 2126–2127 | N/I | |
| 2128 | Shell dish with flowers | –1960s |
| 2129 | Plant pot Rope p70 TSC | 4″h –1960s |
| 2130 | Vase Rope range | |
| 2131 | Posy trough Rope p70 TSC | 8″l –1960s |
| 2132 | Bowl Rope range p70 TSC | 9″l –1960s |
| 2133 | Jardiniere | |
| 2134 | Bowl | |
| 2135 | Bowl | |
| 2136 | Vase p72 TSC | 5½″h –1960s |
| 2137 | Vase p72 TSC | 8″h –1960s |
| 2138 | Tray on feet p72 TSC | 11½″l –1960s |
| 2139 | Vase p72 TSC | 7″h –1960s |
| 2140 | Wall vase p72/73 TSC | 8½″h –1960s |
| 2141 | Bowl | |
| 2142 | Bowl p73 TSC | 7½″l –1960s |
| 2143 | Bowl | –1960s |
| 2144 | Vase p72 TSC | 11″h –1960s |
| 2145 | Bowl | |
| 2146 | Bowl | |
| 2147 | Vase p72 TSC | 8″h 4½″w |
| 2148 | Bowl | |
| 2149 | N/I | |
| 2150 | Plant pot Rope range | 6¾″dia |
| 2151 | Wall vase Rope range p70 TSC | 8¾″h –1960s |
| 2152 | Bulb bowl Autumn range | –1960s |
| 2153 | Bowl | |
| 2154 | Bow wall vase p36 TSS | 5″w –1960s |
| 2155 | Holder | |
| 2156 | Wall vase Autumn range | |
| 2157 | N/I | |
| 2158 | Pixie on toadstool | 3¼″h –1960s |
| 2159 | Jardiniere Autumn range | 5½″h 13½″l – 1960s |
| 2160 | Bowl Rope range p70 TSC | 6″l –1960s |
| 2161 | Vase Rope range | 3″h –1960s |
| 2162 | Vase Rope range p70 TSC | 7″l –1960s |
| 2163 | Vase Rope range | 7″h –1960s |
| 2164 | Vase | |
| 2165 | Cream jug Thistle | 2½″h |
| 2166 | Sugar bowl Thistle | 2½″h |
| 2167 | Jardiniere Thistle | 2⅝″h 6⅞″l |
| 2168 | Candle holder | |
| 2169 | Tray | |
| 2170 | Tray | |
| 2171 | Plant pot Raphique range | –1960s |
| 2172 | Honey Raphique range p59 TSS | 4½″h –1960s |

| | | |
|---|---|---|
| 2173 | Plant pot incised | 4½"h |
| 2174 | Candle holder | |
| 2175 | Vase | |
| 2176 | Vase Raphique range | –1960s |
| 2177 | Honey Raphique range | 4½"h –1960s |
| 2178 | Posy trough Raphique | 8¼"l –1960s |
| 2179 | Butter dish Raphique | 5¾"l |
| 2180 | Jardiniere Raphique | –1960s |
| 2181 | Wall vase Raphique | 8¾"h –1960s |
| 2182 | Bulb bowl Raphique | –1960s |
| 2183 | Pot | |
| 2184 | Cruet set Raphique range p59 TSS | –1960s |
| 2185 | Cream jug Raphique | –1960s |
| 2186 | Cruet | |
| 2187 | Posy trough Rope range p70 TSC | 15"l –1960s |
| 2188 | Teapot Raphique range | –1960s |
| 2189 | Vase Raphique range | –1960s |
| 2190 | Sugar bowl Raphique | –1960s |
| 2191 | Bowl Raphique range | –1960s |
| 2192 | Vase Raphique range | –1960s |
| 2193 | Wall vase | |
| 2194 | Pot | |
| 2195 | Wall vase | |
| 2196 | Cheese dish | |
| 2197 | Butter dish | |
| 2198 | Vase Raphique range | 5¼"h |
| 2199 | Vase | |
| 2200 | Sugar bowl | |
| 2201 | Cream jug | |
| 2202 | Tray | |
| 2203 | Teapot | |
| 2204 | Pot | |
| 2205 | Vase | |
| 2206 | Candle holder | |
| 2207 | N/I | |
| 2208 | Wall vase floral p36 TSS | 7"h |
| 2209 | Plant pot Cactus SCC/14 | |
| 2210 | Cream jug | |
| 2211 | Toast rack | |
| 2212 | Vase Lace range | 4¾"h |
| 2213 | Jardiniere Raphique no handles | 7"l |
| 2214 | Tray | |
| 2215 | Posy trough | |
| 2216 | Bowl | |
| 2217 | Pot | |
| 2218 | Vase horn shaped | |
| 2219 | Vase | |
| 2220 | Vase with incised circles | 6½"h 4½"w |
| 2221 | Lamp | |
| 2222 | Wall vase | |
| 2223 | Dish Lace range floral | 5¼"acr –1960s |
| 2224 | N/I | |
| 2225 | Dish with incised circles | 5¼"acr –1960s |
| 2226 | Honey Cactus range flowers on lid | –1960s |
| 2227 | Bulb bowl Rope range p70 TSC | 12"l –1960s |
| 2228 | N/I | |
| 2229 | Plant pot with circles | |
| 2230 | Bulb bowl with circles | 3½"h 6¼"l |
| 2231 | Vase | |
| 2232 | Pot | |
| 2233 | Pot | |
| 2234 | N/I | |
| 2235 | Wall vase with circles | 7"h |
| 2236 | Bowl with circles | 4½"h 9½"l |
| 2237 | Vase | |
| 2238 | Vase Rope range | 8"l |
| 2239 | Bowl | |
| 2240 | Bowl | |
| 2241 | N/I | |
| 2242 | Bowl | |
| 2243 | Pot | |
| 2244 | Candy box Lace range | 1¾"h |
| 2245 | Dish Cactus with flowers | 5¼"l –1960s |
| 2246 | Vase Cactus range | 6"h |

| | | |
|---|---|---|
| 2247 | Wall vase Cactus range | –1960s |
| 2248 | Bulb bowl Cactus range | –1960s |
| 2249 | Bulb bowl Cactus range | 4½"h 6½"l –1960s |
| 2250 | Pot | |
| 2251 | Bulb bowl Cactus range | –1960s |
| 2252 | Vase Cactus range SCC/14 | 8"h –1960s |
| 2253 | Pot | |
| 2254 | Vase Cactus range | 7"h 5"l –1960s |
| 2255 | Vase Lace range | 6"h |
| 2256 | Bowl | |
| 2257 | N/I | |
| 2258 | Vase | |
| 2259 | Bowl Shell range p66 TSC | 12"l –1970 |
| 2260 | Vase New Style Floral p93 TSC | –1960s |
| 2261 | Tray | 6½"dia |
| 2262 | Wall vase Cactus range | 6½"h –1960s |
| 2263 | Wall vase Cactus range | 5¼"h |
| 2264 | Jardiniere Rope range p70 TSC | 14"l –1960s |
| 2265 | Vase Rope range | 5"h –1960s |
| 2266 | Vase Rope range p70 TSC | 8"h –1960s |
| 2267 | Vase New Style Floral p93 TSC | 5¼"h –1960s |
| 2268 | Vase Lace range | 6¾"h |
| 2269 | Wall vase Lace range | 8¾"h –1960s |
| 2270 | Flower pot Lace range | 4¾"h –1960s |
| 2271 | Honey pot Lace range | 3½"h –1960s |
| 2272 | Vase | |
| 2273 | N/I | |
| 2274 | Wall vase Lace range | 7¼"h |
| 2275 | Log posy with novelty p31 TSS | 5"l –1970s |
| 2276 | Basket posy with novelty p31 TSS | 5"l –1970s |
| 2277 | Watering can with novelty p32/54 TSS | 3"h –1970s |
| 2278 | Flower pot with novelty p32/54 TSS | 3"h –1970s |
| 2279 | Bowl | |
| 2280 | Jardiniere Rope range p70 TSC | 12"l –1970s |
| 2281 | Vase p54 TSS | 7"h –1960s |
| 2282 | Vase p54 TSS | 7"h –1960s |
| 2283 | N/I | |
| 2284 | Posy trough Lace range | 7½"acr –1960s |
| 2285 | Tray | |
| 2286 | N/I | |
| 2287 | Vase | |
| 2288 | Vase p54 TSS | 7"h –1960s |
| 2289 | Bulb bowl with pixie p53 TSS | 5½"l –1960s |
| 2290 | Bowl Lace range | 6"acr |
| 2291 | Pot | |
| 2292 | N/I | |
| 2293 | Wall vase Cactus range | –1960s |
| 2294 | Flower pot Lace range | 5½"h |
| 2295 | Acorn with pixie p53/86 TSS | 7"dia –1982 |
| 2296 | Jardiniere Cactus range | –1960s |
| 2297 | Cheeseboard | |
| 2297 also | Posy, round, curvy edges, centre holder Lace range | 8¼"acr –1960s |
| 2298 | Cruet Lace range 3pce set | –1960s |
| 2299 | Shallow dish Lace range | 11"acr –1960s |
| 2300 | Jardiniere Lace range | 12"acr –1960s |
| 2301 | Bulb bowl Lace range | 9¾"acr –1960s |
| 2302 | Vase | |
| 2303 | Vase | |
| 2304 | Vase | |
| 2305 | Vase Cactus range | 7½"h –1960s |
| 2306 | Wall vase | |
| 2307 | Bowl | |
| 2308 | Bulb bowl Cactus range | –1960s |
| 2309 | Posy holder Lace range | 4½"acr |
| 2310 | Wall vase | |
| 2311 | Basket also with flowers p31 TSS | s/s |
| 2312 | Vase New Style Floral p93 TSC | 5"h –1960s |
| 2313 | Holder | |
| 2314 | Vase Privet range p37 TSS | 4¾"h |
| 2315 | Sweet dish New Style Floral p93 TSC | 1"h 5"l –1960s |
| 2316 | Bowl Floral line | –1960s |
| 2317 | Bowl New Style Floral p93 TSC | –1960s |

| | | |
|---|---|---|
| **2318** | Bowl New Style Floral p93 TSC | –1960s |
| **2319** | Tray Nuleef range sim to 2355 | 11¼"l |
| **2320** | Bulb bowl Rope Range p70 TSC | 7"acr –1970s |
| **2321** | Vase Hyacinth p71 TSC | 7"h –1982 |
| **2322** | Wall vase | |
| **2323** | Candle holder Lace range | 2½"h –1960s |
| **2324** | N/I | |
| **2325** | Sweet dish | s/s –1960s |
| **2326** | Sweet dish sim to 2325 l/s | 3¾"h 7¼"l –1960s |
| **2327** | Cheese dish Lace range | 7¾"acr –1960s |
| **2328** | Vase | |
| **2329** | Vase | 5"h –1970s |
| **2330** | Vase | |
| **2331** | Boxer puppy p42 TSS p39 TSC | 5¼"h –1960s |
| **2332** | Babies bootee | 3¼"h |
| **2333** | Bowl Nuleef p48 TSC | 6½"h 10"l –1960s |
| **2334** | Vase Nuleef p48 TSC | 5½"h –1960s |
| **2335** | Honey Nuleef p48 TSC | –1960s |
| **2336** | Sweet dish Nuleef p48 TSC | –1960s |
| **2337** | Vase sim to 741/2352 | 10¼"h –1960s |
| **2338** | Vase | |
| **2339** | Bulb bowl with pixie sim to 2346 p53 TSS | 9"acr –1960s |
| **2340** | Jardiniere Lace range | 8¼"acr |
| **2341** | Jug Nuleef p48 TSC | –1960s |
| **2342** | Beaker Nuleef p48 TSC | 4½"h –1960s |
| **2343** | Tankard horses head p88 TSS p63 TSC | 4½"h –1982 |
| **2344** | Tankard | |
| **2345** | Vase Plume range | 7"h |
| **2346** | Bulb bowl with pixie p53 TSS sim to 2339 | 7½"acr –1960s |
| **2347** | Sweet dish Lace range | 5¼"acr |
| **2348** | Toastrack Nuleef p48 TSC | –1960s |
| **2349** | Cruet set Nuleef p48 TSC | 2¾"h 9½"l –1960s |
| **2350** | N/I | |
| **2351** | Jug Nuleef p48 TSC 3 sizes | 5"h (size 2) –1960s |
| **2352** | Vase sim to 741/2337 p73 TSC | 6"h –1960s |
| **2353** | Salad dish Nuleef p48 TSC | 11½"l –1960s |
| **2354** | Twin tray Nuleef p48 TSC | –1960s |
| **2355** | Sweet dish Nuleef p48 TSC | 8¼"l –1960s |
| **2356** | Butter dish Nuleef p48 TSC | –1960s |
| **2357** | Cheese dish Nuleef p48 TSC | –1960s |
| **2358** | Triple tray Nuleef p48 TSC | –1960s |
| **2359** | Dish Nuleef sim to 2355 | 12"l |
| **2360** | Plant pot Nuleef p48 TSC | –1960s |
| **2361** | Bulb bowl Nuleef p48 TSC | –1960s |
| **2362** | Sugar bowl Nuleef p48 TSC | 4"dia –1960s |
| **2363** | Cream jug Nuleef p48 TSC | –1960s |
| **2364** | Posy trough Nuleef p48 TSC | –1960s |
| **2365** | Bowl | |
| **2366** | Wall vase Nuleef p48 TSC | –1960s |
| **2367** | Fruit bowl Nuleef p48 TSC | –1960s |
| **2368** | Jardiniere Nuleef | 6"h 10½"l |
| **2369** | Butter dish | |
| **2370** | Tray | |
| **2371** | Bowl | s/s |
| **2372** | N/I | |
| **2373** | Basket jug also with flowers p73 TSC | |
| **2374** | N/I | |
| **2375** | Tankard hound p88 TSS p63 TSC | 4½"h –1982 |
| **2376** | Tankard fox p63 TSC | 4½"h –1982 |
| **2377** | N/I | |
| **2378** | Plant pot p73 TSC | 4¾"h –1960s |
| **2379** | Jardiniere p73/92 TSC | 8"l –1960s |
| **2380** | Bowl | |
| **2381** | Bowl Fir Cone range | |
| **2382** | N/I | |
| **2383** | Vase | |
| **2384** | Vase | |
| **2385** | Posy trough Plume p69 TSC | –1960s |
| **2386** | Wall vase Plume p69 TSC | –1960s |
| **2387** | Bowl | |
| **2388** | Plant pot Plume p69 TSC | –1960s |
| **2389** | N/I | |

| | | |
|---|---|---|
| **2390** | Vase | |
| **2391** | Vase | |
| **2392** | Pot | |
| **2393** | Bowl | |
| **2394** | Tankard | |
| **2395** | Tankard | |
| **2396** | Mother duck p32/37/50/66 TSS | –1960s |
| **2397** | Baby duck p32/66 TSS | 2¼"h 2¼l –1960s |
| **2398** | Baby duck p32/66 TSS | 2¼"h 2¼l –1960s |
| **2399** | Bowl | |
| **2400** | Fruit bowl Plume p69 TSC | 4"h 11½"l –1960s |
| **2401** | Bulb bowl Plume p69 TSC | 3½"h 6¼"l –1960s |
| **2402** | Bowl Plume range p69 TSC | –1960s |
| **2403** | Cheese dish Plume p69 TSC | –1960s |
| **2404** | Vase Plume | 6¼"h |
| **2405** | Bowl | |
| **2406** | Jardiniere Plume p69 TSC | 4"h 8½"l –1960s |
| **2407** | Vase Plume p69 TSC | –1960s |
| **2408** | Vase Plume p69 TSC | 5½"h –1960s |
| **2409** | Cruet set Plume p69 TSC | – 1960s |
| **2410** | Honey Plume p69 TSC | –1960s |
| **2411** | Butter dish Plume p69 TSC | –1960s |
| **2412–2413** | N/I | |
| **2414** | Bowl | |
| **2415** | Bowl | |
| **2416** | Bowl | |
| **2417** | Bowl | |
| **2418** | Vase | |
| **2419** | Vase Nuleef p48 TSC | –1960s |
| **2420** | Vase Nuleef with grid | 8¼"h |
| **2421** | Dog with barrel around neck p42 TSS | 4¾"h –1970 |
| **2422** | Dog | |
| **2423** | N/I | |
| **2424** | Terrier dog ashtray p54 TSS | 5½"l –1960s |
| **2425** | Chimney also with cat, stork or owl p61 TSS | 4"h –1960s |
| **2426** | N/I | |
| **2427** | Rabbit | |
| **2428** | Giraffe (probably for palm vase 2430) | |
| **2429** | Elephant (probably for palm vase 2430) | |
| **2430** | Palm vase also with hippo, elephant or giraffe on base | 4"h –1960s |
| **2431** | Spaniel dog ashtray p54 TSS | 5½" –1960s |
| **2432** | Horse tankard | |
| **2433** | Tankard | |
| **2434** | Tankard | |
| **2435** | Horse tankard | |
| **2436** | Tankard | |
| **2437** | Fox tankard | |
| **2438** | Pekinese dog ashtray p54 TSS | 5¾"l –1960s |
| **2439** | Vase Nautilus p70 TSC | 6"h –1960s |
| **2440** | Vase Nautilus p70 TSC | 6½" –1960s |
| **2441** | Vase Nautilus p70 TSC | 10"h –1960s |
| **2442** | Vase | |
| **2443** | Owl (probably for chimmey 2425) | |
| **2444** | Stork (probably for chimney 2425) | |
| **2445** | Vase | |
| **2446** | Vase | 6"h –1960s |
| **2447** | Vase | 6"h –1960s |
| **2448** | Vase | |
| **2449** | Vase Nautilus p62 TSS p70 TSC | 8¼"h –1960s |
| **2450** | Pot | |
| **2451** | 'Toby' Toothache dog sim to 2455/3093/3183 p42 TSS | 11½"h –1970 |
| **2452** | Vase Hyacinth p71 TSC | 9¼"h –1982 |
| **2453** | Vase Hyacinth p71/110 TSC | 11¼"h –1982 |
| **2454** | Bowl | |
| **2455** | 'Toby' Toothache dog sim to 2451/3093/3183 p42 TSS | 8¼–8½"h –1970s |
| **2456** | Vase Hyacinth p71 TSC | 10"l –1982 |
| **2457** | Vase Squirrel range p113 TSC | 5¾"h –1960s |
| **2458** | Bowl | |

| | | | |
|---|---|---|---|
| 2459 | Twin vase Squirrel range p113 TSC | 5¾"h –1960s | |
| 2460 | Vase | | |
| 2461 | Fern pot Jewel range | 4¾"h –1970 | |
| 2462 | N/I | | |
| 2463 | Urn Vase p92 TSC | 8¼"h –1960s | |
| 2464 | N/I | | |
| 2465 | Bowl on cupid stand Moselle p79 TSC | 9"h –1970s | |
| 2466 | Water wheel (possibly Le Moulin de Lecq Inn p39 TSC) | | |
| 2467 | Jardiniere also with flower | 7"l –1960s | |
| 2468 | Posy trough Squirrel range p87 TSS p113 TSC | 5¾"l –1960s | |
| 2469–2471 | N/I | | |
| 2472 | Vase with lilacs p31 TSS | 5"h | |
| 2473 | Yorkshire Terrier p42 TSS | 4⅛"h 5½"l | |
| 2474 | Bowl on stand Moselle p79 TSC | 10½"l –1970 | |

**Circa 1960** During the previous decade the new Shaw & Copestake factory was built, being completed in 1962. The two potteries combined as one, and Thomas Lawrence ceased trading in 1962. Shaw & Copestake were now at their peak and output was considerable as can be seen from the following schedule

| | | | |
|---|---|---|---|
| 2475 | N/I | | |
| 2476 | Vase with lilacs p31 TSS | 5"h | |
| 2477 | Dog | | |
| 2478 | Bowl Hyacinth p71 TSC | 14½"l –1970 | |
| 2479 | Bowl with 8 hand painted flowers | | |
| 2480 | Wall vase | | |
| 2481 | Bowl | | |
| 2482 | Bowl Hyacinth p71 TSC | 6¾"l –1982 | |
| 2483 | Plant pot Hyacinth p71 TSC | 5"h –1982 | |
| 2484 | Jardiniere Hyacinth p71 TSC | 13"l –1982 | |
| 2485 | Bowl Hyacinth p71 TSC | 10½"l –1982 | |
| 2486 | Posy trough Hyacinth p71 TSC | 8"l –1982 | |
| 2487 | Wall vase Hyacinth p71 TSC | 9"h –1982 | |
| 2488 | Jardiniere Hyacinth p71 TSC | 8¼"l –1982 | |
| 2489 | Plant pot Hyacinth p71 TSC | 6"h –1982 | |
| 2490 | N/I | | |
| 2491 | Vase with lilac p31 TSS | 3½"h 5"l | |
| 2492 | N/I | | |
| 2493 | St. Bernard dog p48 TSS p19 TSC | 4½"h –1982 | |
| 2494 | Urn Vase p92 TSC | 6¼"h | |
| 2495 | Urn Vase p92 TSC | 10¼"h | |
| 2496 | Springer spaniel? | 7¼"h | |
| 2497 | Springer spaniel p48 TSS | 4¼"h | |
| 2498 | Bowl with 7 hand painted flowers p31 TSS | | |
| 2499 | Bowl with 10 hand painted flowers p31 TSS p73 TSC | | |
| 2500 | Bowl with 12 hand painted flowers | | |
| 2501 | Tray | | |
| 2502 | Collie dog p48 TSS | 5½"h –1975 | |
| 2503 | Fox Terrier p48 TSS | 4"h –1970 | |
| 2504 | Boston Terrier p19 TSC (no number on photo) | 4½"h –1970 | |
| 2505 | Vase sim to 1346 p99 TSC | 15"h | |
| 2506 | Vase | | |
| 2507 | Bowl Squirrel range p113 TSC | 5¾"l | |
| 2508 | N/I | | |
| 2509 | Barrel, also with cat | 2¼"h | |
| 2510 | Bowl with 4/5 hand painted flowers p31 TSS | | |
| 2511 | Tray | | |
| 2512 | Bowl Squirrel range p86 TSS p113 TSC | 7½"acr | |
| 2513 | Bowl also with separate leaves draped over side p104 TSS | 7¼"dia | |
| 2514 | Urn vase p92 TSC | 7¼"h | |
| 2515 | Vase | | |
| 2516 | Hound ashtray p63 TSC | 6½"dia –1982 | |
| 2517 | Fox ashtray p63 TSC | 6½"dia –1982 | |
| 2518 | Horse ashtray p63 TSC | 6½"dia –1982 | |
| 2519 | Leaf probably for 2513 | | |
| 2520 | Leaf probably for 2513 | | |
| 2521 | Horse bookends p66 TSS | 4¼"h –1975 | |
| 2522 | Fish bookends p66 TSS | 3¾"h | |
| 2523 | Squirrel | | |
| 2524 | Bloodhound dog p61 TSS | 4½"h | |
| 2525 | Bowl also with 14 hand painted flowers p31 TSS | | |
| 2526 | Bowl | | |
| 2527 | Pot | | |
| 2528 | Setter dog p48 TSS | 4¾"h | |
| 2529 | Squirrel | | |
| 2530 | N/I | | |
| 2531 | Trough | | |
| 2532 | N/I | | |
| 2533 | Ashtray round p66 TSS | 7½"dia | |
| 2534 | N/I | | |
| 2535 | Bowl, also with 3 hand painted flowers | | |
| 2536 | Dog | | |
| 2537 | Greyhound dog p48 TSS p20 TSC | 7½"l –1982+ | |
| 2538 | Airedale dog p48 TSS | 5"h –1975 | |
| 2539 | N/I | | |
| 2540 | Dog | | |
| 2541 | Bowl | | |
| 2542 | Bowl | | |
| 2543 | Vase | | |
| 2544 | Vase | | |
| 2545 | Smooth haired terrier p48 TSS | 4¼"h | |
| 2546 | Plant pot Laronde range | 5½"h | |
| 2547 | Bowl Bamboo range | 3¾"h | |
| 2548 | Vase Moselle range | | |
| 2549 | Cat p61/84 TSS | 5"h | |
| 2550 | Pot | | |
| 2551 | Fern pot sim to 2559 Jewel range | 5½"h –1970 | |
| 2552 | Bookend | | |
| 2553 | Vase | | |
| 2554 | Jug re-numbered 4044 | | |
| 2555 | Honey Kitchen range Reg. No. 897226 (1960) see 2586 for description p93 TSS | 4–5"h | |
| 2556 | Sugar | | |
| 2557 | Cream | | |
| 2558 | Fern pot | | |
| 2559 | Fern pot sim to 2551 Jewel range | 4"h –1970 | |
| 2560 | Shoe | | |
| 2561 | N/I | | |
| 2562 | Comport Moselle p79 TSC with cupid stand | 7¾"h –1970 | |
| 2563 | Tray | | |
| 2564 | Vase Moselle p79 TSC sometimes marked STAFFORDSHIRE HEIRLOOMS | 8½"h –1970 | |
| 2565 | N/I | | |
| 2566 | Comport Moselle p79 TSC | 12"acr | |
| 2567 | Plant pot Laronde | 4¼"h | |
| 2568 | Plant pot Laronde p49 TSC | 4¾"h | |
| 2569 | Bowl | | |
| 2570 | Beaker | | |
| 2571 | Teapot re-numbered 4046 | | |
| 2572 | Seal | | |
| 2573 | Holder | | |
| 2574 | Bull dog | | |
| 2575 | Cheese | | |
| 2576 | Mustard pot & lid | 2½"h | |
| 2577 | Hot water jug | | |
| 2578 | Bowl | | |
| 2579 | Cat | | |
| 2580 | Dog | | |
| 2581 | Jug | | |
| 2582 | Jug re-numbered 4043 | | |
| 2583 | Jug | | |
| 2584 | Dog howling p61 TSS | 7½"h | |
| 2585 | Butter dish | | |

| | | |
|---|---|---|
| **2586** | Storage jar Reg.No.897228 (1960) embossed with kitchen utensils. Red particularly rare. Probably some of the preceeding and following items were from this range p93 TSS | 5½"h inc lid |
| **2587** | Storage Jar | |
| **2588** | Storage Jar re-numbered 4041 | |
| **2589** | Sugar sifter | |
| **2590** | Jug re-numbered 4045 | |
| **2591** | Cress dish | |
| **2592** | Mixing bowl | |
| **2593** | Wall vase Squirrel range p113 TSC | 8"h |
| **2594** | N/I | |
| **2595** | Dachshund p61 TSS | 4 h 6½"l |
| **2596** | N/I | |
| **2597** | Bootee | 2¼"h 3¼"l |
| **2598** | Bowl Squirrel range p113 TSC | 14"l |
| **2599** | Flower holder | |
| **2600** | Bowl Squirrel range p113 TSC | 10"acr |
| **2601** | Gondola bowl also with hand painted flowers | 6½"l |
| **2602** | Dish Laronde p49 TSC | |
| **2603** | Tankard Moulin De Lecq Inn see 3546 | 4½"h |
| **2604** | Teapot re-numbered 4047 | |
| **2605** | Teapot | |
| **2606** | Bowl | |
| **2607** | Wall vase Laronde range | 6½"h |
| **2608** | Posy bar Laronde p49 TSC | 7¾"l |
| **2609** | Vase Laronde range | 7"h |
| **2610** | Bowl Laronde range | 6½"l |
| **2611** | Basket Laronde p49 TSC | 7¾"l |
| **2612** | Cruet Laronde p49 TSC | |
| **2613** | Trough Laronde p49 TSC | 14"l |
| **2614** | Vase Laronde p49 TSC | 10½"l |
| **2615** | Honey Laronde p49 TSC | 5"h |
| **2616** | Vase Laronde p49 TSC | 10"h |
| **2617** | Vase Laronde p49 TSC | 8"h |
| **2618** | Vase Laronde range | 6"h |
| **2619** | Cheese dish Laronde p49 TSC | |
| **2620** | Dish Laronde range | 12½"l |
| **2621** | Shallow dish Laronde p49 TSC | |
| **2622** | Mixing bowl | |
| **2623** | Spaniel dog | |
| **2624** | N/I | |
| **2625** | Bowl Moselle two cupids | 14"l |
| **2626** | Horn vase Moselle with cupid p79 TSC sometimes marked STAFFORDSHIRE HEIRLOOMS | 8¾"h –1982 |
| **2627** | Holder | |
| **2628** | N/I | |
| **2629** | Bowl | |
| **2630** | Bowl | |
| **2631** | Jardiniere | |
| **2632** | Vase | |
| **2633** | Sugar shaker | |
| **2634** | Triple dish Laronde p49 TSC | |
| **2635** | N/I | |
| **2636** | Bowl Laronde p49 TSC | 11"acr |
| **2637** | N/I | |
| **2638** | Bowl Laronde p49 TSC | 9¾"l |
| **2639** | Posy round Laronde | |
| **2640–2641** | N/I | |
| **2642** | Horse Tankard | |
| **2643** | Jardiniere | |
| **2644** | N/I | |
| **2645** | Vase Ivyleaf p68 TSC | 10"h |
| **2646** | Vase Ivyleaf p68 TSC | 7½"h |
| **2647** | Trough Ivyleaf p68 TSC | 15"l |
| **2648** | Posy holder round Ivyleaf p68 TSC | 7"dia |
| **2649** | Jardiniere Ivyleaf p68 TSC | 12"l |
| **2650** | N/I | |
| **2651** | Jardiniere Ivyleaf range | 7"h 10"l |
| **2652** | Vase Ivyleaf range | 8¼"h |

| | | |
|---|---|---|
| **2653** | Vase Ivyleaf range | 6¼"h |
| **2654** | N/I | |
| **2655** | Vase with lamb p31 TSS | 5"h |
| **2656** | Vase with lamb p31 TSS | 5"h |

**Circa 1961**

| | | |
|---|---|---|
| **2657** | N/I | |
| **2658** | Vase with lamb p31 TSS | 5"h |
| **2659** | Vase | |
| **2660** | Vase with tennis dog or city dog or french poodle p31 TSS | 5"h |
| **2661** | Trough curved Ivyleaf p68 TSC | 1¼"h |
| **2662** | N/I | |
| **2663** | Plate | |
| **2664–2666** | N/I | |
| **2667** | Bambi | |
| **2668** | Lamb (for 2655/6/8) | |
| **2669** | Novelty dog (for 2660) p31 TSS | |
| **2670** | Novelty dog (for 2660) p31 TSS | |
| **2671** | Novelty dog (for 2660) p31 TSS | |
| **2672** | Dog | |
| **2673** | Bowl | |
| **2674** | N/I | |
| **2675** | Old English Sheepdog p19 TSC | 5"h |
| **2676** | Vase | |
| **2677** | N/I | |
| **2678** | Jardiniere with wavy top, on feet | 10½"l |
| **2679** | Scottie dog standing | 3½"h 3¾"l –1970s |
| **2680** | Vase | |
| **2681** | Anvil | |
| **2682** | N/I | |
| **2683** | Horn vase Moselle with cupid p79 TSC | 5½"l –1982 |
| **2684** | Tray on stand with handles | 7½"l |
| **2685** | Chest | |
| **2686** | Ashtray round | 2¾"h 6¼"dia |
| **2687** | Skis rabbit | |
| **2688** | Rabbit | |
| **2689** | Skis rabbit | |
| **2690** | Bowl embossed houses and trees | 3½"h 6" dia |
| **2691** | Bowl | |
| **2692** | Vase | |
| **2693** | Dog | |
| **2694** | Urn vase | 6"h –1970s |
| **2695** | Urn vase | 6"h |
| **2696** | Bowl on stand with handles | 7½"l |
| **2697–2698** | N/I | |
| **2699** | Swan posy | 7¼"l –1982 |
| **2700** | N/I | |
| **2701** | Bowl | |
| **2702** | N/I | |
| **2703** | Lemon Squeezer | |
| **2704** | Fern pot | |
| **2705** | Jardiniere Jewel range | 5½"h 12¼"l |
| **2706** | Vase Jewel range | 8"h 6"w |
| **2707** | Bowl Jewel range | 15"l |
| **2708** | Bowl Jewel range | 4½"h 7½"acr |
| **2709** | Jardiniere Jewel range | 7¼"l |
| **2710** | Jardiniere Jewel range | 10½"l |
| **2711** | Posy Jewel range | 8"l |
| **2712** | Vase Jewel range p100 TSC | 10"h 7¼"w |
| **2713** | Vase Jewel range | 6"h |
| **2714** | Fern pot | 7¼"h |
| **2715–2717** | N/I | |
| **2718** | Twin vase Bamboo | 6"h 3¾"l |
| **2719** | N/I | |
| **2720** | Lantern Wall vase | 9¾"h |
| **2721** | Egg Separater | |
| **2722** | Cat sitting sim to 2794 and 2795 | m/s |
| **2723** | Holder | |
| **2724** | Vase | |
| **2725** | Tray | |
| **2726** | Cress dish and stand | |
| **2727** | Swan holder | 9¼"l –1982 |
| **2728** | N/I | |

| | | | |
|---|---|---|---|
| 2729 | Cupid posy Moselle p79 TSC | 5½"l –1982 | |
| 2730 | Dog | | |
| 2731 | Dog | | |
| 2732 | Vase Bamboo | 7"h | |
| 2733 | Vegetable dish | | |
| 2734 | Dish | | |
| 2735 | Bowl | | |
| 2736 | Boy | | |
| 2737 | N/I | | |
| 2738 | Monkey jug | | |
| 2739 | Jardiniere | 20"l –1970s | |
| 2740 | Bowl Bamboo | | |
| 2741 | Wall vase Bamboo | 8"h | |
| 2742 | Plant pot Bamboo | | |
| 2743 | Vase Bamboo | 8¼"h | |
| 2744 | Planter | | |
| 2745 | Posy Bamboo | | |
| 2746 | Jardiniere | | |
| 2747 | Plant pot Bamboo | | |
| 2748 | Twin vase | s/s | |
| 2749 | Posy bar Bamboo | 6¼"l –1970s | |
| 2750 | Posy bar curved Bamboo | 8½"l –1970s | |
| 2751 | Vase | 9¼" | |
| 2752 | Vase Bamboo | 7½" | |
| 2753 | Vase | 10" | |
| 2754 | Vase | 6½" | |
| 2755 | N/I | | |
| 2756 | Cat | | |
| 2757 | Seal | | |
| 2758 | Owl | | |
| 2759 | Dog | | |
| 2760 | Dog | | |
| 2761 | Dog | | |
| 2762 | Dog | | |
| 2763 | Egg cup | | |
| 2764 | Dog | | |
| 2765 | N/I | | |
| 2766 | Posy trough Bamboo | 6¼"acr –1970s | |
| 2767 | Posy 'L' shape Bamboo | 6"l | |
| 2768 | Bowl on stand Corinthus | 8"acr | |
| 2769 | Pot | | |
| 2770 | Vase ribbed base | 8¼"h | |
| 2771 | Wall vase | | |
| 2772 | Vase | | |
| 2773 | Vase Lattice range | 8½"h 5½"dia | |
| 2774 | Jardiniere fan shape sim to 2780 | 5½"h 10½"l | |
| 2775 | Wall vase | | |
| 2776 | Vase | | |
| 2777 | Vase bamboo decoration | 6¼"h 4¼"dia | |
| 2778 | N/I | | |
| 2779 | Vase | | |
| 2780 | Jardiniere fan shape sim to 2774 also with Bamboo decoration no handles | 7"l | |
| 2781 | Vase | | |
| 2782 | Swan | | |
| 2783 | Posy Moselle p79 TSC with Cupid | 5½"l –1982 | |
| 2784 | Bulb bowl embossed basket weave | 6"l –1970s | |
| 2785 | Plant pot p86 TSC also Autumn Chintz | 5½–5¾"h –1982+ | |
| 2786 | Vase | | |
| 2787 | Bowl | | |
| 2788 | Basket Bamboo range | 8¼"h 8¼"l | |
| 2789 | Crib | | |
| 2790 | Plant pot p86 TSC also Autumn Chintz | 4¾"h –1982+ | |
| 2791 | Vase | | |
| 2792 | Jardiniere Cone range | 6¼"h 10"l | |
| 2793 | Posy | | |
| 2794 | Cat flat sim to 2722 and 2795 | s/s | |
| 2795 | Cat flat sim to 2722 and 2794 p105 TSS | l/s 6½"h 4½"w | |
| 2796 | Plant pot | 4¼"h –1982+ | |
| 2797 | Dog | | |
| 2798 | Owl and tree trunk SCC/15 | 3"h | |
| 2799 | Gnome and bamboo | 3"h | |
| 2800 | Fox and pine cone | 3"h | |
| 2801 | Jardiniere Lattice | 5½"h 10¼"l | |
| 2802 | N/I | | |
| 2803 | Vase on stand | 6"h | |
| 2804 | Jardiniere p99 TSC (numbered 2894 in error) | 7½"l | |
| 2805 | Bowl | | |
| 2806 | N/I | | |
| 2807 | Coconut with two monkeys sim to 1190 | 3"h | |
| 2808 | Pot | | |
| 2809 | Coffee jug re-numbered 4048 | | |
| 2810 | Bird stand | | |
| 2811 | Jardiniere | | |
| 2812 | Bowl on stand Corinthus | 14¼"l | |
| 2813 | Monkey jug | | |
| 2814 | Vase on stand Corinthus | 7"h | |
| 2815 | Burns Toby | | |
| 2815 | Shakespeare character jug new number 4491 in 1969 | 5"h | |
| 2816 | Jardiniere scalloped rim Bamboo | 4¼"h 7¼"l | |
| 2817 | Jardiniere fan shape Lattice range p100 TSC | 6¾"h 3"w | |
| 2818 | N/I | | |
| 2819 | Vase on stand Corinthus | 10"h | |
| 2820 | Vase | | |
| 2821 | Vase Lattice range | 10"h | |
| 2822 | Figure | | |
| 2823 | Bowl | | |
| 2824 | Figure St. Francis of Assisi (proto-type, not produced) | 8½"h | |
| 2825 | Pot | | |
| 2826 | Bookend | | |
| 2827 | Vase on stand Corinthus | 8"h | |
| 2828 | Bowl on stand Corinthus | 9¾"acr | |
| 2829 | Pen holder often with girl or boy attached p116 TSC | 3¾"h | |
| 2830 | Pot Cone range | | |
| 2831 | Vase Cone range | 7"h | |
| 2832 | Trough Cone range | | |
| 2833 | Trough Cone range | | |
| 2834 | Jardiniere Cone range | | |
| 2835 | Bowl Cone range | 3¼"h 6½"l | |
| 2836 | Jardiniere Cone range | | |
| 2837 | N/I | | |
| 2838 | Wall vase | | |
| 2839 | N/I | | |
| 2840 | Vase | | |
| 2841 | Shakespeare book vase p111 TSS | 6⅛"h | |
| 2842 | Figure | | |
| 2843 | Trough Lattice range | 13½"l | |
| 2844 | Vase | | |
| 2845 | Girl | | |
| 2846 | Vase Oakleaf range | 6½–7"h | |
| 2847 | Vase | | |
| 2848 | Vase | | |
| 2849 | Pot | | |
| 2850–2951 | N/I | | |
| 2852 | Jardiniere | | |
| 2853 | N/I | | |
| 2854 | Bowl | | |
| 2855–2859 | N/I | | |
| 2860 | Vase | 8¼"h | |
| 2861 | Vase | | |
| 2862 | Gondola bowl | | |
| 2863 | Dutch clog embossed windmill, girl and boy | 4½"l | |
| 2864 | Goblet vase p86 TSC | 7"h –1970s | |
| 2865 | Goblet vase | | |
| 2866 | Bookend | | |
| 2867 | Shell | | |
| 2868 | Shell | | |
| 2869 | Shell | | |
| 2870 | Vase Apple Blossom p74 TSC | 8¼"h –1970s | |
| 2871 | N/I | | |
| 2872 | Jardiniere Apple Blossom p74 TSC | 10½"l –1970s | |

| | | | |
|---|---|---|---|
| **2873** | Bowl | | |
| **2874** | Bowl on feet Apple Blossom p74 TSC | 7″l –1970s | |
| **2875** | Posy bar Apple Blossom p74 TSC | 7¾″l –1970s | |
| **2876** | Vase Apple Blossom p74 TSC | 6¼″h –1970s | |
| **2877** | Plant pot Apple Blossom p74 TSC | 5¾″h –1970s | |
| **2878** | Plant pot Apple Blossom p74 TSC | 4¾″h –1970s | |
| **2879** | Pot | | |
| **2880** | Tray | | |
| **2881** | Goblet vase | | |
| **2882** | Bowl Apple Blossom p74 TSC | 7″l –1970s | |
| **2883** | Bowl Apple Blossom p74 TSC | 10¼″l –1970s | |
| **2884** | Trough Apple Blossom p74 TSC | 14″l –1970s | |
| **2885** | Plate Apple Blossom p74 TSC | 9¼″acr –1970s | |
| **2886** | Posy bar | | |
| **2887** | Figure | | |
| **2888** | Uncle Sam Character jug SCC/8 | | |
| **2889** | Trough | | |
| **2890** | Bowl two handles | | |
| **2891** | Bowl | | |
| **2892** | Abraham Lincoln Character jug | | |
| **2893** | Vase Bracken range embossed bracken leaves | Tall | |
| **2894** | Jardiniere Bracken range | 3¾″h 8½″l | |
| **2895** | Figure | | |
| **2896** | Vase | 6″h –1970s | |
| **2897** | Stocking | | |
| **2898** | N/I | | |
| **2899** | John F. Kennedy Character jug | 6¼″h | |
| **2899 also** | Cheese dish Wyka range | 6¾″acr | |
| **2900** | Vase | | |
| **2901** | Chinese vase | | |
| **2902** | Vase | | |
| **2903** | Figure St. Nicholas and child (proto-type, not produced) SCC/19 | 8½″h | |
| **2904** | Jardiniere Bracken range | 6¼″h 9½″l | |
| **2906** | Plant Pot Bracken | 6–7″h | |
| **2907** | Jardiniere Jewel range | 3¾″h 6½″l | |
| **2908** | N/I | | |
| **2909** | Bowl Bracken range (number indistinct) | 4″h 8¾″l | |
| **2910** | Pot | | |
| **2911** | N/I | | |
| **2912** | Giraffe p61 TSS | 5½″h | |
| **2913** | Tray | | |
| **2914** | Vase | | |
| **2915** | Vase | | |
| **2916** | Biscuit jar | | |
| **2917** | Wall vase | | |
| **2918** | N/I | | |
| **2919** | Bowl | | |
| **2920** | Vase | | |
| **2921–2922** | N/I | | |
| **2923** | Bowl Oakleaf | 3½″h | |
| **2924** | N/I | | |
| **2925** | Jardiniere Oakleaf | 11″l | |
| **2926** | N/I | | |
| **2927** | Vase Oakleaf p98 TSC | 8″h | |
| **2928–2929** | N/I | | |
| **2930** | Colour code denoting hand painted natural colours example p37 TSS | | |
| **2931** | Jardiniere Oakleaf | 6½″h 10½″l | |
| **2932** | Jardiniere Oakleaf | 6″h 7″l | |
| **2933** | Giraffe p61 TSS | 6″h | |
| **2934** | Vase | | |
| **2935** | Vase | | |
| **2936** | Vase | | |
| **2937** | Vase Apple Blossom p74 TSC | 10″h –1970s | |
| **2938** | Dog long face p24 TSC | 4″h –1982 | |
| **2939** | Barrow | | |
| **2940** | Serviette ring | | |
| **2941** | Jug 2 pint | 6½″h | |
| **2942** | Vase | | |
| **2943** | N/I | | |
| **2944** | Jug | | |
| **2945** | Mug Avon shape p50/63 TSC | 4¼″h –1982 | |
| **2946** | Zebra | | |
| **2947** | Beaker | | |
| **2948** | Bowl | | |
| **2949** | Vase | | |
| **2950** | Dog long face p24 TSC | 5¼″h –1982 | |
| **2951** | Dog long face p24 TSC | 7″h –1982 | |
| **2952** | N/I | | |
| **2953** | Bowl | | |
| **2954** | Jardiniere Magnolia p75 TSC | 9″l –1970s | |
| **2955** | Crouching bunny p61 TSS limited edition re-produced c1990 | 8½″l | |
| **2956** | Honey Wyka range | 4½″h | |
| **2957** | Cheese dish | | |
| **2958** | Honey pot | | |
| **2959** | Butter dish | | |
| **2960** | Tray | | |
| **2961** | Salad bowl | | |
| **2962** | Poodle dog p20 TSC s/s sim to 5025/5031 | 5¼″h –1982 | |
| **2963** | Shell containing hand painted china flowers | 2½″h | |
| **2964** | Shell | | |
| **2965** | Pot | | |
| **2966** | Teapot | | |
| **2967** | Teapot | | |
| **2968** | Sugar bowl | | |
| **2969** | Teapot | | |
| **2970** | Ashtray/posy 'With compliments' p39 TSC | 4½″l | |
| **2971** | Poodle dog playing | 6½″l –1970s | |
| **2972** | Vase | | |
| **2973** | Dachshund dog curled up | 5″l | |
| **2974** | Mongrel pup p20 TSC | 5½″h –1982+ | |
| **2975** | Vase | | |
| **2976** | Teapot Avon p50 TSC | 5¾″h –1982 | |
| **2977** | Sugar bowl Avon p50/63 TSC | 3¼″acr –1982 | |
| **2978** | Cream jug Avon p50 TSC s/s | 3″h –1982 | |
| **2979** | Vase embossed Bracken | 8″h | |
| **2980** | Rabbit p61 TSS | 6″h | |
| **2981** | Vase Magnolia p75 TSC | 9″h –1970s | |
| **2982** | Teapot Avon p50 TSC s/s | 5″h –1970s | |
| **2983** | Vase | 9″h | |
| **2984** | Basket | | |
| **2985** | Bowl | | |
| **2986** | Cress dish and stand | 9½″acr | |
| **2987** | Basket | | |
| **2988** | Tray | | |
| **2989** | Bowl | | |
| **2990** | Cress dish and stand | | |
| **2991** | Jardiniere Oak Leaf p98 TSC | 5″h 7½″l | |
| **2992** | Vase Magnolia p75 TSC | 6¼″h –1970s | |
| **2993** | Jardiniere no handles Magnolia range p75 TSC | 6¾″l –1970s | |
| **2994** | N/I | | |
| **2995** | Plant pot Magnolia p75 TSC | 5″h –1970s | |
| **2996** | Cream jug Wyka range | 2¾″h | |
| **2997** | Vase Wyka range | 10½″h | |
| **2998** | Butter dish Wyka range | 7″l | |
| **2999** | Cheese dish | | |
| **3000** | Salad bowl Wyka range | 11″acr | |
| **3001** | Cruet Wyka three piece | 3½″h (mustard) | |
| **3002** | Sandwich tray Wyka range | 11½″l | |
| **3003** | Twin tray Wyka range | 11½″l | |
| **3004** | Triple tray Wyka range | 15″l | |
| **3005** | Toast rack Wyka range | 9½″l | |
| **3006** | Vase Wyka range | 12½″h | |
| **3007** | Cress dish and stand Wyka | 8¼″acr | |
| **3008** | N/I | | |
| **3009** | Jug Wyka range | 8″h | |
| **3010** | Cheese dish Wyka range | 7″l | |
| **3011** | Vase | 8¼″h | |
| **3012** | Beaker Wyka range | 4½″h | |
| **3013** | Sugar bowl Wyka range | 3¼″acr | |
| **3014** | N/I | | |

**Circa 1962**

| | | |
|---|---|---|
| 3015 | Jardiniere Oak Leaf | 3½"h 8"l |
| 3016 | N/I | |
| 3017 | Posy | |
| 3018 | Posy embossed Bracken | |
| 3019 | Pig money box 1/s p119 TSC Caricature range | 4¼–4½"h 7½"l –1982 |
| 3020 | Pot | |
| 3021 | N/I | |
| 3022 | Plant pot Magnolia p75 TSC | 5¾"h –1970s |
| 3023 | Jardiniere embossed Bracken | 4"h 8½"l |
| 3024 | N/I | |
| 3025 | Vase Slymcraft p76 TSC | 6¼"h –1982 |
| 3026 | Vase | |
| 3027 | Vase | |
| 3028 | Vase | |
| 3029 | Vase Slymcraft | 11¾"h |
| 3030 | Vase Slymcraft p76 TSC | 7½"h – 1982+ |
| 3031 | Vase Chesterfield range | 6"h |
| 3032 | Vase Slymcraft | 8¾"h |
| 3033 | Vase | |
| 3034 | Vase | |
| 3035 | Vase | |
| 3036 | Vase Slymcraft p76 TSC | 7¾"h –1982 |
| 3037 | Vase Slymcraft p76 TSC | 9¾"h –1982 |
| 3038 | Vase Slymcraft | 9¾"h |
| 3039 | Vase Slymcraft p76 TSC | 9¾"h –1982+ |
| 3040 | Vase Slymcraft p63/76 TSC | 3¾"h –1982 |
| 3041 | Vase | |
| 3042 | Vase Slymcraft | 7¾"h |
| 3043 | Vase Slymcraft p76 TSC | 5¾"h –1982+ |
| 3044 | Vase Slymcraft p76 TSC | 7¾"h –1982 |
| 3045 | Vase | |
| 3046 | Vase Slymcraft | 7¾"h |
| 3047 | Vase Slymcraft p76 TSC | 9¾"h –1982 |
| 3048 | Vase Slymcraft p76 TSC | 7¾"h –1982 |
| 3049 | Vase Slymcraft | 12"h |
| 3050 | Vase round | 2¾"h |
| 3051 | Vase Slymcraft p76 TSC | 7½"h –1982 |
| 3052 | Vase Slymcraft | 6½"h |
| 3053 | Vase Chesterfield range | 10¼"h |
| 3054 | Vase Chesterfield range | 8¼"h |
| 3055 | Vase Slymcraft | 9¾"h |
| 3056 | Vase Slymcraft | 9¾"h |
| 3057 | Plant pot Chesterfield | 5"h |
| 3058 | Plant pot Chesterfield | 6"h |
| 3059 | Vase Slymcraft | 7¾"h |
| 3060 | Vase | |
| 3061 | Vase Slymcraft | 9¾"h |
| 3062 | Vase Slymcraft | 7½"h |
| 3063 | Vase Slymcraft p76 TSC | 5½"h –1982 |
| 3064 | Vase p67 TSC | 10"h –1982+ |
| 3065 | Vase Slymcraft p76 TSC | 3½"h –1982 |
| 3066 | Vase Slymcraft p76 TSC | 5¾"h –1982 |
| 3067 | Vase Slymcraft p76 TSC | 10"h –1982 |
| 3068 | Bowl Slymcraft | 5½"acr |
| 3069 | Jardiniere Chesterfield | 9¼"l |
| 3070 | Vase | |
| 3071 | Bowl Slymcraft | 7¾"dia |
| 3072 | Jardiniere Chesterfield | 6¼"l |
| 3073 | Vase | |
| 3074 | Dog | |
| 3075 | Manx cat sim to frightened cat 1046 | 3⅜"h |
| 3076 | Flower holder | |
| 3077 | Dachshund dog sitting | 6½"h –1970s |
| 3078 | Dachshund dog sitting | 5"h –1970s |
| 3079 | N/I | |
| 3080 | Basket | |
| 3081 | Bowl | |
| 3082 | Vase | |
| 3083 | Bowl | |
| 3084 | Trough | |
| 3085 | Dish Slymcraft p76 TSC | 10¼"l |
| 3086 | Ashtray round, advertising SylvaC, 1,000 made for dealers and stockists SCC/5 | 6¼"acr |

| | | |
|---|---|---|
| 3087 | N/I | |
| 3088 | Zebra | |
| 3089 | Vase | |
| 3090–3091 | N/I | |
| 3092 | 'Sammy Spaniel' sim to 1246 and 1247 | 4"h |
| 3093 | 'Toby' Toothache dog sim to 2451/2455/3183 | 4"h |
| 3094–3095 | N/I | |
| 3096 | Terrier dog p61 TSS | 4½"h |
| 3097 | Chipmunk p61 TSS | 5½"h |
| 3098 | Vase Lily range | 6½"l |
| 3099 | Candle holder | |
| 3100 | Posy trough Chesterfield | 7½"l |
| 3101 | Posy holder Lily range | 10"l |
| 3102 | Kitten chasing tail | |
| 3103 | N/I | |
| 3104 | Vase | |
| 3105 | Ashtray | |
| 3106 | Robert Burns Character jug | 5¾"h |
| 3107 | Vase | |
| 3108–3109 | N/I | |

**THE FOLLOWING MOULD NUMBERS WERE ISSUED TO THE FALCON POTTERY circa 1947 – 1957**

| | | |
|---|---|---|
| 3110 | Poodle dog p41 TSS | 4¾"h –1970 |
| 3111 | Wall vase | |
| 3111 also | Girl Pam p37 TSS | 3"h |
| 3112 | Boy Paul p37 TSS | 2¾"h |
| 3113 | Boy Pete p37 TSS | 3¼"h |
| 3114 | Puppy dog p37/38 TSS | 3"h |
| 3115 | Duckling p37 TSS | 1½"h |
| 3116 | Puppy dog p37/38 TSS | 2¼"h |
| 3117 | Duckling p37 TSS | 2"h |
| 3118 | Puppy dog p37 TSS | 3½"h |
| 3119 | Horse p48 TSS | 5½"h |
| 3120 | Hare p37 TSS | 4"h |
| 3121 | Cat p37 TSS | 2½"h |
| 3122 | Ashtray p37 TSS | |
| 3123 | Mongrel sitting smiling | 5¾"h |
| 3124 | Dachshund p48 TSS | 4½"h –1970s |
| 3125 | Dog | |
| 3126 | Griffon dog lying | 4"h |
| 3127 | Rabbit | |
| 3128 | Corgi dog p41 TSS p19 TSC | 4¼"h –1982+ |
| 3129 | Horse with saddle | 5½"h |
| 3130 | Horse standing | 5½"h |
| 3131 | Donkey | |
| 3132 | Dog with panniers p38 TSS | 2¼"h |
| 3133 | Corgi puppy sitting p41/43 TSS | 2½"h –1970s |
| 3134 | Corgi puppy playing p43 TSS | 1½"h |
| 3135 | Corgi puppy lying p43 TSS | 2"h |
| 3136 | Corgi dog standing p41/43 TSS | 3¾–4"h –1970s |
| 3137 | Corgi puppy standing p41/43 TSS | 2¾"h –1970s |
| 3138 | Donkey with panniers or cart p2 TSS | 4"h –1970s |
| 3139 | Donkey p2 TSS | 4"h –1982 |
| 3140 | 'Dumbo' elephant p29 TSC | 5"l |
| 3141 | Boxing monkey p50 TSS | 4¾"h |
| 3142 | Dog | |
| 3143 | Dog | |
| 3144 | Horse grazing p48 TSS | 5"h –1982 |
| 3145 | Foal standing p48 TSS | 4¼"h –1982 |
| 3146 | Cockerel | |
| 3147 | Laughing donkey | |
| 3148 | N/I | |
| 3149 | Horse | |
| 3150 | Foal standing p48 TSS | 4"h –1982 |
| 3151 AM | Cat sitting p80 TSS | 5½"h 8¼"l |
| 3151 also | Vase | |
| 3152 AM | Horse/Zebra p80 TSS | 10"h |
| 3153 AM | Tigress sitting p80 TSS | 5½"h 7½"l |
| 3154 AM | Stag sitting p37/80 TSS | 6½"h 7¼"l |
| 3155 | Cart horse p48 TSS | 6½"h –1982 |
| 3156 | Swallow wall plaque p47 TSS | 6½"l –1970s |

| | | | |
|---|---|---|---|
| 3157 | Swallow wall plaque p47 TSS | 5″l –1970s | |
| 3158 | Swallow wall plaque p47 TSS | 5″l –1970s | |
| 3159–3161 | N/I | | |
| 3162 | Grebe to go in bowl 702 p50/54 TSS | 3½″h 6″l | |
| 3163 | Cat | | |
| 3164 | Pekinese puppy p41 TSS | 2½″h –1970s | |
| 3165 | Pekinese dog p41 TSS p20 TSC | 3″h 4½″l –1982+ | |
| 3166 | Staffordshire Bull Terrier p41 TSS p20 TSC | 4½″h –1982+ | |
| 3167 | Cat sitting p42 TSS | 5″h | |
| 3168 | Kitten in wool p32/84 TSS | 2¾″h | |
| 3169 | Golden Retriever p20 TSC p41 TSS | 5¼″h –1982+ | |
| 3170 | Alsatian standing p41/77 TSS | 5¾″h –1970s | |
| 3171 | Alsatian standing p41 TSS | 4″h | |
| 3172 | Goat standing p47 TSS | 5¼″h –1970s | |
| 3173 | Chow dog standing p41 TSS p19 TSC | 4¾″h –1982+ | |
| 3174 | Poodle playing p42 TSS | 5¾″h | |
| 3175 | Dachshund on hind legs p42 TSS | 5½″h | |
| 3176 | Horse standing p48 TSS | 7¼″h –1982+ | |
| 3177 | Sealyham puppy p42 TSS | 5″h | |
| 3178 | Dog | | |
| 3179 | Sealyham dog p42 TSS | 4″h | |
| 3180 | Horse p48 TSS p32 TSC also with Governess trap | 9″h –1982 17½″l | |
| 3181 | N/I | | |
| 3182 | 'Goofy' dog p42 TSS | 5½″h –1970s | |
| 3183 | 'Toby' Toothache dog p42 TSS sim to 2451/2455/3192 | 5¼″h –1970s | |
| 3184 | N/I | | |
| 3185 | Bowl | | |
| 3186 | Tray | | |

## CONTINUATION OF SYLVAC WARE MOULD NUMBERS
**Circa 1962**

| | | | |
|---|---|---|---|
| 3187 | Dog Cruet p59 TSS | | |
| 3188 | Bowl Chesterfield fluted | 7″l | |
| 3189 | Trough Slymcraft p76/106 TSC | 14¾″l –1982 | |
| 3190 | Bowl Chesterfield fluted | 9¼″l | |
| 3191 | Bowl | | |
| 3192 | Vase | | |
| 3193 | Bulb bowl brick design | 9″l –1970s | |
| 3194 | Bulb bowl brick design | 6¼″l –1970s | |
| 3195 | Bowl | | |
| 3196 | Bowl Magnolia p75 TSC | 8″acr –1970s | |
| 3197 | Basket | | |
| 3198–3202 | N/I | | |
| 3203 | Hot water jug 1¼pint | 5¾″h –1970s | |
| 3204 | Cream jug Avon p50/63 TSC | 3¾″h –1982 | |
| 3205 | N/I | | |
| 3206 | Butter dish Avon p50 TSC | 7″l –1982 | |
| 3207 | Cheese dish Avon p50 TSC | 8½″l –1982 | |
| 3208 | Sandwich tray Avon p50 TSC | 12½″l –1982 | |
| 3209 | Honey Avon p50/63 TSC | 4″h –1982 | |
| 3210 | Post trough Trellis design | 2″h 7¾″l (top) | |
| 3211 | Jardiniere | | |
| 3212 | Bowl | | |
| 3213 | Bowl Magnolia p75 TSC | 13½″l –1970s | |
| 3214 | Bowl Magnolia p75 TSC | 9¼″l –1970s | |
| 3215 | Trough Magnolia p75 TSC | 7½″l –1970s | |
| 3216 | Vase Magnolia p75 TSC | 10″h –1970s | |
| 3217 | Vase Magnolia p75 TSC | 8″h –1970s | |
| 3218 | Bowl Magnolia p75 TSC | 6½″l –1970s | |
| 3219 | Tankard with horses | 5″h –1970s | |
| 3220 | Tankard with fish | 5″h –1970s | |
| 3221 | Jardiniere Magnolia p75 TSC | 12″l –1970s | |
| 3222 | Bowl | | |
| 3223 | Log | | |
| 3224 | Bowl | | |
| 3225 | Jardiniere Slymcraft p109 TSC | 12¾–14″l –1982 | |
| 3226 | Tankard with wild ducks | 5″h –1970s | |
| 3227 | Bowl | | |
| 3228 | Vase | | |
| 3229 | N/I | | |

| | | | |
|---|---|---|---|
| 3230 | Vase fish shape | 7″h | |
| 3231 | Candle holder, three holders on oval plate | 2½″h 13″l | |
| 3232 | Vase | | |
| 3233 | Log bowl | 8″l | |
| 3234 | Log bowl | 4½″l | |
| 3235 | Log bowl | 4¾″l | |
| 3236 | Vase | | |
| 3237 | Tray | | |
| 3238 | Cup Avon shape p50 TSC | 3″h –1982 | |
| 3238 also | Saucer Avon shape p50 TSC | 5½″dia –1982 | |
| 3239 | Elephant money box or with flowers p29 TSC sim to 1153 | 4¼″h (with flowers) | |
| 3240 | Pig | | |
| 3241 | Dog | | |
| 3242 | N/I | | |
| 3243 | Bowl | 8¾″l | |
| 3244 | Bowl | 6″l | |
| 3245 | Pot | | |
| 3246 | Bowl | | |
| 3247 | Vase Lily range | 10″h | |
| 3248 | N/I | | |
| 3249 | Bowl | | |
| 3250 | Vase | | |
| 3251 | Bowl | | |
| 3252 | Vase "Lager" shape sim to 3323 and 3324 | m/s | |
| 3253 | Cup | | |
| 3254 | Bowl | | |
| 3255 | Vase Chesterfield fluted | 10″h | |
| 3256 | Vase Chesterfield fluted | 8″h | |
| 3257 | Plate with scroll handles | 9″dia | |
| 3258 | Cream jug | | |
| 3259 | Bowl | | |
| 3260 | Bowl | | |
| 3261 | Jardiniere Fuchsia range | 1/s | |
| 3261 also | Plate (plaque) p67 TSC | 10″dia –1982 | |
| 3262 | Bowl boat shaped Fuchsia range | 3½″h 14″l | |
| 3262 also | Plate Nursery range p63/64 TSS | 8″acr –1982+ | |
| 3263 | Plate Nursery and Avon p63/64 TSS p50 TSC | 6½″acr –1982+ | |
| 3263 also | Vase Fuchsia range | | |
| 3264 | Cereal dish Nursery and Avon p63/64 TSS p50 TSC | 6¼″acr –1982+ | |
| 3265 | Posy trough Fuchsia range | 7¾″l | |
| 3265 also | Fruit dish | | |
| 3266 | Jardiniere Fuchsia range | 4″h 6¾″l | |
| 3266 also | Bread and butter plate Avon shape p50 TSC | 11″dia –1982 | |
| 3267 | Cake stand single tier | 8″dia | |
| 3268 | Cake stand Avon shape two tier p50 TSC | 9½″dia –1982 | |
| 3269 | Vase Fuchsia range p99 TSC | 7¾″h | |
| 3269 also | Fruit bowl Avon shape p50 TSC | 8½″dia –1982 | |
| 3270 | Plant pot Fuchsia range | 5″h | |
| 3270 also | Soup bowl | | |
| 3271 | Plant pot Fuchsia range | | |
| 3272 | Jardiniere Fuschia range | 5″h 12″l | |
| 3273 | Tankard with fox p63 TSC | 3¾″h –1982 | |
| 3274 | Tankard with hound p63 TSC | 3¾″h –1982 | |
| 3274 also | Tankard as above but with Stoke City shield and STOKE CITY WEMBLEY CUP FINAL 1972 embossed | 3¾″h | |
| 3275 | Spaniel with pipe p39 TSC | 5¼″h | |
| 3276 | Spaniel with ball p103 TSS | 3¼″h 6½″l | |
| 3277 | Vase | | |
| 3278 | Tankard with horse p88 TSS p63 TSC | 3¾″h –1982 | |
| 3279 | George Bernard Shaw character jug renumbered 4492 | 5½″h –1970s | |
| 3280 | Log bowl | 6″l | |
| 3281 | Cup | | |
| 3282 | Flower jug | 15″h | |
| 3283 | Vase Lily range | 8¼″h | |
| 3284 | Vase | | |
| 3285 | Jardiniere Lily range | 10″l | |
| 3286 | Vase Lily range | 12″h | |

| | | |
|---|---|---|
| 3287 | Bowl Lily range | 9¾"l |
| 3288 | Plant pot Lily range | 8"acr |
| 3289 | Posy trough Lily range | 7¼"h |
| 3290 | Jardiniere Lily range | 11¾"h |
| 3291 | Plant pot Lily range | 7"acr |
| 3292 | Bowl Lily range | 6½"l |
| 3293–3295 | N/I | |
| 3296 | Cruet three piece on stand Avon shape p50 TSC | –1982 |
| 3297 | Cheese board and knife Avon shape p50 TSC | 9¾"l –1970s |
| 3298 | Vase | |
| 3299 | Toast rack Avon shape p50 TSC | 7½"l –1982 |
| 3300–3302 | N/I | |
| 3303 | Vase | |
| 3304 | Beaker | |
| 3305 | Vase | |
| 3306 | Tankard | |
| 3307 | Cat, long neck, flat face | |
| 3308 | Jardiniere | |
| 3309 | Jardiniere | 15½"l –1970s |
| 3310 | Jardiniere Slymcraft range | 9"l –1982 |

**From 12th December 1962 the modellers initials appear next to the mould numbers.**

| | | |
|---|---|---|
| 3311 C | Bowl with bird attached | |
| 3312 RT | Vase sim to 3316 | 6½"h |
| 3313 SC | Cupid flower holder oval | 3¾"h |
| 3314 SC | Smooth haired fox terrier p110 TSS | 5¾"h |
| 3315 JL | Coffee pot Avon shape 2pnt p50 TSC | 9"h –1982 |
| 3316 RT | Vase sim to 3312 | 8½"h |
| 3317 SC | Wire Haired Fox Terrier standing | 5½"h |
| 3318 SC | Wire Haired Fox Terrier lying down curled up p104 TSS | 1¾"h 5"acr |
| 3319 SC | 'Silly Pup' sitting | |

**January 1963**

| | | |
|---|---|---|
| 3320 SC | Dachshund puppy sitting | s/s |
| 3321 SC | Alsatian sitting | 6"h –1970s |
| 3322 JL | Lop eared rabbit | m/s |
| 3323 JL | Vase 'Lager' shape s/s sim to 3252/3324 | 6¼"h |
| 3324 JL | Vase 'Lager' shape l/s sim to 3252/3323 | 10"h |
| 3325 SC | Cupid flower holder round | 4½"h |
| 3326 JL | Lop eared rabbit | l/s |
| 3327 JL | Rabbit ears erect | |
| 3328 JL | Rabbit ears erect | 8"h |
| 3329 SC | Vase Shell | 7"h |
| 3330 JL | Vase | 8"h |
| 3331 SC | Plant pot round ribbed | |
| 3332 SC | Plant pot square ribbed | |
| 3333 SC | Cupid flower holder cornucopia | 4½"h |
| 3334 | Flower holder sea shell base of 3260 | 5"l |
| 3335 SC | Spaniel sitting | |
| 3336 SC | Flower pot square ribbed | |
| 3337 JL | Pig | 3½"l |
| 3338 SC | West Highland Terrier sitting | |
| 3339 RT | Osprey Prestige Pieces p14/50 TSS | 8½"h –1982 |
| 3340 | Ginger jar with cover | 6"h |
| 3341 JL | Jardiniere Opelle oval fluted sides p108 TSC | |
| 3342 JL | Vase | 7"h |
| 3343 JL | Vase | 5½"h |
| 3344 JL | Vase | 5"h |
| 3345 JL | Jardiniere/small trough | s/s |
| 3346 JL | Pig head money box | |
| 3347 | Vase fluted panel curvy top | 7½"h |
| 3348 JL | Jardiniere | 10½"l |
| 3349 RT | Jardiniere Pebbles p77 TSC (no handles) | 10"l –1970s |

| | | |
|---|---|---|
| 3350 JL | Vase Pebbles range p77 TSC | 6¾"h –1970s |
| 3351 JL | Planter pattern as 3347 | |
| 3352 RT | Ginger jar embossed | |
| 3353 JL | Coffee pot | s/s |
| 3354 RT | Jar square with cover | |
| 3355 JL | Bowl Pebbles range p77 TSC | 6¾"dia –1970s |
| 3356 RT | Bowl oblong log with novelty | 2¼"h |
| 3357 RT | Jar Blossom | |
| 3358 JL | Vase Pebbles range p77 TSC | 9"h –1970s |
| 3359 RT | Jar square engraved pattern | |
| 3360 RT | Posy Pebbles p77/107 TSC | 11½"l –1970s |
| 3361 JL | Plant pot Pebbles p77 TSC | 4½"l –1970s |
| 3362 | Vase flat sides as 3374 | 5"h |
| 3363 JL | Posy bar pattern as 3347 | 8½"l |
| 3364 RT | Vase sim to 3369 Alpine | 8"h |
| 3365 JL | Posy bar pattern as 3347 | 6½"l |
| 3366 JL | Posy bar pattern as 3347 | 4"l |
| 3367 RT | Jar square engraved pattern | |
| 3368 JL | Vase Pebbles p77/108 TSC | 11¼"h –1970s |
| 3369 RT | Vase rope handles sim to 3364 Alpine range | 8"h |
| 3370 SC | Seahorse bowl on stand p109 TSC | 10"h |
| 3371 RT | Vase rope handles sim to 3369 Alpine range | 11"h |
| 3372 RT | Tea Caddy 'Sita Jar' with elephant head handles 100,000 made for Rington's Tea Company special Christmas offer 1963 SCC/13 | 7½"h |
| 3373 JL | Jardiniere pattern as 3347 | 3¼"h 7½"l |
| 3374 RT | Vase sim to 3362 engraved pattern | 5½"h |
| 3375 RT | Vase sim to 3362, embossed and incised as 3490 | 5½"h |
| 3376 JL | Jardiniere pattern as 3347 | 5½"h 10½"l |
| 3377 C | Plant pot | 5"h |
| 3378 C | Tray Feather range | 7½"l –1970s |
| 3379 JL | Vase rope handles Alpine range sim to 3369 | 8"h |
| 3380 JL | Vase rope handles sim to 3369 Alpine range | 8"h |
| 3381 JL | Jardiniere Alpine range | 11"h |
| 3382 JL | Vase Alpine range | 6"h |
| 3383 SC | Mule sitting p41/109 TSC | 6½"h |
| 3384 SC | Mule standing p50 TSS p41 TSC | 6½"h |
| 3385 JL | Vase rope seams Alpine | 8"h |
| 3386 JL | Jardiniere rope seams Alpine | s/s |
| 3387 JL | Bowl oval rope seams Alpine | s/s |
| 3388 JL | Bowl oval rope seams Alpine | l/s |
| 3389 JL | Pot rope seams Alpine | l/s |
| 3390 JL | Pot rope seams Alpine | s/s |
| 3391 JL | Posy bar rope seams | |
| 3392 SC | Long neck cat embossed with flowers p28 TSC | 12¾"h –1970s |
| 3393 RT | Duck | 4½"h |
| 3394 SC | Pipe ashtray woodgrain | 4¾"l –1970s |
| 3395 JL | Fern pot sim to 3351 | s/s |
| 3396 JL | Fern pot sim to 3351 | l/s |
| 3397 JL | Flower jug sim to 3351 | 10"h |
| 3398 JL | Vase sim to 3351 | 9"h |
| 3399 JL | Vase sim to 3351 | 8"h |
| 3400 JL | Vase Alpine sim to 3351 | 6"h |
| 3401 JL | Bowl Oval Alpine sim to 3351 | l/s |
| 3402 JL | Bowl oval sim to 3351 | s/s |
| 3403 SC | Long neck cat | 7"h |
| 3404 SC | Long neck cat p107 TSC | 6½"h –1970s |
| 3405 SC | Jar flower pattern | 6"h |
| 3406 SC | Cat, back paw to ear p106 TSS | 4¾"h |
| 3407 SC | Cat, front paw to ear p106 TSS | 4½"h |
| 3408 SC | Beaker | |
| 3409 SC | Pipe ashtray briar | 4¾"l –1970s |
| 3410 SC | Box ashtray | |
| 3411 JL | Mug | |
| 3412 JL | Vase | |
| 3413 SC | Beaker wheat pattern | |
| 3414 SC | Seahorse vase p108 TSC | 8"h |
| 3415 JL | Plant pot Pebbles p77/107 TSC | 6"h –1970s |

| | | |
|---|---|---|
| 3416 JL | Vase | |
| 3417 SC | Jar with cover | |
| 3418 SC | Shetland Sheepdog puppy | |
| 3419 JL | Bowl Pebbles range p77 TSC | 6½"l –1970s |
| 3420 JL | Posy trough Pebbles p77 TSC | 7¾"l –1970s |
| 3421 JL | Honey pot | |
| 3422 SC | Spaniel 'Funnies' range | 3¾"h 3½"l |
| 3423 SC | Old English Sheepdog 'Funnies' range p38 TSS | 3"h |
| 3424 SC | Pekinese 'Funnies' range | 2¾"h |
| 3425 SC | Alsatian 'Funnies' range | 3½"h 4¾"l |
| 3426 SC | Dachshund 'Funnies' p38 TSS | 3"h |
| 3427 SC | St. Bernard 'Funnies' range | 3"h 4¼"l |
| 3428 SC | Poodle 'Funnies' p38 TSS | 3⅝"h |
| 3429 SC | Bulldog 'Funnies' range | |
| 3430 SC | Shetland sheepdog 'Funnies' | 3¾"h 3¾"l |
| 3431 SC | Scottie dog 'Funnies' range | 3¼"h 4½"l |
| 3432 SC | Yorkshire Terrier 'Funnies' p38 TSS | 3¼"h |
| 3433 SC | Yawning dog 'Funnies' range p38 TSS | 4¼"h |
| 3434 JL | Trough Pebbles range p77 TSC | 13½"l –1970s |
| 3435 SC | Ashbox horses | |
| 3436 SC | Ashbox fish | |
| 3437 SC | Ashbox duck | |
| 3438 RT | Plinth Cyder Ad (sic) | |
| 3439 JL | Bowl Pebbles range p77 TSC | 9¾"l –1970s |
| 3440 JL | Bowl Pebbles range p77 TSC | 6½"l –1970s |
| 3441 RT | Vase | 6"h |
| 3442 SC | Jar | |
| 3443 SC | Vase oval 'Chequers' range alternate coloured squares | 8"h |
| 3444 SC | Vase 'Chequers' range | |
| 3445 SC | Seahorse stand sim to 3370 | s/s |
| 3446 RT | Basket | |
| 3447 RT | Cairn Terrier (modelled on Wendy, Reg Thompson's own beloved pet) p19 TSC | 5"h |
| 3448 SC | Vase or decanter | |
| 3449 JL | Vase Opelle range sim to 3341 | 6"h |
| 3450 JL | Vase Opelle range m/s | 8"h |
| 3451 JL | Vase Opelle range l/s | 10"h |
| 3452 RT | Cup "TEA" embossed | |
| 3453 JL | Posy bar Opelle range | |
| 3454 | Tray round with two handles and six dishes | |
| 3455 JL | Plant pot Opelle range | l/s |
| 3456 JL | Plant Pot Opelle range | s/s |
| 3457 SC | Long neck cat p107 TSC | 13"h –1970s |
| 3458 JL | Jardiniere Opelle range | |
| 3459 JL | Otter with fish Prestige range p14 TSS | 9½"l –1982 |
| 3460 SC | Seahorse vase p100 TSC | 10"h |
| 3461 JL | Bowl oblong Opelle range | l/s |
| 3462 JL | Bowl oblong Opelle range | s/s |
| 3463 JL | Bulb bowl square | |
| 3464 JL | Planter | 15" |
| 3465 JL | Float bowl Opelle range (withdrawn 1969) p107 TSC | 2¾"h 9½"l |
| 3466 JL | Wall vase Opelle p107 TSC | |
| 3467 RT | Ashtray 'Peter Rumsey' Abergavenny | |
| 3468 RT | Cup fluted | |
| 3469 | Boots reserved. (Probably means the number was reserved but not used.) | |
| 3470 SC | Seahorse posy s/s | 8"l |
| 3471 SC | Seahorse posy l/s | 8½"l |
| 3472 SC | Seahorse vase s/s | 6"h |
| 3473 | Seahorse jardiniere | s/s |
| 3474 SC | Seahorse bowl | l/s |
| 3475 SC | Seahorse bowl s/s | 5"h 9½"l |
| 3476 | Seahorse planter | |
| 3477 JL | Jardiniere Tudor | s/s |
| 3478 JL | Shaving mug sim to 4964 l/s | 4¼"h |
| 3479 SC | Bowl | |
| 3480 JL | Plant pot Pebbles p77 TSC | 5¼"h –1970s |
| 3481 JL | Ashtray Pebbles p77 TSC | 5¾"l –1970s |

| | | |
|---|---|---|
| 3482 JL | Dish Pebbles range p77 TSC | 12¾"l –1970s |
| 3483 JL | Vase flat front shape as 3441 | 5"h |
| 3484 | Celery tray Feather range | 13¾"l |
| 3485 | Salad bowl Feather range | 12"dia |
| 3486 JL | Grapefruit/Sundae bowl | 3½"h |
| 3487 JL | Vase, panel on front | 10"h |
| 3488 | Tankard ½pint, also Nottingham Forest Football Club Centenary 1865–1965 | 3¾"h |
| 3489 | Powder bowl ribbed with cover sim to 1821 | |
| 3490 RT | Vase Tudor range, incised panel on front | 6"h |
| 3491 RT | Vase Tudor range | 8"h |
| 3492 RT | Vase Tudor range p108 TSC | 10"h |
| 3493 RT | Jardiniere Tudor range | l/s |
| 3494 RT | Jardiniere Tudor range | s/s |
| 3495 RT | Bowl (low) Tudor range | |
| 3496 RT | Pot Tudor range | l/s |
| 3497 RT | Pot Tudor range | s/s |
| 3498 RT | Posy Tudor range | l/s |
| 3499 RT | Posy Tudor range | s/s |
| 3500 RT | Labrador p19/20 TSC | 5"h –1982+ |
| 3501 SC | Vase ribbed top | 9"h |
| 3502 W | Twin tray for butter and marmalade Feather range | 10"l 9"w |
| 3503 W | Triple tray Feather range | 12"l –1970s |
| 3504 W | Dish Feather range | 12¼"l –1970s |
| 3505 W | Cruet Feather range | 8¾"l (stand) |
| 3506 W | Twin tray Feather range | 11"l –1970s |
| 3507 W | Cress dish with stand Feather range | 10"acr –1970s |
| 3508 W | Cheese dish Feather range | |
| 3509 W | Cooky jar Feather range | |
| 3510 W | Tray four sections Feather | 14½"l –1970s |
| 3511 W | Butter dish oblong Feather | 6½"l (lid) |
| 3512 W | Twin preserve dish Feather | 11"l –1970s |
| 3513 W | Beaker Feather range | |
| 3514 W | Honey pot Feather range | |
| 3515 W | Dish Feather range | 5½"l –1970s |
| 3516 | Teacup | |
| 3517 | Pot panel on front | l/s |
| 3518 | Pot panel on front | s/s |

**Circa 1964**

| | | |
|---|---|---|
| 3519 JL | Cup | |
| 3520 JL | Butter dish square | |
| 3521 JL | Posy bar | |
| 3522 SC | Spaniel | |
| 3523 SC | Vase New Shell range | 8"h |
| 3524 SC | Vase New Shell p62 TSS | 10"h |
| 3525 SC | Jardiniere New Shell range | l/s |
| 3526 SC | Jardiniere New Shell s/s | 5¾"h 6¼"l |
| 3527 SC | Wall vase New Shell range | |
| 3528 SC | Posy New Shell range | 11"l |
| 3529 SC | Flower holder New Shell | 4¼"h 7½"l |
| 3530 SC | Bowl New Shell range s/s | 3¾"h 6½"l |
| 3531 SC | Bowl New Shell range | l/s |
| 3532 SC | Posy bar New Shell p62 TSS | 2⅛"h 7½"l |
| 3533 SC | Bowl with foot s/s | 6"h |
| 3534 SC | Bowl with foot l/s | 9"h |
| 3535 JL | Jardiniere | l/s |
| 3536 JL | Posy bar | |
| 3537 SC | Bowl fluted | |
| 3538 JL | Vase | 6"h |
| 3539 RT | Vase Tudor range | 6"h |
| 3540 JL | Vase sim to 3051 | 8"h |
| 3541 RT | Vase Tudor range | 8"h |
| 3542 RT | Mr. SylvaC with dog, 500 originally made for dealers but small quantity reissued 1989/90 by Crown Winsor (Pottery) Ltd. p43 TSS p15 TSC | 8"h |
| 3543 JL | Cup | |
| 3544 JL | Cup | |
| 3545 RT | Bowl | |
| 3546 RT | Tankard featuring Le Moulin de Lecq Inn, Jersey about 3,000 produced sim to 2603 | 3¾"h |

| Code | Description | Dimensions |
|------|-------------|------------|
| 3547 W | Cup and Saucer Magnolia | |
| 3548 JL | Vase on pedestal | 8″h |
| 3549 JL | Vase on pedestal | 8″h |
| 3550 RT | Lamp straight sides | 15½″h |
| 3551 JL | Vase on pedestal | 8″h |
| 3552 RT | Pug dog p20 TSC | 4½″h –1982+ |
| 3553 JL | Urn vase Vintage range | 7″h –1981 |
| 3554 RT | Butter dish Butterfly handle | |
| 3555 JL | Bowl on pedestal Evening Fantasy or for Grapefruit | 3⅞″acr –1970s |
| 3556 RT | Posy log also with novelty | |
| 3557 RT | Vase Lily range | 8″h |
| 3558 SC | Vase lower half ribbed | 13″h |
| 3559 JL | Urn Vintage range s/s | 5″h |
| 3560 RT | Bowl "wall" with dog p38 TSS | 3¼″h |
| 3561 SC | Bassett Hound p22 TSC | 6¾″h 5¾″l –1982+ |
| 3561 also | Cockerel | |
| 3562 SC | Bowl New Shell range | 12″ |
| 3562 also | Cockerel | |
| 3563 SC | Bassett Hound sitting up | 6¾″h –1970s |
| 3564 RT | Cup Butterfly handle | 3⅛″h |
| 3565 SC | Scottie dog for novelties p38 TSS (top right on 2054) | 2¾″h |
| 3566 RT | Barrel ashbox | |
| 3567 SC | Spaniel dog novelty used with 1996 basket | 2⅝″l |
| 3568 SC | Giraffe | 10″h |
| 3569 JL | Jug one pint Avon shape p50 TSC | 5½″h –1982 |
| 3570 SC | Elephant sitting | |
| 3571 SC | Basket and kitten novelty | |
| 3572 | Jardiniere with handles | |
| 3573 | Grapefruit bowl | |
| 3574 RT | Cricketers Schweppes Ad (see page 128 TSC) one off | |
| 3575 SC | Hare shell pattern | 7″h |
| 3576 RT | Honey Butterfly handle p86 TSS | 4½″h |
| 3577 SC | Jardiniere rose pattern shape as 3572 | |
| 3578 JL | Urn vase Vintage range | 9¼″h –1981 |
| 3579 JL | Urn vase Vintage range | 11¼″h –1981 |
| 3580 SC | Frog shell pattern | 4″h |
| 3581 JL | Vegetable dish | |
| 3582 JL | Porridge or soup dish | |
| 3583 SC | Penguin shell pattern | |
| 3584 JL | Flower jug on pedestal | 11″h |
| 3585 SC | Toucan shell pattern | |
| 3586 SC | Dog lying down shell pattern | |
| 3587 SC | Vase on feet | 8″h |
| 3588 RT | Bowl fluted | 11″acr |
| 3589 JL | Cheeseboard with fitted container | |
| 3590 RT | Pot raffia | 4″h |
| 3591 SC | Vase sim to 3587 | 6″h |
| 3592 JL | Bowl on pedestal | 11″ |
| 3593 RT | Vase or bottle | 6″h |
| 3594 JL | Meat dish oval | 15½″ |
| 3595 SC | Vase | 8″h |
| 3596 JL | Jug feather pattern | |
| 3597 RT | Pot 16ozs sim to 3590 | |
| 3598 JL | Vase oval | 8″h |
| 3599 JL | Sugar bowl feather | |
| 3600 JL | Jug feather | s/s |
| 3601 JL | Jug feather | l/s |
| 3602 SC | Vase shape as 3595 embossed | |
| 3603 SC | Vase shape as 3595 embossed | |
| 3604 JL | Jug Butterfly handle | |
| 3605 RT | Pot 12ozs | |
| 3606 JL | Cream jug Butterfly handle | |
| 3607 JL | Sugar bowl Butterfly | |
| 3608 RT | Bowl fluted | 3″h 6″dia |
| 3609 JL | Coffee can | |
| 3610 SC | Cat shell pattern | |
| 3611 JL | Gravy boat and stand | |
| 3612 SC | Mouse shell pattern | 4″h |
| 3613 RT | Honey pot hive | 4½″h |
| 3614 SC | Dog sitting | 5″h |
| 3615 SC | Dog sitting | 5″h |
| 3616 RT | Pot embossed 12ozs | |
| 3617 RT | Baby mug two handles p63/64 TSS | 3¼″h –1982+ |
| 3618 SC | Jardiniere (glass) | 11″l |
| 3619 JL | Cruet on stand Butterfly | |
| 3620 JL | Teapot Butterfly handle | |
| 3621 RT | Ashtray oblong | 6″l |
| 3622 SC | Jar triangle | |
| 3623 RT | Pot embossed 16ozs | |
| 3624 RT | Bowl Privet range p97 TSC | 7″acr –1981 |
| 3625 RT | Bowl (stones) | |
| 3626 RT | Top hat | 4″h |
| 3627 SC | Jar round | |
| 3628 JL | Coffee pot | |
| 3629 SC | Jar triangle embossed | |
| 3630 JL | Coffee pot | |
| 3631 SC | Vase | 8″h |
| 3632 RT | Tankard lining halfpint p89 TSC | 5″h –1982 |
| 3633 JL | Meat dish | 12″ |
| 3634 JL | Beaker | |
| 3635 JL | Sugar bowl | |
| 3636 RT | Cheese and biscuit tray | 14½″acr –1970s |
| 3637 SC | Jar embossed | 6″h |
| 3638 SC | Bowl stonewall pattern | 9½″ |
| 3639 RT | Jardiniere with handles | 13″ |
| 3640 JL | Coffee pot embossed | |
| 3641 RT | Ashtray | |
| 3642 SC | Basset Hound p22 TSC | 5″l –1982 |
| 3643 SC | Vase stonewall pattern | 9″h |
| 3644 RT | Mixing bowl | |
| 3645 RT | Tray | |
| 3646 JL | Beaker pattern as 3640 embossed | |
| 3647 JL | Coffee pot web pattern | |
| 3648 JL | Sugar bowl | |
| 3649 JL | Sugar bowl | |
| 3650 JL | Beaker web pattern | |
| 3651 JL | Jardiniere "tear drops" | 13″ |
| 3652 JL | Jardiniere | s/s |
| 3653 SC | Jardiniere stonewall pattern | |
| 3654 JL | Jardiniere l/s | 11″ |
| 3655 JL | Vase on pedestal | 10″h |
| 3656 JL | Vase | 8″h |
| 3657 JL | Vase | 6″h |
| 3658 JL | Pot | s/s |
| 3659 JL | Pot | l/s |
| 3660 SC | Ashtray three feet | 8″ |
| 3661 RT | Tankard lining one pint | 5½″h |
| 3662 SC | Vase | 6″h |
| 3663 JL | Bowl on pedestal | s/s |
| 3664 JL | Beaker on pedestal | |
| 3665 JL | Bowl on pedestal | m/s |
| 3666 JL | Bowl on pedestal | l/s |
| 3667 JL | Sugar bowl on pedestal | 2½″h |
| 3668 JL | Teapot on pedestal | 6″h |
| 3669 JL | Cream jug on pedestal | 3½″h |
| 3670 JL | Coffee pot fluted | |
| 3671 JL | Cup on pedestal | 3″h |
| 3672 JL | Cup embossed on pedestal | |
| 3673 JL | Cheese dish round on pedestal | |
| 3674 SC | Tyre ashtray | 5¾″dia |
| 3675 JL | Grandfather clock | 2″ |
| 3675 also | Dog | |
| 3676 RT | Vase/Jar | 6″h |
| 3677 JL | Cheese dish square pedestal | |
| 3678 RT | Vase Palm Leaf range | 8″h |
| 3679 JL | Cheese dish oblong Butterfly handle | |
| 3680 SC | Pot New Shell range | |
| 3681 RT | Bowl fluted sim to 3588/3608 | m/s |
| 3682 RT | Ashtray | 4″l |
| 3683 RT | Lamp Pebbles range | 12″h |
| 3684 SC | Shell shape posy holder | 6½″h |
| 3685 JL | Honey pot pattern as 3673 | |
| 3686 JL | Butter dish oblong pedestal pattern as 3673 | |
| 3687 JL | Coffee pot on pedestal pattern as 3673 | l/s |

| | | |
|---|---|---|
| **3688 JL** | Beaker pattern as 3673 | |
| **3689 SC** | Jardiniere | |
| **3690 RT** | Vase Palm Leaf range | 8"h |
| **3691 RT** | Bowl with cover | 4"h |
| **3692 SC** | Jardiniere Chequers range | l/s |
| **3693 SC** | Vase Chequers range | |
| **3694 SC** | Vase Chequers range | 8⅛"h |
| **3695 SC** | Jardiniere Chequers range | s/s |
| **3696 SC** | Bowl on foot New Shell range | 4"h 5¾"l |
| **3697 SC** | Bulb bowl oval l/s | 10" |
| **3698 SC** | Bulb bowl Chequers range s/s | 3½"h 6¾"l |
| **3699 SC** | Plant pot Chequers range | l/s |
| **3700 SC** | Plant pot Chequers range | m/s |
| **3701** | Plant pot Chequers range | s/s |
| **3702 SC** | Posy bar | |
| **3703** | Posy trough | s/s |
| **3704 SC** | Trough | 4½"h 6½"l |
| **3705 SC** | Vase Chequers range | 6¼"h |
| **3706 SC** | Menu card | 6"h |
| **3707 SC** | Posy on pedestal | |
| **3708 JL** | Butter/cheese dish square, square knob. Changed to 3554 | |
| **3709** | Place card | 3"l |
| **3710 RT** | Bowl Palm Leaf range | 4½"h 6½"l |
| **3711 RT** | Harp vase Ireland | 4⅝"h |
| **3712 JB** | Ashtray square | 2"h |
| **3713 JL** | Cruet with tray | 8¾"l |
| **3714 RT** | Jardiniere Palm Leaf range | 6¾"h 13½"l |
| **3715 RT** | Plant pot Palm Leaf range | 6"h –1970s |
| **3716 RT** | Bulb bowl oval Palm Leaf | 10¼"l –1970s |
| **3717 RT** | Posy or slipper Palm Leaf | |
| **3718 RT** | Posy bowl Palm Leaf range | l/s |
| **3719 RT** | Posy boat Palm Leaf range | s/s |
| **3720 RT** | Trough Palm Leaf range | 2⅜"h 8½"l |
| **3721 RT** | Wall vase Palm Leaf range | |
| **3722 RT** | Fern pot Palm Leaf range | 4¾"h –1970s |
| **3723 RT** | Jardiniere no handles Palm Leaf range | |
| **3724 RT** | Vase Palm Leaf range | 10"h |
| **3725 RT** | Vase Palm Leaf range | 6"h |
| **3726 RT** | Bowl oval Palm Leaf range | 6¾"l –1970s |
| **3727 JL** | Jug one pint on pedestal | |
| **3728 JL** | Cream jug | |
| **3729 JL** | Cream jug Web pattern | |
| **3730 JL** | Ashtray square | 3"h |
| **3731 JL** | Vase Oslo range | 9¾"h –1970s |
| **3732 JL** | Vase Oslo range | 8"h –1970s |
| **3733 JL** | Vase Oslo range | 6"h –1970s |
| **3734 JL** | Bowl Oslo range | l/s |
| **3735 JL** | Bowl Oslo range m/s | 7¾"dia –1969 |
| **3736 JL** | Bowl Oslo range s/s | 5¾"dia –1970s |
| **3737 JL** | Plant pot Oslo range | 4¾"h –1970 |
| **3738 JL** | Plant pot Oslo range | 6¼"h –1970 |
| **3739 JL** | Posy Oslo range | –1969 |
| **3740 JL** | Jardiniere Oslo range | 6¼"l –1970s |
| **3741 JL** | Jardiniere Oslo range | 9¼"l –1970s |
| **3742 RT** | Baby mug one handle p63/64 TSS | 3¼"h – 1982+ |
| **3743 JL** | Grapefruit bowl Oslo range | 3¾"dia –1970s |
| **3744 RT** | Bread and butter plate Butterfly range | |
| **3745** | Sandwich plate Butterfly | 12½"l |
| **3746 RT** | Teapot Butterfly range | |

**Circa 1965–1967**

| | | |
|---|---|---|
| **3747 RT** | Mug half pint Tudor range | |
| **3748 RT** | Mug half pint ribbed | |
| **3749 RT** | Mug half pint embossed | |
| **3750 RT** | Mug pineapple | |
| **3751 RT** | Mug fluted | |
| **3752 JL** | Vase | 10"h |
| **3753 SC** | Vase/Jar | |
| **3754 SC** | Cats head money box | |
| **3755 RT** | Bird | 4"h |
| **3756 RT** | Birds head pie funnel | 2" |
| **3757 JL** | Cup on pedestal | |

| | | |
|---|---|---|
| **3758 SC** | Jar flower pattern shape as 3753 | |
| **3759 RT** | Plate fluted (casted) | 10"dia |
| **3760** | Ash bowl | 5½" |
| **3761 JL** | Tray oblong | 15" |
| **3762 RT** | Horse | |
| **3763 SC** | Lifeboat mans head money box | |
| **3764 JL** | Jar square | |
| **3765 SC** | Scottie dog sitting | |
| **3766 SC** | Poodle dog sitting | 6"h |
| **3767 SC** | Corgi dog sitting | 6"h |
| **3768 RT** | Triple tray | |
| **3769 JL** | Jardiniere no handles | 10½"l |
| **3770 SC** | Cats head money box | |
| **3771** | Cheese oblong Wishing Well range | |
| **3772** | Honey pot Wishing Well range | |
| **3773** | Butter dish square Wishing Well | |
| **3774–3787** | These numbers were reserved for further Wishing Well items, but not used | |
| **3788** | Egg cup (cast and jollied) p63/64 TSS | 3"dia –1982+ |
| **3789 JL** | Stork | 9" |
| **3790 JL** | Stork | 6" |
| **3791** | Baby plate (jollied) p63/64 TSS | 6"dia –1982+ |
| **3792 JL** | Vase | |
| **3793** | Vase/Jar square | |
| **3794 RT** | Vase/Jar round | 6"h |
| **3795 SC** | Vase/Jar round | |
| **3796 JL** | Jardiniere no handles | |
| **3797 SC** | Vase/Jar | |
| **3798 SC** | Spaniel dog sitting | |
| **3799 SC** | Character jug lifeboat man Seaman Jones | |
| **3800 RT** | Vase/Jar square | |
| **3801 SC** | Vase/Jar round | |
| **3802 SC** | Seaman Jones money box | s/s |
| **3803 RT** | Lamp Tudor range | 10"h |
| **3804 RT** | Lamp 1807 vase right way up | 9¾"h |
| **3805** | Lamp 1807 vase upside down | 9¾"h |
| **3806 RT** | Bowl oblong | 10½"l |
| **3807 SC** | Fern pot Wall pattern l/s | 5½"h –1970s |
| **3808 SC** | Fern pot Wall pattern m/s | 4¾"h –1970s |
| **3809 SC** | Fern pot Wall pattern s/s | 4½"h –1970s |
| **3810 SC** | Vase Wall pattern | 10"h |
| **3811 SC** | Vase Wall pattern | 8"h |
| **3812 SC** | Vase Wall pattern | 6"h |
| **3813 SC** | Bowl oblong Wall pattern | s/s |
| **3814 SC** | Twin bowl Wall pattern | 13" |
| **3815 SC** | Bowl oblong Wall pattern | 12" |
| **3816 SC** | Jardiniere Wall pattern | s/s |
| **3817 SC** | Bowl oblong Wall pattern | 14" |
| **3818 SC** | Tray Wall pattern s/s | 7"l |
| **3819 SC** | Posy bar Wall pattern | 14"l |
| **3820 SC** | Posy bar Wall pattern | s/s |
| **3821 RT** | Bowl oblong Glost pattern | 7½"l |
| **3822 RT** | Bowl oval Glost pattern | 11"l |
| **3823 RT** | Bowl oval Glost pattern | l/s |
| **3824 RT** | Jardiniere Privet range | 5"h 11"l –1968 |
| **3825 RT** | Vase Privet range | 7"h |
| **3826 SC** | Bowl oblong Wall pattern | 12"l |
| **3827 SC** | Spaniel with slipper p39 TSC | 5"h |
| **3828 RT** | Coffee pot long spout Avon | 8¼"h |
| **3829 SC** | Scottie dog | |
| **3830 SC** | Posy or slipper Wall pattern | |
| **3831 SC** | Tray Wall pattern | 13"l |
| **3832 RT** | Jug | |
| **3833** | Jar | |
| **3834 RT** | Jug embossed Wisdom and Providence sim to 4788 | 8½"h |
| **3835 SC** | Bowl oblong | |
| **3836 RT** | Coffee pot | |
| **3837 SC** | Teddy bear police money box | |
| **3838 SC** | Bowl Manhattan range | 10¼"l –1970s |
| **3839 SC** | Bunnies bank money box | |
| **3840 SC** | Cowboy money box | |
| **3841 SC** | Indian money box | |
| **3842 RT** | Vase Privet range p97 TSC | 8½"h –1981 |

| | | |
|---|---|---|
| 3843 JL | Bowl and fish | |
| 3844 RT | Vase Privet range p97 TSC | 10¼"h –1981 |
| 3845 RT | Vase Privet range | 6"h –1968 |
| 3846 RT | Bulb bowl oval Privet range | 10"l |
| 3847 RT | Laughing cat (no fur) | 6"h |
| 3848 SC | Scottie dog | 4"h |
| 3849 RT | Fish on pedestal | |
| 3850 JL | Vase Linton range s/s | 4"h |
| 3851 JL | Vase Linton range medium s/s | 6"h |
| 3852 JL | Vase Linton range middle/s | 8"h |
| 3853 JL | Vase Linton range | l/s |
| 3854 JL | Posy Linton range | s/s |
| 3855 JL | Planter Linton range | 12"l |
| 3856 JL | Jardiniere Linton range | s/s |
| 3857 JL | Jardiniere Linton range | l/s |
| 3858 JL | Pot Linton range | s/s |
| 3859 JL | Pot Linton range | l/s |
| 3860 JL | Bowl Linton range | s/s |
| 3861 JL | Bowl Linton range | l/s |
| 3862 JL | Posy slipper Linton range | |
| 3863 JL | Vase Begonia range s/s | 4"h |
| 3864 JL | Vase Begonia range Medium s/s | 6"h |
| 3865 JL | Vase Begonia range | 8"h |
| 3866 JL | Vase Begonia range | 10"h |
| 3867 JL | Posy Begonia range p112 TSS | 7¼"l |
| 3868 JL | Planter Begonia range | |
| 3869 JL | Jardiniere Begonia range s/s | 4¼"h 6¾"l (top) |
| 3870 JL | Jardiniere Begonia range | l/s |
| 3871 JL | Pot Begonia range | s/s |
| 3872 JL | Pot Begonia range | l/s |
| 3873 JL | Bowl Begonia range | s/s |
| 3874 JL | Bowl Begonia range | l/s |
| 3875 JL | Slipper Begonia range | |
| 3876 JL | Tray Begonia range | |
| 3877 JL | Vase Texture range s/s | 4"h |
| 3878 JL | Vase Texture range medium/s | 6"h |
| 3879 JL | Vase Texture range middle/s | 8"h |
| 3880 JL | Vase Texture range l/s | 10"h |
| 3881 JL | Posy Texture range | s/s |
| 3882 JL | Planter Texture range | |
| 3883 JL | Jardiniere Texture range | s/s |
| 3884 JL | Jardiniere Texture range | l/s |
| 3885 JL | Pot Texture range | s/s |
| 3886 JL | Pot Texture range | l/s |
| 3887 JL | Bowl Texture range s/s | 3½"h 6¾"l (top) |
| 3888 JL | Bowl Texture range | l/s |
| 3889 JL | Slipper posy Texture range | |
| 3890 JL | Tray Texture range | |
| 3891 | Number not used | |
| 3892 RT | Cat laughing, as 3847 but with fur | |
| 3893 JL | Tray Coral range | |
| 3894 RT | Bowl round Privet range | |
| 3895 RT | Plant pot Privet range s/s p97 TSC | 4⅞"h –1981 |
| 3896 RT | Plant pot Privet range l/s p97 TSC | 5¾"h –1981 |
| 3897 JL | Vase Coral range | 6"h |
| 3898 JL | Jardiniere Coral range | m/s |
| 3899 RT | Posy ring Privet range | 6½"acr |
| 3900 RT | Posy bar Privet range | 8"l |
| 3901 JL | Vase Coral range | 8"h |
| 3902 JL | Posy bar Coral range | 9½"l |
| 3903 RT | Jardiniere Privet range | 10¼"acr |
| 3904 JL | Vase Coral range | 10"h |
| 3905 JL | Jardiniere Coral range | s/s |
| 3906 JL | Pot Coral range | |
| 3907 JL | Jardiniere Coral range l/s p62 TSS | 9"h 15½"l |
| 3908 RT | Sugar bowl to match 3828 | |
| 3909 RT | Cream jug to match 3828 | |
| 3910 JL | Pot Coral range | l/s |
| 3911 RT | Dish | 1¼"h 7"l 4"w |
| 3912 RT | Squirrel sitting (no paws) | |
| 3913 RT | Jack Russell Terrier p19 TSC | 3½"h –1982+ |
| 3914 RT | Egg cup Avon shape | 1½"h |
| 3915 RT | Bread and butter plate square Lisbon range | |
| 3916 GM | Vase | m/s |
| 3917 GM | Vase | s/s |
| 3918 GM | Fox | |
| 3919 RT | Mug half pint embossed flowers and leaves | 3¾"h |
| 3920 RT | Mug half pint | |
| 3921 GM | Hunchback dog sim to 3923 | 4"h 6¾"l |
| 3922 RT | Mug half pint | |
| 3923 GM | Hunchback dog sim to 3921 | 2"h 4¾"l |
| 3924 GM | Vase on pedestal | 10"h |
| 3925 GM | Bambi (mould eight parts) | |
| 3926 RT | Mug | |
| 3927 GM | Fox and chicken p133 TSC | 7"h |
| 3928 RT | Lamp base | |
| 3929 GM | Tree vase, twin rabbits | |
| 3930 RT | Bull Prestige pieces p57 TSS | 14½"l –1982 |
| 3931 RT | Jar | 6"h |
| 3932 GM | Vase sim to 3924 | 12"h |
| 3933 GM | Pomeranian dog sitting | 4⅜"h |
| 3934 GM | Pot Cactus range | 3"h |
| 3935 GM | Squirrel money box re-numbered 5105 also re-named Chipmunk | 5¾"h |
| 3936 GM | Pot Cactus range | 3"h |
| 3937 RT | Tankard half pint Wisdom and Providence | 5"h |
| 3938 GM | Vase Manhattan range | 6¼"h –1970s |
| 3939 GM | Vase Manhattan range | 8"h –1970s |
| 3940 GM | Bowl Manhattan range | 6¼"l –1970s |
| 3941 GM | Plant pot Manhattan range | 6½"dia –1970s |
| 3942 GM | Plant pot Manhattan range | 5¾"dia –1970s |
| 3943 GM | Plant pot Manhattan range | 5"dia –1970s |
| 3944 GM | Jardiniere Manhattan range | 7½"l –1970s |
| 3945 GM | Posy bar Manhattan range | 7½"l –1970s |
| 3946 GM | Vase Manhattan range | 8"h |
| 3947 GM | Vase Manhattan range | 10¼"h –1970s |
| 3948 GM | Tray oval Manhattan range | 12¾"l –1970s |
| 3949 GM | Bowl Manhattan range | 10"l –1970s |
| 3950 GM | Tray Manhattan range | 6¼"l –1970s |
| 3951 GM | Posy bar Manhattan range | 5"l –1970s |
| 3952 GM | Posy bar Manhattan range | 10¼"l –1970s |
| 3953 RT | Ashtray maple leaf Montreal Canada | 5½"dia |
| 3954 RT | Tankard maple pattern | |
| 3955 RT | Tray maple leaf | |
| 3956 GM | Jardiniere Manhattan range | 11½"l –1970s |
| 3957 GM | Fox | |
| 3958 | Lamp base Hyacinth range | |
| 3959 | Lamp base 3880 vase | 10"h |
| 3960 RT | Prowling Manx cat (this was never actually produced) see 4077 | 6" |
| 3961 | Lamp base (Macklestone pot) | s/s |
| 3962 | Lamp base | 12"h |
| 3963 | Extension to above lamp (top half) | 8"h |
| 3964 GM | Jardiniere boar fight | 10" |
| 3965 RT | Jardiniere embossed 3225 | 14"l |
| 3966 RT | Vase with three feet | 9"h |
| 3967 RT | Jardiniere on stand | |
| 3968 GM | Dachshund dog | |
| 3969 RT | Vase | |
| 3970 RT | Vase embossed 3037 | 9¾"h |
| 3971 GM | Horse shoe wall vase | |
| 3972 GM | Vase | 4"h |
| 3973 RT | Mug to coffee set | |
| 3974 GM | Vase | 5"h |
| 3975 RT | Tankard Wisdom and Providence | 4¼"h –1970s |
| 3976 | Lamp base (Macklestone vase) | 10"h |
| 3977 RT | Cheese dish Totem p54 TSC | 7½"l –1970s |
| 3978 RT | Tankard Wisdom and Providence | 5¾"h –1970s |
| 3979 | Lamp base (Macklestone) | |
| 3980 RT | Vase | |
| 3981 RT | Coffee beaker | |
| 3982 GM | Honey pot Totem p54 TSC | 4½"h –1970s |
| 3983 RT | Jardiniere | 13½"l |
| 3984 GM | Cat | |
| 3985 RT | Coffee pot | s/s |

| | | | |
|---|---|---|---|
| 3986 GM | Butter dish Totem p54 TSC | 6″l –1970s | |
| 3987 GM | Posy bar Totem | | |
| 3988 RT | Irish Terrier | 5″h –1970s | |
| 3989 RT | Pot | s/s | |
| 3990 GM | Pot | l/s | |
| 3991 RT | Tray tulip | | |
| 3992 GM | Jardiniere | s/s | |
| 3993 RT | Vase | 6″h | |
| 3994 RT | Vase sim to 3998 but with round foot | 3½″h | |
| 3995 RT | Vase Maple range p81 TSC | 10¼″h | |
| 3996 RT | Ashtray with suede cover p89 TSC | 5¼″dia –1982 | |
| 3997 GM | Vase | 8″h | |
| 3998 RT | Urn vase Olympus p80 TSC as 3994 with square foot | 4″h –1970s | |
| 3999 RT | Vase embossed | 10″h | |
| 4000 GM | Vase sim to 3980 | 6″h | |
| 4001 RT | Jardiniere Maple range l/s no handles p81 TSC | 10¼″l –1982+ | |
| 4002 RT | Plant pot Maple p81 TSC m/s | 5¾″dia –1982+ | |
| 4003 RT | Plant pot fluted | | |
| 4004 RT | Plant pot Maple p81 TSC l/s | 7″dia –1982+ | |
| 4005 RT | Pot Wall pattern | 3½″h | |
| 4006 RT | Plant pot Maple p81 TSC s/s | 5¼″dia –1982+ | |
| 4007 RT | Bulb bowl | l/s | |
| 4008 RT | Jardiniere Maple range s/s no handles p81 TSC | 7″l –1982+ | |
| 4009 RT | Ashtray with suede cover p89 TSC | 7⅝″dia –1982 | |
| 4010 RT | Vase Maple range p81 TSC | 6″h –1982+ | |
| 4011 RT | Vase Maple range p81 TSC | 8″h –1982+ | |
| 4012 RT | Jardiniere Manhattan range | 9″l –1970s | |
| 4013 RT | Bulb bowl Maple p81 TSC s/s | 7½″dia –1982+ | |
| 4014 GM | Cruet Totem range p54 TSC | 3½″h –1970s | |
| 4015 GM | Bulb bowl | s/s | |
| 4016 GM | Posy bar | 9″l | |
| 4017 GM | Bulb bowl round | | |
| 4018 RT | Bulb bowl Maple p81 TSC | 6¾″l –1982+ | |
| 4019 GM | Bowl Manhattan range s/s | 3¾–4″acr –1970s | |
| 4020 | Fruit dish Totem range | s/s | |
| 4021 RT | Coffee perculator (mono) | | |
| 4022 GM | Tray and oil/vinegar bottles with stoppers Totem p54 TSC | 7¾″l –1970s | |
| 4023 RT | Posy bar Maple p81 TSC | 8″l –1982+ | |
| 4024 GM | Bowl Manhattan range | 8½″dia –1970s | |
| 4025 | Coffee Perculator | | |
| 4026 GM | Sugar bowl | | |
| 4027 GM | Ashtray round (four part mould) l/s | 6½″dia | |
| 4028 GM | Cream jug for coffee set | | |
| 4029 GM | Toast rack Totem p54 TSC | 7¼″l –1970s | |
| 4030 GM | Cheese board Totem p54 TSC | 9¾″l –1970s | |
| 4031 GM | Egg tray and four cups Totem range p54 TSC | 6½″dia –1970s | |
| 4032 RT/GM | Triple tray Totem p54 TSC | 13¼″l –1970s | |
| 4033 GM | Sugar bowl Totem p54 TSC | 4″acr –1970s | |
| 4034 GM | Beaker Toronto Totem pattern | | |
| 4035 RT/GM | Double tray Totem range | 10¾″l –1970s | |
| 4036 GM | Sandwich tray Totem p54 TSC | 13″l –1970s | |
| 4037 GM | Coffee jug Totem p54 TSC | 8¼″h –1970s | |
| 4038 GM | Mug Totem range p54 TSC | 4″h –1970s | |
| 4039 RT/GM | Cream jug Totem p54 TSC | 4″h –1970s | |
| 4040 RT/GM | Jug one pint Totem p54 TSC | 5¼″h –1970s | |
| 4041 RT | Storage jar Nouveau kitchen ware available in red, blue, yellow and some green previously 2588 | l/s | |
| 4042 RT | Storage jar Nouveau | s/s | |
| 4043 RT | Jug Nouveau (2582) | l/s | |
| 4044 RT | Jug Nouveau (2554) | m/s | |
| 4045 RT | Jug Nouveau (2590) | s/s | |
| 4046 RT | Teapot Nouveau (2571) | l/s | |
| 4047 RT | Teapot Nouveau (2604) | s/s | |
| 4048 RT | Coffee jug Nouveau (2809) | | |
| 4049 RT | Cheese dish Nouveau | | |
| 4050 RT | Butter dish Nouveau | | |
| 4051 RT | Sugar bowl Nouveau | | |
| 4052 RT | Beaker Nouveau | | |
| 4053 RT | Sugar shaker Nouveau | | |
| 4054 RT | Honey pot Nouveau | | |
| 4055 | Mixing bowl Nouveau | l/s | |
| 4056 | Mixing bowl Nouveau | s/s | |
| 4057 | Egg separator Nouveau | | |
| 4058 | Lemon squeezer Nouveau | | |
| 4059 | Cruet Nouveau | | |
| 4060 GM | Vinegar bottle Nouveau | | |
| 4061 RT | Spice jar Nouveau | 3½″h | |
| 4062 | Not used | | |
| 4063 | Vase Nouveau | | |
| 4064 | Vase Nouveau | | |
| 4065 | Mug "Tea Taster" | | |
| 4066 RT | Ashtray (four parts) | s/s | |
| 4067 RT | Coffee pot | | |
| 4068 | Acorn and squirrel vase sim to 330/1115/1958/1959 and 1993 | 8½″h –1982 | |
| 4069 | Stork vase sim to 475/1138 and 1960 | 10″h –1982 | |
| 4070 | Flower jug "rabbit climbing into furze" sim to 1318/1978 | 8½″h –1970s | |
| 4071 RT | Double egg cup | s/s | |
| 4072 RT | Coffee egg strainer with handle | | |
| 4073 GM | Beaker | | |
| 4074 GM | Preserve jar | | |
| 4075 GM | Preserve jar Totem range | | |
| 4076 RT | Coffee pot | | |
| 4077 | Manx cat s/s 3960 p104 TSS | 3″h 4″l | |
| 4078 GM | Pot square foot | 2nd/s | |
| 4079 GM | Urn pot | 3rd/s | |
| 4080 GM | Urn pot Olympus p80 TSC | 6¼″h –1970s | |
| 4081 GM | Urn pot Olympus p80 TSC | 7″h –1970s | |
| 4082 RT | Coffee perculator (mono) sim to 4021 | s/s | |
| 4083 GM | Pot square foot | 11″h | |
| 4084 GM | Urn pot Olympus p80 TSC | 9½″h –1970s | |
| 4085 GM | Bowl square foot | | |
| 4086 GM | Bowl Olympus p80 TSC | 10¼″dia –1970s | |
| 4087 RT | Cream jug (mono) to match 4021 | | |
| 4088 RT | Sugar bowl (mono) to match 4021 | | |
| 4089 RT | Cream jug (mono) without handle | 3½″h | |
| 4090 RD | Tankard (fish) | | |
| 4091 GM | Vase | 8″h | |
| 4092 GM | Vase | 10″h | |
| 4093 GM | Vase Olympus p80 TSC | 8″h –1970s | |
| 4094 RT | Lamp base Manhattan range | | |
| 4095 | Tea cup Totem range to go with 4141 saucer | 3″h –1970s | |
| 4096 GM | Vase | 5″h | |
| 4097 RT | King Charles Spaniel p20 TSC (mould sold to another pottery) | 4¾″h –1982+ | |
| 4098 GM | Vase Olympus p80 TSC | 10″h –1970s | |
| 4099 RT | Coffee strainer with handle | | |
| 4100 GM | Vase | 12″h | |
| 4101 RT | Coffee strainer no handle | | |
| 4102 RT | Coffee strainer Totem sim to 4172 goes with 4106 p54 TSC (bottom left) | 5″dia –1970s | |
| 4103 GM | Vase Olympus p80 TSC | 5″h –1970s | |
| 4104 GM | Bowl on square stand | 7½″h | |
| 4105 GM | Vase Olympus p80 TSC | 12″h –1970s | |
| 4106 GM | Coffee pot Totem goes with 4102 p54 TSC (bottom left) | 6¼″h –1970s | |
| 4107 GM | Bowl on round stand | 7½″dia | |
| 4108 JR | Mug | | |
| 4109 GM | Bowl on round stand embossed | 7½″dia | |
| 4110 GM | Horseshoe vase horses head, shamrock, "Good luck from Ireland" | 4¾″h | |
| 4111 RT | Log posy shamrock ashtray "Ireland" | 6″l | |
| 4112 GM | Candleholder | 8″ | |
| 4113 GM | Great Dane dog | 6″ | |

| No. | Description | Dimensions |
|---|---|---|
| 4114 RT | Vase | 8″h |
| 4115 GM | Bowl on stand Olympus p80 TSC | 7″h –1970s |
| 4116 GM | Vase Seaweed and shells | 8″h |
| 4117 RT | Vase floral pattern sim to 2147 | 8″h |
| 4118 RT | Ashtray square | 4″ |
| 4119 RT | Vase fruit pattern | 8″h |
| 4120 GM | Ashtray square | 5½″ |
| 4121 RT | Vase cornflower | 8″h |
| 4122 GM | Bowl on square stand | l/s |
| 4123 GM | Bowl on square stand | s/s |
| 4124 GM | Jug square one pint | |
| 4125 GM | Ashtray golf p63 TSC | 5½″dia –1982 |
| 4126 RT | Vase embossed shape as 3051 | 7½″h |
| 4127 GM | Vase Sycamore p83 TSC | 6″h –1970s |
| 4128 GM | Vase Sycamore range | 6½″h |
| 4129 GM | Bowl Sycamore p83 TSC | 8½″dia –1970s |
| 4130 GM | Bowl Olympus p80 TSC | 4″h –1970s |
| 4131 GM | Bowl Olympus p80 TSC | 5″h –1970s |
| 4132 GM | Plant pot Hyacinth | 7″dia –1982 |
| 4133 GM | Storage jar | |
| 4134 GM | Teapot for Totem | |
| 4135 GM | Teapot | |
| 4136 GM | Ashtray briar square | |
| 4137 GM | Cup | |
| 4137 also | Mixing bowl | |
| 4138 RT | Vase | 6″h |
| 4139 GM | Spice jar | |
| 4140 GM | Teapot Totem p54 TSC s/s | 5″h –1970s |
| 4141 | Saucer for 4095 cup Totem | 6¼″acr –1970s |
| 4142 GM | Breakfast cup Totem | 3¼″h 3¼″acr –1970s |
| 4143 GM | Storage jar Totem | 7″h –1970s |
| 4144 GM | Teapot Totem 6/8 cup l/s | 6½″h –1970s |
| 4145 GM | Ashtray Totem range | 4″ |
| 4146 GM | Mixing bowl Totem s/s | 8½″l –1970s |
| 4147 GM | Mixing bowl Totem l/s | 11½″l –1970s |
| 4148 GM | Spice jar Totem range | 3¾″h –1970s |
| 4149 GM | Cheese dish Totem l/s | 8¼″l –1970s |
| 4150 GM | Storage jar Totem l/s | 8″h –1970s |
| 4151 GM | Egg separator Totem | 3½″h –1970s |
| 4152 RT | Vase Marina l/s p78 TSC | 8″h –1970s |
| 4153 RT | Plant pot Marina p78 TSC | 7″dia –1970s |
| 4154 RT | Tray Marina p78 TSC | 6½″l –1970s |
| 4155 RT | Plant pot Marina s/s p78 TSC | 4½″h –1970s |
| 4156 RT | Plant pot Marina l/s p78 TSC | 5½″h –1970s |
| 4157 RT | Vase Marina m/s p78 TSC | 6¼″h –1970s |
| 4158 RT | Posy bar Marina p78 TSC | 8″l –1970s |
| 4159 RT | Flower holder Marina round p78 TSC | 8½″dia –1970s |
| 4160 RT | Jardiniere Marina l/s p78 TSC | 10½″l –1970s |
| 4161 RT | Bowl Marina s/s p62 TSS p78 TSC | 6½″l –1970s |
| 4162 | Jardiniere Marina s/s p78 TSC | 7″l –1970s |
| 4163 RT | Vase Marina s/s p78 TSC | 5″h –1970s |
| 4164 RT | Vase Flora range p82 TSC | 8″h –1970s |
| 4165 RT | Vase Flora range p82 TSC | 6″h –1970s |
| 4166 RT | Jardiniere Flora s/s p82 TSC | 9¼″l –1970s |
| 4167 RT | Posy ring Flora range | 6″dia |
| 4168 RT | Jardiniere Flora l/s p82 TSC | 12½″l –1970s |
| 4169 RT | Plant pot Flora range l/s p82 TSC | 5½″h –1970s |
| 4170 RT | Plant pot Flora range s/s p82 TSC | 4¾″h –1970s |
| 4171 RT | Bowl Flora s/s p82 TSC | 6½″l –1970s |
| 4172 RT | Posy bar Flora p82 TSC | 8″l –1970s |
| 4173 RT | Bowl on stand Flora s/s 4130 shape p82 TSC | 4½″dia –1970s |
| 4174 RT | Vase Flora s/s 3037 shape p82 TSC | 10″h –1970s |
| 4175 RT | Bowl Flora l/s | 9¼″dia –1970s |
| 4176 GM | Sugar shaker Totem | 5½″h –1970s |
| 4177 RT | Sauce boat and stand Totem l/s | 9″l –1970s |
| 4178 RT | Posy bar Marina p78 TSC | 5¼″l –1970s |
| 4179 GM | Jug Totem range two pint | 6¼″h –1970s |
| 4180 RT | Coffee perculator incised | |
| 4181 | Jardiniere Knib pattern | |
| 4182 GM | Egg cups and stand Avon shape plain (Totem shape) | 6½″dia –1982 |
| 4183 RT | Tankard plain half pint | |
| 4184 RT | Jar Hound head | |
| 4185 RT | Sugar bowl Ireland sim to 1140 | 2½″h |
| 4186 RT | Cream jug Ireland sim to 1134 | 2½″h |
| 4187 RT | Sugar bowl Ireland sim to 1135 | l/s |
| 4188 RT | Pig money box Ireland sim to 1132 | |
| 4189 RT | Beaker plain | |
| 4190 RT | Coffee perculator basket pattern | |
| 4191 RT | Beaker (country scene) | |
| 4192 RT | Tankard (leather) | |
| 4193 GM | Sauce boat and stand Totem s/s | 7¾″l –1970s |
| 4194 RT | Coffee perculator basket pattern | l/s |
| 4195 RT | Tray round p56/88 TSC | 6½″dia –1970s |
| 4196 RT | Tray triangle p56/88 TSC | 6½″dia –1970s |
| 4197 RT | Tray square p56/88 TSC | 6½″dia –1970s |
| 4198 RT | Tray oblong p56/67/88 TSC | 6½″dia –1970s |
| 4199 RT | Vase crazy paving shape as 223 (Falcon) | 8½″h |
| 4200 RT | Tankard pewter | |
| 4201 | Plant pot Marina s/s fourth size p78 TSC | 4″h –1970s |
| 4202 GM | Coffee pot Totem p54 TSC | 10¾″h –1970s |
| 4203 RT | Vase on foot | |
| 4204 | Plant pot Marina second size p78 TSC | 5″h –1970s |
| 4205 GM | Bowl Sycamore p83 TSC | 6½″l –1970s |
| 4206 GM | Vase Sycamore p83 TSC | 8″h –1970s |
| 4207 GM | Jardiniere Sycamore s/s p83 TSC | 7¼″l –1970s |
| 4208 GM | Vase Sycamore p83 TSC | 10″h –1970s |
| 4209 GM | Jardiniere Sycamore l/s no handles p83 TSC | 11″l –1970s |
| 4210 GM | Bowl Sycamore p83 TSC | 5″dia –1970s |
| 4211 GM | Plant pot Sycamore s/s p83 TSC | 5½″dia –1970s |
| 4212 GM | Plant pot Sycamore l/s p83 TSC | 6¼″dia –1970s |
| 4213 GM | Posy bar Sycamore p83 TSC | 7¾″l –1970s |
| 4214 GM | Low bowl Sycamore p83 TSC | 6″dia –1970s |
| 4215 GM | Vase Sycamore p83 TSC | 6″h –1970s |
| 4216 | Sugar bowl to go with 4135 teapot and Avon cream jug 2978 | |
| 4217 | Pot stand to go with 4265 pot | |
| 4218 GM | Covered bowl Agincourt p62 TSC | 4¼″h –1982 |
| 4219 | Number not used | |
| 4220 | Storage jar Totem s/s | 6½″h –1970s |
| 4221 RT/GM | Plate Totem p54 TSC | 10″dia –1970s |
| 4222 RT/GM | Plate Totem p54 TSC | 8″dia –1970s |
| 4223 RT/GM | Plate Totem p54 TSC | 6½″dia –1970s |
| 4224 | Teapot Totem m/s p54 TSC | 5¾″h –1970s |
| 4225 | Lemon squeezer Totem | 5¾″dia –1970s |
| 4226 | Horseshoe vase Wales embossed Welsh lady | 5″h |
| 4227 | Horseshoe vase Scotland Scottie dog p64 TSS | 5″h |
| 4228 | Horseshoe vase Devon | 5″h |
| 4229 | Horseshoe vase Cornwall | 5″h |
| 4230 | Horseshoe vase Somerset | 5″h |
| 4231 RT | Posy with deer Woodland range p87 TSS p113 TSC | 4¼″l –1982 |
| 4232 | Jardiniere embossed whirl pattern | |
| 4233 RT | Tree vase with squirrel Woodland range p87 TSS p113 TSC | 4½″h –1982 |
| 4234 RT | Rabbit | |
| 4235 RT | Coffee pot Totem short spout | |
| 4236 RT | Horseshoe vase Cheddar p64 TSS | 5″h |
| 4237 RT/GM | Perculator Totem range | 8¾″h –1970s |
| 4238 RT | Perculator | |
| 4239 RT | Posy vase with deer Woodland range p113 TSC | 2¼″h –1970s |
| 4240 RT | Basket with squirrel or deer Woodland p113 TSC | 5½″l –1982 |

| | | | |
|---|---|---|---|
| 4241 GM | Tree vase with squirrel Woodland range p113 TSC | 6″h –1982 | |
| 4242 RT | Tree vase with rabbit Woodland range p113 TSC | 9¼″h –1982 | |
| 4243 GM | Twin tree vase with rabbit Woodland p113 TSC | 7″h –1982 | |
| 4244 RT | Tray p56/88 TSC | 7″l –1970s | |
| 4245 | Tankard p58 TSC also used to commemorate the Hereford Cider Festival (Bulmers) | 4½″h –1970s | |
| 4246 GM | Horseshoe ashtray (re-numbered 5382 p63 TSC) | 6″l –1970s | |
| 4247 RT | Lining | 7″ | |
| 4248 RT | Lining | | |
| 4249 RT | Sweet tray with novelty | | |
| 4250 RT | Squirrel | | |
| 4251 RT | Corgi dog | 3″ | |
| 4252 | Spaniel dog | 3″ | |
| 4253 GM | Tankard p61 TSC | 3¾″h –1970s | |
| 4254 GM | Tankard p61/67 TSC | 4⅝″h –1982 | |
| 4255 GM | Tankard p61/62 TSC | 5½″h –1982 | |
| 4256 RT | Beaker | | |
| 4257 RT | Beaker | | |
| 4258 GM | Vase | | |

**Circa 1968**

| | | | |
|---|---|---|---|
| 4259 GM | Jug with cover p62 TSC | 13½″h –1982 | |
| 4260 | Coffee tankard embossed | | |
| 4261 RT | Lining | 5″ | |
| 4262 RT | Honeypot with pixie on lid, embossed shamrock and Ireland | 5″h | |
| 4263 RT | Vase | | |
| 4264 RT | Vase Autumn Chintz p86 TSC also Marble range | 6″h –1970s | |
| 4265 RT | Plant pot Autumn Chintz p86 TSC also Marble range with pot stand 4217 | 4¾″h–5″h –1982 | |
| 4266 RT | Vase oak leaves | 8″h | |
| 4267 RT | Tankard p61 TSC | 6¼″h –1970s | |
| 4268 RT | Jug pewter | 5″h –1970s | |
| 4269 RT | Honey pot embossed | | |
| 4270 RT | Tankard p61/62 TSC | 4½″h –1982 | |
| 4271 GM | Jug p62 TSC | 4¼″h –1982 | |
| 4272 RT | Jug pewter l/s | 6″h –1970s | |
| 4273 GM | Tankard p61/62 TSC | 4¼″h –1982 | |
| 4274 GM | Tankard p61 TSC | 3½″h –1970s | |
| 4275 GM | Tankard p61 TSC | 3″h –1970s | |
| 4276 GM | Posy bar | | |
| 4277 GM | Jardiniere l/s | 11″l | |
| 4278 GM | Bowl | s/s | |
| 4279 GM | Pot | l/s | |
| 4280 GM | Bowl | 8″l | |
| 4281 GM | Posy bar | 7″l | |
| 4282 GM | Posy | | |
| 4283 | Mug shape as 3749/3922 and 3919 | | |
| 4284 GM | Collon vase No. 1 | l/s | |
| 4285 | Collon vase No. 2 | s/s | |
| 4286 | York vase | | |
| 4287 | Plant pot with deer Woodland range p113 TSC | 4″h –1982 | |
| 4288 RT | Ashtray with deer Woodland range p113 TSC | 6″l –1970s | |
| 4289 RT | Bowl with squirrel Woodland range p113 TSC | 7½″dia –1982 | |
| 4290 | Twin tree vase with deer Woodland range p113 TSC | 3¼″h –1982 | |
| 4291 | Plant pot with squirrel Woodland range p113 TSC | 5″h –1970s | |
| 4292 | Bowl with rabbit Woodland range p113 TSC | 7½″l –1982 | |
| 4293 | Ashtray with deer Woodland range p87 TSS p113 TSC | 4¼″l –1982 | |
| 4294 GM | Bowl oval | 8″l | |
| 4295 GM | Tankard p61 TSC | 5″h –1970s | |

| | | | |
|---|---|---|---|
| 4296 GM | Tankard p61 TSC | 2½″h –1970s | |
| 4297 RT | Horseshoe vase Ireland embossed pixie p64 TSS | 5″h | |
| 4298 | Pot Harmony range | s/s | |
| 4299 | Vase Harmony p84 TSC | 8″h –1970s | |
| 4300 | Posy bar Harmony p84 TSC | 7½″l –1970s | |
| 4301 | Vase Harmony p84 TSC | 10″h –1970s | |
| 4302 | Plant pot Harmony m/s p84 TSC | 7″dia –1970s | |
| 4303 | Plant pot Harmony s/s p84 TSC | 6¼″dia –1970s | |
| 4304 | Vase Harmony p84 TSC | 10¼″h –1970s | |
| 4305 | Jardiniere Harmony s/s p84 TSC | 8½″l –1970s | |
| 4306 | Vase Harmony p84 TSC | 6″h –1970s | |
| 4307 | Jardiniere Harmony l/s no handles p84 TSC | 10¾″l –1970s | |
| 4308 | Bowl Harmony l/s p84 TSC | 9½″l –1970s | |
| 4309 | Plant pot Harmony l/s p84 TSC | 7½″dia –1970s | |
| 4310 | Bowl Harmony s/s p84 TSC | 6¼″l –1970s | |
| 4311 GM | Tankard p61/62 TSC | 5½″h –1982 | |
| 4312 RT | Honey pot | | |
| 4313 | Beaker, Totem shape | | |
| 4314 RT | Honey pot as 4312 embossed | | |
| 4315 GM | Cruet pepper and salt pewter coloured | 5½″h –1970s | |
| 4315 GM also | Mustard pewter coloured | 2½″acr –1970s | |
| 4316 RT | Horseshoe ashtray Ireland embossed horses head | 6″l | |
| 4317 GM | Tankard p61/62 TSC | 4¼″h –1982 | |
| 4318 GM | Tankard p61/62 TSC | 5¼″h –1982 | |
| 4319 RT | Vase Aurora range p88 TSC | 8″h –1970s | |
| 4320 RT | Vase | 8″h | |
| 4321 RT | Vase | 8″h | |
| 4322 RT | Vase | 8″h | |
| 4323 GM | Plant pot Aurora range s/s No.4 p88 TSC | 5″h –1970s | |
| 4324 GM | Plant pot Aurora range m/s No.3 p88 TSC | 5½″h –1970s | |
| 4325 GM | Plant pot Aurora No.2 p88 TSC | 6″h –1970s | |
| 4326 GM | Plant pot Appolo range No.1 | 7½″h –1970s | |
| 4327 GM | Vase Aurora range p88 TSC | 6″h –1970s | |
| 4328 GM | Vase Aurora range p88 TSC | 10″h –1970s | |
| 4329 GM | Vase Aurora range p88 TSC | 4″h –1970s | |
| 4330 GM | Jardiniere Aurora range no handles l/s p88 TSC | 11″l –1970s | |
| 4331 GM | Jardiniere Aurora range no handles s/s p88 TSC | 7½″l –1970s | |
| 4332 GM | Bowl Appolo range s/s | 6½″l –1970s | |
| 4333 RT | Perculator | | |
| 4334 RT | Pot Manhattan shape | | |
| 4335 RT | Shell tray | 6″l | |
| 4336 GM | Bowl Harmony s/s p84 TSC | 4¼″dia –1970s | |
| 4337 GM | Tray oval | | |
| 4338 GM | Plant pot Harmony s/s No.4 p84 TSC | 5″dia –1970s | |
| 4339 RT | Coffee beaker embossed p55 TSC | 3¾″h –1982 | |
| 4340 | Vase Harmony m/s slim p84 TSC | 8¼″h –1970s | |
| 4341 | Number not used | | |
| 4342 RT | Coffee beaker embossed p55 TSC | 3¾″h –1982 | |
| 4343 RT | Coffee beaker embossed Oslo range p55 TSC | 3½″h –1982 | |
| 4344 RT | Coffee beaker | | |
| 4345 GM | Bowl Appolo range l/s | 9½″l –1970s | |
| 4346 GM | Vase embossed shape 4264 | | |
| 4347 GM | Jardiniere | | |
| 4348 RT | Coffee beaker embossed p55 TSC | 3¾″h –1982 | |
| 4349 GM | Pot Olympus sim to 4081 | m/s | |
| 4350 GM | Pot Olympus sim to 4081 | s/s | |
| 4351 GM | Pot Olympus sim to 4084 | l/s | |
| 4352 GM | Tankard | | |
| 4353 RT | Number not used | | |
| 4354 RT | Shell tray three feet | s/s | |
| 4355 RT | Horseshoe ashtray with horse head | 6″l –1970s | |
| 4356 GM | Plate oval Totem range | | |

| | | | |
|---|---|---|---|
| 4357 GM | Steak plate oval Totem | 10¼″l −1970s | |
| 4358 RT | Honey no cover | | |
| 4359 | Shell tray | 6″l | |
| 4360 GM | Pig money box | | |
| 4361 GM | Owl money box (re-numbered 5106) | 4¾″h | |
| 4362 GM | Beaker Starway pattern | 3¾″h −1970s | |
| 4363 GM | Pot | l/s | |
| 4364 GM | Vase | 6″h | |
| 4365 GM | Vase | 6″h | |
| 4366 GM | Vase | 6″h | |
| 4367 GM | Vase | 8″h | |
| 4368 GM | Jug pewter colour | 6″h | |

**Circa 1969**

| | | |
|---|---|---|
| 4369 RT | Lining quarter pint | |
| 4370 GM | Coffee pot | |
| 4371 GM | Jardiniere s/s also used for Evening Fantasy range | 4″h 6″l −1970s |
| 4372 GM | Cup (re-numbered 4508) | |
| 4373 GM | Vase | |
| 4374 RT | Vase embossed | |
| 4375 GM | Vase Riverside range with swan p114 TSC | 8⅛″h −1982 |
| 4376 RT | Pot | |
| 4377 GM | Vase Riverside range with swan p87 TSS p114 TSC | 6″h −1982 |
| 4378 GM | Coffee pot Starway pattern | 10½″h −1970s |
| 4379 GM | Jardiniere also used for Evening Fantasy range | 9½l −1970s |
| 4380 GM | Pot | l/s |
| 4381 GM | Ashtray round | 6″dia |
| 4382 GM | Sugar bowl | |
| 4383 RT | Cigarette box | 4½″x3″ |
| 4384 | Cream jug Starway pattern | 4″h −1970s |
| 4385 RT | Vase Riverside range with swan p114 TSC | 4″h −1982 |
| 4386 | Beaker (re-numbered 4501) | |
| 4387 RT | Cod's head tankard p118 TSC sim to 4566/4577 | 6″h −1970s |
| 4388 | Ashtray square (jollied) Evening Fantasy range | 4¾″dia −1970s |
| 4389 RT | Tobacco jar | |
| 4390 GM | Sugar bowl Starway pattern | 4″dia −1970s |
| 4391–4392 | Numbers not used | |
| 4393 | Twin vase Riverside range with swan p87 TSS p114 TSC | 3⅜″h −1982 |
| 4394 RT | Bowl Riverside range with swan p114 TSC | 7⅝″l −1982 |
| 4395 RT | Candle holder Riverside range with swan p114 TSC | 2¾″h −1970s |
| 4396 | Candle holder Hollyberry range p53 TSC | 4¼″dia −1970s |
| 4397 RT | Ashtray square | 4″acr |
| 4398 | Tray Hollyberry range l/s p53 TSC | 8″l −1970s |
| 4399 | Tray Hollyberry range s/s p53 TSC | 6″l −1970s |

Some TOBY JUGS and CHARACTER JUGS were outside modelled by Longton New Art Pottery Co. Ltd., and originally produced by them under their trade name of Kelsboro Ware. They continued to be produced after 1982 by Crown Winsor, and it is thought some of the moulds were sold after the closure of Crown Winsor (Pottery) Ltd in 1989, as some dubious examples have been sighted.

| | | |
|---|---|---|
| 4400 | Mine Host Character jug | l/s |
| 4401 | New Toby l/s p126 TSC | 7¼″h −1982+ |
| 4402 | New Toby m/s p126 TSC | 5¼″h −1982+ |
| 4403 | New Toby s/s p126 TSC | 3¾″h −1982+ |
| 4404 | Old Toby l/s p126 TSC | 8″h −1982+ |
| 4405 | Old Toby m/s p126 TSC | 4″h −1982+ |
| 4406 | Old Toby s/s p126 TSC | 3″h −1982+ |
| 4407 | Coachman m/s p126 TSC | 5½″h −1982+ |
| 4408 | Coachman s/s | 4″h −1970s |
| 4409 | Auld Mac m/s p125 TSC | 4½″h −1982+ |
| 4410 | Auld Mac s/s | 2½″h −1970s |

| | | |
|---|---|---|
| 4411 | Squire m/s p126 TSC | 4″h −1982+ |
| 4412 | Squire s/s | 2½″h −1970s |
| 4413 | Jolly Roger | m/s |
| 4414 | Jolly Roger | s/s |
| 4415 | Gaffer m/s p126 TSC | 3¾″h −1982+ |
| 4416 | Gaffer s/s p127 TSC | 2½″h −1982+ |
| 4417 | Fisherman s/s p125 TSC | 2¼″h 1980–1982+ |
| 4418 | Nellie | s/s |
| 4419 | James | s/s |
| 4420 | Colonel s/s p125 TSC | 3¼″h −1982+ |
| 4421 | Silas Sly s/s | 3¼″h −1970s |
| 4422 | King Neptune l/s | 4¼″h −1970s |
| 4423 | King Neptune m/s p125 TSC | 3″h −1982+ |
| 4424 | King Neptune s/s | 2″h −1970s |
| 4425 | King Neptune | xl/s |
| 4426 | Santa Claus | xl/s from 1982+ |
| 4427 | Santa Claus | l/s from 1982+ |
| 4428 | Santa Claus m/s | 3¼″h from 1982+ |
| 4429 | Santa Claus | s/s |
| 4430 | Mr. Pickwick | x/ls |
| 4431 | Mr. Pickwick l/s p88 TSS p127 TSC | 4¼″h −1982+ |
| 4432 | Mr. Pickwick m/s p127 TSC | 3¼″h −1982+ |
| 4433 | Mr. Pickwick s/s p127 TSC | 2″h −1982+ |
| 4434 | Tony Weller | xl/s |
| 4435 | Tony Weller l/s | 4½″h −1970s |
| 4436 | Tony Weller m/s p127 TSC | 3¼″h −1982+ |
| 4437 | Tony Weller s/s | 2¼″h −1970s |
| 4438 | Sam Weller | xl/s |
| 4439 | Sam Weller p88 TSS l/s | 4¼″h −1970s |
| 4440 | Sam Weller m/s p88 TSS p127 TSC | 3¼″h −1982+ |
| 4441 | Sam Weller s/s | 2″h −1970s |
| 4442 | Mrs. Bardwell | xl/s |
| 4443 | Mrs. Bardwell | l/s |
| 4444 | Mrs. Bardwell | m/s |
| 4445 | Mrs. Bardwell | s/s |
| 4446 | Mr. Winkle | xl/s |
| 4447 | Mr. Winkle l/s | 4½″h −1970s |
| 4448 | Mr. Winkle m/s p127 TSC | 3¼″h −1982+ |
| 4449 | Mr. Winkle s/s | 2¼″h −1970s |
| 4450 | Watchman l/s | 4½″h −1970s |
| 4451 | Watchman m/s | 3½″h −1970s |
| 4452 | Watchman s/s p125 TSC | 2″h −1982+ |
| 4453 | Cavalier | m/s |
| 4454 | Cavalier | s/s |
| 4455 | George | m/s |
| 4456 | George | s/s |
| 4457 | Simon m/s | 3¾″h −1970s |
| 4458 | Simon s/s | 2½″h −1970s |
| 4459 | Mr. Wolfe m/s p127 TSC | 3½″h −1982+ |
| 4460 | Mr. Wolfe s/s p88 TSS p127 TSC | 2¼″h −1982+ |
| 4461 | Mandolin player | l/s |
| 4462 | Mandolin player m/s p125 TSC | 8″h −1982 |
| 4463 | Mandolin player | s/s |
| 4464 | Louis | s/s |
| 4465 | Marie | s/s |
| 4466 | Charles s/s p127 TSC | 2¾″h −1982+ |
| 4467 | Cabby s/s p127 TSC | 2¾″h −1982+ |
| 4468 | Milady | m/s |
| 4469 | Musketeer m/s p125 TSC | 5⅞″h −1982+ |
| 4470 | Ann Hathaway l/s | 5¼″h −1970s |
| 4471 | Ann Hathaway m/s p127 TSC | 3″h −1982+ |
| 4472 | Ann Hathaway | s/s |
| 4473 | William Shakespears l/s | 4¾″h −1970s |
| 4474 | William Shakespeare m/s p127 TSC | 3″h −1982+ |
| 4475 | William Shakespeare | s/s |
| 4476 GM | Churchill m/s p125 TSC | 4¼″h −1982+ |
| 4477 | Welsh lady s/s p127 TSC | 3″h −1982+ |
| 4478 | Shylock l/s p125 TSC | 6½″h −1982+ |
| 4479 | Falstaff l/s p125 TSC | 6″h −1982+ |
| 4480 | Touchstone | l/s |
| 4481 | Romeo | l/s |
| 4482 | Juliet | l/s |
| 4483 | Irish leprechaun | m/s |
| 4484 | 'Duffy' the pixie | m/s |
| 4485 | Hamlet | |

| | | |
|---|---|---|
| **4486 RT** | Dick Turpin p35 TSS | 4¾"h –1970s |
| **4487 RT** | Cavalier (old number 306) p35/88 TSS p126 TSC | 4¾"h –1982+ |
| **4488 RT** | Henry VIII p35/88 TSS p126 TSC | 4"h –1982+ |
| **4489 RT** | Yeoman of the guard p35 TSS p126 TSC (old number 312) | 4¼"h –1982+ |
| **4490 GM** | Life Guard (Household Cavalry) p126 TSC | 5"h 1978–1982+ |
| **4491 RT** | William Shakespeare (old number 2815) p126 TSC | 5"h –1982+ |
| **4492 RT** | George Bernard Shaw (old number 3279) | 5½"h –1970s |
| **4493 GM** | Chelsea Pensioner p126 TSC | 4¼"h 1978–1982+ |
| **4494 GM** | Grenadier Guardsman p126 TSC | 5"h 1978–1982+ |
| **4495 GM** | Leprechaun p125 TSC | 4½"h 1980–1982+ |
| **4496 GM** | Fisherman l/s p125 TSC | 5"h 1980–1982+ |
| **4497 GM** | Harrods doorman, originally produced for Harrods only and contained tea. Mould was sold to Carlton Ware who produced it with their mark until closure of the factory in 1989 p14/15 TSC | 4¼"h from 1981+ |
| **4498–4499** | Numbers not used | |
| **4500 GM** | Teapot (Christmas pudding) | |
| **4501 GM** | Concord mug (old number 4386) | |
| **4502 GM** | Cruet three piece on stand sim to Totem | |
| **4503 GM** | Sugar bowl | |
| **4504 GM** | Cream jug | |
| **4505 GM** | Butter dish oblong | |
| **4506 GM** | Cheese dish | |
| **4507** | Sandwich tray | |
| **4508** | Cup | |
| **4509 GM** | Sandwich/sweet tray oval | 9"l |
| **4510 GM** | Coffee pot 1½pints | s/s |
| **4511** | Steak plate oval | |
| **4512** | Coffee pot 2½pint | l/s |
| **4513** | Honey pot | |
| **4514** | Plate | 8"dia |
| **4515–4520** | Numbers not used | |
| **4521 RT** | Plant pot | l/s |
| **4522 RT** | Teapot | |
| **4523** | Vase rose pattern | 6"h |
| **4524 RT** | Ashtray with swan Riverside range p114 TSC | 4½"dia –1982 |
| **4525 GM** | Cheesedish with cat and mouse | 6½"l –1982+ |
| **4526 RT** | Plant pot Rhapsody range p88 TSC | 6½"dia –1982 |
| **4527 RT** | Ashtray | |
| **4528 RT** | Vase with platform for animal p43 TSS | 8¾"h –1970s |
| **4529 RT** | Vase Gossamer range p85 TSC | 7"h –1970s |
| **4530** | Honey pot Hollyberry range p53 TSC | 4"h –1970s |
| **4531 RT** | Dolphin | 8" |
| **4532 RT** | Vase | |
| **4533** | Number not used | |
| **4534** | Vase | 10"h |
| **4535 RT** | Vase Privet range p97 TSC | 5"h –1981 |
| **4536 RT** | Plant pot Privet range m/s p97 TSC | 4"h –1981 |
| **4537 RT** | Vase Privet range p97 TSC | 4"h –1981 |
| **4538 RT** | Posy bar Privet range | 4"l |
| **4539 RT** | Plant pot Privet range s/s p97 TSC | 3¼"h –1981 |
| **4540 RT** | Vase Privet range p97 TSC | 7⅛"h –1981 |
| **4541 GM** | Cow creamer jug possibly comic type with bell | |
| **4542 RT** | Vase Adam and Eve | 10"h |
| **4543 GM** | Cow butter dish | 7"l |
| **4544 RT** | Bowl triangular Privet range | |
| **4545** | Vase Spectrum range p87 TSC | 7¾"h –1970s |
| **4546** | Egg cups and stand with fox p133 TSC | 5½"h 7¼"w |

| | | |
|---|---|---|
| **4547 RT** | Float bowl with swan Riverside range p114 TSC | 10¼"acr –1970s |
| **4548 RT** | Vase plain | 8"h |
| **4549 GM** | Apple sauce 'face pot' p59 TSS | 4¾"h –1982 |
| **4550 RT** | Vase Tristan sim to 4552, shape as 4554 | 6"h |
| **4551 GM** | Bread Sauce 'face pot' (changed to 4557) | 4"h |
| **4551 GM** | Vase Autumn Chintz range m/s (probably 4557 p86 TSC) | 8¼"h |
| **4552** | Vase shape as 4548 | 6"h |
| **4553 GM** | Beetroot 'face pot' p59 TSS | 5"h –1982 |
| **4554** | Vase Rhapsody range p88 TSC | 8¼"h –1982 |
| **4555 RT** | Jardiniere Autumn Chintz range s/s | 7"l –1970s |
| **4556** | Vase Autumn Chintz range l/s p86 TSC | 10"h –1970s |
| **4557** | Bread Sauce 'face pot' p59 TSS (previously 4551) | 4"h –1982 |
| **4557 also** | Vase Autumn Chintz m/s p86 TSC (see 4551) | 8¼"h –1970s |
| **4558** | Vase Autumn Chintz range s/s p86 TSC | 6"h –1970s |
| **4559** | Jardiniere Autumn Chintz range no handles l/s p86 TSC | 10⅛"l –1970s |
| **4560** | Posy bar Autumn Chintz p86 TSC | 7⅝"l –1970s |
| **4561** | Plant pot Gossamer range p85 TSC | 5½"dia –1970s |
| **4562** | Plant pot Tristan | |
| **4563** | Vase Tristan also Evening Fantasy | 8"h 5"dia (top) |
| **4564 RT** | Vase Tristan | |
| **4565 GM** | Cucumber 'face pot' p59 TSS | 6"h –1982 |
| **4566** | Fish head tankard sim to 4387 and 4567 | 5⅛"h –1970s |
| **4567** | Fish head tankard sim to 4387 and 4566 | 4⅜"h –1970s |
| **4568** | Vase usually Evening Fantasy | 8"h –1970s |
| **4569** | Urn vase Evening Fantasy | 6¼"h –1970s |
| **4570 GM** | Skull tankard p88 TSS p118/63 TSC | 4"h –1982+ |
| **4570 also** | Skull teapot (collector assures me this number is correct) | 4"h 6"acr –1982+ |
| **4571 RW** | Perculator | |
| **4572 GM** | Sauce boat and stand Pisces range p63 TSS p62 TSC | 7¾"l –1982 |
| **4573 TR** | Vase Assyria range p79 TSS | 8"h –1970s |
| **4574 GM** | Drinking horn tankard p63/118 TSC | 5¾"h –1982 |
| **4575** | Bowl Autumn Chintz p86 TSC | 4¾"dia –1970s |
| **4576** | Cheese dish Hollyberry p53 TSC | 7¼"l –1970s |
| **4577** | Cruet Hollyberry range p53 TSC | 6¾"l –1970s |
| **4578** | Number not used | |
| **4579** | Posy bar Hollyberry range p53 TSC | 6¾"l –1970s |
| **4580** | Posy ring Hollyberry p53 TSC | 7"dia –1970s |
| **4581 RT** | Vase Tristan part ribbed | 10"h |
| **4582** | Candle holder Hollyberry range to fit 4580 posy ring p53 TSC | 3"acr –1970s |
| **4583 GM** | Pot Tristan part ribbed | |
| **4584 GM** | Riding boot tankard p63/118 TSC | 5¾"h –1982 |
| **4585 GM** | Cruet (duck) | |
| **4586 RT** | Vase Tristan part ribbed | 6"h |
| **4587 GM** | Hot milk jug with lid Starway | 5¾"h –1970s |
| **4588 RT** | Vase Tristan part ribbed | 6"h |
| **4589** | Posy bar or cow cheese dish | |
| **4590** | Bowl Tristan round on stand part ribbed sim to 4595 | 5" |
| **4591** | Bowl Tristan oval part ribbed sim to 4593/4597 | 6" |
| **4592** | Vase incised | 6"h |
| **4593 GM** | Jardiniere Tristan part ribbed sim to 4591/4597 | l/s |
| **4594** | Vase Gossamer range p85 TSC | 9"h –1970s |

| | | |
|---|---|---|
| 4595 | Jardiniere Tristan part ribbed sim to 4590 | s/s |
| 4596 | Plant pot Gossamer range p85 TSC | 6¼"dia –1970s |
| 4597 GM | Jardiniere Tristan sim to 4590 and 4593 | l/s |
| 4598 GM | Posy bar Tristan part ribbed | |
| 4599 | Vase Gossamer range p85 TSC | 5"h –1970s |

**Circa 1970**

| | | |
|---|---|---|
| 4600 GM | Round barrel butter dish with comical cow on lid | 5¼"dia |
| 4601 | Hoop pot two handles six feet | |
| 4602 RT | Vase incised | 10"h –1970s |
| 4603 RT | Jardiniere Gossamer range p85 TSC no handles | 9½"l –1970s |
| 4604 RT | Bowl Gossamer range p85 TSC | 4"dia –1970s |
| 4605 RT | Posy bar Gossamer range p85 TSC | 7"l –1970s |
| 4606 RT | Jardiniere Gossamer s/s p85 TSC no handles | 6"l –1970s |
| 4607 GM | Jardiniere no handles | 10"l |
| 4608 | Vase Rhapsody range p88 TSC | 6"h –1982 |
| 4609 GM | Jardiniere sim to 4607 | s/s |
| 4610 GM | Vase shape as 4542 | 10"h |
| 4611 GM | Bowl | 9"l |
| 4612 GM | Plant pot Rhapsody s/s p88 TSC | 5¾"dia –1982 |
| 4613 RT | Plant pot Rhapsody l/s p88 TSC | 8¾"dia –1982 |
| 4614 RT | Jardiniere Rhapsody l/s | 10¼"l –1970s |
| 4615 RT | Jardiniere Rhapsody s/s | 7"l –1970s |
| 4616 RT | Bowl and cover (fish) | 6"l |
| 4617 GM | Vase | 10"h |
| 4618 GM | Vase | 6"h |
| 4619 GM | Vase | 8"h |
| 4620 RT | Bowl Rhapsody range p88 TSC | 9"dia –1982 |
| 4621 | Tankard plain shape as 4342 | |
| 4622 | Tankard hound head | |
| 4623 | Tankard fox head | |
| 4624 | Tankard horse head | |
| 4625 | Vase plain s/s | 6"h |
| 4626 GM | Vase | 7"h 5"dia |
| 4627 | Lochness monster (souvenir of Scotland) | s/s |
| 4628 | Drinking horn tankard | 8"h |
| 4629 | Vase Hollyberry range p53 TSC | 6"h –1970s |
| 4630 GM | Vase | 6"h |
| 4631 GM | Vase Spectrum range p87 TSC | 6"h –1970s |
| 4632 GM | Riding boot tankard one pint | |
| 4633 | Beaker (mug) Hollyberry p53 TSC | 3½"h –1970s |
| 4634 | Tray Hollyberry range l/s p53 TSC | 9½"l –1982 |
| 4635 GM | Bowl Spectrum range low foot | |
| 4636 GM | Vase Spectrum range | 10"h |
| 4637 GM | Plant pot Spectrum range l/s p87 TSC | 6"dia –1970s |
| 4638 RT | Vase Rhapsody range l/s p88 TSC | 10"h –1982 |
| 4639 RT | Comport Rhapsody range | 9"dia |
| 4640 GM | Plant pot Spectrum range | m/s |
| 4641 RT | Bowl Rhapsody range p88 TSC | 5¼"h –1982 |
| 4642 GM | Posy bar Spectrum range p87 TSC | 7¾"l –1970s |
| 4643 GM | Jardiniere Spectrum s/s p87 TSC no handles | 6½"l –1970s |
| 4644 GM | Plant pot Spectrum s/s p87 TSC | 3½"dia –1970s |
| 4645 RT | Bowl Rhapsody range p88 TSC | 9½"l –1982 |
| 4646 | Jardiniere Hollyberry s/s p53 TSC no handles | 7½"l –1970s |
| 4647 GM | Bowl Spectrum range s/s p87 TSC | 5½"dia –1970s |
| 4648 | Jardiniere Spectrum l/s p87 TSC no handles | 10"l –1970s |
| 4649 GM | Comport Spectrum range p87 TSC | 8¾"dia –1970s |
| 4650 RT | Badger | 4" |
| 4651 GM | Vase Spectrum range p87 TSC | 4¾"h –1975 |

| | | |
|---|---|---|
| 4652 GM | Bowl Spectrum range p87 TSC | 7¼"dia –1975 |
| 4653 GM | Bowl low Spectrum | |
| 4654–59 GM | Vases | 6"h |
| 4660 GM | Jardiniere | s/s |
| 4661 GM | Vase | 8"h |
| 4662 GM | Vase | 10"h |
| 4663 GM | Vase | 8"h |
| 4664 | Vase two handles six feet hoop pattern as 4601 | 8"h |
| 4665 RT | Bowl Rhapsody range p88 TSC | 4½"dia –1982 |
| 4666 RT | Bowl Rhapsody range p88 TSC with handles | 5"h –1982 |
| 4667 RT | Flower holder | 6"h |
| 4668 GM | Cup Starway range | 3"h –1975 |
| 4669 GM | Cruet Pisces range p62 TSC | 3½"h –1982 |
| 4670 | Bowl round with foot | 3¼" |
| 4671 RT | Posy ring ribbed | 6½"dia –1975 |
| 4672 RT | Horse shoe shaped posy ribbed | 6½"dia –1975 |
| 4673 RT | Posy bar ribbed | 4½"l –1975 |
| 4674 | Posy bar ribbed | 6¾"l –1975 |
| 4675 RT | Posy bar ribbed | 8¾"l –1975 |
| 4676 RT | Posy bar ribbed | 13¼"l –1975 |
| 4677 RT | Posy tray ribbed | 7¾"l –1975 |
| 4678 | Fern pot Assyria l/s p79 TSS | 7"dia –1975 |
| 4679–4681 | Numbers not used | |
| 4682 RD | Mug embossed owl | |
| 4683 GM | Mint sauce jug and stand p60 TSC | 5½"l –1982 |
| 4684 GM | Plate Pisces range p62 TSC | 9½"dia –1982 |
| 4685 GM | Plate oval Pisces range p62 TSC | 12½"l –1982 |
| 4686 GM | Saucer Starway range | 5½"dia –1975 |
| 4687–4688 | Numbers not used | |
| 4689 GM | Vase on foot | 8"h |
| 4690 GM | Plate Assyria range p79 TSS | 12¼"dia –1975 |
| 4691 GM | Bowl barrel oval two handles hoop pattern | |
| 4692 GM | Vase | 6½"h |
| 4693 GM | Vase Assyria range p79 TSS | 6¼"h –1975 |
| 4694 GM | Vase | 6½"h |
| 4695 GM | Vase p98 TSC | 6½"h |
| 4696 GM | Plant pot three feet | |
| 4697 GM | Plant pot three feet stag fighters | |
| 4698 GM | Bowl on foot | |
| 4699 GM | Plant pot Assyria p79 TSS | 5½"dia –1975 |
| 4700 GM | Honey pot | |
| 4701 GM | Vase | 7"h |
| 4702 GM | Vase Etruscan range p89 TSC | 8"h –1982+ |
| 4703 GM | Tray or saucer leaf | |
| 4704 GM | Vase Assyria range | |
| 4705 | Plate Pisces range p62 TSC | 5"dia –1982 |
| 4706 GM | Plate Pisces range p63 TSS p62 TSC | 6¾"dia –1982 |
| 4707 | Horse and rider (previously Falcon number 21) p45/85 TSS | 9"l –1975 |
| 4708 | Pony and rider p45 TSS | 5¾"l –1975 |
| 4709 | Hound lying p45/85 TSS | 4"l –1975 |
| 4710 | Hound on scent p45 TSS | 3½"l –1975 |
| 4711 | Hound standing p45 TSS | 4"l –1975 |
| 4712 GM | Golf ball honey pot | 3½"acr –1975 |
| 4713 GM | Football honey pot | 3½"acr –1975 |
| 4714 GM | Cricket ball honey pot | 3½"acr –1975 |
| 4715 GM | Rugby ball honey pot | 4¾"h –1975 |
| 4716 GM | Tennis ball honey pot | |
| 4717 | Hockey honey pot | |
| 4718 | Bowls honey pot | |
| 4719 GM | Golf ball tankard p88 TSS p63 TSC | 3¾"h –1982 |
| 4720 GM | Cricket ball tankard | 3¾"h –1975 |
| 4721 GM | Football tankard p88 TSS | 3¾"h –1975 |
| 4722 GM | Rugby ball tankard | 4½"h –1975 |
| 4723 GM | Tennis tankard | 3¾"h –1975 |
| 4724 GM | Hockey tankard | 3¾"h –1975 |
| 4725 GM | Bowls tankard p88 TSS | 3¾"h –1975 |
| 4726 RT | Sailing tankard capstan | 4"h –1975 |
| 4727 GM | Fishing tankard fish handle p88 TSS | 3¾"h –1975 |
| 4728 GM | Soccer tankard | 3¾"h –1975 |
| 4729–4730 | Numbers not used | |

| | | |
|---|---|---|
| 4731 | Bowl on foot | |
| 4732 | Bison p34 TSS | 8"l –1975 |
| 4733 | Buffalo p34 TSS | 9½"l –1975 |
| 4734 | Honey pot barrel six feet hoop pattern | |
| 4735 | Tankard | |
| 4736 | Thistle tankard Scotland | 3¾"h |
| 4737–4743 | Numbers not used | |
| 4744 RT | Jug as leaves SCC/6 | 4"h –1975 |
| 4745 RT | Jug beech leaves SCC/14 | 4"h –1975 |
| 4746 RT | Jug as leaves | 4"h –1975 |
| 4747 | Jug ash leaves and berries | 4"h –1975 |
| 4748–4749 | Numbers not used | |
| 4750 GM | Coleslaw 'facepot' p59 TSS | 4¾"h –1982 |
| 4751 GM | Tomato 'facepot' | 4¾"h –1972 |
| 4752 GM | Piccalilli 'facepot' p59 TSS | 5"h –1982 |
| 4753 GM | Chutney 'facepot' p59 TSS | 5"h –1982 |
| 4754 GM | Parsley 'facepot' p59 TSS | 4¾"h –1982 |
| 4755 GM | Pickled cabbage 'facepot' p59 TSS | 5¼"h –1982 |
| 4756 | Onion 'facepot' p59 TSS | 4¾"h –1982 |
| 4757 | Plant pot six feet hoop pattern 2nd size | 5"h 5"dia |
| 4758 GM | Bottle | 10"h |
| 4759 | Mint sauce jug | |
| 4760 GM | Humpty Dumpty egg separator | 4½"h –1975 |
| 4761 | Bowl round hoop pattern | 5"dia |
| 4762 | Bowl oval hoop pattern | 7"dia |
| 4763 | Plant pot two handles six feet hoop pattern 3rd size p112 TSS | 4¼"h |
| 4764 | Plant pot two handles six feet hoop pattern 4th size | |
| 4765 GM | Stand | 3¾"acr |

**Circa 1971**

| | | |
|---|---|---|
| 4766 RT | Gnome | l/s |
| 4767 GM | Spirit measure for leather range | |
| 4768 GM | Dish round embossed thistles in centre 'good luck from bonnie Scotland' round edge 'Made in Gt.Britain' on base | 6"dia |
| 4769 RT | Gnome new for Lazy Pixie range, can be seen on 707 p112 TSC s/s | 2½"l –1975 |
| 4770 GM | Candle holder Chrys Ware | |
| 4771 GM | Ice jug without handle | |
| 4772 GM | Vase Etruscan range p89 TSC | 6"h –1982+ |
| 4773 | Vase Etruscan range p89 TSC | 5"h –1982+ |
| 4774 GM | Bowl Etruscan range p89 TSC | 4"dia –1982+ |
| 4775 | Vase Etruscan range | 4"h |
| 4776 GM | Plant pot Etruscan p89 TSC | 5½"dia –1982+ |
| 4777 GM | Plant pot Etruscan p89 TSC | 4¼"dia –1982+ |
| 4778 | Plant pot Etruscan p89 TSC | 6½"dia –1982+ |
| 4779 GM | Bowl low Etruscan range | 10"dia |
| 4780 | Bowl Etruscan range s/s | 6"dia |
| 4781 | Bowl on stand Etruscan m/s p89 TSC | 7½"dia |
| 4782 | Bowl on stand Etruscan s/s | |
| 4783 GM | Miniature bowl on stand Etruscan range | 2½"h –1982 |
| 4784 GM | Miniature vase Rhapsody | 2¾"h –1982 |
| 4785 GM | Miniature jug antique gold or metallic black | 3"h –1982 |
| 4786 GM | Miniature vase 'Aztec' style | 3"h –1982 |
| 4787 GM | Miniature vase ridged and with raised circles | 3"h –1982 |
| 4788 | Miniature jug sim to 3834 | 3"h |
| 4789 GM | House in the Glen vase p115 TSC | 8"h –1975 |
| 4790 GM | House in the Glen twin vase p115 TSC | 7"h –1975 |
| 4791 GM | House in the Glen vase p115 TSC | 6"h –1975 |
| 4792 | Moustache cup with handle | |
| 4793 | Coffee pot Starway range | s/s |
| 4794 | Moustache cup no handle | |
| 4795 | Ice jug with handle | |

| | | |
|---|---|---|
| 4796 RT | Vase | 10"h |
| 4797 GM | Coffee pot Medway p51 TSC | 8½"h –1975 |
| 4798 RT | Bird | |
| 4799 RT | Vase sim to 4796 with panel | |
| 4800 GM | Vase Bamboo range | 8"h |
| 4801 GM | Mug Medway range p51 TSC | 3¾"h –1975 |
| 4802 GM | Sugar bowl Medway p51 TSC | 3½"h –1975 |
| 4803 | Vase Floral | 6" |
| 4804 RT | Vase with Dolphin (altered and re-numbered 5186) | |
| 4805 RT | Vase | 8"h |
| 4806 GM | Cream jug Medway p51 TSC | 4"h –1975 |
| 4807 RT | Coffee pot Brazil p51 TSC | 8¾"h –1973 |
| 4808 GM | Jardiniere oblong Bamboo | 7"l |
| 4809 RT | Teapot Croft range p58 TSS | 5¾"h –1982+ |
| 4810 RT | Miniature tankard embossed village | 3"h –1972 |
| 4811 GM | Plate Croft range p58 TSS (this number was previously a vase re-numbered 4884) | 8"acr –1982+ |
| 4812 RT | Honey pot Croft p58 TSS | 4½"h –1982+ |
| 4813 RT | Cream jug Croft | 3¼"h –1982+ |
| 4814 RT | Sugar bowl Croft | 3½"dia –1982+ |
| 4815 GM | Cheese dish Croft p58 TSS | 7"l –1982+ |
| 4816 GM | Butter dish Croft | 5"dia –1982+ |
| 4817 RT | Mug Croft range p58 TSS | 4½"h –1982+ |
| 4818 RT | Cup Croft range | 3"h –1982+ |
| 4819 RT | Saucer Croft range | 5½"dia –1982+ |
| 4820 RT | Plate Croft range (crazy paving) | 6½"dia |
| 4821 RT | Plate Croft range (crazy paving) | 8"dia |
| 4822 GM | Plate Croft range (embossed cottage) (this number was previously log with two blue tits re-numbered 4885) | 6¾"h –1982+ |
| 4823 GM | Plant pot Fleur range embossed flowers | 4¾"h –1975 |
| 4824 GM | Jardiniere Fleur range | 6¾"l –1975 |
| 4825 GM | Plant pot Fleur range s/s | 4"h –1975 |
| 4826 GM | Jardiniere Fleur range l/s | 9¼"l –1975 |
| 4827 GM | Vase Fleur range | 7"h –1975 |
| 4828 GM | Vase Fleur range | 5"h –1975 |
| 4829 GM | Vase Fleur range | 9"h –1975 |
| 4830 GM | Bowl on foot Fleur range | 5"h –1975 |
| 4831 RT | Thimble cottage p122 TSC | 1¾"h –1982 |
| 4832 GM | Cruet Croft range p58 TSS four piece or two piece | 9"l –1982+ 3½"h p & s |
| 4833 GM | Storage jar Croft range | 7½"h –1982+ |
| 4834 GM | Teapot Croft range s/s | 4¾"h –1982+ |
| 4835 TH | Flower holder leaf with novelty attached | 4" |
| 4836 TH | Stand plain round for novelties and whisky tot 4767 | 4¼" |
| 4837 | Spaniel dog 115 made smaller | |
| 4838 | Twin rabbits 1590 made smaller | |
| 4839 RT | Galloway bull s/s to go on tray 4972 p39 TSC | 2¼"h 4"l |
| 4840 TH | Flower holder Privet range novelty attached | 4¾"l |
| 4841 RT | Top hat with cat and dog | |
| 4842 GM | Jardiniere | l/s |
| 4843 GM | Cup Medway range p51 TSC | 3"h –1975 |
| 4844 GM | Saucer Medway range p51 TSC | 6¼"dia –1975 |
| 4845 RT | Vase with dots and lumps | 6"h |
| 4846 RT | St. Bernard dog | |
| 4847 | Gnome | |
| 4848 | Bowl Bamboo range | |
| 4849 RT | Picture frame flower holder | 6"h |
| 4850 RT | Leaf saucer Brazil range p51 TSC | 5½"acr –1975 |
| 4851 RT | Cup Brazil range p51 TSC | 2¾"h –1975 |
| 4852 RT | Sugar bowl Brazil p51 TSC | 3½"acr –1975 |
| 4853 RT | Cream jug Brazil p51 TSC | 4¼"h –1975 |
| 4854 GM | Vase like a rock | |
| 4855 GM | Vase Medway range | 5"h –1975 |
| 4856 GM | Vase Medway range | 5"h –1975 |
| 4857 GM | Vase Medway range | 5"h –1975 |
| 4858 GM | Vase Medway range | 7"h –1975 |
| 4859 GM | Vase Medway range | 7"h –1975 |

| | | |
|---|---|---|
| 4860 GM | Vase Medway range | 9"h –1975 |
| 4861 GM | Vase Medway range | 6"h –1975 |
| 4862 GM | Vase Medway range | 10"h –1975 |
| 4863 GM | Vase Medway range | 7"h –1975 |
| 4864 | Number not used | |
| 4865 RT | Basket honey base only p57 TSC | 3"h –1975 |
| 4866 RT | Lid for 4865 strawberry | 4"h complete |
| 4867 RT | Lid for 4865 blackberry or raspberry | 3¾"h complete |
| 4868 RT | Lid for 4865 plum or damson all on p57 TSC | 4"h complete |
| 4869 RT | Orange lid (not used) | |
| 4870 RT | Lemon lid (not used) | |
| 4871 RT | Leaf honey base only used with above lids p57 TSC | 2¾"h –1975 |
| 4872 RT | Shire horse with or without harness p46 TSS p33 TSC | 28"l with cart |
| 4873 RT | Boot tankard | |
| 4874 RT | Cruet Medway range p51 TSC | 4¼"h –1975 |

**Circa 1972 Numbers start to be used out of sequence**

| | | |
|---|---|---|
| 4875 RT | Plate Medway range p51 TSC | 6¾"acr –1975 |
| 4876 RT | Honey pot Medway p51 TSC | 4½"h –1975 |
| 4877 RT | Cheese dish Medway p51 TSC | 7½"l –1975 |
| 4878 RT | Steak plate Medway p51 TSC | 10"l –1975 |
| 4879 RT | Soup bowl Medway p51 TSC | 5½"l –1975 |
| 4880 RT | Teapot Medway p51 TSC | 5½"h –1975 |
| 4881 RT | Sandwich tray Medway p51 TSC | 12¼"l –1975 |
| 4882 RT | Butter dish Medway p51 TSC | 5"acr –1975 |
| 4883 | Number not used | |
| 4884 | Vase (previously 4811) | 7"h |
| 4885 | Log with two blue tits (previously 4822) | |
| 4886 GM | House in the Glen range bowl p115 TSC | 8"l –1975 |
| 4887 GM | House in the Glen range basket p115 TSC | 5½"l |
| 4888 GM | House in the Glen range tray p115 TSC | 4½"acr –1975 |
| 4889 GM | House in the Glen range posy (round table centre) p115 TSC | 8¾"acr –1975 |
| 4890 GM | House in the Glen range posy p87 TSS p115 TSC | 4¾"l –1975 |
| 4891–4894 | Numbers not used | |
| 4895 GM | Lemon face honey pot SCC/13 | 4½"h |
| 4896 GM | Orange face honey pot | 3½"h |
| 4897 GM | Plum face honey pot | |
| 4898 GM | Bramble/raspberry face honey | 3¾"h |
| 4899 GM | Strawberry face honey pot SCC/13 | 3½"h |
| 4900 | Number not used | |
| 4901 | Cereal dish | |
| 4902 GM | Beef dripping holder | 3¾"h –1982 |
| 4903 GM | Pork dripping holder | 3¾"h –1982 |
| 4904 GM | Lard holder | 3¾"h –1982 |
| 4905 GM | Soup bowl sim to 4908 | l/s |
| 4906 GM | Holder with different lids pan scourer, beef stock chicken stock cubes p57 TSC | 3¼"h –1982 |
| 4907 | Sink tidy bowl | |
| 4908 RT | Soup bowl with handle and lid embossed with vegetables sim to 4905 s/s | 5½"h |
| 4909–4912 | Numbers not used | |
| 4913 GM | Container for bath salts | |
| 4914 GM | Fish beaker | |
| 4915 GM | Tartare sauce 'face pot' p59 TSS (originally used as denture holder) | 3¾"h –1982 |
| 4916 GM | Fish soap tray | |
| 4917 GM | Spare toilet roll holder | |
| 4918 | Talcum powder shaker | |
| 4919 GM | Fish toothbrush holder | |
| 4920 | Number not used | |
| 4921 RT | Hexagon plant pot/vase | l/s |

| | | |
|---|---|---|
| 4922 RT | Hexagon plant pot/vase | m/s |
| 4923 RT | Hexagon plant pot/vase | s/s |
| 4924 RT | Moustache tankard (shaving mug) | |
| 4925 RT | Moustache tankard | |
| 4926 RT | Moustache tankard | |
| 4927 RT | Moustache tankard | |
| 4928 GM | Rabbit (for House in the Glen) p115 TSC | 2"h |
| 4929 GM | Pixie (for House in the Glen) p115 TSC | |
| 4930 | Swan (pomade) | |
| 4931 GM | Tea strainer set p59 TSC | 3½"h –1982 |
| 4932 RT | Vase | |
| 4933 RT | Vase mushroom shape | l/s |
| 4934 GM | Vase mushroom shape s/s | 5"h |
| 4935 GM | Vase mushroom shape m/s | 6½"h |
| 4926 | Vase | |
| 4937—4944 | Numbers not used | |
| 4945 GM | Coffin ashtray | |
| 4946 RT | Vase incised | 5"h |
| 4947 RT | Vase incised (sim to 4932) | |
| 4948 RT | Vase incised | 10"h |
| 4949 GM | Bowl incised | |
| 4950 GM | Vase incised square foot | 7"h |
| 4951 GM | Basket incised floral | |
| 4952 RT | Vase incised | 8"h |
| 4953–4958 | Numbers not used | |
| 4959 | Tankard sim to 4924 | |
| 4960 | Tankard sim to 4925 | |
| 4961 | Tankard sim to 4926 | |
| 4962 | Tankard sim to 4927 | |
| 4963 RT | Shire horse p46 TSS | 7"h 10¾"l –1982 |
| 4964 | Shaving mug plain sim to 3478 s/s | 3¾"h |
| 4965 GM | Denture holder Mosaic | 3"h |
| 4966 GM | Bath salts Mosaic p110 TSS | 5"h |
| 4967 GM | Beaker Mosaic | 3¾"h |
| 4968 | Soap tray Mosaic | |
| 4969 GM | Toilet roll holder Mosaic | 4¼"h |
| 4970 GM | Toothbrush holder Mosaic | 4"h |
| 4971 GM | Shaving mug Mosaic | 4"h |
| 4972 RT | Tray for Galloway bull 4839 sim to 4288. Limited edition made for the Galloway Bull Society p39 TSC | 1½"h 6¼"acr |
| 4973 GM | Boy and dog | |
| 4974 GM | Chicken pomander | |
| 4975 GM | Floral ball pomander | |
| 4976 GM | Ships lantern bookends p109 TSS | 5¾"h |
| 4977 GM | Kittens in a boot p84 TSS | 4¾"h –1982 |
| 4978 RT | Shire horse p46 TSS to make pair with 4963 | 7"h 10¼"l –1982 |
| 4979 GM | Vase embossed flower basket base | |
| 4980–4985 | Numbers not used | |
| 4986 RT | Dachshund dog p18 TSC | 7¾"l –1982 |
| 4987 RT | Basket wicker base | 4" |
| 4988 RT | West Highland White Terrier p18 TSC | 6¼"l –1982+ |
| 4989 | Frog pomander as 1399 | 2½"h |
| 4990 | Mouse pomander as 105 | |
| 4991 | Squirrel pomander (woodland) | |
| 4992 RT | Boxer dog | 5¾"h. clay size |
| 4993 GM | Vase Florence range | 5½"h c.s. |
| 4994 GM | Vase Florence range | 5½"h c.s. |
| 4995 GM | Vase Florence grapevine | 5½"h c.s. |
| 4996 GM | Vase Florence two handles | 5½"h c.s. |
| 4997 GM | Vase Florence range | 5½"h c.s. |
| 4998 GM | Vase Florence cottage | 5½"h c.s. |
| 4999 RT | Spaniel dog standing | |
| 5000 RT | Rough Collie dog p22 TSC | 9"l –1982 |
| 5001 GM | Saucer fabric with rose embossed possibly Milady | |
| 5002 GM | Cup fabric with rose embossed possibly Milady range | |

**June, July and August 1974**

| | | |
|---|---|---|
| 5003 GM | Vase Churnet range (leaves) | 8″h |
| 5004 GM | Vase Churnet range | 6″h |
| 5005 GM | Fern pot Churnet range | 5″h |
| 5006 GM | Fern pot Churnet range | 5½″h |
| 5007 GM | Vase Churnet range | 10″h |
| 5008 GM | Fern pot Churnet range | 4¾″–5″h |
| 5009 GM | Bowl Churnet range | 7″h |
| 5010 GM | Fern pot Churnet range | 7″h |
| 5011 GM | Plinth for 5010 pot | |
| 5012–5014 | Numbers not used | |

**July 1972**

| | | |
|---|---|---|
| 5015 GM | Vase Milton faint rib | 8″h |
| 5016–5018 | Numbers not used | |
| 5019 GM | Pot | 6″h 7″acr |
| 5020 GM | Bowl | |
| 5021 GM | Bowl | 5″ |
| 5022 GM | Rose bowl and cover | |

**June 1974**

| | | |
|---|---|---|
| 5023 RT | Shetland sheepdog s/s p21 TSC | 6¼″h –1982+ |
| 5024 RT | Shetland sheepdog l/s | 7″h |
| 5025 RT | Poodle dog sitting l/s sim to 2962/5031 | 11¼″h |

**August 1972**

| | | |
|---|---|---|
| 5026 GM | Vase irregular shape panelled | 5¾″h |
| 5027 RT | Yorkshire terrier p18 TSC | 5½″h –1982+ |
| 5028 GM | Log flower holder with kingfisher | |
| 5029 GM | Flower holder Pebble range | |
| 5030 RT | Tankard half pint 'Coco de Mer' | |
| 5031 RT | Poodle dog sitting sim to 2962/5025 m/s | 8½″h |
| 5032 RT | Boxer dog p18 TSC | 7¾″l –1982 |
| 5033 GM | Celery jug p60 TSC | 7½″h –1982+ |
| 5034 RT | Dalmation dog p22 TSC | 9″l –1982 |
| 5035 RT | Horse Hunter standing | 11½″h –1982 |
| 5036 GM | Dog money box | |
| 5037 GM | Frog money box | |
| 5038 GM | Tea bag holder p59 TSC | 6″l –1982 |
| 5039 RT | Owl money box | 8″ |
| 5040 RT | Eagle (American) | |
| 5041 GM | Coffee bag holder p59 TSC | 6″l –1982 |
| 5042 GM | Spring onion jar p60 TSC | 4½″h –1982+ |
| 5043 GM | Corn on the cob dish p60 TSC | 9″l –1982+ |
| 5044 OM | Resin container triangle | |
| 5045 OM | Resin container fluted cone | |
| 5046 OM | Resin container plain cone | |
| 5047 GM | Tea bag dispenser | |
| 5048 GM | Horseradish 'face pot' p59 TSS | 4¼″h –1982 |
| 5049 RT | Beagle dog p18 TSC | 8½″l –1982+ |
| 5050 RT | Swans head pie funnel | |
| 5051 GM | Vase incised pattern | 6″h |

**1st October 1980**

| | | |
|---|---|---|
| 5052 GM | Pigs head thimble | |
| 5053 GM | Castle thimble p122 TSC | 1¼″h –1982 |
| 5054 GM | Rose thimble | |
| 5055 GM | Daffodil thimble | |
| 5056 GM | Heart thimble | |
| 5057 GM | Leaning tower of Pisa thimble p122 TSC | 1⅜″h –1982 |
| 5058 GM | Windmill thimble p122 TSC | 1¼″h –1982 |
| 5059 GM | Circus clown thimble p122 TSC | 1¼″h –1982 |

**1st October 1979**

| | | |
|---|---|---|
| 5060 GM | Wishing Well thimble p122 TSC | 1¼″h –1982 |
| 5061 GM | Unicorn thimble | |
| 5062 | Lion thimble | |

**Thimbles came in attractive matching boxes**

**November 1972**

| | | |
|---|---|---|
| 5063 GM | Cigarette box (treasure chest) | 2″h 4¼″w |
| 5064 OM | Ashtray (Resin container) | |
| 5065 GM | Ashtray (ships wheel) | |
| 5066 GM | Vase Trentham leaf pattern | 5″h |
| 5067 GM | Vase Trentham | 8″h |
| 5068 GM | Vase Trentham | 5¼″h |
| 5069 GM | Plant pot Trentham | 5″h |
| 5070 GM | Plant pot Trentham | 6″h |
| 5071 GM | Vase Trentham | 7¾″h |
| 5072 GM | Bowl on foot Trentham | 6″h |
| 5073 GM | Bowl low Trentham | 2″h |
| 5074 GM | Bowl oval Trentham | 1″h |
| 5075 GM | Vase Trentham | 4¼″h |
| 5076 RT | Spaniel dog p17/18 TSC | 7¾″l –1982+ |
| 5077 GM | Coffee bag dispenser | |
| 5078 GM | Cup Avon shape hammered pattern gold or silver colours | 3″h |
| 5079 GM | Saucer Avon shape hammered pattern | 5½″acr |
| 5080 GM | Plate Avon shape hammered pattern | 6½″acr |
| 5081 GM | Sugar bowl Avon shape hammered pattern | 3¼″h |
| 5082 GM | Cream jug Avon shape hammered pattern | 3¾″h |
| 5083 GM | Coffee pot Avon shape hammered pattern | 9″h |

**January 1973**

| | | |
|---|---|---|
| 5084 GM | Bread and butter plate Avon shape hammered pattern | 11″acr |
| 5085 GM | Sandwich tray Avon hammered pattern | 12½″l |
| 5086 GM | Salt and Pepper Avon hammered pattern | 3¼″h |
| 5087 GM | Tea pot s/s Avon hammered | 5″h |
| 5088 GM | Tea pot l/s Avon hammered | 5¾″h |
| 5089 GM | Individual cream jug Avon s/s hammered pattern | 3″h |
| 5090 GM | Tankard Avon shape hammered pattern | 4¼″h |

**August 1978**

| | | |
|---|---|---|
| 5091 GM | Tortoise money box (eyes altered from 5101) | 5¾″l |
| 5092 GM | Owl money box (eyes altered from 5106) | 4¾″h |
| 5093 GM | Squirrel money box (eyes altered from 5105) | 5¾″h |
| 5094–5095 | Numbers not used | |
| 5096 GM | Bulldog Optical money box p119 TSC | 5¾″h –1982+ |
| 5097 GM | Frog Optical money box p119 TSC (see article in SCC/18) | 5¼″h –1982 |

**February and March 1973**

| | | |
|---|---|---|
| 5098 | Tankard half pint (3278 old number) | 3¾″h |
| 5099 | Moustache tankard half pint (3278 old number) | 3¾″h |
| 5100 GM | Pen tray (Motivil) | |
| 5101 GM | Tortoise money box Optical and Caricature p119 TSC | 5¾″l –1982+ |
| 5102 GM | Elephant Caricature money box p119 TSC | 5″l –1982 |
| 5103 GM | Bloodhound Caricature money box p119 TSC | 5¼″h –1982+ |
| 5104 GM | Teddy bear Caricature money box p119 TSC | 5¼″h –1982+ |
| 5105 GM | Chipmunk Optical and Caricature money box (old number 3935) p119 TSC | 5¾″h –1982+ |

| | | |
|---|---|---|
| **5106 GM** | Owl Optical and Caricature money box (old number 4361) p119 TSC (See article in SCC/18) | 4¾"h –1982 |
| **5107 RT** | Siamese cat p47/84 TSS | 8½"l –1982+ |
| **5108 RT** | Afghan hound p21 TSC | 8¾"l –1982+ |
| **5109 GM** | Cucumber bowl | |
| **5110 GM** | Grapefruit bowl on stand (jollied) | |
| **5111 RT** | Siamese cat p47 TSS | 8¾"h –1982+ |
| **5112 RT** | Alsation (German Shepherd dog) p21 TSC | 9¾"l –1982+ |
| **5113 GM** | Friar Tuck Character jug p127 TSC | 6¾"h –1981 |
| **5114 GM** | Robin Hood Character jug p127 TSC | 6"h –1981 |
| **5115 GM** | Sheriff of Nottingham Character jug p127 TSC | 6"h –1981 |
| **5116 GM** | Little John Character jug p127 TSC | 6¾"h –1981 |
| **5117 GM** | Maid Marion Character jug p127 TSC | 6¼"h –1981 |
| **5118 GM** | Allan A Dale Character jug p127 TSC | 6¼"h –1981 |
| **5119 OM** | Mallard duck p50 TSS | 6½"l –1982+ |

**May 1973**

| | | |
|---|---|---|
| **5120 OM** | Golden Eye duck p50 TSS | 6"l –1982+ |
| **5121 OM** | Gosling | |
| **5122 OM** | Shoveller duck p37 TSS | 6½"l –1982+ |
| **5123 OM** | Tufted duck | |
| **5124 GM** | Beaker | |
| **5125 RT** | Shire horse smaller version of 4963 p46 TSS | 8¾"l –1982 |
| **5126** | Onion 'face pot' s/s p59 TSS | 4"h –1982 |
| **5127** | Beetroot 'face pot' s/s p59 TSS | 4¼"h –1982 |
| **5128 GM** | Strawberry bowl jollied (Brazil saucer 4850 as stand) | |
| **5129 GM** | Raspberry bowl jollied (Brazil saucer 4850 as stand) | |
| **5130 GM** | Ashtray with cover | |
| **5131 RT** | Donkey p50 TSS also with saddle or panniers | 10½"l –1982 |

**September and October 1973**

| | | |
|---|---|---|
| **5132 GM** | Vase Florence range (candle grease effect) | 7½"h |
| **5133 GM** | Vase Florence range | 2¾"h |
| **5134 GM** | Vase Florence range | 9"h |
| **5135 GM** | Plant pot Florence range | 5½"h |
| **5136 GM** | Candle holder Florence range | |
| **5137 GM** | Plant pot Florence range | 4½"h |
| **5138 GM** | Twin candle holder Florence | 2¾"h 6¼"w |
| **5139 GM** | Candle holder jug Florence | 3½"h |
| **5140 GM** | Bowl on foot Florence | s/s |
| **5141** | Number not used | |
| **5142 GM** | Jardiniere Florence | l/s |
| **5143 OM** | Ham stand made for Rodek limited edition of 100 (Rodek was a promotional and advertising company) | |
| **5144 OM** | Ashtray made for Rodeks own use. Limited edition | |
| **5145 OM** | Ashtray made for Lesney, sand coloured and mounted with a model Sand Buggy. Limited edition of 600 | |
| **5146 OM** | Ashtray made for Lesney, grey coloured and mounted with an aeroplane. Limited edition of 600 | |
| **5147 GM** | Muffin/scone dish on stand with lid | |
| **5148 GM** | Mayonaise jug and stand p60 TSC | 6½"l –1982 |
| **5149** | Pickwick pomander s/s based on number 4433 | |

| | | |
|---|---|---|
| **5150 RT** | Dobermann Pinscher p21 TSC | 8½"l –1982+ |
| **5151 GM** | Banana Split dish (open tray) | |
| **5152 GM** | Elephant based on 5102 money box | 5"l |
| **5153 GM** | Coffee beaker | |
| **5154 GM** | Coffee beaker | |
| **5155 GM** | Coffee beaker | |
| **5156 GM** | Coffee beaker embossed leaves and berries | |

**14th January 1974**

| | | |
|---|---|---|
| **5157 GM** | Coffee beaker embossed diamond shapes | 3⅞"h |
| **5158 GM** | Coffee beaker embossed flowers | 3⅞"h |
| **5159 GM** | Coffee beaker embossed sticks | 3⅞"h |
| **5160 GM** | Coffee beaker embossed flowers | 3⅞"h |
| **5161 GM** | Coffee beaker embossed leaves | 3⅞"h |
| **5162 GM** | Coffee beaker embossed circles (shape as 5155) | 3⅞"h |
| **5163 GM** | Coffee beaker embossed elongated triangles | 3⅞"h |
| **5164** | Number not used | |
| **5165 GM** | Bust of Winston Churchill p76 TSS | 8"h |
| **5166 GM** | Rhinoceros p31 TSC | 10½"l –1982 |
| **5167 RT** | Labrador p21/22 TSC | 9½"l –1982+ |
| **5168 GM** | Butter dish round basket base sunflower lid | 5"acr |

**25th January 1974**

| | | |
|---|---|---|
| **5169 GM** | Butter dish oblong basket base sunflower lid | 5⅞"l |
| **5170 RT** | Setter p17/21 TSC | 9¼"l –1982+ |
| **5171 GM** | Coffee pot Alton range fluted with embossed flowers | 10¼"h |
| **5172 GM** | Cream jug Alton range | 3⅞"h |
| **5173 GM** | Cup Alton range | 2⅞"h |
| **5174 GM** | Cruet Alton range (two piece) | 3½"h |
| **5175 GM** | Sugar bowl Alton range | 3½"acr |
| **5176 GM** | Saucer Alton range fluted only | 5⅝"acr |
| **5177 GM** | Tea plate Alton fluted only | 6¾"acr |
| **5178 GM** | Teapot Alton range | 6¼"h –1982+ |
| **5179 GM** | Bread and butter plate Alton range fluted only | 10¼"acr |
| **5180 GM** | Butter dish Alton range | 5¼"l |
| **5181 GM** | Cheese dish Alton range | 7¼"l |
| **5182 GM** | Honey pot Alton range | 4¾"h |
| **5183 GM** | Cereal dish Alton fluted only | 6¼"acr |

**28th March 1974**

| | | |
|---|---|---|
| **5184** | Number not used | |
| **5185 RT** | Bowl Dolphin novelty range (l/s dolphin) | 7½"l |
| **5186 RT** | Vase Dolphin range (taken from number 4084) (s/s dolphin) | 4"h |
| **5187 RT** | Tray Dolphin (s/s dolphin) | |
| **5188 RT** | Vase Dolphin (l/s dolphin) p62 TSS | 5¾"h |
| **5189 RT** | Plant pot Dolphin (l/s dolphin) | 4"h |
| **5190 RT** | Posy trough Dolphin (s/s dolphin) | 5"l |
| **5191 RT** | Basket Dolphin (s/s dolphin) | 6"l |
| **5192 RT** | Twin vase Dolphin (s/s dolphin) | 3¼"h |
| **5193 GM** | Bowl plain | 2½"h |

**July 1975**

| | | |
|---|---|---|
| **5194 GM** | Doggy's Dinner bowl embossed dog's head on lid and bones and biscuits around bowl | 5"acr |
| **5195 GM** | Pussy's Dinner bowl embossed cat's head on lid and fish around bowl | 5"acr |

| | | |
|---|---|---|
| **5196 RT** | Chestnut vase (renumbered from 5398) | |

**Circa 1974**

| | | |
|---|---|---|
| **5197 RT** | Galloway bull l/s | 5″h |
| **5198 GM** | Fisherman character jug | 5″h |
| **5199 GM** | Clerk character jug | 5″h |
| **5200 GM** | Horse dealer character jug | 5″h |
| **5201 GM** | Miner character jug | 5″h |
| **5202 GM** | Bricklayer character jug | 5″h |
| **5203 GM** | Cook character jug | 5″h |
| **5204 GM** | Coffee beaker | |
| **5205 RT** | Welsh Sheepdog (Border Collie) p21 TSC | 9¾″l –1982+ |
| **5206 RT** | John Kennedy character jug | 6¼″h |
| **5207 RT** | Galloway bull m/s 5197 made smaller p41 TSC (error in height) | 4¾″h 8″l |
| **5208 RT** | Beaker with orange face | |
| **5209 RT** | Fox Prestige range p14 TSS | 10½″l –1982+ |
| **5210 GM** | Gazelle Modus 80 p79 TSS | 9½″l –1982 |
| **5211 GM** | Squirrel Prestige range p14 TSS | 7″h –1982 |
| **5212 GM** | Cheetah Modus 80 p79 TSS | 10″l –1982 |
| **5213 GM** | Horse Modus 80 p79 TSS | 8½″h –1982 |
| **5214 RT** | Loving cup three handles American scenes | |
| **5215 RT** | Tankard embossed George Washington | |
| **5216 OM** | Badger with front paw on rock | 5″h 10″l |
| **5217 GM** | Tankard three quarters pint | 4″h |
| **5218 GM** | Tankard three quarters pint | 4″h |
| **5219 GM** | Tankard three quarters pint | 4″h |
| **5220** | Number not used | |

**17th March 1981**

| | | |
|---|---|---|
| **5221 GM** | Volvo Tankard | |
| **5222 OM** | Benskins Indian Head Tankard limited edition p128/129 TSC | 5¾″h |

**December 1974**

| | | |
|---|---|---|
| **5223 RT** | Vase embossed | 8″h |
| **5224 RT** | Vase embossed | 8″h |
| **5225 RT** | Vase plain | 8″h |
| **5226 RT** | Vase ribbed | 10″h |
| **5227 RT** | Vase plain | 7″h |

**Circa 1975**

| | | |
|---|---|---|
| **5228 RT** | Vase plain | 6″h |
| **5229 GM** | Hippopotamus p46 TSS | 6″l –1982 |
| **5230 GM** | Camel p46 TSS | 5¼″l –1982 |
| **5231 GM** | Bear | 3″h 6″l |
| **5232 GM** | Two monkeys p46 TSS | 4⅛″h –1982 |
| **5233 GM** | Lion p46 TSS | 6¼″l –1982 |
| **5234 GM** | Giraffe p46 TSS | 5″h –1982 |
| **5235 RT** | Cushion (for 5236 cat) p47 TSS | 9″x6″ –1982 |
| **5236 RT** | Long haired cat p47 TSS this was modelled on Mr. Thompson's own cat, originally a stray | 8¼″ – 1982 |
| **5237 RT** | Cat p47 TSS | 11½″l –1982+ |
| **5238 GM** | Polar Bear Modus 80 p79 TSS | 7″h –1982 |
| **5239 GM** | Badger | 5½″h 11″l |
| **5240 RT** | Plant pot plain | 6¼″h |
| **5241 RT** | Cup | |
| **5242 GM** | Dish mop holder | 6⅛″h –1982 |

**Circa 1977**

| | | |
|---|---|---|
| **5243 GM** | Flower jug Harvest Time range p116 TSC | 7¾″h –1982 |
| **5244 GM** | Basket Harvest Time p116 TSC | 6″l –1982 |
| **5245 GM** | Plant pot Harvest Time p116 TSC | 5″h –1982 |
| **5246 GM** | Vase Harvest Time p87 TSS p116 TSC | 4½″h –1982 |
| **5247 GM** | Twin vase Harvest Time p116 TSC | 6″h –1982 |
| **5248 GM** | Posy Bowl Harvest Time p116 TSC | 5″l –1982 |
| **5249 GM** | Bulb bowl Harvest Time p116 TSC | 6″acr –1982 |
| **5250 GM** | Jardiniere Harvest Time p116 TSC (originally intended to have handles but don't know if any were produced) | 6¾″l –1982 |
| **5251 GM** | Mouse for Harvest Time l/s | 2½″h c.s. –1982 |
| **5252 GM** | Mouse for Harvest Time s/s | 1¾″h c.s. –1982 |
| **5253** | Number not used | |

**16th December 1980**

| | | |
|---|---|---|
| **5254 GM** | Mouse | |
| **5255 GM** | Fox | |
| **5256 GM** | Vase | 6″h |
| **5257 GM** | Rabbit | |

**26th February 1979**

| | | |
|---|---|---|
| **5258** | Great Dane Supreme Dogs p17 TSC | 8⅞″l –1982+ |
| **5259 OM** | Schnauzer Supreme Dogs p17 TSC | 7″l –1982+ |
| **5260 GM** | Whippet Supreme Dogs p17 TSC | 6″l –1982+ |
| **5261 OM** | Cat crouching p47 TSS | 10½″l –1982+ |
| **5262 GM** | Long hair cat half sitting p47 TSS | 7⅛″l –1982+ |

**21st July 1983**

| | | |
|---|---|---|
| **5263 GM** | Poodle dog standing (lion clip) | 5½″h 6½″l –1982+ |
| **5264–5265** | Numbers not used | |
| **5266** | Vase (unconfirmed) | 7–8″h |

**15th July 1975**

| | | |
|---|---|---|
| **5267 GM** | Vase with squares and circles | 5½″h |
| **5268 RT** | Vase as 5227 but incised pattern | 7″h |
| **5269 RT** | Vase as 5228 but incised pattern | 6⅜″h |

**1st January 1977**

| | | |
|---|---|---|
| **5270 RT** | Tankard half pint p76 TSC | 4¼″h –1982 |
| **5271 RT** | Tankard quarter pint p76 TSC | 3¼″h –1982 |
| **5272 GM** | Covered bowl p60/63 TSC | 4¼″acr –1982 |
| **5273** | Bowl 4641 made smaller | |

**Circa 1975**

| | | |
|---|---|---|
| **5274 GM** | Bowl Vintage range embossed grapes and vine leaves with pedestal base | 7¾″acr –1981 |
| **5275 GM** | Urn vase Vintage range | 9″h –1981 |
| **5276 GM** | Plant pot Vintage range | 6⅞″h –1981 |
| **5277 GM** | Fruit stand Vintage range | 10½″acr –1981 |
| **5278 GM** | Vase Vintage range | 6⅞″h –1981 |
| **5279 GM** | Bamboo vase single stem | |
| **5280 GM** | Urn vase Vintage range | 9″h |
| **5281 RT** | Tankard p58/76 TSC | 5¾″h –1982 |
| **5282 RT** | Tankard p58 TSC | 8⅛″h –1982 |
| **5283 RT** | Tankard lining for leather holder | Gill size |
| **5284 RT** | Tankard p58 TSC | 5¾″h –1982 |
| **5285 GM** | Leaf (for ashtrays) | |
| **5286 GM** | Bowl for dish cloth | 3¾″h –1982 |
| **5287 GM** | Eagle | 8″h |
| **5288 RT** | Ashtray (Geest) with centre piece | |
| **5289 GM** | Novelty lop ear rabbit l/s | 7″h –1982 |
| **5290 GM** | Novelty lop ear rabbit m/s | 5¼″h –1982 |
| **5291 GM** | Novelty lop ear rabbit s/s | 3⅞″h –1982 |
| **5292 GM** | Novelty dog l/s p24 TSC | 7⅛″h –1982 |

| | | |
|---|---|---|
| 5293 GM | Novelty dog m/s p24 TSC | 5½"h –1982 |
| 5294 GM | Novelty dog s/s p24 TSC | 3⅞"h –1982 |
| 5295 GM | Novelty dog l/s p24 TSC | 7"h –1982 |
| 5296 GM | Novelty dog m/s p24 TSC | 5¼"h –1982 |
| 5297 GM | Novelty dog s/s p24 TSC | 3¾"h –1982 |
| 5298 GM | Novelty cat l/s p84 TSS p27 TSC | 7⅛"h –1982 |
| 5299 GM | Novelty cat m/s p27 TSC | 5¼"h –1982 |
| 5300 GM | Novelty cat s/s p84 TSS p27 TSC | 3⅞"h –1982 |

**18th February 1976**

| | | |
|---|---|---|
| 5301 GM | Novelty sheep dog l/s p24 TSC | 7"h |
| 5302 GM | Novelty sheep dog m/s p24 TSC | 5¼"h |
| 5303 GM | Novelty sheep dog s/s p24 TSC | 3¾"h |
| 5304 RT | Corgi dog | 7½"h |
| 5305 GM | Rabbit straight ears l/s | |
| 5306 | Rabbit straight ears m/s | |
| 5307 | Rabbit straight ears s/s | |
| 5308 GM | Tea bag pot | 4½"h –1982 |
| 5309 RT | Ashtray plain square | 5¾"acr |
| 5310 RT | Ashtray plain oblong | 7"l |
| 5311 RT | Ashtray plain oval | |
| 5312 RT | Corgi dog | 6½"h |
| 5313 GM | Emily with dog Staffordshire Rustics | 10"h |
| 5314 GM | Alice with goat Staffordshire Rustics p34 TSC | 10¾"h |
| 5315 GM | Adam the gamekeeper Staffordshire Rustics p34 TSC | 10¼"h |
| 5316 GM | Katie the goosegirl Staffordshire Rustics | 10¼"h |

**9th March 1977**

| | | |
|---|---|---|
| 5317 RT | Candle holder plain | 6"h |
| 5318 RT | Candle holder embossed | 6"h |

**May 1976**

| | | |
|---|---|---|
| 5319 RT | Chihuahua Supreme Dogs p18 TSC | 5¾"h –1982+ |
| 5320 RT | St. Bernard Supreme Dogs p22 TSC | 9½"l –1982+ |
| 5321 RT | Corgi Supreme Dogs p18 TSC | 6¾"l –1982+ |

**March 1975**

| | | |
|---|---|---|
| 5322 RT | Old English Sheepdog Supreme Dogs p17 TSC | 7"l –1982+ |
| 5323 RT | Sealyham Supreme Dogs p17 TSC | 7½"l –1982+ |
| 5324 RT | Pyrennean Mountain dog Supreme Dogs p17 TSC | 10"l –1982+ |

**11th August 1976**

| | | |
|---|---|---|
| 5325 GM | Jug New Cavalier range | 8"h –1982 |
| 5326 GM | Punch bowl New Cavalier range | 10½"acr –1982 |
| 5327 RT | Wall plaque New Cavalier range | 10"acr –1982 |
| 5328 GM | Tankard New Cavalier range l/s | 5¾"h –1982 |
| 5329 GM | Jug New Cavalier range s/s | 5⅞"h –1982 |
| 5330 GM | Goblet New Cavalier range | 5"h –1982 |
| 5331 GM | Ashtray square New Cavalier range | 5⅞"acr –1982 |
| 5332 GM | Loving cup three handles New Cavalier range | 5¼"h –1982 |
| 5333 GM | Tankard s/s New Cavalier range | 4⅛"h –1982 |
| 5334 GM | Decanter New Cavalier range | 9¾"h –1982 |
| 5335 GM | Hanging bowl 'Right Herbert' s/s | |
| 5336 RT | Hanging bowl 'Right Herbert' | |
| 5337 GM | Jug Cordon Brun Kitchen Ware p55 TSC | 6¼"h –1982 |
| 5338 GM | Jug Cordon Brun p55 TSC | 5½"h –1982 |
| 5339 GM | Jug Cordon Brun p55 TSC | 4¾"h –1982 |
| 5340 GM | Jug Cordon Brun p55 TSC | 3¾"h –1982 |
| 5341 GM | Storage jar Cordon Brun p63 TSS | 6¾"h –1982 |

| | | |
|---|---|---|
| 5342 GM | Storage jar Cordon Brun p63 TSS | 5"h –1982 |
| 5343 GM | Cruet two piece Cordon Brun | 4½"h –1982 |
| 5344 GM | Salt jar Cordon Brun | 7½"h –1982 |
| 5345 GM | Honey pot Cordon Brun p55 TSC | 4"h –1982 |
| 5346 GM | Coffee pot Cordon Brun p55 TSC | 8¼"h –1982 |
| 5347 GM | Teapot Cordon Brun p55 TSC | 5¾"h –1982 |
| 5348 GM | Beaker Cordon Brun p55 TSC | 4¼"h –1982 |

**19th January 1977**

| | | |
|---|---|---|
| 5349 GM | Butter dish Cordon Brun | 5¼"l –1982 |
| 5350 GM | Cheese dish Cordon Brun | 7¼"l –1982 |
| 5351 GM | Jam pot holder Cordon Brun | 4"h |
| 5352 GM | Cup Cordon Brun p55 TSC | 3½"h –1982 |
| 5353 RT | Saucer Cordon Brun p55 TSC | 5½"acr –1982 |
| 5354 RT | Plate s/s Cordon Brun p55 TSC | 6½"acr –1982 |
| 5355 RT | Plate m/s Cordon Brun p55 TSC | 8"acr –1982 |
| 5356 RT | Egg cup with saucer Cordon Brun | 5"acr –1982 |
| 5357 GM | Sugar sifter Cordon Brun | 5¼"h –1982 |
| 5358 GM | Spoon rest Cordon Brun | 8"l –1982 |
| 5359 RT | Egg separator Cordon Brun | 3¼"h –1982 |
| 5360 RT | Lemon squeezer Cordon Brun | 4½"h –1982 |
| 5361 GM | Herb/Spice jars Cordon Brun | 3¾"h –1982 |
| 5362 GM | Mixing bowl Cordon Brun | 6½"acr –1982 |
| 5363 GM | Sweet/Fruit stand Cordon Brun | |
| 5364 RT | Double egg cup | 4½"l –1982 |
| 5365 RT | Teapot stand Cordon Brun p55 TSC | 6¼"acr –1982 |
| 5366 GM | Toast rack Cordon Brun p55 TSC | 7½"l –1982 |
| 5357 OM | Ashtray | l/s |
| 5368 GM | Ashtray | s/s |
| 5369 GM | Plant pot Bamboo range p95 TSC | 5¼"acr –1982 |
| 5370 GM | Vase Bamboo range p95 TSC | 7¾"h –1982 |
| 5371 GM | Plant pot Bamboo range p95 TSC | 6½"acr –1982 |
| 5372 GM | Vase Bamboo range p95 TSC | 10"h –1982 |
| 5373 GM | Vase Bamboo range p95 TSC | 12"h –1982 |
| 5374 GM | Vase Bamboo range p95 TSC | 6"h –1982 |
| 5375 GM | Posy bar m/s Bamboo range p95 TSC | 8"l –1982 |
| 5376 GM | Posy bar l/s Bamboo range p95 TSC | 11¾"l –1982 |
| 5377 GM | Posy bar s/s Bamboo range p95 TSC | 5¾"l –1982 |
| 5378 GM | Plant pot Bamboo range p95 TSC | 7½"acr –1982 |
| 5379 GM | Plant pot Bamboo range p95 TSC | 8¾"acr –1982 |
| 5380 GM | English sheepdog | |
| 5381 GM | Skye Terrier | 3½"h |
| 5382 RT | Horse shoe ashtray (old number 4246) p63 TSC | 6"l –1982 |
| 5383 GM | Bee honey pot p60 TSC | 4⅞"h –1982+ |
| 5384 GM | Ashtray (jollied) | 8"x2" c.s. |
| 5385 GM | Pomander | |
| 5386 GM | Tray Lincoln range hand decorated with stylised leaves | 7¼"l |
| 5387 GM | Vase two handles Lincoln range | 8"h |
| 5388 GM | Flower jug Lincoln range | 8"h |
| 5389 GM | Plant pot Lincoln ornamental handles | 5¾"h |
| 5390 GM | Fruit bowl Lincoln range | 12½"l |
| 5391 GM | Vase Lincoln range | 10"h |
| 5392 RT | Vase plain | 8"h |
| 5393 RT | Ginger jar Canton range p95 TSC | 11½"h –1982 |
| 5394 RT | Ginger jar Canton range p95 TSC | 9½"h –1982 |
| 5395 RT | Ginger jar Canton range p95 TSC | 7"h –1982 |
| 5396 RT | Jar Canton range p95 TSC | 13"h –1982 |
| 5397 RT | Jar Canton range p95 TSC | 9¼"h –1982 |

| | | | |
|---|---|---|---|
| 5398 RT | Covered bowl Canton range p95 TSC | 9″h –1982 | |
| 5399 RT | Covered bowl Canton range p95 TSC | 9½″acr –1982 | |
| 5400 GM | Cruet two piece p49 TSC | 3½″h –1982 | |
| 5401 OM | Bathroom jar made for 'Boots' | 7″h | |

**February 1980**

| | | | |
|---|---|---|---|
| 5402 GM | Cheese dish plain p49 TSC | 8¾″l –1982 | |
| 5403 GM | Ashtray | | |

**August 1977**

| | | | |
|---|---|---|---|
| 5404 RT | Leyland lorry for British Leyland limited edition p33 TSS | | |
| 5405 GM | Ashtray | 3¾″ 5″ c.s. | |
| 5406 RT | Bowl ribbed | 5″h 8¾″w | |
| 5407 RT | Ashtray | 2½″h 3¼″w | |
| 5408 RT | Tray (jollied) | 5½″ c.s. | |
| 5409 RT | Teapot English Rose p56 TSC | 5″h –1982 | |
| 5410 RT | Sugar bowl English Rose p56 TSC | 4″acr –1982 | |
| 5411 RT | Cream jug English Rose p56 TSC | 3″h –1982 | |
| 5412 GM | Saucer English Rose p56 TSC | 5½″acr –1982 | |
| 5413 GM | Tea plate English Rose p56 TSC | 6¾″acr –1982 | |
| 5414 GM | Cup English Rose range p56 TSC | 3″h –1982 | |
| 5415 GM | Cruet English Rose range | 3⅜″h –1981 | |
| 5416 GM | Honey pot English Rose range | | |
| 5417 GM | Cheese dish English Rose range | 7⅝″h –1981 | |
| 5418 GM | Butter dish English Rose range | 5¾″l –1981 | |

**November 1980**

| | | | |
|---|---|---|---|
| 5419 GM | Teapot 'Dutch' shape p49 TSC | 5½″h –1982 | |
| 5420 GM | Jug No. 4 'Dutch' shape s/s | 4″h –1982 | |
| 5421 GM | Beaker | 4″h –1982 | |
| 5422 GM | Honey pot | 5″h –1982 | |
| 5423 GM | Teatime set teapot and beaker with clockface set at 3 pm | 4½″h teapot 3″h beaker | |
| 5424 GM | Butter dish | 5¾″l –1982 | |
| 5425 GM | Teapot 'Three Tea Bag Pot' p59 TSC | 5½″h –1982+ | |
| 5426 GM | Teapot 'Two Tea Bag Pot' p59 TSC | 4¾″h –1982+ | |
| 5427 GM | Teapot 'One Tea Bag Pot' p59 TSC | 4″h –1982+ | |
| 5428 GM | Teapot stand p59 TSC | 6″acr –1982+ | |
| 5429 GM | Jug No.3 'Dutch' shape m/s p49 TSC | 4½″h –1982 | |
| 5430 GM | Jug No.2 'Dutch' shape l/s | 4¾″h –1982 | |

**Circa 1978**

| | | | |
|---|---|---|---|
| 5431 GM | Owl lamp base | 4¼″h | |
| 5432 GM | Tortoise lamp base | 3½″h | |
| 5433 GM | Hound lamp base | 5″h | |
| 5434 RT | Springer spaniel p17 TSC | 8″l –1982 | |
| 5435 OM | Jug 'Pipers Whisky' limited edition | | |
| 5436 OM | Ashtray 'Pipers Whisky' limited edition | | |
| 5437 OM | Guinness ashtray limited edition | | |
| 5438 OM | Bell and dove | | |
| 5439 GM | Soap dish | | |
| 5440 OM | Tyre ashtray | | |
| 5441 GM | Miniature 'teapot' flower jug Hollington range sim to 5470/5476 | 3″h | |
| 5442 GM | Miniature flower jug, handle at top | 3″h | |
| 5443 GM | Miniature flower jug incised swirl pattern | 3″h | |
| 5444 GM | Miniature flower jug Hollington range sim to 5469/5475 | | |

| | | | |
|---|---|---|---|
| 5445 GM | Miniature flower jug Hollington range sim to 5472/5474 | 3″h | |
| 5446 GM | Miniature flower jug Hollington range sim to 5471/5473 | 3″h | |
| 5447 GM | Honey pot Anniversary range p52 TSC | 5″h –1981 | |
| 5448 GM | Goblet Anniversary range p52 TSC | 5″h –1981 | |
| 5449 GM | Teapot Anniversary range p52 TSC | 6¾″h –1981 | |
| 5450 GM | Plate Anniversary range p52 TSC | 10″acr –1981 | |
| 5451 GM | Trinket box Anniversary p52 TSC | 4½″l –1981 | |
| 5452 GM | Cream jug Anniversary p52 TSC | 3¾″h –1981 | |
| 5453 GM | Cup Anniversary range | | |
| 5454 GM | Saucer Anniversary range | | |
| 5455 GM | Tea plate Anniversary range | | |
| 5456 GM | Loving cup Anniversary p52 TSC | 7½″acr –1981 | |
| 5457 | Bowl Anniversary range (similar to Hudson tray) | | |
| 5458 GM | Ashtray Anniversary range p52 TSC | 5½″l –1981 | |
| 5459 GM | Candle holder Anniversary p52 TSC | 6¾″h –1981 | |
| 5460 GM | Bell Anniversary range p52 TSC | 5¼″h –1981 | |
| | PLEASE NOTE: ANNIVERSARY RANGE WAS ALSO USED AS COMMEMORATIVE WARE | | |
| 5461–5462 | Numbers not used | | |
| 5463 GM | Egg cup first chicken (not used) | | |
| 5464 GM | Egg cup second chicken (not used) | | |
| 5465 GM | Egg cup third chicken p60 TSC | 4″l –1982 | |
| 5466 GM | Egg cup stand p60 TSC | 8″acr –1982 | |
| 5467 OM | Yorkshire hod | | |
| 5468 OM | "Nessie" Cruet set p56 TSS | 13″l –1982 | |
| 5469 GM | Flower jug Hollington p97 TSC sim to 5444/5475 | 9″h –1981 | |
| 5470 GM | Teapot flower jug Hollington sim to 5441/5476 p97 TSC | 9″h –1981 | |
| 5471 GM | Flower jug Hollington p97 TSC sim to 5446/5473 | 9″h –1981 | |
| 5472 GM | Flower jug Hollington p97 TSC sim to 5445/5474 | 9″h –1981 | |
| 5473 GM | Flower jug Hollington p97 TSC sim to 5446/5471 | 6½″h –1981 | |
| 5474 GM | Flower jug Hollington p97 TSC sim to 5445/5472 | 6½″h –1981 | |
| 5475 GM | Flower jug Hollington p97 TSC sim to 5444/5469 | 6½″h –1981 | |
| 5476 GM | Teapot flower jug Hollington p97 TSC sim to 5441/5470 | 6½″h –1981 | |
| 5477 | Number not used | | |

**Circa 1981**

| | | | |
|---|---|---|---|
| 5478 GM | Egg cup 'truck' Nursery Ware p64 TSS | 2⅜″l –1982 | |
| 5479 GM | Salt 'engine' Nursery Ware p64 TSS | 4″l –1982 | |
| 5480 GM | Teddy bear honey pot | | |

**Circa 1979**

| | | | |
|---|---|---|---|
| 5481 GM | Vase High Tide swirling waves hand decorated rocks and shells on base | 5¾″h | |
| 5482 GM | Bowl High Tide range | 7¾″l | |
| 5483 GM | Plant pot High Tide range | 4″h 3½″dia | |
| 5484 GM | Plant pot High Tide range | 5″h | |
| 5485 GM | Vase High Tide range | 7¾″h | |
| 5486 GM | Vase High Tide range | 4½″h | |
| 5487 GM | Basket High Tide range | 8¼″l | |
| 5488 GM | Flower holder High Tide range | 8½″acr | |

| | | |
|---|---|---|
| 5489 GM | Bowl High Tide range | 5¼"l |
| 5490 GM | Acorn vase | |

**9th February 1982**

| | | |
|---|---|---|
| 5491–5494 | Vases | |
| 5495–5498 | Numbers not used | |

**Circa 1979**

| | | |
|---|---|---|
| 5499 GM | Vase Autumn Leaves embossed leaves hand decorated in Autumn tints | 6"h |
| 5500 GM | Flower pot Autumn Leaves range | 5⅝"h |
| 5501 GM | Jug vase Autumn Leaves range | 8"h |
| 5502 GM | Vase Autumn Leaves range | 10"h |
| 5503 GM | Covered bowl on pedestal Autumn Leaves range | 6½"h |
| 5504 GM | Flower holder Autumn Leaves range | 11½"l |
| 5505 GM | Plant pot Autumn Leaves range | 5"h |
| 5506 GM | Plant pot Autumn Leaves range | 7"h |
| 5507 GM | Covered trinket box Autumn Leaves | 4"h 6"l |
| 5508 GM | Candleholder Autumn Leaves range | 5½"acr |
| 5509 GM | Jug vase Autumn Leaves range | 7"h |
| 5510 OM | Vase for single flower | |
| 5511 OM | Vase for single flower | |
| 5512 OM | Vase for single flower leaves/bud Solo range | 4¼"h –1981 |
| 5513 OM | Vase Solo range embossed leaves | 6¼"h –1981 |
| 5514 OM | Vase Solo range embossed leaves single bud vase | 4"h –1981 |
| 5515 OM | Vase Solo range embossed leaves single bud vase | 6⅛"h –1981 |
| 5516 GM | Vase corn on the cob Solo range single bud vase | 6⅛"h –1981 |
| 5517 GM | Brooch/pendant Retriever head only (in box) p51 TSS | 4"x3"x⅞" (box) –1982 |
| 5518 GM | Brooch/pendant Cairn p51 TSS | –1982 |
| 5519 GM | Brooch/pendant Poodle p51 TSS | –1982 |
| 5520 GM | Brooch/pendant Bulldog p51 TSS | –1982 |
| 5521 GM | Brooch/pendant Spaniel p51 TSS | –1982 |
| 5522 GM | Brooch/pendant Collie p51 TSS | –1982 |
| 5523 GM | Brooch/pendant horse p51 TSS | –1982 |
| 5524 GM | Brooch/pendant horse p51 TSS | –1982 |
| 5525 GM | Brooch/pendant horse p51 TSS | –1982 |
| 5526–5528 | Numbers not used | |
| 5529 OM | Salt and Pepper (½pint beer mug) | |
| 5530 OM | Money box (½pint beer mug) | |
| 5531 GM | Salt (½ pint beer mug 'froth') | |
| 5532 GM | Money box (½ pint beer mug 'froth') | |
| 5533 | Plain pot remodelled from Privet range flower pot 4536 | 4"h |
| 5534 | Number not used | |
| 5535 GM | Bell Croft range p58 TSS | 4¾"h –1982 |
| 5536 GM | Jug Croft range | 7"h –1982+ |
| 5537 GM | Coffee pot Croft p58 TSS | 9"h –1982+ |
| 5538 GM | Clock Croft range p58 TSS clock movement made in West Germany sim to plate 4811 on page 58 TSS | 8"acr –1981 |
| 5539–5546 | Numbers not used | |
| 5547 OM | Clown honey pot | |

**Circa 1980**

| | | |
|---|---|---|
| 5548 HH | 'Nosey Parker' vinegar bottle (face with hat and large nose) | 5¾"h |
| 5549 HH | 'Nosey Parker' Pepper | 5"h |
| 5550 HH | 'Nosey Parker' Salt | 4¾"h |
| 5551 GM | Tray to go with plant pots 2790 and 2785 | l/s & s/s |
| 5552 GM | Tray to go with plant pot 2796 | s/s |

**Circa 1981**

| | | |
|---|---|---|
| 5553 GM | Cradle | 3½"h 4½"l |
| 5554 GM | Pair of baby bootees p120 TSC | 3½"h |
| 5555 GM | Stork carrying bundle p120 TSC | 4½"h |
| 5556–5558 | Numbers not used | |
| 5559 EB | Wall disc miniature plaque | 4¼"acr |
| 5560 EB | Wall dish miniature plaque | 3½"acr |
| 5561–5562 | Numbers not used | |

**Circa 1980**

| | | |
|---|---|---|
| 5563 HH | Tray | |
| 5564 HH | Toilet roll holder | |
| 5565 HH | Bath salt jar with cover | |
| 5566 HH | Tooth brush holder | |
| 5567 HH | Denture bowl | |
| 5568–5570 | Numbers not used | |

**Circa 1981**

| | | |
|---|---|---|
| 5571 GM | Plant pot Giant Panda range p117 TSC | 4½"h –1982 |
| 5572 GM | Twin vase Giant Panda range p117 TSC | 6¼"h –1982 |
| 5573 GM | Flower jug Giant Panda range p117 TSC | 9"h –1982 |
| 5574 GM | Flower jug Giant Panda range | 7½"h –1982 |
| 5575 GM | Bowl Giant Panda p117 TSC | 8½"l –1982 |
| 5576 GM | Money box Giant Panda range p87 TSS p117 TSC | 4¼"h –1982 |
| 5577 | Number not used | |
| 5578 EB | Panda sitting (for Giant Panda range) | 2¼"h –1982 |
| 5579 EB | Panda standing (for Giant Panda range) | 1½"h 2¾"l –1982 |

**Circa 1977**

| | | |
|---|---|---|
| 5580 RT | Disc | s/s |
| 5581 RT | Disc | l/s |
| 5582 RT | Disc Martingale s/s p80 TSS | 3½"dia –1982 16½"l (set of three) |
| 5583 RT | Disc Martingale p80 TSS (leather by Strand Leathergoods Ltd) | l/s –1982 25"l (set of three) |

**Circa 1980**

| | | |
|---|---|---|
| 5584 GM | Trinket box Milady range | 5¼"l –1982 |
| 5585 GM | Ring stand Milady range | 4½"acr –1982 |
| 5586 GM | Plant pot Milady p94 TSC | 6¾"acr –1982 |
| 5587 GM | Tray oval Milady range | 10"l –1982 |
| 5588 GM | Powder bowl or pin cushion p94 TSC (supplied with powder puff or pin cushion) | 4½"acr –1982 |
| 5589 GM | Candle holder Milady range | 4"h –1982 |
| 5590 GM | Plant pot Milady p94 TSC | 5½"acr –1982 |
| 5591 GM | Plant pot Milady p94 TSC | 4¾"acr –1982 |
| 5592 GM | Vase Milady range p94 TSC | 8"h –1982 |
| 5593 GM | Vase Milady range p94 TSC | 6"h –1982 |
| 5594 GM | Hand mirror Milady range | 8¾"l –1982 |
| 5595 GM | Bud vase Milady p94 TSC | 6¾"h –1982 |

**Circa 1981**

| | | |
|---|---|---|
| 5596 GM | Vase '1904' range p33 TSS | 8⅝"h –1982+ |
| 5597 GM | Flower jug '1904' p33 TSS | 9"h –1982+ |
| 5598 GM | Vase '1904' range p33 TSS | 9⅝"h –1982+ |
| 5599 GM | Vase '1904' range p33 TSS | 9¼"h –1982+ |
| 5600 GM | Vase '1904' range p33 TSS | 9⅛"h –1982+ |
| 5601–5605 | Numbers not used | |
| 5606 GM | Vase Belgravia range p96 TSC | 8¼"h –1982+ |

| | | | |
|---|---|---|---|
| **5607 GM** | Vase Belgravia range p96 TSC | 6¾"h | –1982+ |
| **5608 GM** | Vase Belgravia range p96 TSC | 6"h | –1982 |
| **5609 GM** | Jardiniere Belgravia p96 TSC no handles | 6¼"l | –1982+ |
| **5610 GM** | Bowl Belgravia range p96 TSC | 7¾"l | –1982+ |
| **5611 GM** | Plant pot Belgravia p96 TSC | 4⅝"h | –1982+ |
| **5612 GM** | Plant pot Belgravia p96 TSC | 5"h | –1982 |
| **5613 GM** | Plant pot Belgravia p96 TSC | 5½"h | –1982+ |
| **5614 GM** | Plant pot Belgravia p96 TSC | 6½"h | –1982+ |
| **5615 GM** | Plant pot Belgravia p96 TSC | 7½"h | –1982+ |

**Belgravia range re-introduced by Portmeirion Potteries Ltd 1992+**

| | |
|---|---|
| **5616–5618** | Numbers not used |

**Circa 1980**

| | | | |
|---|---|---|---|
| **5620 GM** | Cup Tapestry range | 3⅛"h | –1982 |
| **5621 GM** | Saucer Tapestry range | 5¾"acr | –1982 |
| **5622 GM** | Tea plate Tapestry range | 6¾"acr | –1982 |
| **5623 GM** | Beaker Tapestry range | 4½"h | –1982 |
| **5624 GM** | Sugar bowl Tapestry range | 3¼"acr | –1982 |
| **5625 GM** | Cream jug Tapestry range | 3½"h | –1982 |
| **5626 GM** | Teapot Tapestry range | 5"h | –1982 |
| **5627 GM** | Sandwich tray Tapestry range | 11¾"l | –1982 |
| **5628 GM** | Cruet two piece Tapestry | 3½"h | –1982 |
| **5629 GM** | Butter dish Tapestry range | 5¼"l | –1982 |
| **5630 GM** | Cheese dish Tapestry range | 7½"l | –1982 |
| **5631 GM** | Honey pot Tapestry p112 TSS | 3½"h | –1982 |
| **5632–5633** | Numbers not used | | |

**4th March 1982**

| | | |
|---|---|---|
| **5634 GM** | Teapot | l/s |
| **5635 GM** | Teapot | l/s |
| **5636 GM** | Teapot | s/s |
| **5637 GM** | Teapot | s/s |
| **5638–5643** | Numbers not used | |

**Circa 1981**

| | | | |
|---|---|---|---|
| **5644 GM** | Wedding cake thimble | | |
| **5645–5654** | Numbers not used | | |
| **5655 GM** | Pig beaker | | |
| **5656 GM** | Panda/Teddy Bear money box Optical range p33 TSS | 5¼"h | –1982+ |
| **5657 GM** | Pig money box p33 TSS Optical range | 5½"h | –1982+ |
| **5658 GM** | Rabbit/Chipmunk money box Optical range p33 TSS | 5¾"h | –1982+ |
| **5659 GM** | Elephant money box p33 TSS Optical range | 5¾"h | –1982+ |
| **5660 GM** | 'Cheshire' cat money box | 6¼"l | –1982+ |

| | | | |
|---|---|---|---|
| | Optical range p33 TSS | | |
| **5661 GM** | Bassett hound money box Optical range p33 TSS | 5⅝"h | –1982+ |
| **5662 GM** | Fish money box p33 TSS Optical range (See article in SCC/18) | 6⅝"l | –1982+ |
| **5663–5668** | Numbers not used | | |
| **5670 GM** | Teapot Tudor Cottage Ware p62 TSS | 5½"h | –1982+ |
| **5671 GM** | Sugar bowl Tudor Cottage Ware p62 TSS | 3"acr | –1982+ |
| **5672 GM** | Cream jug Tudor Cottage Ware p62 TSS | 3¼"h | –1982+ |
| **5673 GM** | Butter dish Tudor Cottage Ware p62 TSS | 5¾"l | –1982+ |
| **5674 GM** | Cheese dish Tudor Cottage Ware p62 TSS | 7"l | –1982+ |
| **5675 GM** | Honey pot Tudor Cottage Ware p62 TSS | 4½"h | –1982+ |
| **5676 GM** | Cruet two piece Tudor Cottage Ware p62 TSS | 3¼"h | –1982+ |
| **5677–5995** | Numbers not used | | |

**Circa 1978**

| | | | |
|---|---|---|---|
| **5996 GM** | Newspaper holder Desk Top range p121 TSC | 4⅝"h | –1981 |
| **5997 GM** | Matchbox tray Desk Top range p121 TSC | 5⅜"l | –1981 |
| **5998 GM** | Matchbox pen holder Desk Top range p121 TSC | 4⅛"h | –1981 |
| **5999 GM** | Sack pen holder Desk Top range p121 TSC | 4¼"h | –1981 |
| **6000 OM** | Scrap paper tray Desk Top range p121 TSC | 5¼"l | –1982 |
| **6001 OM** | Gift Parcel box Desk Top range p121 TSC | 4½"l | –1982 |
| **6002 OM** | Carrier Bag pen holder Desk Top range p121 TSC also used by and marked Harrods Food Halls, and originally contained tea, (in Harrods colours) | 4"h | –1982 |
| **6003 OM** | Parcel money box Desk Top range p121 TSC | 4"l | –1982 |
| **6004 OM** | Letter paper weight Desk Top range p121 TSC | 5¼"l | –1982 |
| **6005 OM** | Ball of String string dispenser Desk Top range p121 TSC | 3⅝"h | –1982 |
| **6006 OM** | Beer can | | |
| **6007–6127** | Numbers not used | | |
| **6128 GM** | Alphabet 'P' money box | | |

# ILLUSTRATION INDEX

A quick reference guide to illustrations found in The SylvaC Story and The SylvaC Companion. The Falcon Ware numbers have been separated from the OLD Shaw & Copestake numbers, to avoid confusion. The mould number is in the first column, followed by page number and book title. Compiled by Brian Stalley.

## Falcon Ware

| No. | Page | Book | No. | Page | Book | No. | Page | Book | No. | Page | Book | No. | Page | Book |
|---|---|---|---|---|---|---|---|---|---|---|---|---|---|---|
| 15 | 106 | TSC | 170 | 41 | TSS | 282 | 86 | TSS | 427 | 102 | TSC | 591 | 53 | TSS |
| 15 | 107 | TSC | 176 | 42 | TSS | 287 | 105 | TSC | 431 | 37 | TSS | 591 | 86 | TSS |
| 15 | 48 | TSS | 177 | 42 | TSS | 292 | 145 | TSC | 455 | 148 | TSC | 599 | 72 | TSC |
| 16 | 22 | TSC | 177 | 43 | TSS | 293 | 145 | TSC | 455 | 57 | TSS | 603 | 92 | TSC |
| 16 | 48 | TSS | 178 | 43 | TSS | 294 | 151 | TSC | 463 | 102 | TSC | 615 | 92 | TSC |
| 18 | 19 | TSC | 183 | 50 | TSS | 297 | 140 | TSC | 465 | 148 | TSC | 616 | 92 | TSC |
| 18 | 42 | TSS | 184 | 50 | TSS | 300 | 151 | TSC | 468 | 57 | TSS | 618 | 92 | TSC |
| 18 | 41 | TSS | 184 | 84 | TSS | 300 | 35 | TSS | 469 | 86 | TSS | 619 | 59 | TSS |
| 25 | 37 | TSS | 185 | 43 | TSS | 304 | 151 | TSC | 471 | 53 | TSS | 621 | 59 | TSS |
| 26 | 37 | TSS | 188 | 43 | TSS | 304 | 35 | TSS | 473 | 86 | TSS | 623 | 103 | TSC |
| 27 | 37 | TSS | 188 | 42 | TSS | 305 | 151 | TSC | 475 | 66 | TSS | 626 | 102 | TSC |
| 28 | 37 | TSS | 192 | 138 | TSC | 305 | 35 | TSS | 476 | 66 | TSS | 628 | 91 | TSC |
| 29 | 37 | TSS | 196 | 67 | TSC | 306 | 88 | TSS | 479 | 143 | TSC | 628 | 94 | TSC |
| 31 | 38 | TSS | 196 | 144 | TSC | 307 | 151 | TSC | 485 | 105 | TSC | 629 | 91 | TSC |
| 43 | 137 | TSC | 196 | 102 | TSC | 307 | 35 | TSS | 486 | 102 | TSC | 630 | 91 | TSC |
| 44 | 137 | TSC | 197 | 67 | TSC | 309 | 151 | TSC | 488 | 105 | TSC | 631 | 91 | TSC |
| 44 | 70 | TSS | 198 | 67 | TSC | 310 | 151 | TSC | 489 | 72 | TSC | 632 | 91 | TSC |
| 45 | 137 | TSC | 199 | 67 | TSC | 320 | 54 | TSS | 490 | 143 | TSC | 636 | 72 | TSC |
| 68 | 31 | TSC | 203 | 42 | TSS | 323 | 54 | TSS | 493 | 105 | TSC | 636 | 73 | TSC |
| 68 | 107 | TSC | 205 | 97 | TSS | 325 | 151 | TSC | 494 | 105 | TSC | 639 | 72 | TSC |
| 68 | 47 | TSS | 207 | 48 | TSS | 328 | 151 | TSC | 497 | 86 | TSS | 645 | 91 | TSC |
| 72 | 103 | TSS | 209 | 42 | TSS | 330 | 112 | TSC | 500 | 143 | TSC | 646 | 91 | TSC |
| 73 | 106 | TSS | 210 | 42 | TSS | 331 | 141 | TSC | 501 | 143 | TSC | 648 | 91 | TSC |
| 74 | 124 | TSC | 214 | 2 | TSS | 332 | 141 | TSC | 509 | 66 | TSC | 649 | 91 | TSC |
| 75 | 124 | TSC | 216 | 138 | TSC | 334 | 140 | TSC | 510 | 66 | TSC | 656 | 90 | TSC |
| 81 | 124 | TSC | 218 | 147 | TSC | 335 | 151 | TSC | 511 | 66 | TSC | 673 | 72 | TSC |
| 82 | 52 | TSS | 221 | 144 | TSC | 337 | 140 | TSC | 512 | 66 | TSC | 674 | 94 | TSC |
| 83 | 52 | TSS | 221 | 138 | TSC | 338 | 141 | TSC | 513 | 66 | TSC | 675 | 94 | TSC |
| 87 | 52 | TSS | 222 | 97 | TSS | 339 | 141 | TSC | 514 | 66 | TSC | 675 | 103 | TSC |
| 92 | 31 | TSC | 222 | 138 | TSC | 340 | 151 | TSC | 516 | 59 | TSC | 676 | 94 | TSC |
| 92 | 107 | TSC | 223 | 67 | TSC | 341 | 151 | TSC | 524 | 143 | TSC | 679 | 85 | TSS |
| 92 | 47 | TSS | 225 | 138 | TSC | 342 | 140 | TSC | 530 | 148 | TSC | 684 | 94 | TSC |
| 96 | 31 | TSC | 226 | 147 | TSC | 343 | 140 | TSC | 535 | 86 | TSS | 684 | 103 | TSC |
| 96 | 47 | TSS | 226 | 138 | TSC | 344 | 140 | TSC | 536 | 148 | TSC | 689 | 86 | TSS |
| 97 | 31 | TSC | 228 | 138 | TSC | 345 | 141 | TSC | 540 | 148 | TSC | 697 | 31 | TSS |
| 97 | 47 | TSS | 230 | 138 | TSC | 350 | 140 | TSC | 541 | 148 | TSC | 702 | 54 | TSS |
| 98 | 31 | TSC | 233 | 138 | TSC | 351 | 140 | TSC | 542 | 148 | TSC | 707 | 112 | TSC |
| 98 | 47 | TSS | 236 | 145 | TSC | 352 | 140 | TSC | 544 | 14 | TSS | 707 | 54 | TSS |
| 99 | 47 | TSS | 236 | 138 | TSC | 353 | 53 | TSS | 545 | 14 | TSS | 707 | 32 | TSS |
| 100 | 47 | TSS | 237 | 138 | TSC | 353 | 86 | TSS | 546 | 73 | TSC | 708 | 31 | TSS |
| 101 | 47 | TSS | 238 | 138 | TSC | 354 | 54 | TSS | 546 | 72 | TSC | 710 | 90 | TSC |
| 102 | 47 | TSS | 239 | 138 | TSC | 355 | 57 | TSS | 546 | 92 | TSC | 711 | 72 | TSC |
| 102 | 84 | TSS | 240 | 138 | TSC | 355 | 86 | TSS | 548 | 86 | TSS | 712 | 72 | TSC |
| 103 | 47 | TSS | 246 | 147 | TSC | 365 | 140 | TSC | 549 | 72 | TSC | 713 | 72 | TSC |
| 104 | 84 | TSS | 249 | 67 | TSC | 366 | 140 | TSC | 550 | 86 | TSS | 714 | 72 | TSC |
| 107 | 50 | TSS | 252 | 105 | TSC | 368 | 142 | TSC | 557 | 76 | TSC | 716 | 72 | TSC |
| 108 | 52 | TSS | 252 | 145 | TSC | 376 | 147 | TSC | 557 | 102 | TSC | 718 | 90 | TSC |
| 110 | 52 | TSS | 252 | 144 | TSC | 380 | 102 | TSC | 561 | 101 | TSC | 718 | 73 | TSC |
| 113 | 124 | TSC | 253 | 145 | TSC | 380 | 144 | TSC | 562 | 101 | TSC | 721 | 54 | TSS |
| 114 | 41 | TSS | 258 | 103 | TSC | 383 | 103 | TSC | 564 | 102 | TSC | 724 | 70 | TSC |
| 114 | 42 | TSS | 259 | 67 | TSC | 384 | 37 | TSS | 566 | 102 | TSC | 725 | 90 | TSC |
| 115 | 42 | TSS | 259 | 144 | TSC | 385 | 102 | TSC | 567 | 61 | TSS | 726 | 70 | TSC |
| 115 | 41 | TSS | 259 | 101 | TSC | 386 | 101 | TSC | 568 | 61 | TSS | 727 | 72 | TSC |
| 116 | 41 | TSS | 260 | 144 | TSC | 387 | 103 | TSC | 569 | 86 | TSS | 732 | 54 | TSS |
| 116 | 42 | TSS | 260 | 101 | TSC | 393 | 101 | TSC | 571 | 102 | TSC | 733 | 54 | TSS |
| 129 | 31 | TSS | 262 | 47 | TSC | 394 | 101 | TSC | 572 | 86 | TSS | 736 | 54 | TSS |
| 134 | 30 | TSC | 266 | 47 | TSC | 399 | 147 | TSC | 582 | 68 | TSS | 739 | 73 | TSC |
| 136 | 37 | TSS | 267 | 47 | TSC | 400 | 66 | TSS | 582 | 59 | TSS | 741 | 73 | TSC |
| 145 | 41 | TSS | 268 | 47 | TSC | 406 | 57 | TSS | 582 | 86 | TSS | 747 | 53 | TSS |
| 146 | 41 | TSS | 272 | 101 | TSC | 409 | 92 | TSC | 583 | 59 | TSS | 749 | 73 | TSC |
| 147 | 41 | TSS | 272 | 144 | TSC | 409 | 104 | TSC | 583 | 86 | TSS | 752 | 73 | TSC |
| 148 | 41 | TSS | 273 | 145 | TSC | 410 | 53 | TSS | 583 | 69 | TSS | 753 | 70 | TSC |
| 152 | 31 | TSS | 275 | 47 | TSC | 418 | 142 | TSC | 585 | 86 | TSS | 756 | 70 | TSC |
| 155 | 41 | TSS | 276 | 47 | TSC | 426 | 101 | TSC | 585 | 59 | TSS | | | |
| 166 | 23 | TSC | 277 | 47 | TSC | 426 | 102 | TSC | 586 | 38 | TSS | | | |
| 169 | 36 | TSS | 280 | 76 | TSS | 427 | 101 | TSC | 587 | 86 | TSS | | | |

**Shaw & Copestake**

| Ref | No. | Type | Ref | No. | Type | Ref | No. | Type | Ref | No. | Type | Ref | No. | Type | Ref | No. | Type |
|---|---|---|---|---|---|---|---|---|---|---|---|---|---|---|---|---|---|
| | | | 962 | 124 | TSC | 1175 | 101 | TSC | 1296 | 84 | TSS | 1390 | 30 | TSC | 1455 | 17 | TSS |
| 19 | 98 | TSS | 964 | 37 | TSC | 1176 | 71 | TSC | 1298 | 28 | TSC | 1390 | 45 | TSS | 1457 | 17 | TSS |
| 30 | 98 | TSS | 981 | 105 | TSS | 1179 | 106 | TSS | 1298 | 44 | TSS | 1391 | 45 | TSS | 1457 | 61 | TSS |
| 36 | 20 | TSS | 989 | 95 | TSS | 1181 | 38 | TSS | 1299 | 44 | TSS | 1393 | 17 | TSS | 1458 | 74 | TSS |
| 127 | 36 | TSC | 990 | 28 | TSC | 1181 | 17 | TSS | 1300 | 44 | TSS | 1393 | 62 | TSS | 1459 | 15 | TSS |
| 273 | 35 | TSC | 990 | 44 | TSS | 1182 | 17 | TSS | 1302 | 28 | TSC | 1394 | 17 | TSS | 1462 | 74 | TSS |
| 337 | 35 | TSC | 990 | 21 | TSS | 1184 | 45 | TSC | 1302 | 44 | TSS | 1394 | 62 | TSS | 1464 | 25 | TSC |
| 371 | 81 | TSS | 992 | 18 | TSS | 1184 | 86 | TSS | 1302 | 87 | TSS | 1395 | 66 | TSC | 1467 | 85 | TSS |
| 374 | 35 | TSC | 1022 | 18 | TSS | 1189 | 67 | TSC | 1303 | 44 | TSS | 1395 | 105 | TSC | 1473 | 95 | TSS |
| 419 | 35 | TSC | 1024 | 124 | TSC | 1190 | 42 | TSC | 1303 | 87 | TSS | 1397 | 56 | TSS | 1475 | 39 | TSC |
| 421 | 35 | TSC | 1026 | 28 | TSC | 1190 | 56 | TSS | 1304 | 44 | TSS | 1399 | 17 | TSS | 1479 | 56 | TSS |
| 425 | 35 | TSC | 1026 | 21 | TSS | 1191 | 39 | TSC | 1304 | 87 | TSS | 1400 | 41 | TSS | 1480 | 90 | TSC |
| 432 | 81 | TSS | 1026 | 44 | TSS | 1191 | 61 | TSS | 1305 | 56 | TSS | 1400 | 38 | TSS | 1480 | 56 | TSS |
| 436 | 54 | TSS | 1027 | 21 | TSS | 1192 | 39 | TSC | 1307 | 90 | TSC | 1400 | 44 | TSS | 1481 | 56 | TSS |
| 509 | 81 | TSS | 1027 | 44 | TSS | 1193 | 39 | TSS | 1311 | 32 | TSS | 1400 | 17 | TSS | 1484 | 56 | TSS |
| 540 | 95 | TSS | 1028 | 28 | TSC | 1194 | 39 | TSC | 1311 | 17 | TSS | 1401 | 2 | TSS | 1484 | 38 | TSS |
| 559 | 97 | TSS | 1028 | 21 | TSS | 1195 | 56 | TSS | 1312 | 54 | TSS | 1401 | 15 | TSS | 1485 | 18 | TSS |
| 560 | 38 | TSC | 1028 | 44 | TSS | 1196 | 56 | TSS | 1312 | 56 | TSS | 1402 | 15 | TSS | 1485 | 31 | TSS |
| 573 | 38 | TSC | 1033 | 36 | TSC | 1201 | 67 | TSC | 1315 | 16 | TSS | 1402 | 2 | TSS | 1485 | 84 | TSS |
| 573 | 83 | TSS | 1039 | 96 | TSS | 1203 | 23 | TSC | 1318 | 56 | TSS | 1403 | 17 | TSS | 1487 | 56 | TSS |
| 575 | 35 | TSC | 1044 | 37 | TSC | 1205 | 40 | TSS | 1320 | 18 | TSS | 1403 | 2 | TSS | 1490 | 104 | TSC |
| 578 | 35 | TSC | 1046 | 28 | TSC | 1205 | 41 | TSS | 1326 | 16 | TSS | 1404 | 101 | TSC | 1491 | 104 | TSC |
| 578 | 81 | TSS | 1046 | 45 | TSS | 1206 | 40 | TSS | 1327 | 16 | TSS | 1406 | 96 | TSS | 1492 | 30 | TSC |
| 600 | 35 | TSC | 1046 | 84 | TSS | 1207 | 41 | TSS | 1328 | 17 | TSS | 1407 | 103 | TSC | 1492 | 44 | TSS |
| 604 | 37 | TSC | 1064 | 27 | TSC | 1207 | 40 | TSS | 1330 | 17 | TSS | 1409 | 101 | TSC | 1494 | 18 | TSS |
| 605 | 82 | TSS | 1064 | 17 | TSS | 1208 | 40 | TSS | 1331 | 17 | TSS | 1410 | 96 | TSS | 1496 | 95 | TSS |
| 605 | 83 | TSS | 1065 | 21 | TSS | 1209 | 39 | TSC | 1332 | 15 | TSS | 1410 | 101 | TSC | 1497 | 18 | TSS |
| 606 | 42 | TSC | 1065 | 44 | TSS | 1209 | 40 | TSS | 1332 | 40 | TSS | 1412 | 40 | TSS | 1498 | 30 | TSC |
| 606 | 82 | TSS | 1067 | 28 | TSC | 1209 | 41 | TSS | 1333 | 15 | TSS | 1413 | 17 | TSS | 1498 | 50 | TSS |
| 614 | 42 | TSC | 1067 | 21 | TSS | 1211 | 18 | TSS | 1334 | 15 | TSS | 1414 | 45 | TSS | 1498 | 44 | TSS |
| 649 | 83 | TSS | 1067 | 44 | TSS | 1213 | 45 | TSC | 1334 | 2 | TSS | 1414 | 42 | TSS | 1499 | 30 | TSC |
| 650 | 83 | TSS | 1070 | 71 | TSC | 1214 | 67 | TSC | 1334 | 50 | TSS | 1415 | 42 | TSS | 1499 | 44 | TSS |
| 680 | 96 | TSS | 1086 | 18 | TSS | 1216 | 45 | TSC | 1334 | 17 | TSS | 1415 | 40 | TSS | 1499 | 50 | TSS |
| 693 | 96 | TSS | 1090 | 45 | TSC | 1221 | 124 | TSC | 1336 | 16 | TSS | 1416 | 56 | TSS | 1500 | 18 | TSS |
| 698 | 96 | TSS | 1091 | 45 | TSC | 1227 | 40 | TSS | 1337 | 16 | TSS | 1417 | 97 | TSS | 1504 | 18 | TSS |
| 700 | 54 | TSS | 1092 | 123 | TSC | 1238 | 29 | TSC | 1340 | 17 | TSS | 1418 | 101 | TSC | 1505 | 18 | TSS |
| 700 | 96 | TSS | 1109 | 36 | TSC | 1245 | 40 | TSS | 1342 | 101 | TSC | 1419 | 95 | TSS | 1506 | 18 | TSS |
| 703 | 109 | TSS | 1110 | 108 | TSS | 1246 | 42 | TSS | 1343 | 103 | TSC | 1420 | 30 | TSC | 1508 | 18 | TSS |
| 704 | 37 | TSC | 1113 | 142 | TSC | 1246 | 56 | TSS | 1344 | 101 | TSC | 1420 | 17 | TSS | 1508 | 18 | TSS |
| 709 | 107 | TSS | 1114 | 42 | TSC | 1247 | 42 | TSS | 1346 | 94 | TSC | 1421 | 17 | TSS | 1509 | 16 | TSS |
| 711 | 96 | TSS | 1115 | 42 | TSC | 1250 | 45 | TSC | 1349 | 17 | TSS | 1422 | 45 | TSS | 1509 | 28 | TSC |
| 714 | 96 | TSS | 1115 | 56 | TSS | 1250 | 16 | TSS | 1350 | 17 | TSS | 1423 | 56 | TSS | 1510 | 54 | TSS |
| 715 | 96 | TSS | 1116 | 42 | TSS | 1253 | 67 | TSC | 1351 | 17 | TSS | 1424 | 30 | TSC | 1510 | 16 | TSS |
| 718 | 96 | TSS | 1116 | 84 | TSS | 1253 | 102 | TSC | 1352 | 15 | TSS | 1424 | 17 | TSS | 1510 | 86 | TSS |
| 722 | 96 | TSS | 1117 | 37 | TSC | 1255 | 45 | TSC | 1353 | 15 | TSS | 1425 | 17 | TSS | 1511 | 44 | TSS |
| 726 | 96 | TSS | 1118 | 40 | TSS | 1259 | 40 | TSS | 1357 | 17 | TSS | 1426 | 17 | TSS | 1512 | 18 | TSS |
| 727 | 96 | TSS | 1119 | 17 | TSS | 1261 | 40 | TSS | 1357 | 87 | TSS | 1426 | 18 | TSS | 1513 | 56 | TSS |
| 743 | 37 | TSC | 1120 | 39 | TSC | 1262 | 40 | TSS | 1360 | 2 | TSS | 1427 | 45 | TSS | 1513 | 53 | TSS |
| 769 | 18 | TSS | 1121 | 40 | TSS | 1265 | 44 | TSS | 1360 | 15 | TSS | 1428 | 50 | TSS | 1513 | 86 | TSS |
| 772 | 107 | TSS | 1122 | 40 | TSS | 1265 | 17 | TSS | 1365 | 86 | TSS | 1428 | 2 | TSS | 1514 | 56 | TSS |
| 776 | 37 | TSC | 1123 | 40 | TSS | 1270 | 27 | TSC | 1366 | 17 | TSS | 1428 | 45 | TSS | 1514 | 57 | TSS |
| 780 | 42 | TSC | 1126 | 108 | TSS | 1270 | 17 | TSS | 1366 | 38 | TSS | 1431 | 45 | TSS | 1514 | 53 | TSS |
| 784 | 37 | TSC | 1127 | 110 | TSC | 1271 | 104 | TSC | 1366 | 87 | TSS | 1432 | 17 | TSS | 1514 | 86 | TSS |
| 785 | 83 | TSS | 1127 | 32 | TSS | 1272 | 66 | TSC | 1367 | 101 | TSC | 1433 | 41 | TSS | 1517 | 16 | TSS |
| 788 | 18 | TSS | 1132 | 119 | TSC | 1274 | 42 | TSC | 1369 | 40 | TSS | 1433 | 17 | TSS | 1518 | 18 | TSS |
| 795 | 33 | TSC | 1132 | 32 | TSS | 1274 | 56 | TSS | 1370 | 42 | TSC | 1433 | 87 | TSS | 1519 | 18 | TSS |
| 804 | 83 | TSS | 1132 | 18 | TSS | 1277 | 66 | TSC | 1370 | 56 | TSS | 1435 | 15 | TSS | 1520 | 18 | TSS |
| 818 | 25 | TSC | 1138 | 56 | TSS | 1278 | 66 | TSC | 1371 | 44 | TSS | 1436 | 15 | TSS | 1521 | 18 | TSS |
| 827 | 37 | TSC | 1139 | 96 | TSS | 1278 | 70 | TSS | 1372 | 17 | TSS | 1437 | 15 | TSS | 1522 | 18 | TSS |
| 829 | 42 | TSC | 1140 | 18 | TSS | 1279 | 66 | TSC | 1373 | 45 | TSS | 1437 | 86 | TSS | 1523 | 44 | TSS |
| 839 | 37 | TSC | 1142 | 45 | TSS | 1280 | 66 | TSC | 1374 | 45 | TSS | 1438 | 15 | TSS | 1525 | 44 | TSS |
| 843 | 27 | TSC | 1143 | 45 | TSS | 1282 | 66 | TSC | 1374 | 50 | TSS | 1439 | 15 | TSS | 1526 | 44 | TSS |
| 861 | 99 | TSS | 1144 | 45 | TSS | 1284 | 27 | TSC | 1375 | 17 | TSS | 1440 | 15 | TSS | 1527 | 18 | TSS |
| 881 | 36 | TSC | 1145 | 45 | TSS | 1284 | 47 | TSS | 1376 | 50 | TSS | 1441 | 15 | TSS | 1528 | 18 | TSS |
| 898 | 71 | TSC | 1146 | 45 | TSS | 1284 | 56 | TSS | 1376 | 17 | TSS | 1442 | 15 | TSS | 1529 | 44 | TSS |
| 898 | 104 | TSC | 1147 | 84 | TSS | 1285 | 56 | TSS | 1378 | 40 | TSS | 1443 | 15 | TSS | 1530 | 44 | TSS |
| 903 | 37 | TSC | 1147 | 96 | TSS | 1286 | 27 | TSC | 1378 | 41 | TSS | 1445 | 15 | TSS | 1531 | 18 | TSS |
| 919 | 36 | TSC | 1150 | 71 | TSC | 1288 | 27 | TSC | 1379 | 41 | TSS | 1446 | 15 | TSS | 1532 | 16 | TSS |
| 920 | 36 | TSC | 1156 | 110 | TSS | 1288 | 37 | TSS | 1379 | 40 | TSS | 1447 | 45 | TSS | 1534 | 18 | TSS |
| 920 | 85 | TSS | 1157 | 26 | TSC | 1289 | 27 | TSC | 1380 | 41 | TSS | 1447 | 50 | TSS | 1538 | 104 | TSC |
| 930 | 95 | TSS | 1158 | 26 | TSC | 1290 | 27 | TSC | 1380 | 40 | TSS | 1450 | 17 | TSS | 1540 | 16 | TSS |
| 931 | 36 | TSC | 1163 | 35 | TSC | 1292 | 27 | TSC | 1384 | 36 | TSC | 1451 | 56 | TSS | 1543 | 18 | TSS |
| 944 | 37 | TSC | 1165 | 95 | TSS | 1293 | 27 | TSC | 1386 | 28 | TSC | 1454 | 17 | TSS | 1544 | 18 | TSS |
| 945 | 37 | TSC | 1173 | 71 | TSC | 1294 | 27 | TSC | 1386 | 44 | TSS | 1454 | 38 | TSS | 1545 | 18 | TSS |
| 957 | 96 | TSS | 1174 | 99 | TSS | 1295 | 40 | TSS | 1388 | 44 | TSS | 1455 | 32 | TSS | 1546 | 32 | TSS |
| 961 | 18 | TSS | 1175 | 67 | TSC | 1296 | 56 | TSS | 1389 | 44 | TSS | 1455 | 38 | TSS | 1546 | 16 | TSS |

| | | | | | | | | | | | | | | | | | |
|---|---|---|---|---|---|---|---|---|---|---|---|---|---|---|---|---|---|
| 1547 | 18 | TSS | 1801 | 35 | TSS | 2090 | 68 | TSC | 2356 | 48 | TSC | 2493 | 48 | TSS | 2729 | 79 | TSC |
| 1548 | 18 | TSS | 1807 | 145 | TSC | 2093 | 66 | TSS | 2357 | 48 | TSC | 2494 | 92 | TSC | 2783 | 79 | TSC |
| 1548 | 42 | TSS | 1807 | 102 | TSC | 2111 | 36 | TSS | 2358 | 48 | TSC | 2495 | 92 | TSC | 2785 | 86 | TSC |
| 1548 | 41 | TSS | 1808 | 145 | TSC | 2112 | 36 | TSS | 2360 | 48 | TSC | 2497 | 48 | TSS | 2790 | 86 | TSC |
| 1551 | 16 | TSS | 1818 | 60 | TSS | 2113 | 36 | TSS | 2361 | 48 | TSC | 2498 | 31 | TSS | 2795 | 105 | TSS |
| 1552 | 16 | TSS | 1820 | 36 | TSS | 2119 | 36 | TSS | 2362 | 48 | TSC | 2499 | 73 | TSC | 2804 | 99 | TSC |
| 1553 | 16 | TSS | 1821 | 36 | TSS | 2122 | 73 | TSS | 2363 | 48 | TSC | 2499 | 31 | TSS | 2817 | 100 | TSC |
| 1561 | 18 | TSS | 1822 | 36 | TSS | 2122 | 31 | TSS | 2364 | 48 | TSC | 2502 | 48 | TSS | 2829 | 116 | TSC |
| 1562 | 94 | TSC | 1824 | 101 | TSC | 2124 | 68 | TSC | 2366 | 48 | TSC | 2503 | 48 | TSS | 2841 | 111 | TSS |
| 1563 | 94 | TSC | 1826 | 104 | TSC | 2129 | 70 | TSC | 2367 | 48 | TSC | 2504 | 19 | TSC | 2864 | 86 | TSC |
| 1564 | 94 | TSC | 1827 | 104 | TSC | 2131 | 70 | TSC | 2373 | 73 | TSC | 2505 | 99 | TSC | 2870 | 74 | TSC |
| 1565 | 95 | TSS | 1829 | 105 | TSC | 2132 | 70 | TSC | 2375 | 63 | TSC | 2507 | 113 | TSC | 2872 | 74 | TSC |
| 1566 | 16 | TSS | 1830 | 105 | TSC | 2136 | 72 | TSC | 2375 | 88 | TSS | 2510 | 31 | TSS | 2874 | 74 | TSC |
| 1570 | 103 | TSC | 1831 | 103 | TSC | 2137 | 72 | TSC | 2376 | 63 | TSC | 2512 | 113 | TSC | 2875 | 74 | TSC |
| 1571 | 103 | TSC | 1832 | 103 | TSC | 2138 | 72 | TSC | 2378 | 73 | TSC | 2512 | 86 | TSS | 2876 | 74 | TSC |
| 1572 | 45 | TSC | 1833 | 103 | TSC | 2139 | 72 | TSC | 2379 | 73 | TSC | 2513 | 104 | TSS | 2877 | 74 | TSC |
| 1573 | 18 | TSS | 1834 | 103 | TSC | 2140 | 73 | TSC | 2379 | 92 | TSC | 2514 | 92 | TSC | 2878 | 74 | TSC |
| 1575 | 103 | TSC | 1835 | 103 | TSC | 2140 | 72 | TSC | 2385 | 69 | TSC | 2516 | 63 | TSC | 2882 | 74 | TSC |
| 1578 | 102 | TSC | 1836 | 103 | TSC | 2142 | 73 | TSC | 2386 | 69 | TSC | 2517 | 63 | TSC | 2883 | 74 | TSC |
| 1579 | 45 | TSC | 1837 | 103 | TSC | 2144 | 72 | TSC | 2388 | 69 | TSC | 2518 | 63 | TSC | 2884 | 74 | TSC |
| 1580 | 45 | TSC | 1849 | 60 | TSS | 2147 | 72 | TSC | 2396 | 50 | TSS | 2521 | 66 | TSS | 2885 | 74 | TSC |
| 1581 | 45 | TSC | 1849 | 86 | TSS | 2151 | 70 | TSC | 2396 | 32 | TSS | 2522 | 66 | TSS | 2912 | 61 | TSS |
| 1581 | 86 | TSS | 1849 | 60 | TSS | 2154 | 36 | TSS | 2396 | 37 | TSS | 2524 | 61 | TSS | 2927 | 98 | TSC |
| 1582 | 45 | TSC | 1850 | 60 | TSS | 2160 | 70 | TSC | 2396 | 66 | TSS | 2525 | 31 | TSS | 2933 | 61 | TSS |
| 1583 | 45 | TSC | 1858 | 83 | TSS | 2162 | 70 | TSC | 2397 | 32 | TSS | 2528 | 48 | TSC | 2937 | 74 | TSC |
| 1584 | 45 | TSC | 1862 | 86 | TSS | 2172 | 59 | TSS | 2397 | 66 | TSS | 2533 | 66 | TSS | 2938 | 24 | TSC |
| 1585 | 45 | TSC | 1867 | 68 | TSS | 2172 | 86 | TSS | 2398 | 32 | TSS | 2537 | 20 | TSC | 2945 | 63 | TSC |
| 1586 | 45 | TSC | 1867 | 86 | TSS | 2184 | 59 | TSS | 2398 | 66 | TSS | 2537 | 48 | TSS | 2945 | 50 | TSC |
| 1587 | 45 | TSC | 1868 | 86 | TSS | 2187 | 70 | TSC | 2400 | 69 | TSC | 2538 | 48 | TSS | 2950 | 24 | TSC |
| 1589 | 45 | TSC | 1869 | 86 | TSS | 2208 | 36 | TSS | 2401 | 69 | TSC | 2545 | 48 | TSS | 2951 | 24 | TSC |
| 1590 | 18 | TSS | 1870 | 86 | TSS | 2227 | 70 | TSC | 2402 | 69 | TSC | 2549 | 84 | TSS | 2954 | 75 | TSC |
| 1591 | 45 | TSC | 1871 | 86 | TSS | 2259 | 66 | TSC | 2403 | 69 | TSC | 2549 | 61 | TSS | 2955 | 61 | TSS |
| 1614 | 88 | TSC | 1873 | 86 | TSS | 2260 | 93 | TSC | 2406 | 69 | TSC | 2555 | 93 | TSS | 2956 | 86 | TSS |
| 1620 | 72 | TSC | 1909 | 31 | TSS | 2264 | 70 | TSC | 2407 | 69 | TSC | 2562 | 79 | TSC | 2962 | 20 | TSC |
| 1622 | 38 | TSS | 1937 | 86 | TSS | 2266 | 70 | TSC | 2408 | 69 | TSC | 2564 | 79 | TSC | 2970 | 39 | TSC |
| 1623 | 101 | TSC | 1956 | 57 | TSS | 2267 | 93 | TSC | 2409 | 69 | TSC | 2566 | 79 | TSC | 2974 | 20 | TSC |
| 1625 | 101 | TSC | 1959 | 57 | TSS | 2275 | 31 | TSS | 2410 | 69 | TSC | 2568 | 49 | TSC | 2976 | 50 | TSC |
| 1646 | 39 | TSC | 1960 | 57 | TSS | 2276 | 31 | TSS | 2411 | 69 | TSC | 2584 | 61 | TSS | 2977 | 50 | TSC |
| 1647 | 39 | TSC | 1964 | 90 | TSC | 2277 | 54 | TSS | 2419 | 48 | TSC | 2586 | 93 | TSS | 2977 | 63 | TSC |
| 1653 | 104 | TSC | 1965 | 90 | TSC | 2277 | 32 | TSS | 2421 | 42 | TSS | 2593 | 113 | TSC | 2978 | 50 | TSC |
| 1654 | 105 | TSC | 1966 | 90 | TSC | 2278 | 54 | TSS | 2424 | 54 | TSS | 2595 | 61 | TSS | 2980 | 61 | TSS |
| 1655 | 42 | TSC | 1967 | 90 | TSC | 2278 | 32 | TSS | 2425 | 61 | TSS | 2598 | 113 | TSC | 2981 | 75 | TSC |
| 1655 | 101 | TSC | 1969 | 42 | TSC | 2280 | 70 | TSC | 2431 | 54 | TSS | 2600 | 113 | TSC | 2982 | 50 | TSC |
| 1667 | 38 | TSS | 1969 | 57 | TSS | 2281 | 54 | TSS | 2438 | 54 | TSS | 2600 | 64 | TSS | 2991 | 98 | TSC |
| 1667 | 32 | TSS | 1970 | 101 | TSC | 2282 | 54 | TSS | 2439 | 70 | TSC | 2602 | 49 | TSC | 2992 | 75 | TSC |
| 1678 | 30 | TSC | 1971 | 101 | TSC | 2288 | 54 | TSS | 2440 | 70 | TSC | 2608 | 49 | TSC | 2993 | 75 | TSC |
| 1679 | 30 | TSC | 1990 | 60 | TSS | 2289 | 53 | TSS | 2441 | 70 | TSC | 2610 | 49 | TSC | 2995 | 75 | TSC |
| 1679 | 69 | TSS | 1992 | 90 | TSC | 2295 | 53 | TSS | 2449 | 70 | TSC | 2611 | 49 | TSC | 3001 | 86 | TSS |
| 1680 | 30 | TSC | 1993 | 66 | TSS | 2295 | 86 | TSS | 2449 | 62 | TSS | 2612 | 49 | TSC | 3003 | 86 | TSS |
| 1685 | 101 | TSC | 1996 | 38 | TSS | 2311 | 31 | TSS | 2451 | 42 | TSS | 2613 | 49 | TSC | 3005 | 86 | TSS |
| 1695 | 86 | TSS | 1997 | 36 | TSS | 2312 | 93 | TSC | 2452 | 71 | TSC | 2614 | 49 | TSC | 3010 | 86 | TSS |
| 1698 | 68 | TSS | 2024 | 32 | TSS | 2314 | 37 | TSS | 2453 | 71 | TSC | 2615 | 49 | TSC | 3012 | 86 | TSS |
| 1715 | 60 | TSS | 2024 | 61 | TSS | 2315 | 93 | TSC | 2453 | 110 | TSC | 2616 | 49 | TSC | 3019 | 119 | TSC |
| 1732 | 104 | TSC | 2025 | 32 | TSS | 2317 | 93 | TSC | 2455 | 42 | TSS | 2617 | 49 | TSC | 3022 | 75 | TSC |
| 1745 | 101 | TSC | 2025 | 61 | TSS | 2318 | 93 | TSC | 2456 | 71 | TSC | 2619 | 49 | TSC | 3025 | 76 | TSC |
| 1747 | 46 | TSC | 2027 | 68 | TSC | 2320 | 70 | TSC | 2457 | 113 | TSC | 2621 | 49 | TSC | 3030 | 76 | TSC |
| 1748 | 46 | TSC | 2032 | 68 | TSS | 2321 | 71 | TSC | 2459 | 113 | TSC | 2626 | 79 | TSC | 3036 | 76 | TSC |
| 1758 | 102 | TSC | 2033 | 68 | TSC | 2331 | 39 | TSC | 2463 | 92 | TSC | 2634 | 49 | TSC | 3037 | 76 | TSC |
| 1774 | 35 | TSS | 2039 | 68 | TSC | 2331 | 42 | TSS | 2465 | 79 | TSC | 2636 | 49 | TSC | 3039 | 76 | TSC |
| 1775 | 88 | TSS | 2044 | 68 | TSC | 2333 | 48 | TSC | 2468 | 113 | TSC | 2638 | 49 | TSC | 3040 | 63 | TSC |
| 1777 | 105 | TSC | 2046 | 68 | TSC | 2334 | 48 | TSC | 2468 | 87 | TSS | 2645 | 68 | TSC | 3040 | 76 | TSC |
| 1777 | 31 | TSS | 2046 | 86 | TSS | 2335 | 48 | TSC | 2472 | 31 | TSS | 2646 | 68 | TSC | 3043 | 76 | TSC |
| 1780 | 105 | TSC | 2047 | 68 | TSC | 2336 | 48 | TSC | 2473 | 42 | TSS | 2647 | 68 | TSC | 3044 | 76 | TSC |
| 1782 | 42 | TSC | 2049 | 86 | TSS | 2339 | 53 | TSS | 2474 | 79 | TSC | 2648 | 68 | TSC | 3047 | 76 | TSC |
| 1782 | 101 | TSC | 2050 | 68 | TSC | 2341 | 48 | TSC | 2476 | 31 | TSS | 2649 | 68 | TSC | 3048 | 76 | TSC |
| 1783 | 104 | TSC | 2051 | 32 | TSS | 2342 | 48 | TSC | 2478 | 71 | TSC | 2655 | 31 | TSS | 3051 | 76 | TSC |
| 1784 | 102 | TSC | 2054 | 38 | TSS | 2343 | 63 | TSC | 2482 | 71 | TSC | 2655 | 64 | TSS | 3063 | 76 | TSC |
| 1786 | 104 | TSC | 2064 | 68 | TSC | 2343 | 88 | TSS | 2483 | 71 | TSC | 2656 | 31 | TSS | 3064 | 67 | TSC |
| 1787 | 104 | TSC | 2068 | 68 | TSC | 2346 | 53 | TSS | 2484 | 71 | TSC | 2656 | 64 | TSS | 3065 | 76 | TSC |
| 1791 | 105 | TSC | 2071 | 111 | TSS | 2348 | 48 | TSC | 2485 | 71 | TSC | 2658 | 31 | TSS | 3066 | 76 | TSC |
| 1794 | 97 | TSS | 2079 | 36 | TSS | 2349 | 48 | TSC | 2486 | 71 | TSC | 2658 | 64 | TSS | 3067 | 76 | TSC |
| 1794 | 102 | TSC | 2083 | 36 | TSS | 2351 | 48 | TSC | 2487 | 71 | TSC | 2660 | 31 | TSS | 3085 | 76 | TSC |
| 1795 | 102 | TSC | 2084 | 36 | TSS | 2352 | 73 | TSC | 2488 | 71 | TSC | 2661 | 68 | TSC | 3096 | 61 | TSS |
| 1796 | 105 | TSC | 2086 | 36 | TSS | 2353 | 48 | TSC | 2489 | 71 | TSC | 2675 | 19 | TSC | 3097 | 61 | TSS |
| 1797 | 46 | TSC | 2088 | 68 | TSC | 2354 | 48 | TSC | 2491 | 31 | TSS | 2683 | 79 | TSC | 3110 | 41 | TSS |
| 1798 | 46 | TSC | 2089 | 68 | TSC | 2355 | 48 | TSC | 2493 | 19 | TSC | 2712 | 100 | TSC | 3111 | 37 | TSS |

| | | | | | | | | | | | | | | | | | |
|---|---|---|---|---|---|---|---|---|---|---|---|---|---|---|---|---|---|
| 3112 | 37 | TSS | 3196 | 75 | TSC | 3434 | 77 | TSC | 4037 | 54 | TSC | 4233 | 113 | TSC | 4385 | 114 | TSC |
| 3113 | 37 | TSS | 3197 | 59 | TSS | 3439 | 77 | TSC | 4038 | 54 | TSC | 4233 | 87 | TSS | 4387 | 118 | TSC |
| 3114 | 38 | TSS | 3204 | 63 | TSC | 3440 | 77 | TSC | 4039 | 54 | TSC | 4236 | 64 | TSS | 4393 | 114 | TSC |
| 3114 | 37 | TSS | 3204 | 50 | TSC | 3447 | 19 | TSC | 4040 | 54 | TSC | 4239 | 113 | TSC | 4393 | 87 | TSS |
| 3115 | 37 | TSS | 3206 | 50 | TSC | 3447 | 107 | TSC | 4077 | 104 | TSS | 4240 | 113 | TSC | 4394 | 114 | TSC |
| 3116 | 38 | TSS | 3207 | 50 | TSC | 3457 | 107 | TSC | 4080 | 80 | TSC | 4241 | 113 | TSC | 4395 | 114 | TSC |
| 3116 | 37 | TSS | 3208 | 50 | TSC | 3459 | 107 | TSC | 4081 | 80 | TSC | 4242 | 113 | TSC | 4396 | 53 | TSC |
| 3117 | 37 | TSS | 3209 | 50 | TSC | 3459 | 14 | TSS | 4084 | 80 | TSC | 4243 | 113 | TSC | 4398 | 53 | TSC |
| 3118 | 37 | TSS | 3209 | 63 | TSC | 3460 | 100 | TSC | 4086 | 80 | TSC | 4244 | 56 | TSC | 4399 | 53 | TSC |
| 3119 | 48 | TSS | 3213 | 75 | TSC | 3465 | 107 | TSC | 4093 | 80 | TSC | 4244 | 88 | TSC | 4401 | 126 | TSC |
| 3120 | 37 | TSS | 3214 | 75 | TSC | 3466 | 107 | TSC | 4097 | 20 | TSC | 4245 | 58 | TSC | 4401 | 88 | TSS |
| 3121 | 37 | TSS | 3215 | 75 | TSC | 3480 | 77 | TSC | 4098 | 80 | TSC | 4245 | 88 | TSS | 4402 | 126 | TSC |
| 3122 | 37 | TSS | 3216 | 75 | TSC | 3481 | 77 | TSC | 4102 | 54 | TSC | 4253 | 61 | TSC | 4403 | 126 | TSC |
| 3124 | 48 | TSS | 3217 | 75 | TSC | 3482 | 77 | TSC | 4103 | 80 | TSC | 4254 | 61 | TSC | 4404 | 126 | TSC |
| 3128 | 19 | TSC | 3218 | 75 | TSC | 3492 | 108 | TSC | 4105 | 80 | TSC | 4254 | 67 | TSC | 4405 | 126 | TSC |
| 3128 | 108 | TSC | 3221 | 75 | TSC | 3500 | 20 | TSC | 4106 | 54 | TSC | 4255 | 61 | TSC | 4406 | 126 | TSC |
| 3128 | 41 | TSS | 3225 | 109 | TSC | 3500 | 19 | TSC | 4115 | 80 | TSC | 4255 | 62 | TSC | 4407 | 126 | TSC |
| 3132 | 38 | TSS | 3238 | 50 | TSC | 3524 | 62 | TSS | 4125 | 63 | TSC | 4259 | 62 | TSC | 4409 | 125 | TSC |
| 3133 | 41 | TSS | 3239 | 29 | TSC | 3532 | 62 | TSS | 4127 | 83 | TSC | 4264 | 86 | TSC | 4411 | 126 | TSC |
| 3133 | 43 | TSS | 3261 | 67 | TSC | 3542 | 15 | TSC | 4129 | 83 | TSC | 4265 | 86 | TSC | 4411 | 88 | TSS |
| 3134 | 43 | TSS | 3262 | 64 | TSS | 3542 | 34 | TSS | 4130 | 80 | TSC | 4267 | 61 | TSC | 4415 | 126 | TSC |
| 3135 | 43 | TSS | 3262 | 63 | TSS | 3552 | 20 | TSC | 4131 | 80 | TSC | 4270 | 62 | TSC | 4416 | 127 | TSC |
| 3136 | 43 | TSS | 3263 | 50 | TSC | 3560 | 38 | TSS | 4140 | 54 | TSC | 4270 | 61 | TSC | 4417 | 125 | TSC |
| 3136 | 41 | TSS | 3263 | 63 | TSS | 3561 | 22 | TSC | 4152 | 78 | TSC | 4271 | 62 | TSC | 4420 | 125 | TSC |
| 3137 | 41 | TSS | 3263 | 64 | TSS | 3565 | 38 | TSS | 4153 | 78 | TSC | 4273 | 61 | TSC | 4423 | 125 | TSC |
| 3137 | 43 | TSS | 3264 | 50 | TSC | 3567 | 38 | TSS | 4154 | 78 | TSC | 4273 | 62 | TSC | 4431 | 127 | TSC |
| 3138 | 2 | TSS | 3264 | 63 | TSS | 3569 | 50 | TSC | 4155 | 78 | TSC | 4274 | 61 | TSC | 4431 | 88 | TSS |
| 3139 | 2 | TSS | 3264 | 64 | TSS | 3576 | 86 | TSS | 4156 | 78 | TSC | 4275 | 61 | TSC | 4432 | 127 | TSC |
| 3140 | 29 | TSC | 3266 | 50 | TSC | 3617 | 64 | TSS | 4157 | 78 | TSC | 4287 | 113 | TSC | 4433 | 127 | TSC |
| 3141 | 50 | TSS | 3268 | 50 | TSC | 3617 | 63 | TSS | 4158 | 78 | TSC | 4288 | 113 | TSC | 4436 | 127 | TSC |
| 3144 | 48 | TSS | 3269 | 99 | TSC | 3624 | 97 | TSC | 4159 | 78 | TSC | 4289 | 113 | TSC | 4439 | 88 | TSS |
| 3145 | 48 | TSS | 3269 | 50 | TSC | 3632 | 89 | TSC | 4160 | 78 | TSC | 4290 | 113 | TSC | 4440 | 127 | TSC |
| 3150 | 48 | TSS | 3273 | 63 | TSC | 3642 | 22 | TSC | 4161 | 78 | TSC | 4291 | 113 | TSC | 4440 | 88 | TSS |
| 3151 | 80 | TSS | 3274 | 63 | TSC | 3711 | 64 | TSS | 4161 | 62 | TSS | 4292 | 113 | TSC | 4448 | 127 | TSC |
| 3152 | 80 | TSS | 3275 | 39 | TSC | 3742 | 64 | TSS | 4162 | 78 | TSC | 4293 | 113 | TSC | 4452 | 125 | TSC |
| 3153 | 80 | TSS | 3276 | 103 | TSS | 3742 | 63 | TSS | 4163 | 78 | TSC | 4293 | 87 | TSS | 4459 | 127 | TSC |
| 3154 | 37 | TSS | 3278 | 63 | TSC | 3788 | 63 | TSS | 4164 | 82 | TSC | 4295 | 61 | TSC | 4460 | 127 | TSC |
| 3154 | 70 | TSS | 3278 | 88 | TSS | 3788 | 64 | TSS | 4165 | 82 | TSC | 4296 | 61 | TSC | 4460 | 88 | TSS |
| 3154 | 80 | TSS | 3296 | 50 | TSC | 3791 | 63 | TSS | 4166 | 82 | TSC | 4297 | 64 | TSS | 4462 | 125 | TSC |
| 3155 | 48 | TSS | 3297 | 50 | TSC | 3791 | 64 | TSS | 4168 | 82 | TSC | 4299 | 84 | TSC | 4466 | 127 | TSC |
| 3156 | 47 | TSS | 3299 | 50 | TSC | 3827 | 39 | TSC | 4169 | 82 | TSC | 4300 | 84 | TSC | 4467 | 127 | TSC |
| 3157 | 47 | TSS | 3314 | 110 | TSS | 3842 | 97 | TSC | 4170 | 82 | TSC | 4301 | 84 | TSC | 4469 | 125 | TSC |
| 3158 | 47 | TSS | 3315 | 50 | TSC | 3844 | 97 | TSC | 4171 | 82 | TSC | 4302 | 84 | TSC | 4471 | 127 | TSC |
| 3162 | 50 | TSS | 3318 | 104 | TSS | 3867 | 112 | TSS | 4172 | 82 | TSC | 4303 | 84 | TSC | 4474 | 127 | TSC |
| 3164 | 41 | TSS | 3339 | 107 | TSC | 3895 | 97 | TSC | 4173 | 82 | TSC | 4304 | 84 | TSC | 4476 | 125 | TSC |
| 3165 | 20 | TSC | 3339 | 14 | TSS | 3896 | 97 | TSC | 4174 | 82 | TSC | 4305 | 84 | TSC | 4477 | 127 | TSC |
| 3165 | 107 | TSC | 3339 | 50 | TSS | 3907 | 62 | TSS | 4178 | 78 | TSC | 4306 | 84 | TSC | 4478 | 125 | TSC |
| 3165 | 41 | TSS | 3341 | 108 | TSC | 3913 | 19 | TSC | 4182 | 50 | TSC | 4307 | 84 | TSC | 4479 | 125 | TSC |
| 3166 | 20 | TSC | 3349 | 77 | TSC | 3927 | 133 | TSC | 4195 | 56 | TSC | 4308 | 84 | TSC | 4487 | 126 | TSC |
| 3166 | 41 | TSS | 3350 | 77 | TSC | 3930 | 57 | TSS | 4195 | 88 | TSC | 4309 | 84 | TSC | 4487 | 35 | TSS |
| 3167 | 42 | TSS | 3355 | 77 | TSC | 3977 | 54 | TSC | 4196 | 56 | TSC | 4310 | 84 | TSC | 4487 | 88 | TSS |
| 3168 | 32 | TSS | 3358 | 77 | TSC | 3982 | 54 | TSC | 4196 | 88 | TSC | 4311 | 61 | TSC | 4488 | 126 | TSC |
| 3168 | 84 | TSS | 3360 | 77 | TSC | 3982 | 86 | TSS | 4197 | 56 | TSC | 4311 | 62 | TSC | 4488 | 35 | TSS |
| 3168 | 69 | TSS | 3360 | 107 | TSC | 3986 | 54 | TSC | 4197 | 88 | TSC | 4317 | 61 | TSC | 4488 | 88 | TSS |
| 3169 | 20 | TSC | 3361 | 77 | TSC | 3995 | 81 | TSC | 4198 | 67 | TSC | 4317 | 62 | TSC | 4489 | 35 | TSS |
| 3169 | 41 | TSS | 3368 | 77 | TSC | 3996 | 89 | TSC | 4198 | 56 | TSC | 4318 | 61 | TSC | 4489 | 126 | TSC |
| 3170 | 41 | TSS | 3368 | 108 | TSC | 3998 | 80 | TSC | 4198 | 88 | TSC | 4318 | 62 | TSC | 4490 | 126 | TSC |
| 3170 | 77 | TSS | 3370 | 109 | TSC | 4001 | 81 | TSC | 4201 | 78 | TSC | 4319 | 88 | TSC | 4491 | 126 | TSC |
| 3171 | 41 | TSS | 3383 | 41 | TSC | 4002 | 81 | TSC | 4202 | 54 | TSC | 4323 | 88 | TSC | 4493 | 126 | TSC |
| 3172 | 47 | TSS | 3383 | 109 | TSC | 4004 | 81 | TSC | 4204 | 78 | TSC | 4324 | 88 | TSC | 4494 | 126 | TSC |
| 3173 | 19 | TSC | 3384 | 41 | TSC | 4006 | 81 | TSC | 4205 | 83 | TSC | 4325 | 88 | TSC | 4495 | 125 | TSC |
| 3173 | 41 | TSS | 3384 | 50 | TSS | 4008 | 81 | TSC | 4206 | 83 | TSC | 4327 | 88 | TSC | 4496 | 125 | TSC |
| 3174 | 42 | TSS | 3392 | 28 | TSC | 4009 | 89 | TSC | 4207 | 83 | TSC | 4328 | 88 | TSC | 4497 | 15 | TSC |
| 3175 | 42 | TSS | 3404 | 107 | TSC | 4010 | 81 | TSC | 4208 | 83 | TSC | 4329 | 88 | TSC | 4524 | 114 | TSC |
| 3176 | 48 | TSS | 3406 | 108 | TSC | 4011 | 81 | TSC | 4209 | 83 | TSC | 4330 | 88 | TSC | 4526 | 88 | TSC |
| 3177 | 42 | TSS | 3407 | 108 | TSS | 4013 | 81 | TSC | 4210 | 83 | TSC | 4331 | 88 | TSC | 4528 | 43 | TSS |
| 3179 | 42 | TSS | 3414 | 108 | TSC | 4014 | 54 | TSC | 4211 | 83 | TSC | 4336 | 84 | TSC | 4529 | 85 | TSC |
| 3180 | 32 | TSC | 3415 | 77 | TSC | 4018 | 81 | TSC | 4212 | 83 | TSC | 4338 | 84 | TSC | 4530 | 53 | TSC |
| 3180 | 107 | TSC | 3415 | 107 | TSC | 4022 | 54 | TSC | 4213 | 83 | TSC | 4339 | 55 | TSC | 4535 | 97 | TSC |
| 3180 | 108 | TSC | 3419 | 77 | TSC | 4023 | 81 | TSC | 4214 | 83 | TSC | 4340 | 84 | TSC | 4536 | 97 | TSC |
| 3180 | 48 | TSS | 3420 | 77 | TSC | 4029 | 54 | TSC | 4215 | 83 | TSC | 4342 | 55 | TSC | 4537 | 97 | TSC |
| 3182 | 42 | TSS | 3423 | 38 | TSS | 4030 | 54 | TSC | 4218 | 62 | TSC | 4343 | 55 | TSC | 4539 | 97 | TSC |
| 3183 | 42 | TSS | 3426 | 38 | TSS | 4031 | 54 | TSC | 4224 | 54 | TSC | 4348 | 55 | TSC | 4540 | 97 | TSC |
| 3187 | 59 | TSS | 3428 | 38 | TSS | 4032 | 54 | TSC | 4227 | 64 | TSS | 4375 | 114 | TSC | 4545 | 87 | TSC |
| 3189 | 76 | TSC | 3432 | 38 | TSS | 4033 | 54 | TSC | 4231 | 113 | TSC | 4377 | 114 | TSC | 4546 | 133 | TSC |
| 3189 | 106 | TSC | 3433 | 38 | TSS | 4036 | 54 | TSC | 4231 | 87 | TSS | 4377 | 87 | TSS | 4547 | 114 | TSC |

| ID | Val | Type | ID | Val | Type | ID | Val | Type | ID | Val | Type | ID | Val | Type | ID | Val | Type |
|---|---|---|---|---|---|---|---|---|---|---|---|---|---|---|---|---|---|
| 4549 | 59 | TSS | 4709 | 45 | TSS | 4978 | 46 | TSS | 5245 | 116 | TSC | 5395 | 95 | TSC | 5598 | 33 | TSS |
| 4553 | 59 | TSS | 4709 | 85 | TSS | 4986 | 18 | TSC | 5246 | 116 | TSC | 5396 | 95 | TSC | 5599 | 33 | TSS |
| 4554 | 88 | TSC | 4710 | 45 | TSS | 4988 | 18 | TSC | 5246 | 87 | TSS | 5397 | 95 | TSC | 5600 | 33 | TSS |
| 4555 | 86 | TSC | 4711 | 45 | TSS | 5000 | 22 | TSC | 5247 | 116 | TSC | 5398 | 95 | TSC | 5606 | 96 | TSC |
| 4556 | 86 | TSC | 4713 | 86 | TSS | 5023 | 21 | TSC | 5248 | 116 | TSC | 5399 | 95 | TSC | 5607 | 96 | TSC |
| 4557 | 86 | TSC | 4719 | 63 | TSC | 5027 | 18 | TSC | 5249 | 116 | TSC | 5400 | 49 | TSC | 5608 | 96 | TSC |
| 4557 | 59 | TSS | 4719 | 88 | TSS | 5032 | 18 | TSC | 5250 | 116 | TSC | 5402 | 49 | TSC | 5609 | 96 | TSC |
| 4558 | 86 | TSC | 4721 | 88 | TSS | 5033 | 60 | TSC | 5258 | 17 | TSC | 5404 | 33 | TSS | 5610 | 96 | TSC |
| 4559 | 86 | TSC | 4725 | 88 | TSS | 5034 | 22 | TSC | 5259 | 17 | TSC | 5409 | 56 | TSC | 5611 | 96 | TSC |
| 4560 | 86 | TSC | 4727 | 88 | TSS | 5038 | 59 | TSC | 5260 | 17 | TSC | 5410 | 56 | TSC | 5612 | 96 | TSC |
| 4561 | 85 | TSC | 4732 | 34 | TSS | 5041 | 59 | TSC | 5261 | 47 | TSS | 5411 | 56 | TSC | 5613 | 96 | TSC |
| 4565 | 59 | TSS | 4733 | 34 | TSS | 5042 | 60 | TSC | 5262 | 47 | TSS | 5412 | 56 | TSC | 5614 | 96 | TSC |
| 4570 | 63 | TSC | 4750 | 59 | TSS | 5043 | 60 | TSC | 5270 | 76 | TSS | 5413 | 56 | TSC | 5615 | 96 | TSC |
| 4570 | 118 | TSC | 4752 | 59 | TSS | 5048 | 59 | TSS | 5271 | 76 | TSC | 5414 | 56 | TSC | 5631 | 112 | TSS |
| 4570 | 88 | TSS | 4753 | 59 | TSS | 5049 | 18 | TSC | 5272 | 60 | TSC | 5416 | 86 | TSS | 5656 | 33 | TSS |
| 4572 | 62 | TSS | 4754 | 59 | TSS | 5053 | 122 | TSC | 5272 | 63 | TSC | 5419 | 49 | TSC | 5657 | 33 | TSS |
| 4572 | 63 | TSS | 4755 | 59 | TSS | 5057 | 122 | TSC | 5281 | 58 | TSC | 5425 | 59 | TSC | 5658 | 33 | TSS |
| 4573 | 79 | TSS | 4756 | 59 | TSS | 5058 | 122 | TSC | 5281 | 76 | TSC | 5426 | 59 | TSC | 5659 | 33 | TSS |
| 4574 | 118 | TSC | 4763 | 112 | TSS | 5059 | 122 | TSC | 5282 | 58 | TSC | 5427 | 59 | TSC | 5660 | 33 | TSS |
| 4574 | 63 | TSC | 4772 | 89 | TSC | 5060 | 122 | TSC | 5284 | 58 | TSC | 5428 | 59 | TSC | 5661 | 33 | TSS |
| 4575 | 86 | TSC | 4773 | 89 | TSC | 5076 | 18 | TSC | 5292 | 24 | TSC | 5429 | 49 | TSC | 5662 | 33 | TSS |
| 4576 | 53 | TSC | 4774 | 89 | TSC | 5076 | 17 | TSC | 5293 | 24 | TSC | 5434 | 17 | TSC | 5670 | 62 | TSS |
| 4577 | 53 | TSC | 4776 | 89 | TSC | 5096 | 119 | TSC | 5294 | 24 | TSC | 5447 | 52 | TSC | 5671 | 62 | TSS |
| 4579 | 53 | TSC | 4777 | 89 | TSC | 5097 | 119 | TSC | 5295 | 24 | TSC | 5448 | 52 | TSC | 5672 | 62 | TSS |
| 4580 | 53 | TSC | 4778 | 89 | TSC | 5101 | 119 | TSC | 5296 | 24 | TSC | 5449 | 52 | TSC | 5673 | 62 | TSS |
| 4582 | 53 | TSC | 4781 | 89 | TSC | 5102 | 119 | TSC | 5297 | 24 | TSC | 5450 | 52 | TSC | 5674 | 62 | TSS |
| 4584 | 63 | TSC | 4789 | 115 | TSC | 5103 | 119 | TSC | 5298 | 27 | TSC | 5451 | 52 | TSC | 5675 | 62 | TSS |
| 4584 | 118 | TSC | 4790 | 115 | TSC | 5104 | 119 | TSC | 5298 | 84 | TSS | 5452 | 52 | TSC | 5676 | 62 | TSS |
| 4594 | 85 | TSC | 4791 | 115 | TSC | 5105 | 119 | TSC | 5299 | 27 | TSC | 5456 | 52 | TSC | 5996 | 121 | TSC |
| 4596 | 85 | TSC | 4797 | 51 | TSC | 5106 | 119 | TSC | 5300 | 27 | TSC | 5458 | 52 | TSC | 5997 | 121 | TSC |
| 4599 | 85 | TSC | 4801 | 51 | TSC | 5107 | 47 | TSS | 5300 | 84 | TSS | 5459 | 52 | TSC | 5998 | 121 | TSC |
| 4603 | 85 | TSC | 4802 | 51 | TSC | 5107 | 84 | TSS | 5301 | 24 | TSC | 5460 | 52 | TSC | 5999 | 121 | TSC |
| 4604 | 85 | TSC | 4806 | 51 | TSC | 5108 | 21 | TSC | 5302 | 24 | TSC | 5465 | 60 | TSC | 6000 | 121 | TSC |
| 4605 | 85 | TSC | 4807 | 51 | TSC | 5111 | 47 | TSS | 5303 | 24 | TSC | 5466 | 60 | TSC | 6001 | 121 | TSC |
| 4606 | 85 | TSC | 4809 | 58 | TSS | 5112 | 21 | TSC | 5314 | 34 | TSC | 5468 | 56 | TSS | 6002 | 121 | TSC |
| 4608 | 88 | TSC | 4811 | 58 | TSS | 5113 | 127 | TSC | 5315 | 34 | TSC | 5469 | 97 | TSC | 6003 | 121 | TSC |
| 4612 | 88 | TSC | 4812 | 58 | TSS | 5114 | 127 | TSC | 5319 | 18 | TSC | 5470 | 97 | TSC | 6004 | 121 | TSC |
| 4613 | 88 | TSC | 4812 | 86 | TSS | 5115 | 127 | TSC | 5320 | 22 | TSC | 5471 | 97 | TSC | 6005 | 121 | TSC |
| 4620 | 88 | TSC | 4815 | 58 | TSS | 5116 | 127 | TSC | 5321 | 18 | TSC | 5472 | 97 | TSC | | | |
| 4629 | 53 | TSC | 4817 | 58 | TSS | 5117 | 127 | TSC | 5322 | 17 | TSC | 5473 | 97 | TSC | | | |
| 4631 | 87 | TSC | 4831 | 122 | TSC | 5118 | 127 | TSC | 5323 | 17 | TSC | 5474 | 97 | TSC | | | |
| 4633 | 53 | TSC | 4832 | 58 | TSS | 5119 | 50 | TSS | 5324 | 17 | TSC | 5475 | 97 | TSC | | | |
| 4634 | 53 | TSC | 4843 | 51 | TSC | 5120 | 50 | TSS | 5337 | 55 | TSC | 5476 | 97 | TSC | | | |
| 4637 | 87 | TSC | 4844 | 51 | TSC | 5122 | 37 | TSS | 5338 | 55 | TSC | 5478 | 64 | TSS | | | |
| 4638 | 88 | TSC | 4850 | 51 | TSC | 5122 | 50 | TSS | 5339 | 55 | TSC | 5479 | 64 | TSS | | | |
| 4641 | 88 | TSC | 4851 | 51 | TSC | 5125 | 46 | TSS | 5340 | 55 | TSC | 5517 | 51 | TSS | | | |
| 4642 | 87 | TSC | 4852 | 51 | TSC | 5126 | 59 | TSS | 5342 | 63 | TSS | 5518 | 51 | TSS | | | |
| 4643 | 87 | TSC | 4853 | 51 | TSC | 5127 | 59 | TSS | 5345 | 55 | TSC | 5519 | 51 | TSS | | | |
| 4644 | 87 | TSC | 4865 | 57 | TSC | 5131 | 50 | TSS | 5346 | 55 | TSC | 5520 | 51 | TSS | | | |
| 4645 | 88 | TSC | 4871 | 57 | TSC | 5148 | 60 | TSC | 5347 | 55 | TSC | 5521 | 51 | TSS | | | |
| 4646 | 53 | TSC | 4872 | 33 | TSC | 5150 | 21 | TSC | 5348 | 55 | TSC | 5522 | 51 | TSS | | | |
| 4647 | 87 | TSC | 4872 | 46 | TSS | 5165 | 76 | TSS | 5352 | 55 | TSC | 5523 | 51 | TSS | | | |
| 4648 | 87 | TSC | 4874 | 51 | TSC | 5166 | 31 | TSC | 5352 | 63 | TSS | 5524 | 51 | TSS | | | |
| 4649 | 87 | TSC | 4875 | 51 | TSC | 5167 | 21 | TSC | 5353 | 55 | TSC | 5525 | 51 | TSS | | | |
| 4651 | 87 | TSC | 4876 | 51 | TSC | 5167 | 22 | TSC | 5353 | 63 | TSS | 5535 | 58 | TSS | | | |
| 4652 | 87 | TSC | 4877 | 51 | TSC | 5170 | 21 | TSC | 5354 | 55 | TSC | 5537 | 58 | TSS | | | |
| 4665 | 88 | TSC | 4878 | 51 | TSC | 5170 | 17 | TSC | 5354 | 63 | TSS | 5554 | 120 | TSC | | | |
| 4666 | 88 | TSC | 4879 | 51 | TSC | 5188 | 62 | TSS | 5355 | 55 | TSC | 5555 | 120 | TSC | | | |
| 4669 | 62 | TSC | 4880 | 51 | TSC | 5205 | 21 | TSC | 5365 | 55 | TSC | 5571 | 117 | TSC | | | |
| 4669 | 63 | TSS | 4881 | 51 | TSC | 5207 | 41 | TSC | 5366 | 55 | TSC | 5572 | 117 | TSC | | | |
| 4678 | 79 | TSS | 4882 | 51 | TSC | 5209 | 14 | TSS | 5369 | 95 | TSC | 5573 | 117 | TSC | | | |
| 4683 | 60 | TSC | 4886 | 115 | TSC | 5210 | 79 | TSS | 5370 | 95 | TSC | 5574 | 117 | TSC | | | |
| 4684 | 62 | TSC | 4887 | 115 | TSC | 5211 | 14 | TSS | 5371 | 95 | TSC | 5575 | 117 | TSC | | | |
| 4684 | 63 | TSS | 4888 | 115 | TSC | 5212 | 79 | TSS | 5372 | 95 | TSC | 5576 | 117 | TSC | | | |
| 4685 | 62 | TSC | 4889 | 115 | TSC | 5213 | 79 | TSS | 5373 | 95 | TSC | 5576 | 87 | TSS | | | |
| 4685 | 63 | TSS | 4890 | 115 | TSC | 5222 | 129 | TSC | 5374 | 95 | TSC | 5582 | 80 | TSS | | | |
| 4690 | 79 | TSS | 4890 | 87 | TSS | 5229 | 46 | TSS | 5375 | 95 | TSC | 5583 | 80 | TSS | | | |
| 4693 | 79 | TSS | 4899 | 86 | TSS | 5230 | 46 | TSS | 5376 | 95 | TSC | 5586 | 94 | TSC | | | |
| 4695 | 98 | TSC | 4906 | 57 | TSS | 5232 | 46 | TSS | 5377 | 95 | TSC | 5588 | 94 | TSC | | | |
| 4699 | 79 | TSC | 4915 | 59 | TSS | 5233 | 46 | TSS | 5378 | 95 | TSC | 5590 | 94 | TSC | | | |
| 4702 | 89 | TSC | 4931 | 59 | TSC | 5234 | 46 | TSS | 5379 | 95 | TSC | 5591 | 94 | TSC | | | |
| 4705 | 62 | TSC | 4963 | 46 | TSS | 5236 | 47 | TSS | 5382 | 63 | TSC | 5592 | 94 | TSC | | | |
| 4706 | 62 | TSC | 4966 | 110 | TSS | 5237 | 47 | TSS | 5383 | 60 | TSC | 5593 | 94 | TSC | | | |
| 4707 | 45 | TSS | 4972 | 39 | TSC | 5238 | 79 | TSS | 5383 | 86 | TSS | 5595 | 94 | TSC | | | |
| 4707 | 85 | TSS | 4976 | 109 | TSS | 5243 | 116 | TSC | 5393 | 95 | TSC | 5596 | 33 | TSS | | | |
| 4708 | 45 | TSS | 4977 | 84 | TSS | 5244 | 116 | TSC | 5394 | 95 | TSC | 5597 | 33 | TSS | | | |